Certificate Course

# UNDERSTANDI<br>MATHEMAT

Melissa Herbert TALBOT

MR Crowle 5·T·

C.J. Cox & D. Bell

John Murray

© C. J. Cox and D. Bell 1987

First published 1987
by John Murray (Publishers) Ltd
50 Albemarle Street, London W1X 4BD

Reprinted 1987, 1989

Printed in Great Britain by
The Alden Press Ltd, Oxford

British Library Cataloguing in Publication Data

Cox, Christopher J.
    Understanding mathematics 5:
    certificate course.
    1. Mathematics—1961-
    I. Title   II. Bell, D. (David)
    510     QA39.2

ISBN 0-7195-4303-7

# Foreword

*Children's Understanding of Mathematics 11–16*, which was published in 1981, reported the work of the mathematics team of the research project *Concepts in Secondary Mathematics and Science* (CSMS). Christopher Cox is head of department in one of the schools which co-operated with us in the research.

From the beginning he and his colleagues utilised the results we were able to make available. In particular, he noted the lack of success experienced by many children and the errors they committed. This led to the writing of material for use by the mathematics staff in his own and other schools, work which has led to this series of books.

The philosophy behind *Understanding Mathematics* is that, traditionally, the mathematics in secondary school becomes too difficult, too soon, for many children. Thus the exercises here provide a wide range of examples in order to cater for different learning rates, so organised that the learner is encouraged to take some responsibility for the amount of practice needed. The existence and benefits of the calculator and computer are recognised and exercises are provided for their use. Above all, the exercises are full of *interesting* questions and not just lists of sums. Also, the accompanying Teachers' Manuals contain a wide range of very useful copyable resource material, which is additional to the detailed guides to all the exercises.

CSMS showed that many children could not cope with the secondary mathematics they were expected to learn. Other research, particularly that reported in the publication of *Children Reading Mathematics* (edited by H. Shuard and A. Rothery) has pin-pointed the special problems faced in conveying meaning through written text. The writers of this series of books have taken the messages to heart and done something about it. Thus the reader is receiving the benefit of tested and well thought-out material written by enthusiastic and dedicated practising teachers.

Kath Hart

# Preface

*Understanding Mathematics* is a complete course for secondary pupils in the 11–16 age range. It was designed with reference to the findings of the research project *Concepts in Secondary Mathematics and Science* (CSMS)*. The *Foundation Course* has proved to be equally effective with average pupils as with those of the highest ability, its exercise structure providing the flexibility needed to cater for this wide range.

The two-book *Certificate Course* meets the needs of students preparing for GCSE mathematics. The content and achievement levels closely match the GCSE Mathematics Criteria. Book 4 covers sufficient material to achieve level 2 (middle level). The exercises in Book 5 consolidate the material at level 2 then develop the topics to the standard needed for the highest grade of level 3 (upper level). Book 5 also contains comprehensive reference notes on all GCSE topics.

The Topic Matrix on pages vi to xi of the Teachers' Manual to Book 5 shows the full plan of the Foundation and Certificate Courses and the GCSE Syllabus Matrix on pages xii to xviii of the Manual indicates the coverage at each level of the syllabuses.

*Reported in K. Hart's *Children's Understanding of Mathematics 11–16*, John Murray

## Note on this printing

The Reference Notes on transposition of formulae on page 229, and also variation example (b) on page 238, have been amended so that the arrows may be read as 'becomes', following the Understanding Mathematics convention. If using previous editions side-by-side with this edition, or if photocopied Notes from an unamended Teachers' Manual are issued, it is recommended that students alter the original. Alternatively, pages 229 and 238 of this book may be photocopied for class use.

# Acknowledgements

The authors are grateful for advice received from the following: Dr Kath Hart, Brian Bolt (Exeter University), Andrew Rothery (Worcester College of Education), Alec Penfold, Martyn Dunford (Huish Episcopi School), Jacqueline Gilday (Wells Blue School), Hazel Bevan (Millfield School), John Wishlade (Uffculme School), John Halsall, David Symes, Simon Goodenough, Mary Mears.

They are also indebted to Mr. R. A. Batts of Texas Instruments for checking the notes given on calculators.

The authors thank their publishers for their help, their wives for their tolerance, and all the many teachers and pupils who have helped in the testing and revising of the course.

Illustrations by Tony Langham.

The following examination boards have kindly given permission for the use of past examination questions. The authors accept full responsibility for any errors in these questions or in the answers to the same.

**London and East Anglian Group** (LEAG)
East Anglian Examinations Board (EAEB)
London Regional Examining Board (LREB)

**Southern Group** (SEG)
Associated Examining Board (AEB)
Southern Regional Examinations Board (SREB)
South Western Examinations Board (SWEB)

**Wales**
Welsh Joint Education Committee (WELSH)

**Northern Association** (NEA)
Joint Matriculation Board (JMB)
Associated Lancashire Schools Examining Board (ALSEB)

**Midland Group** (MEG)
Oxford and Cambridge Schools Examination Board (O & C) and (MEI)
Southern Universities Joint Board for School Examinations (SUJB)
University of Cambridge Local Examinations Syndicate (U o C)

**Scotland** (Scottish)

# Notes to Students

This book provides exercises and reference material for your final year before GCSE. It should give you enough practice at topics you have already learnt to make you confident, and there are harder questions for those of you aiming for high grades. There are plenty of notes for reference and revision. After working through the book you will be very well prepared for the exams. However, before you start work it is well worth reading the following remarks on students' work from examiners:

Too many candidates only give answers and leave the rest to the imagination . . . . It is impossible for the examiner to give full credit to candidates unless he sees the whole of the working—these candidates are penalising themselves very heavily.

The work of some candidates was so untidy that it was almost indecipherable and almost impossible to mark.

It would be a great help to the examiner and the candidate if they would always draw the figures, even if they are drawn on the question paper already. (Note: You can trace them through your writing paper to save time.)

Candidates should be told that it is extremely rare for marks to be deducted for wrong work; the objective is to give marks for correct work, and any extra evidence the candidate offers should work to his advantage. (This means that you should not cross out any of your work unless you are 100% certain that it is completely wrong and has been replaced by something that is 100% correct.)

$5x^2$ was too often taken to mean $5x \times 5x$.

Calculator answers should be given to a sensible degree of accuracy. (Note: 3 significant figures is often the best level of approximation.)

## How to use the book

The book is organised into two parts, designed to interact with one another. The first part contains questions arranged in **exercises** under main topic headings. The coloured box under the exercise heading shows you which topics are covered in the exercise.

As in Book 4 there are four kinds of question:
**Introductory questions** (common core) are for everyone.
**Starred questions** (reinforcement) need not be done if you are expected to gain a high grade in GCSE.
**Further questions** (development) take the topic to the highest level necessary for GCSE.
**Boxed questions** (extension) challenge the most able students. Many of them are developed from past examination papers.

After the exercises there are twenty homework **Papers**, and five **Reference Sheets** for use when your teacher sets Aural Tests.

The second part of the book, the **REFERENCE SECTION**, contains **Reference Notes**—notes and worked examples on every topic you are likely to meet at GCSE, **You Need to Learn**—a list of *some* of the facts and formulae that are difficult to remember and which you must learn, and a **Glossary**. The Reference Section is for use in two ways—for reference when working the exercises, and for revision.

The **You Need to Know** statement at the start of each exercise indicates which Reference Notes are relevant to the exercise—look at them first, decide if you already know the material well enough, and if not read the Notes until you do. 'Algebra 9', for example, refers you to Note 9 in the section on Algebra (pages 205 to 207 give the page numbers of all the Notes).

For revision purposes, the Reference Notes indicate which exercises in Book 5 contain questions which may be worked for practice in each topic.

Finally there are **Answers** to the exercises—use these sensibly, remembering that your working will need to be shown in an examination.

## Calculators

You will need a scientific calculator for most exercises, and for the examination. Familiarise yourself with the calculator you will be using in your examination.

## Plan for revision

1   Start well before the examination; at least three months before. Cramming at the last minute will muddle you. You need time to keep going back to a topic to check that you understand it.

2   Read the Reference Notes until you nearly know them by heart.

3   Learn all the facts on pages 269 to 275.

4   While learning notes go back to the exercises and do examples, and make sure that you understand them.

5   When working past papers, keep a note of the questions you could not do. Learn to do them, then try again a week later, and then a month later. Keep on doing them until you get them right.

# Contents

# 1 Basic arithmetic (i)

Kinds of numbers

Estimation

Approximation

Standard form

Inequality

(Negative and fractional indices)

## ● You need to know:

**Basic arithmetic 1, 2, 6, 8, 9, 10**
**Algebra 9**

---

**1** A = {15, 16, 17, 18, 19, 20}

From set A, state:
(a) two prime numbers      (b) a square number      (c) a factor of 100
(d) a multiple of 9      (e) a triangular number.

**2** What number, when squared, gives the same answer as its square root?

**3** $n$ is an integer, such that $3 < n \leqslant 5$. Which numbers could $n$ be?

**4** Using a calculator, find:
(a) 1.65 × 14.2 correct to 1 decimal place
(b) 1.65 ÷ 14.2 correct to 2 significant figures.

**5** Figure 1:1 shows a riverside flood-warning post.
(a) At what level is the water now?
(b) If the water rises $1\frac{1}{2}$ feet what level will it be at?
(c) If the water then fell $2\frac{1}{2}$ feet what would be the reading?

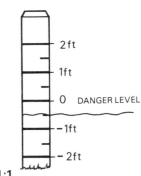

Fig. 1:1

**6** State for 15, 20 and 25:
(a) their highest common factor
(b) their lowest common multiple.

**7** A rational number can be expressed exactly as a common fraction. Are the following rational or irrational?

(a) $\sqrt{4}$      (b) $\sqrt{14}$      (c) $0.\dot{3}$

1

**8** Find for 4 and 6:
   (a) their sum      (b) their difference      (c) their product
   (d) their quotient, giving both possible answers, both as common fractions and decimal fractions.

**9** 'Tower Bridge was completed in 1894, when it opened 6000 times. 119 men were employed to operate it 24 hours a day. In 1985 it opened fewer than 200 times, and had only a staff of 15.'

(*Mark Waters*)

Which numbers above do you think are:
   (a) exact      (b) approximate?

**10** Write as an ordinary number:
   (a) $3.4 \times 10^2$      (b) $6.38 \times 10^{-2}$.

**11** Write in standard form, as in question 10:
   (a) 98.5      (b) 0.46

**12** Write:
   (a) 2/5 as a decimal fraction      (b) 3/5 as a percentage      (c) 0.07 as a common fraction
   (d) 15% as a common fraction as simply as possible.

**\*13** List all six factors of 12.

**\*14** From your answer to question 13 list:
   (a) any odd numbers      (b) any prime numbers      (c) any square numbers
   (d) any factors of 20      (e) any multiples of 4      (f) the three triangular numbers
   (g) the rectangular numbers.

**\*15** Write in figures:
   (a) one thousand      (b) one million      (c) two hundred thousand and fifty-six.

**\*16** Write your answers to question 15 in standard form.

**\*17** A calculator shows 0.000 176 as 1.76  −04. How would it show:
   (a) 0.000 28      (b) 0.0365      (c) 0.842?

**\*18** A 15 cm bar of metal shrinks by 0.1 mm when the temperature drops by 1 °C. What is its new length in:
(a) mm　(b) cm?

**\*19** Simplify:
(a) $2 \times 2 \times 5$　(b) $2 \times 3 \times 3 \times 7$.

**\*20** Express as a product of prime factors, as in question 19:
(a) 18　(b) 39　(c) 42.

**\*21** Write the numbers at points A to E in Figure 1:2
(a) as fractions or mixed numbers　(b) as decimal fractions.

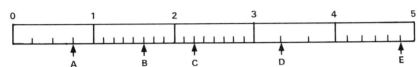

**Fig. 1:2**

**\*22** Copy Figure 1:3. Show with arrows, as in Figure 1:2, the points:
A, 2.3　B, 3.7　C, −1.3　D, −1.8　E, −2.5　F, −0.6

**Fig. 1:3**

**\*23** Using a calculator, a common fraction (e.g. $a/b$) may be changed to a percentage fraction as follows:

$a$ ÷ $b$ = × 100 =

A decimal fraction may be changed to a percentage fraction by multiplying it by 100, then writing the percentage sign.

Change to percentages:
(a) $\frac{1}{2}$　(b) $\frac{1}{4}$　(c) $\frac{3}{5}$　(d) 4/7, correct to the nearest whole number　(e) 0.1875

**\*24** $16\% \Rightarrow \dfrac{16}{100} \to \dfrac{\overset{4}{\cancel{16}}}{\underset{25}{\cancel{100}}} \to \dfrac{4}{25}$

Also $16\% \Rightarrow 16 \div 100 \to 0.16$

Write as a common fraction and as a decimal fraction:
(a) 75%　(b) 24%　(c) $33\frac{1}{3}$%.

**\*25** Suggest the most likely next two terms in the following sequences.
(a) 17, 14, 11, 8　(b) 1, 4, 9, 16　(c) 3, 6, 12, 24　(d) 6, 12, 20, 30
(e) $\frac{1}{2}, \frac{1}{4}, \frac{1}{8}, \frac{1}{16}$　(f) 10, 1, 0.1　(g) 11, 8, 5, 2　(h) 0.6, 0.4, 0.2　(i) 1, 8, 27, 64
(j) 26, 17, 10, 5, 2.

**\*26** The tables in Emma's classroom are arranged in four equal rows. The tables in John's classroom are arranged in six equal rows. Both classrooms have the same number of tables. What is the smallest possible number of tables in each room?

**\*27** Ninety-six packets of butter are to be packed in a box, four packets deep. Find four possible ways of arranging the packets, then choose one of your four as a 'best way', saying why you so consider it.

**\*28** Ten children and two adults are to travel on the school minibus. The cost is 14p per mile, the journey is 200 miles in total, and the adults are to pay twice as much as the children. What charges should be made?

**\*29** Arrange in order of size, largest first:
15%, 4/5, 0.6, 4/7, 1/3, 2/3.

**\*30** On January 11 the temperature at midnight was $-9\,°C$. On July 2 the temperature at midday was $24\,°C$. What is the difference between these two temperatures?

**\*31** (a) The number 0.07 can be written as $\dfrac{7}{c}$. Find $c$.

(b) The number 0.07 can be written as $7 \times 10^n$. Find $n$.

**\*32** Which numbers from 5 to 12 cannot be written as the sum of two prime numbers?

**\*33** If $a$ is an even number, $b$ is an odd number, and $c$ can be either, state whether the answers to the following are odd, even, or either.
(a) $3 \times a$    (b) $3 \times b$    (c) $a + b$    (d) $a + b + c$    (e) $a - b$    (f) $a^2$
(g) $a^2 + b^2$    (h) $a^2 + 2b^2$.

**34** $\dfrac{a \times b}{c}$ is approximately equal to 56. What is an approximate value for $\dfrac{10a \times 20b}{100c}$?

**35** State the reciprocal of:
(a) 2    (b) 7, correct to 3 significant figures    (c) $\frac{3}{4}$    (d) 4/5.

**36** Simplify:
(a) $2^{-1}$    (b) $3^{-2}$    (c) $4^{\frac{1}{2}}$    (d) $4^{-\frac{1}{2}}$    (e) $8^{\frac{2}{3}}$    (f) $8^{-\frac{1}{3}}$    (g) $100^{1\frac{1}{2}}$.

---

**37** A picture frame needs two 15.4 cm lengths and two 12.6 cm lengths of moulding. The moulding comes in 2-metre lengths. How should I cut two 2-metre lengths of moulding to make as many complete frames as possible?

**38** Find a multiple of 7 that leaves remainder 1 when divided by 2, 3, 4, 5 or 6.

**39** The area of Scotland is about $7.88 \times 10^4\,km^2$ and the area of England is about $1.30 \times 10^5\,km^2$. The population of Scotland is about $5.2 \times 10^6$ and the population of England is about $4.65 \times 10^7$.

Giving answers in full (not in standard form) state:
(a) how much larger in area England is than Scotland
(b) how many times as many people live in England as in Scotland
(c) the density of population in each country, in people per $km^2$. Comment on your answer.

**40** Find a four-digit number that reverses when multipled by four.

Investigate for numbers of other lengths.

**41** Find a number $n$ that leaves a remainder of 1 less than the divisor when it is divided by 2, 3, 4, 5, 6, 7, 8, 9 or 10 (e.g. $n \div 7$ leaves remainder 6).

# 2 Basic arithmetic (ii)

The four rules for positive integers, common fractions and decimal fractions

(Brackets)
(Negative numbers)

## ● You need to know:

Basic arithmetic 3, 4, 5, 6

---

**1** (a) $\frac{3}{4} + \frac{5}{6}$   (b) $\frac{3}{4} - \frac{2}{3}$   (c) $\frac{3}{4}$ of $\frac{2}{3}$   (d) $\dfrac{3/4}{7/12}$

**2** (a) $\frac{3}{4} + 1\frac{2}{5}$   (b) $4\frac{3}{5} - 1\frac{3}{4}$   (c) $\frac{2}{5} \times 3\frac{1}{3}$   (d) $2\frac{1}{5} \div 3\frac{2}{3}$

**3** British Airways carried about 14.6 million passengers in 1983, using a fleet of 148 aircraft which flew a total of 138 million miles on 177 routes. For their major long routes they used the 340-ton Boeing-747 jumbo jets. Each jet can carry 407 passengers.

Let us follow a jumbo flight from London to Sydney, Australia. At 2050 on Saturday the plane, carrying 121 tons of fuel and 407 passengers, sets off on the 3627 miles to its first refuelling stop at Muscat. It is on its 10 378th take-off, and has flown for 45 369 hours. The ideal altitude is 37 000 feet, but our journey starts at 27 000 feet until it reaches Austria, when it climbs to 33 000 feet.

The passengers settle down. Those going to Sydney have paid £3796 return, 1st class, or £1822, club class, or £938, economy class.

On landing at Muscat at 0345 Sunday (London time) the crew is changed. The first crew will wait 24 hours, then take over in their turn. This pattern continues for 21 days, when they will be given 6 days' leave in London.

The second stop, Kuala Lumpur, is reached at 1110 London time, then on to Singapore at 1250. Finally, 10 946 miles from its departure point in London, our jumbo lands at Sydney at 2152 on Sunday, London time.

(a) On average, how many passengers were carried each month in 1983?

(b) On average, how many miles were flown per aircraft in 1983?

(c) If the average weight of a passenger and luggage is 80 kg, what is the total weight of the Boeing-747, its passengers and fuel on take-off? (You may take 1 tonne as the same as 1 ton.)

(d) How long does the plane take to reach Muscat?

(e) What is the average speed of the plane between London and Muscat?

(f) Mount Everest is five and a half miles high. One mile is 5280 feet. About how many feet higher than Mount Everest is the plane flying once it has passed Austria?

(g) What is the cost per mile for a club-class passenger travelling from London to Sydney and back again?

(h) How long does the Boeing take (ignoring time on the ground) between
(i) Muscat and Kuala Lumpur     (ii) Kuala Lumpur and Singapore
(iii) Singapore and Sydney     (iv) London and Sydney?

(i) What is the average speed of the plane over the whole journey?

(British Airways)

*4    (a) $\frac{1}{4} + \frac{3}{5}$     (b) $\frac{5}{7} - \frac{2}{3}$     (c) $\frac{7}{9} \times \frac{3}{7}$     (d) $\frac{1}{8} \div \frac{1}{3}$

*5    (a) $1\frac{1}{2} + \frac{3}{8}$     (b) $2\frac{2}{3} - 1\frac{1}{2}$     (c) $\frac{1}{3}$ of $2\frac{2}{5}$     (d) $2\frac{3}{4} \div 6\frac{7}{8}$

*6    Ahmed borrows two-thirds of the cost of his new £54 000 house. How much does he borrow?

*7    An organism grows by cell division. Every cell divides into two cells every 15 minutes. How many cells will develop from one cell during 2 hours?

*8    My video tape records for 195 minutes. Can I record the whole of a pop concert which starts at 5:25 and finishes at 8:45? If so, how many minutes are spare? If not, how many minutes short is the tape?

**\*9** In Figure 2:1 ABC is an equilateral triangle. M and N are midpoints. What fraction of the triangle is area X?

**Fig. 2:1**

**\*10** Jodi travels 18 miles in 20 minutes. What is her average speed in miles per hour?

**11** (a) $(\frac{1}{3} - \frac{1}{4}) \div (\frac{1}{2} - \frac{1}{3})$    (b) $\dfrac{6}{\frac{4}{5} - \frac{2}{3}}$

**12** A teacher gives each pupil 20 marks to start with. A right answer scores +2 marks and a wrong answer scores −3 marks. What will be the final score of a pupil with five correct answers and seven wrong answers?

**13** If $\dfrac{x}{10} = \dfrac{5}{6}$ find $x$.

**14** Find:

(a) $(3 + 5) \div 8$    (b) $3 + (5 \div 8)$    (c) $\dfrac{70\,000 \times 60\,000}{800}$

**15** The formula $C = \dfrac{5(F - 32)}{9}$ converts degrees Fahrenheit to degrees Celsius. What is the Celsius equivalent of:

(a) $0\,°F$    (b) $-10\,°F$?

**16** The flow-chart (Figure 2:2) shows an algorithm (or 'rule') that can be used in a computer program to sort numbers, or words, into order. It is called a Bubble Sort.

Copy and complete the table to show how the example numbers are sorted, then use the flow-chart for five numbers of your own, drawing up your own table.

| | | | | | | |
|---|---|---|---|---|---|---|
| N(1) | 7 | 1 | | | | |
| N(2) | 1 | 7 | | | | |
| N(3) | 4 | 4 | | | | |
| N(4) | 8 | 8 | | | | |
| N(5) | 2 | 2 | | | | |

**Note** In our example you start with A = 1, B = 2.
Then N(A) = N(1) = 7
    N(B) = N(2) = 1.
The answer to 'Is N(A) < N(B)?' is NO because 7 > 1.
So M = 7
    N(1) becomes 1
    N(2) becomes 7.

It is easy to extend the method for more than five numbers, though there are faster but more complex methods for large lists of numbers or words. Write a computer program that will sort a list of five names into alphabetical order.

To arrange five numbers into numerical order

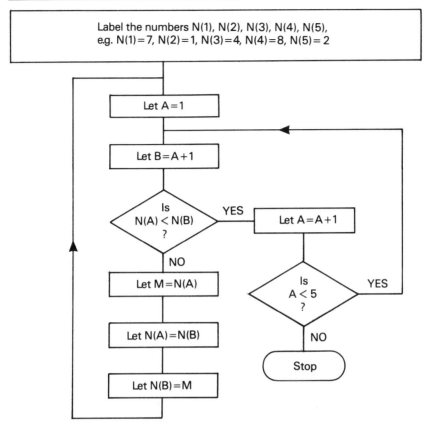

Fig. 2:2

**17** In a sheep-dog trial a dog managed to divide the flock into two equal groups, three equal groups, four equal groups, five equal groups, six equal groups and seven equal groups . . . well, almost. You see, every time the same small sheep escaped from the flock, and was never put into a group. What is the smallest possible number of sheep in the flock?

**18** A factory produces canned fish of three kinds, caviar, salmon and tuna, each in a different size can. Boxes are needed, of one size only, for transportation. Find the size of the smallest possible box that will be completely filled by each type of can, for cans of the following sizes:

Caviar:   6 cm diameter, 4 cm high
Salmon:   8 cm diameter, 6 cm high
Tuna:     12 cm diameter, 8 cm high.

Draw a plan and elevation of the box filled with each kind of can, and say how many of each are in the box.

**19** Split the numbers 28, 35, 42, 44, 48, 61, 63, 77, 84 and 88 into three sets such that the total of the first set is 180, the total of the second is 190 and the total of the third is 200.

# 3  Percentage

% of an amount                          % change

One amount as a % of
   another

## ● You need to know:

### Percentages 1 to 8

---

**1**  Find 9% of £150.

**2**  Alison scores 56 out of 80 in French and 48 out of 60 in German. By changing each to a percentage mark, find which subject she did best in.

**3**  My car insurance premium is £140 less 60% no-claims discount. How much do I actually pay?

**4**  Arlene invests £1800 in some shares. Three months later she sells them for £4800. What is her percentage profit?

**5**  (a)  Figure 3:1 shows a breakdown of a council's income from rates. Check amount (i) is correct, then calculate amounts (ii), (iii) and (iv).

   (b)  In what way is the diagram a bar-chart?

**\*6**  Find:
   (a)  40% of 40
   (b)  $2\frac{1}{2}$% of £3400
   (c)  $5\frac{1}{4}$% of £48.

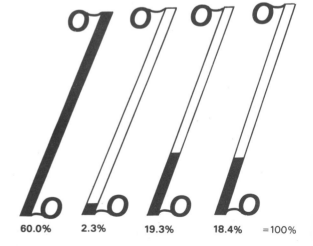

**THE RATES: WHO PAYS?**

| Domestic ratepayers | Industry | Commerce | Other ratepayers |
|---|---|---|---|
| (i) £6.68m | £ (ii) m | £ (iii) m | £ (iv) m |
| 60.0% | 2.3% | 19.3% | 18.4% = 100% |

**Fig. 3:1**          **TOTAL : £11.14m**

*7 A pullover priced at £20 is reduced in a sale by 20%. What is the sale price?

*8 A car which cost £2400 was sold with a loss of 5% of the cost price. What was the selling price?

*9 The cost of a bottle of squash once priced at 36p has increased over the past five years by 50%. What is the present price?

*10 In a sale 15% is taken off the price of a skirt. The original price was £16.40. Calculate the sale price.

*11 The wholesale price of a television is £260. The retailer sells it for £312. What is the retailer's percentage profit?

*12 What percentage profit is made when a car bought for £260 is sold, after a respray costing £250, for £850?

*13 A bicycle bought for £168 was later sold for £126. Find:
(a) the loss      (b) the loss as a percentage of the buying price.

*14 A greengrocer buys lettuce at £1.80 a dozen. For how much must he sell each lettuce to make a profit of 40% on his cost price?

*15 To buy a flat costing £22 500 Tony has to pay a 10% deposit.
(a) How much is the deposit?
(b) How much would he still have left to pay?

*16 A bus fare was increased from 40p to 50p. By what percentage was it increased?

*17 A motorbike has a list price of £400.

(a) Find the cost of insuring the bike if the insurance premium is 8% of the list price.

(b) If the bike is bought for cash a 10% discount is given. Find the cash price.

(c) If the bike is bought on Hire Purchase the terms are 20% deposit and 24 equal monthly payments of £15. Find the total H.P. price.

(d) A customer decides to pay cash for the bike instead of paying by H.P. How much does she save?

*(SWEB)*

*18 A second-hand car is advertised at a price of £2400. If cash is paid for the car a discount of 5% is given.

(a) How much is saved on the advertised price by paying cash?

(b) How much does it cost to insure the car if insurance is charged at £3 on every £100 of the advertised price?

(c) The car may also be bought on Hire Purchase. By this method the customer pays one third of the advertised price plus a regular monthly payment of £80 for 24 months. What is the total Hire Purchase price, and how much is saved by paying cash?

*(SWEB)*

**\*19** A television listed at £240 was bought with a 20% deposit and 24 monthly payments of £9.

(a) Find the total cost of the television.

(b) The set is insured at 15p per £20 of value. Find the cost of the insurance.

(c) The set depreciated in value by 25% in its first year. In its second year it depreciated by 20% of the value it had at the end of the first year. Starting from a value of £240 find the value of the television at the end of the second year.

*(SWEB)*

**\*20** A young couple wish to obtain a television advertised at £280, and to cover it for servicing. Three schemes are available:

RENTAL £9.60 per month including free service.

CASH PURCHASE A 10% discount is offered. The annual service charge is £11.80.

HIRE PURCHASE A deposit of 20% is required plus 24 monthly repayments of £12.40 each. The first two years servicing are free. After that there is an annual charge of £11.80.

(a) Calculate the total cost of each scheme for the three-year period.

(b) Calculate the difference in the cost of buying the set, ignoring service charges, on H.P. and by cash.

*(EAEB)*

**\*21** A club makes the following charges:

Membership per day: 75p per person
Membership per year: £24 single or £39 double
Dinner: £8.50 + VAT at 15%

(a) Find the cost of one day's membership for a party of thirty people.

(b) Find the VAT on a dinner.

(c) Find the total cost of dinner for four club members.

(d) How much is saved by a couple taking out yearly double membership instead of singles?

(e) How many times in a year would a single person have to visit the club to make a yearly payment the cheaper option?

(f) If the following year the charge per day is increased to 90p what is the percentage increase?

(g) Increase the other charges by the same percentage.

*(SWEB)*

**22** Between 1969 and 1985 house prices in my area rose by an average 800%. What was the 1985 value of a house purchased for £5000 in 1969?

**23** The population of the U.K. in 1985 was 56 million. Fifteen per cent of these were aged 65 or over, an increase of 2 million on the 1961 figure, when the population was 55 million.

(a) How many people aged 65 or over were there in the U.K. in 1985?

(b) What percentage of the population were aged 65 or over in 1961?

**24** A car sells for £5650 including 15% VAT. What was its pre-VAT price, correct to the nearest pound?

**25** Freda has an 8% pay rise, giving her earnings of £800 a month. What was her pay before the rise, correct to the nearest pound?

**26** In an M.O.T. testing station 10% of the cars tested one year had faulty brakes and of these 25% had faulty shock-absorbers. What percentage of the cars tested had both faults?

**27** A grocer bought a crate of 50 tins of pineapple at 20p per tin.

  (a) Calculate the total cost of the whole crate.

  (b) He wishes to make a profit of 30%. At what price must he sell each tin?

  (c) The grocer sold ten tins at 26p per tin and then sold off the rest of the crate at 24p per tin.
    (i) Calculate the amount of profit made.
    (ii) Express his profit as a percentage of his total cost.

  (d) He purchased a second crate of pineapple, also containing 50 tins, for £10 and sold these at 25p per tin.
    (i) Which purchase gave him a greater profit?
    (ii) How much extra profit did he make?

*(SREB)*

**28** At the beginning of 1979 a car manufacturer made 15% profit on his cost price by selling a car for £4600. The cost of manufacturing the car was made up of wages, raw materials, electricity, and factory maintenance in the ratios $15:6:3:1$. During 1979 wages rose by 20%, the cost of raw materials rose by $12\frac{1}{2}$%, electricity charges rose by 25% and factory maintenance costs rose by 50%.

  (a) Find the manufacturer's cost price at the beginning of 1979.

  (b) Express the increase in the total cost of manufacturing during 1979 as a percentage of the total cost at the beginning of that year.

  (c) After the rise in costs the manufacturer decided to reduce his profit to 12% of his cost price. Find the new selling price.

  (d) Calculate the increase in the selling price of the car expressed as a percentage, correct to one decimal place, of the original selling price.

*(UoL)*

# 4 Ratio

## ● You need to know:

### Ratio 1 to 10

---

1 State whether the following are examples of direct or inverse proportion.

   (a) The speed of a car and the distance travelled per minute.

   (b) The circumference of a circle and its diameter.

   (c) The number of people travelling on a coach outing and the cost per person if they share the cost of hiring the coach equally.

   (d) The extension of a spring and the load hung on it.

2 Which graph in Figure 4:1 could show that the price of houses has risen less in the last twelve months than in the previous twelve months?

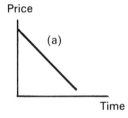

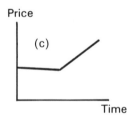

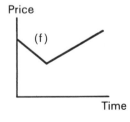

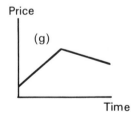

Fig. 4:1

3 Simplify the following ratios:
   (a) $16:8$    (b) 4 cm to 2 m (change them both to cm first)    (c) 15 cm to 10 mm
   (d) $3\frac{1}{4}:2\frac{1}{2}$.

14

**4** Express in the form $n:1$
(a) $12:4$    $12:5$    (c) $6:8$.

**5** The ratio of boys to girls in a youth club of 25 members is $2:3$. How many members are girls?

**6** Tanya and Sandra share their pool winnings in the ratio $5:4$. Tanya receives £300. How much does Sandra receive?

**7** A house plan is drawn to a scale of $1:100$. The front wall is 10 cm long on the plan. How long is it really?

**8** The scale of a map is $1:25\,000$. Find the distance in km represented by 20 cm on the map.

**\*9** To make orange paint, red and yellow are mixed in the ratio $2:3$. If I have 12 litres of yellow paint and 12 litres of red paint, how much orange paint can I make?

**\*10** A 100 franc note is worth about £10. About how much is a 25 franc note worth?

**\*11** A coin is made of three parts copper and five parts nickel.
(a) What fraction of the coin is copper?
(b) What percentage of the coin is copper?
(c) The coin weighs 10.4 g. What weight of copper is in it?

**\*12** Which of the toothpaste packs shown in Figure 4:2 is the best buy?

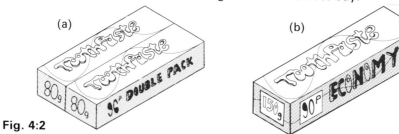

**Fig. 4:2**

**\*13** Taking 8 km = 5 miles, find the equivalent of 60 m.p.h. in km/h.

**\*14** A model aeroplane is to a scale of 1 to 50. The real plane is 50 metres long. How many cm long is the model?

**\*15** Figure 4:3 shows a 3-speed gear box. Wheels A have 60 teeth, wheels B have 40 teeth and wheels C have 20 teeth.

The gear ratio is the number of turns made by shaft X to the number of turns made by shaft Y, either in the form $n:1$ or $1:n$. State three gear ratios obtainable as shaft Y is moved upwards.

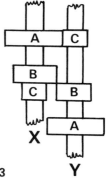

**Fig. 4:3**

**\*16** A builder reckons he will take 12 days to build a garage if he works 8 hours a day. Due to illness he has to complete the job in 10 days. How many hours a day must he now work?

**17** State a formula to find the cost in pounds of *x* articles given that the cost of *y* of the same articles is *z* pounds.

**18** At 0900 one day a six-foot pole casts a nine-foot shadow. At the same time a tree casts a fifteen-foot shadow. How tall is the tree?

**19** A packing machine packs a box of chocolates in 12 seconds, at a rate of 150 chocolates a minute. A newer machine can deliver 250 chocolates per minute. How long will the new machine take to pack a box?

**20** Why is the method shown in Figure 4:4 a good way of dividing a given distance into equal divisions?

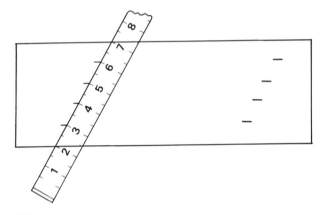

**Fig. 4:4**

**21** Duracolor sells paint in cans of three sizes, 500 ml, 1 litre and $2\frac{1}{2}$ litres. The empty cans cost 15p, 20p and 25p respectively. The paint itself costs £1.75 a litre to produce and the firm allows 30p per litre of paint produced to cover production expenses and overheads. The profit on each can is to be 40% of its total production cost. Work out the price at which Duracolor should sell its paint to the retailers.

**22** In a factory the ratio of the number of articles produced per day to the number of employees is 100:1. New production methods give a 15% cut in the number of employees with a 20% rise in output. What is the new ratio of articles produced to the number of employees, giving your answer in the form *n*:1?

**23** The coefficient of friction ($\mu$) can be worked out from the ratio *F*:*R*, where *F* is the force required to move a block and *R* is the weight of the block plus weights put on it. This is represented in Figure 4:5.

The table gives some experimental results. Plot the points, draw a straight line of best fit, and give a value for $\mu$ for the block being tested.

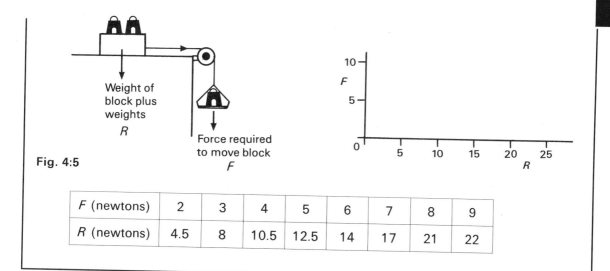

**Fig. 4:5**

| F (newtons) | 2 | 3 | 4 | 5 | 6 | 7 | 8 | 9 |
|---|---|---|---|---|---|---|---|---|
| R (newtons) | 4.5 | 8 | 10.5 | 12.5 | 14 | 17 | 21 | 22 |

## Efficient use of a calculator

● # You need to know:

### Calculators 1 to 6
### Percentages 6 to 8

1   Does your calculator follow the BODMAS rule? See Reference Notes: Calculators 1 if you are not sure.

2   Does your calculator have an accumulating memory and/or a store memory? Explain the differences between them. See Reference Notes: Calculators 3 if you are not sure about this.

3   (a)  $3.6 \times 4.7$     (b)  $8.1 - 9.6$     (c)  $4.15 \div 1.6$     (d)  $4 \times 3.6 + 1$     (e)  $3 + 4 \times 5$

   (f)  $\dfrac{8 \times 6}{7.5}$     (g)  $\dfrac{7}{4.6 \times 2.1}$     (h)  $\dfrac{3}{9.1 \times 7.3}$     (i)  $4.6 \div \frac{3}{4}$     (j)  $\dfrac{2.9 \times 3.1}{4.5 \times 7.6}$

   (k)  $\dfrac{2.3 + 4.7}{1.6 + 24}$     (l)  $\dfrac{4.7}{2.6 + 1.3}$

4   Find, correct to 3 significant figures where appropriate:
   (a)  $x$ if $x^2 = 20$     (b)  $\sqrt{x}$ if $x = 12$     (c)  the reciprocal of 7
   (d)  the reciprocal of the reciprocal of 7.

5   By rounding each number to one-figure accuracy, estimate:
   (a)  $16.1 + 8.9 + 15.1 + 231 + 7.6 + 8.14$
   (b)  $301 + 17.9 + 45.5 + 54.6 + 56.3 + 17.8$
   (c)  $21p + 9p + 86p + 47p + 35p + 10p + 79p$
   (d)  $8.75\,m + 16\,m + 4.17\,m + 121\,m + 9.9\,m.$

6   Use your calculator to work out accurate answers to question 5.

7   Find:
   (a)  16% of £83     (b)  16 out of 83 as a percentage     (c)  14 as a percentage of 25.

8   (a)  Increase £9 by 2%.     (b)  Decrease £18 by 25%.     (c)  Increase £9 by 200%.

9   In 1983 60% of the 22 million homes in the U.K. were owner-occupied, compared with 50% of $19\frac{1}{2}$ million homes in 1971.
   (a)  What was the increase in owner-occupied houses between 1971 and 1983?
   (b)  What was the percentage increase?

*10 (a) £14.60 + £8.30 + £16.10 − £3.50

(b) Find the cost of 145 breeze-blocks at 38p each.

(c) How many 19p stamps can I buy for £5?

*11 (a) $3.8 \times (7.6 \times 5.3)$     (b) $(3.8 + 7.6) \times 5.3$     (c) $\dfrac{4}{7.1 \times 2.8}$

(d) $\dfrac{3.1}{1.6 + 1.7}$     (e) $\dfrac{8.9 \times 360}{4.1 \times 19}$

*12 Between 1971 and 1981 the working population of the U.K. rose from 25 123 thousand to 26 089 thousand.

(a) Find the increase in the working population.

(b) Using '*Increase per cent equals* (*increase divided by original number*) *times a hundred per cent*', find the percentage increase in the working population between 1971 and 1981.

*13 (a) Sum 111, 333, 555, 777 and 999.

(b) Now replace six of the figures in part (a) by zeros so that the total is 1111. (Note: numbers like 007 are allowed.)

14 Find correct to 3 significant figures:

(a) $1.6^5$     (b) $\sqrt[3]{20}$     (c) $\sqrt[3]{0.6}$     (d) $\sqrt[5]{0.14}$

15 (a) Sum all the factors of 220, except 220 itself.

(b) Sum all the factors of 284, except 284 itself.

(*Did you know that*: In October 1986 a Dutch mathematician discovered a method of computing all so-called 'amicable' pairs of numbers like 220 and 284. He used a computer for over 1000 hours to find 1427 amicable pairs less than 10 billion. Eight hundred of these were previously unknown, although Pythagoras knew of 220 and 284 in the 5th century BC. The next pair, 1184 and 1210, were found by a 16-year old boy in 1866.)

16 In 1983 there were 690 thousand births in the U.K. This was 10% more than in 1977 but 29% fewer than in 1964.

How many births in:
(a) 1977     (b) 1964?

17 (a) Take 0.165 away from −3.5.

(b) Take 3.5 away from −0.165.

(c) Multiply −4.6 by −3.8.

(d) Divide 0.15 by −0.04.

18 Sum all the integers from 1 to 17 inclusive.

19 Seats at Bewley Arena cost £10, £8 and £6. Every seat is sold and the total revenue is £10 850. Twice as many £10 seats as £8 seats are sold. Twice as many £8 seats as £6 seats are sold. How many of each seat are sold?

**20** Your answer to question 18 should be 153. This is rather a special number. To find out why:

> Cube its digits and sum the result.
> Now start with any number that is a multiple of 3.
> Cube its digits and sum the result.
> Keep doing this until the answer repeats itself.

What digits make up the repeating answer? Investigate further.

**21** 'Iteration' is a mathematical process of guessing an answer to a problem, then using that answer to find a more accurate answer, and so on until your answer is as accurate as you require.

The equation $2x^3 - 4x - 1 = 0$ has three solutions. They can be found by using the iteration formula:

$$x \to \frac{3x^3 - 1}{x^2 + 4x}$$

One solution is between $x = -1$ and $x = 0$. Starting with $x = 2$, repeatedly use the formula to find this solution correct to 3 significant figures.

Now find two other solutions.

A programmable calculator or a computer will be a big help.

# 6 Measure

S.I. system          Speed
Time                 Reading dials and tables

## ● You need to know:

**Basic arithmetic 7**

---

**1**                       BLACKDOWN RESERVOIR

| | |
|---|---|
| Area of gathering ground | 4120 hectares |
| Capacity of reservoir | 15100 million litres |
| Surface area of full reservoir | 161 hectares |
| Average rainfall | 148.4 mm per year |

(a) A hectare is the area of a square of side 100 metres. How many square metres is the gathering ground?

(b) One litre is a volume of 1000 cm$^3$.
$1 \text{ m}^3 = 100 \text{ cm} \times 100 \text{ cm} \times 100 \text{ cm} = 1 \text{ million cm}^3$
What is the volume of water in the full reservoir, in m$^3$?

(c) The average depth of water multiplied by the surface area gives the volume of water in the reservoir. Calculate the average depth of water in the full reservoir in metres correct to the nearest centimetre.

(d) What volume of water falls on the gathering ground per year in litres? (Hints: Multiply your answer to (a) by the average rainfall in metres. Use the information in part (b) to change your m$^3$ volume to litres.)

**2** This table gives the mileage and train times for a journey from London to Bournemouth.

| Miles | Station | Time |
|------:|---------|------|
| 0 | London Waterloo | 1105 |
| 12 | Surbiton | 1137 |
| 24 | Woking | 1210 |
| 48 | Basingstoke | 1231 |
| 66 | Winchester | 1243 |
| 75 | Southampton | 1309 |
| 93 | Brockenhurst | 1328 |
| 108 | Bournemouth | 1351 |

(a) How many minutes for the whole journey?

(b) How many minutes from Winchester to Southampton?

(c) Figure 6:1 shows a common form of distance chart. What distances should be shown in squares A, B and C?

(d) Calculate the average speed of the whole journey in m.p.h. correct to the nearest mile.

(e) The fare from London to Bournemouth is £12.30. How much is this in pence per mile?

(f) Plot distance vertically against time horizontally to show the information given, and hence find which journey between stations is covered at the fastest average speed.

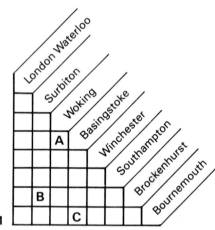

Fig. 6:1

**3** Figure 6:2 is a chart to convert between ounces and grams. Use the chart to find:
(a) how many ounces equal 200 g    (b) how many grams equal 12 ounces.

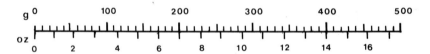

Fig. 6:2

**4** Read the electricity meter in Figure 6:3.

units

Fig. 6:3

5   Figure 6:4 shows a volt/ohm-meter dial. Note that the dial is read clockwise for volts but anticlockwise for ohms. The needle reading is different, depending on the position of the switch. As drawn in Figure 6:4 the dial shows $k\Omega$ from 0 to 1 $k\Omega$, so the needle reads 0.35 $k\Omega$. What is the reading when the needle is at the position shown and the switch is set to:

(a) 5 V     (b) 50 V     (c) 10 V     (d) 500 V     (e) 1 M$\Omega$?

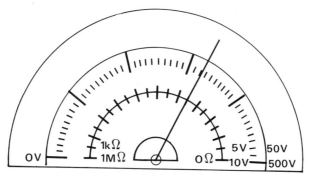

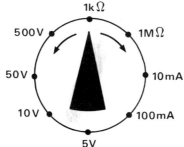

**Fig. 6:4**

6

| SPEED | THINKING | | BRAKING | | TOTAL | |
|---|---|---|---|---|---|---|
| m.p.h. | Time | Distance | Time | Distance | Time | Distance |
| 20 | 0.7 s | 20 ft | 0.7 s | 20 ft | 1.4 s | 40 ft |
| 40 | 0.7 s | 40 ft | 1.4 s | 80 ft | 2.1 s | 120 ft |
| 60 | 0.7 s | 60 ft | 2.1 s | 180 ft | 2.8 s | 240 ft |

This table is drawn up from information given in the Highway Code.

(a)  Read from it:
   (i)  the total stopping distance at 40 m.p.h.
   (ii)  the thinking time at any speed
   (iii)  the braking time at 60 m.p.h.

(b)  Why are the times in the first column the same but those in the second column different?

(c)  Draw a bar-chart showing three bars for each speed, the length of each bar representing the total stopping distance.

*7   Use the following conversion details to draw up an S.I. version of the table in question 6, giving reasonable approximations suitable for everyday use.

$$20 \text{ m.p.h.} \simeq 30 \text{ km/h}$$
$$20 \text{ ft} \simeq 6 \text{ metres}$$

*8  The following table shows part of an insurance company's promotion leaflet. The amount payable on the death of the insured person depends on the Sum Assured, and grows each year for 15 years. If the insured person is still alive after 15 years, he/she will receive the amount shown (the Maturity Value).

| 15 YEAR ENDOWMENT ASSURANCE | | | | | | |
|---|---|---|---|---|---|---|
| Premium | £10 | | £20 | | £30 | |
| Age next birthday | Sum Assured £ | 15 year Maturity Value £ | Sum Assured £ | 15 year Maturity Value £ | Sum Assured £ | 15 year Maturity Value £ |
| Male    Female | | | | | | |
| 15–29    15–33 | 1827 | 3595 | 3763 | 7405 | 5697 | 11 211 |
| 31    35 | 1824 | 3589 | 3757 | 7393 | 5688 | 11 193 |
| 33    37 | 1821 | 3583 | 3751 | 7381 | 5679 | 11 176 |
| 41    45 | 1792 | 3526 | 3690 | 7261 | 5587 | 10 995 |
| 51    55 | 1699 | 3343 | 3498 | 6884 | 5297 | 10 424 |

(a)  For £10 a month:
   (i)  How much could *you* expect to receive in 15 years?
   (ii)  How much would you have paid during those 15 years?

(b)  For £30 a month, for a woman aged 36:
   (i)  How much would she expect to receive in 15 years?
   (ii)  How much would she have paid during those 15 years?

(c)  How much less insurance cover does a 50-year-old man receive than a 30-year-old man if both pay £20 a month?

(d)  Why does a 50-year-old man receive less insurance cover than a 30-year-old man when he pays the same amount?

(e)  How much more insurance cover does a 32-year-old woman receive for £30 a month than a 32-year-old man? Why is there this difference?

*9  Read the gas meter shown in Figure 6:5.

**Fig. 6:5**                                                                                   therms

*10  Draw a gas meter that is reading 24 508 therms.

11  Using the Endowment Assurance table in question 8, plot the Sum Assured for £10 a month on a graph for the ages given. Estimate the Sum Assured the insurance company would offer a man who is 37 next birthday, and a woman who is 50 next birthday.

**12** Figure 6:6 shows the bus stops in the city centre of Leicester.

    (a) Find the London Road (A6). Two buses travel in only one direction along this road. What are their numbers?

    (b) Which bus would you take from London Road Station to the ABC Cinema on Belgrave Gate?

    (c) You catch a number 37 bus on the Haymarket to go to Mowmacre Hill, which is off the top of the map. You catch the same number bus back again, alighting at Welford Road. What city centre streets do you pass along on your return journey?

    (d) A visitor stops his car by the Phoenix Arts Centre and asks you for directions to the ABC Cinema. Advise him.

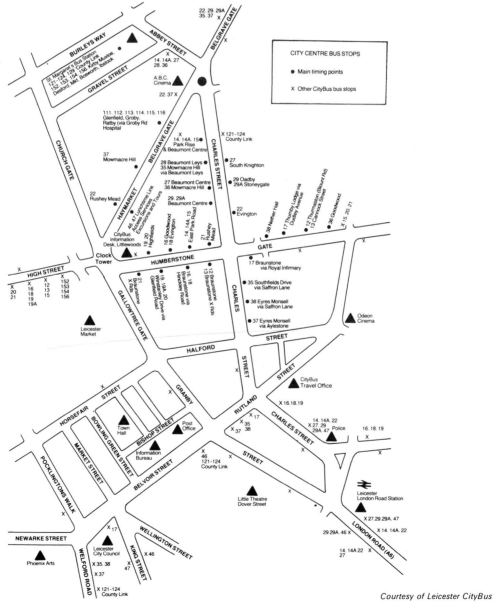

**Fig. 6:6**

*Courtesy of Leicester CityBus*

**13** Wallpaper comes in rolls 10 metres long and 50 cm wide. Design a chart to help customers decide how many rolls to buy for various sizes of rooms, for heights between 2 m and 3.05 m at 15 cm intervals, and for perimeters from 12 m to 20 m at 1 m intervals. Doors and windows should be ignored, as pattern matching and wastage will more than compensate for these.

**14** Figure 6:7 shows InterCity train routes, with fastest journey times to London.

(a) At which London terminus does the Cardiff train arrive?

(b) What is the shortest time for a train journey from Manchester to London?

(c) Use the table in question 2, on page 22, to calculate the mean average speed of the fastest journey from Bournemouth to Waterloo, giving your answer in m.p.h.

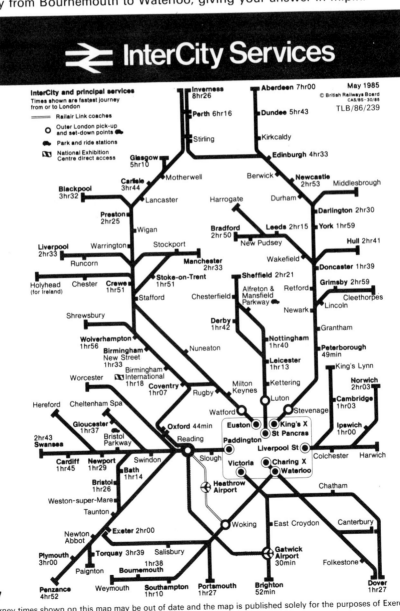

Fig. 6:7

*Note:* The journey times shown on this map may be out of date and the map is published solely for the purposes of Exercise 6, Question 14 in this book.

**15**

| Month | July | Aug | Sept | Oct | Nov | Dec |
|---|---|---|---|---|---|---|
| Workers taken on | 4 | 9 | 6 | 5 | 7 | 4 |
| Output in 1000s | 5 | 15 | 20 | 31 | 40 | 44 |

The table shows how the output of a firm changed as more workers were employed, e.g. in July four extra workers were employed and output was five thousand; in August there were thirteen extra workers and output was fifteen thousand.

Plot the information on a suitable graph, draw the line of best fit, and hence estimate the output in January if a further seven workers are taken on.

**16** The following table gives the purchasing power of the pound from 1881 to 1985, taking the 1881 pound as base.

| 1881 | 1900 | 1913 | 1920 | 1938 | 1946 | 1951 | 1961 | 1971 | 1976 | 1977 |
|---|---|---|---|---|---|---|---|---|---|---|
| 100p | 106p | $97\frac{1}{2}$p | 39p | 62p | $36\frac{1}{2}$p | 28p | 21p | $13\frac{1}{2}$p | 7p | 6p |

| 1978 | 1979 | 1980 | 1981 | 1984 | 1985 |
|---|---|---|---|---|---|
| $5\frac{1}{2}$p | 5p | 4p | $3\frac{1}{2}$p | 3p | 3p |

(a) Sketch a chart to illustrate the changing value of the pound if:
  (i) you wish to emphasise how much the value has dropped
  (ii) you wish to play down the decreasing value of the pound.

(b) Draw an accurate chart for the figures from 1951 onwards. From your chart estimate the purchasing power of the 1881 pound in 1965.

# 7 Finance

● ## You need to know:

### Percentages 1 to 8

___

**1** A family visiting Germany and France changes £210 into German marks at the rate of DM3.8
to the £. They spend DM676 before changing the remaining marks into French francs at the rate
of 3.05 francs to the mark.

(a) Calculate the number of marks they bought.

(b) Calculate the number of francs they bought.

**2** Miriam has to pay the Electricity Board a quarterly charge of £7.50 plus 5.2 pence for every unit
used. Her meter reading at the beginning of the quarter was 14 742 and at the end of the quarter
it is 15 774. How much will Miriam have to pay?

**3**          BRITISH TELECOM charges as at 1.11.1986

| Time allowed for 1 unit @ 4.4p per unit | | |
|---|---|---|
| | Local (L)   Up to 56 km (a)   Over 56 km (b) | |
| Cheap | 6 min          100 s | 45 s |
| Standard | 90 s          34.3 s | 24 s |
| Peak | 60 s          25.7 s | 18 s |
| **Peak**   9 a.m.–1 p.m. Monday–Friday | | |
| **Standard**   8 a.m.–9 a.m. and 1 p.m.–6 p.m. Monday–Friday | | |

Find the cost correct to the nearest penny of:

(a) 6 min from 8:15 a.m. on Tuesday at rate L
(b) 18 min from 1215 on Friday at rate a
(c) 40 min from 1225 on Sunday at rate b.

**4** A television listed at £345 was bought with a £40 deposit and 12 monthly payments of £3

(a) Find the total cost of the monthly payments.

(b) Find the total cost of buying the television.

(c) If cash is paid, a discount of 20% on the list price is given. Find the cash price.

(d) How much less is the cash price than the total cost paid by instalments?

(e) If the same television can be rented for £1.90 per week, how long will it be before the total rent paid becomes greater than the list price?

**5** Niri owns a hundred £5 preference shares in British Metals. Each share pays 8% simple interest per year. What will be her total investment income over five years?

**6** (a) Read about compound interest in the Reference Notes: Percentages 8.

(b) Calculate the amount resulting from
    (i)  £1200 invested for 2 years at 5% p.a.
    (ii)  £1150 invested for 3 years at 8% p.a.
    (iii) £400 invested for 5 years at 4% p.a.

**7** Andrea borrows £20 000 for 5 years at 12% per annum compound interest.

(a) How much will she have to repay altogether?

(b) The loan is repaid by 60 equal monthly repayments. How much is each repayment?

**8** A car bought for £6300 on May 1st 1980 depreciated by 20% in its first year, by 12% in its second year, and by 5% in its third year. What was its value on:
(a) May 1st 1981     (b) May 1st 1982     (c) May 1st 1983?

**9** Over the past five years the value of gold has increased by an average of 7% per year. Five years ago I bought a gold coin for £50. What is its present value?

**10** A building society will advance a mortgage loan equal to $2\frac{1}{2}$ times a person's annual salary, up to a limit of £40 000. How much can be advanced if a person earns £12 000 a year?

**11** A young couple want to buy a flat for £26 000. A building society will give them a 90% mortgage. How much must they find themselves?

**12** An estate agent uses the following scale of charges to work out his commission on any house that he sells: 2% on the first £10 000 and 1% on the remainder. Calculate his commission on a £42 000 house.

**13** Tax relief is granted on the interest paid on a mortgage on one's own home. Find the amount of tax relief and the net cost of a mortgage in a year if the amount of interest to be paid in that year is £2840 and the relief allowed is 29p in the £.

**14** Householders have to pay rates to finance local government (council) spending. The amount to be paid is the rateable value of the house multiplied by the rate in the £ declared by the council. Find the rates to be paid by a householder whose house has a rateable value of £426 when the rate is 105p in the £.

**15** Find the council's income from a penny rate (1p in the £) if the total rateable value of the town is £726 400.

**16** Mr Reynolds earns £11 840 per year and has tax allowances of £4175. How much is his taxable pay, and how much will be left after tax at 29% is paid?

**17** Gary is a salesman. He has a basic salary of £9000 per year and in addition earns commission on his sales as follows:

The first £5000        10%
The next £5000        20%
Sales over £10 000   25% on the remainder.

Find his total salary in a year in which his sales total:
(a) £4500      (b) £8000      (c) £12 000.

**18** Jock Fairhurst is a lorry driver. He is paid a flat rate of £240 per week, and in addition receives:

£9 a day subsistence allowance
6p per mile mileage bonus
30p per tonne tonnage bonus.

One week his records show:

|         | Monday | Tuesday | Wednesday | Thursday | Friday |
|---------|--------|---------|-----------|----------|--------|
| Miles   | 289    | 175     | 348       | 246      | 191    |
| Tonnes  | 25     | 15      | 30        | 20       | 15     |

(a)  What is his subsistence allowance for the week?
(b)  What is his mileage bonus for the week?
(c)  What is his tonnage bonus for the week?
(d)  What is his gross pay for the week?

**19** Julie and Ron insure their home for £45 000 and its contents for £10 000. The rate for buildings is 16p per £100 and that for contents is 27p per £100. Find the total premium.

**\*20** A family changed £480 into German marks at the rate of 4.43 marks to the pound, and during their 14-day stay in Germany they spent an average of 145 marks a day. On their return to England they exchanged their remaining marks back into sterling at the rate of 4.52 marks to the pound. In both exchanges a bank charge of $2\frac{1}{2}$% of the sterling value was made.

Calculate:
(a)  the number of marks they received for £480
(b)  the number of marks left over at the end of their holiday
(c)  how much they received in sterling on their return
(d)  the total amount of bank charges paid
(e)  the average cost of their holiday per day, correct to the nearest 10p.

**\*21** Deepkeep Ltd make freezers. Their best-selling model costs £240 wholesale. The retailers then make a profit of 25% when they sell them to customers. The hire-purchase terms are £80 deposit and twelve monthly payments of £20.60. Insurance of £2.75 per £50 worth of food per year is available, and the freezer uses about 55p of electricity per week.

(a)  Find the retail price of the freezer.

(b)  How much more must the shop charge in order to increase its profit by 15%?

(c)  Find the total hire-purchase price of the freezer.

(d)  Find the total cost of running the freezer for a year and insuring food valued at £150.

(*SWEB*)

*22

| Time in years | 1 | 2 | 3 | 4 | 5 |
|---|---|---|---|---|---|
| Amount of £1 | 1.1556 | 1.3355 | 1.5433 | 1.7835 | 2.0610 |
| Time in years | 6 | 7 | 8 | 9 | 10 |
| Amount of £1 | 2.3818 | 2.7524 | 3.1808 | 3.6758 | 4.2478 |

The table shows the amount of £1 at 15% per annum compound interest, where the interest is added every 6 months. For example, in 7 years £1 will have increased to £2.7524, and £10 will have increased to £27.524.

Find:
(a) the amount of £200 after 4 years
(b) how long, to the nearest year, to double the principal
(c) the minimum sum that would amount to at least £1250 at the end of 5 years
(d) the interest paid on £100 at the end of the first year of a ten-year investment
(e) the interest paid on the £100 investment during the last year of the ten-year period.

(*EAEB*)

*23 Study the finance company's advertisement in Figure 7:1.

23.1% ANY PURPOSE LOANS FOR HOMEBUYERS/OWNERS WITH FREE LIFE INSURANCE,
APR OPTIONAL SICKNESS/REDUNDANCY COVER AVAILABLE

| BORROW | EQUIVALENT WEEKLY REPAYMENTS TO NEAREST PENNY OVER | | | | |
|---|---|---|---|---|---|
| | 36mths £ | 60mths £ | 90mths £ | 120mths £ | 180mths £ |
| **£2000** | 18.00 | 12.93 | 10.58 | 9.55 | n/a |
| **£3000** | 27.01 | 19.39 | 15.88 | 14.33 | n/a |
| **£4000** | 36.01 | 25.86 | 21.17 | 19.11 | n/a |
| **£5000** | 45.01 | 32.32 | 26.46 | 23.89 | 21.87 |
| **£6000** | 54.01 | 38.79 | 31.75 | 28.66 | 26.25 |

E.G. £2500 × 36 MTHS AT £97.52 PER MTH = £3510.72. BIG REBATES OF INTEREST FOR EARLY SETTLEMENT. LOANS ARE SECURED ON PROPERTY FOR LOW COST

**Fig. 7:1**

(a) What is a finance company?

(b) What interest rate ('Annual Percentage Rate') is quoted by the company?

(c) If you borrow £4000 over 10 years, how much will you have to pay back: (i) each week (ii) altogether?

(d) Building societies were charging about 13% interest at the time of the advertisement. Why do you think the finance company charges so much more?

(e) If the interest payable per year is calculated on the amount owing at the start of the year, how much of the first year's payments repay part of the £4000 loan?

*24 (a) Find, in pounds, the income from a 1p rate for a district with a total rateable value of £4 500 000.

(b) If the rate charged by a local council is 80p in the £ and the rateable value of a house is £300, find the rates to be paid that year by the householder.

*25 Study the table, which shows part of a building society leaflet. It shows details of a £15 000 mortgage over 25 years at 10% (7% net) interest.

How much of the debt is paid off at the end of:
(a) year 1    (b) year 10    (c) year 20
(d) year 25?

| Year | Monthly payment £ | Year-end debt £ |
|------|-------------------|-----------------|
| 1    | 107.26            | 14 762.88       |
| 5    | 107.26            | 13 636.38       |
| 10   | 107.26            | 11 723.84       |
| 15   | 107.26            | 9 041.41        |
| 20   | 107.26            | 5 279.15        |
| 25   | 107.26            | REPAID          |

Total cost £32 180.39

*26 A sewing-machine salesman is paid a basic salary of £575 per month plus a commission of £15 for each machine that he sells.

(a) In May he sells 35 machines. How much does he receive?
(b) If he needs to earn at least £750 a month, how many sewing machines must he aim to sell?
(c) What will be his new basic salary after a 6% pay rise?

*27 A petrol-pump attendant is paid at the rate of £2.40 per hour for a basic working week of 40 hours. Deductions from these earnings total £20.50. Calculate her net weekly income.

If she works overtime, she is paid at time and a half. A deduction of 30% of any overtime pay is made. Calculate the hourly rate for overtime after deductions, and the total net income for a week in which she works seven hours overtime.

*28 A family insures their house for £45 000 and its contents for £10 000. Find their total annual premium if the rate for buildings is 36p per £100 and that for contents is 37p per £100.

*29 Carlo has to travel 16 km a day, 5 days a week, 46 weeks a year. The bus fare is £1.40 per day. Carlo decides it might be cheaper to buy a motorcycle to ride to work. He sees a second-hand one advertised for £200 cash, or a deposit of £50 followed by twelve monthly instalments of £13.50.

(a) How much will Carlo save by paying cash rather than using hire purchase?

(b) Carlo decides to buy the motorcycle on hire purchase, and during the first year his running costs average 3p per kilometre. Which is cheaper, and by how much: going to work by bus or going to work by motorcycle?

(c) In the next year bus fares go up by $12\frac{1}{2}$% and running costs on the motorcycle by 1p per km. Which is now the cheaper means of getting to work, and by how much?

30 The flow-chart (Figure 7:2) illustrates some of the decisions that you will have to reach when you consider buying your first house.

If you were a building society manager, what would your advice be to the following couples, who all wish to buy a £45 000 house?

(a) Girish and Sharma: Annual income £15 000, savings £5000.
(b) Joe and Marissa: Annual income £20 000, savings £9000.
(c) John and Vicky: Annual income £13 000, savings £3000.

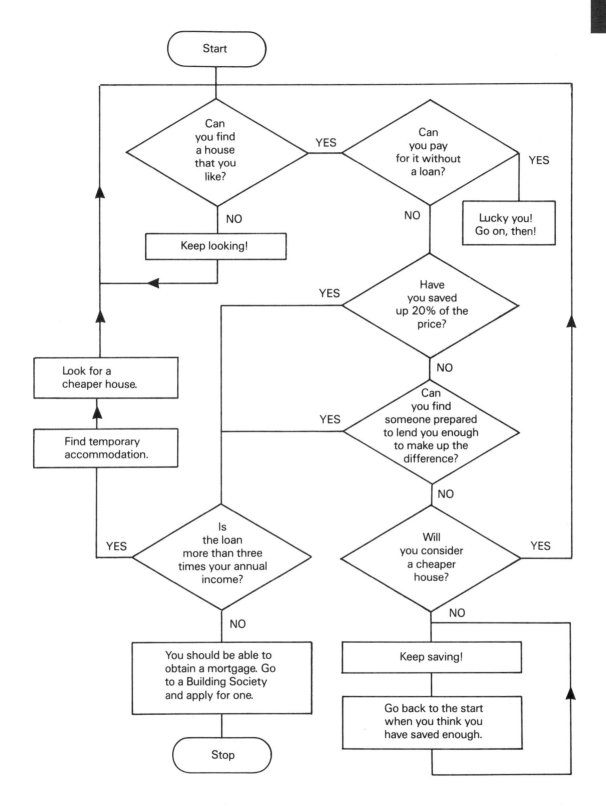

**Fig. 7:2**

**31** The Western Building Society pays compound interest on the amount in your account on the 28th day of each month. The monthly rate of interest is one-twelfth of the yearly rate. If you pay in £50 on the 1st of each month in a year when the interest rate is 8% per annum, how much will you have in your account at the end of six months?

**32** The estimated cost of building a house is £42 000, of which 55% is for wages and the rest is for materials. If during the work wages are increased by 7% and materials rise in cost by an average 15%, calculate the new cost of building the house.

**33** Study the Mortgage Saver Account details in Figure 7:3. Part of the bank's leaflet (not shown) gave a detailed example for a 'typical saver'. Write such an example to help customers understand the implications of the scheme.

Your Mortgage Saver Account gives you guaranteed access to a mortgage from us. Under this guarantee, which remains open for 6 months after you have completed your savings, you may apply for a mortgage:

- up to 95% of the value of the house you want to buy (or the purchase price if that is lower)

- up to 3 times your gross annual income if you are the main income earner and $1\frac{1}{2}$ times the second income earner

- between £12 000 and £40 000.

The amount you eventually borrow will depend on the property you choose and your ability to meet repayments.

You may apply for a mortgage greater than £40 000 (up to a maximum of £150 000) but in these circumstances different criteria will apply.

The following table illustrates the different ways in which the total savings could be accumulated.

| Monthly savings £ | over 18 ms | over 24 ms | over 36 ms |
|---|---|---|---|
| 50 | 900 | 1 200 | 1 800 |
| 75 | 1 350 | 1 800 | 2 700 |
| 100 | 1 800 | 2 400 | 3 600 |
| 200 | 3 600 | 4 800 | 7 200 |
| 500 | 9 000 | 12 000 | 18 000 |

To keep the examples as simple as possible the interest and bonus on the Mortgage Saver Account, paid to you each half year, is not included in these figures.

**Fig. 7:3**

**34** From a man's salary of £17 750 p.a. the following allowances were deducted before income tax payable was calculated:

**A** £3575 personal allowance

**B** The annual interest payable on his £35 000 endowment mortgage. (In this type of mortgage, only the interest is paid each year; the whole loan is repaid at the end of the fixed term by a life insurance on the borrower.)

The rate of income tax was 30% and the mortgage rate was $12\frac{1}{2}$%.

(a) Calculate his taxable income.
(b) Calculate his net monthly salary.

**35** A greengrocer bought 50 kg of tomatoes for £10 and marked their price up so as to make 75% profit. When he had sold 30 kg they began to go squiggy, so he reduced the selling price by two-fifths. At this reduced price he was able to sell all but 5 kg of them.

(a) Calculate the total income from his sales.

(b) Calculate the average selling price per kg of the tomatoes he sold, correct to the nearest penny.

(c) Calculate the profit he made as a percentage of the cost price.

(*SUJB*)

| Co-ordinates | $(ax^2 + bx + c)$ |
|---|---|
| $y =$ and $f(x)$ notation for | $(ax^3 + d)$ |
| $ax + b$, $ax^2$, $a/x$ | $(k/x^2)$ |
| Gradient | (Solution of equations) |

## ● You need to know:

**Graphs 1 to 6**

---

**1** Look at Figure 8:1.

(a) Write the co-ordinates of the ends of:
   (i) line AB     (ii) line IJ.

(b) State the equation of:
   (i) line AB     (ii) line AD     (iii) line AF.

(c) Which line can be described as $f(x) = 1 - x$?

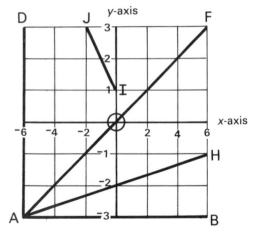

Fig. 8:1

**2** Draw axes, $x$ from $-3$ to $3$ and $y$ from $0$ to $10$. On your axes draw the graphs:
   (a) $y = 2x + 1$     (b) $y = x^2$     (c) $f(x) = \frac{1}{2}x^2$.

**3** (a) Copy the tables for $f(x) = 1/x$, then use a calculator to help you to complete them, giving $f(x)$ correct to 2 d.p.

| $x$ | $-5$ | $-4.5$ | $-4$ | $-3.5$ | $-3$ | $-2.5$ | $-2$ | $-1.5$ | $-1$ | $-0.5$ |
|---|---|---|---|---|---|---|---|---|---|---|
| $f(x)$ | | | | | | | | | | |

| $x$ | $5$ | $4.5$ | $4$ | $3.5$ | $3$ | $2.5$ | $2$ | $1.5$ | $1$ | $0.5$ |
|---|---|---|---|---|---|---|---|---|---|---|
| $f(x)$ | | | | | | | | | | |

(b) A problem arises when $x = 0$. Why?

(c) $\frac{1}{0}$ is taken to have the value infinity ($\infty$), although such a value does not exist except as a mathematical idea. Figure 8:2 shows a sketch of the graph of $f(x) = 1/x$. Use your table values to construct an accurate graph.

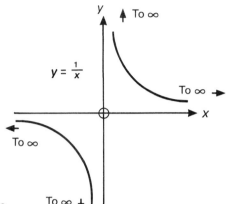

**Fig. 8:2**

**4** Look at Figure 8:1 again.

The gradient, or slope, of line AH is $\frac{1}{6}$. If you start at point A and go towards B for 6 units (3 squares), then 1 unit up takes you back to the line AH again, reaching it at $-2$. Six across, one up, gives the gradient $\frac{1}{6}$.

Remember that if a line slopes backwards ($\backslash$) then the gradient is negative.

State the gradient of:
(a) line AF      (b) line IJ.

*5 If $x - y = 5$, state the value of $x$ when $y$ is:
(a) 0     (b) 3     (c) 5     (d) $-1$     (e) $-2$     (f) $-4$.

*6 Draw one pair of axes, both from $-6$ to 6. Draw on your grid the straight lines from:
(a) (0, 3) to (3, 6)     (b) (3, $-5$) to (5, $-1$)     (c) (1, 1) to (5, 3)
(d) (0, $-3$) to (1, 0)     (e) (0, $-6$) to (6, $-5$)     (f) (0, 0) to ($-3$, 3)
(g) ($-4$, 5) to (0, 4)     (h) ($-6$, $-1$) to ($-4$, $-4$)   (i) ($-3$, $-3$) to (0, $-5$).

*7 State in as simple a form as possible the slope of each line given in question 6.

*8 Draw one pair of axes from $-6$ to 6 each. Draw on your grid the straight lines:
(a) $x = -1$     (b) $y = x$     (c) $y = x - 4$     (d) $y = x + 4$.

*9 Repeat question 8 for:
(a) $y = 6$     (b) $x + y = 3$     (c) $x + y = 6$     (d) $y - x = 4$     (e) $y = \frac{1}{2}x - 6$
(f) $y + \frac{1}{2}x = -6$.

*10 Repeat question 8 for:
(a) $y = 2x$     (b) $y = 2x - 3$     (c) $x + y = 2$     (d) $x + y = -2$.

*11 (a) On axes from −6 to 6 each shade the regions A and B where:
   (i) A = {(x, y) : −4 ⩽ x ⩽ 5; 1 ⩽ y ⩽ 3}
   (ii) B = {(x, y) : y ⩽ x; −4 ⩽ x ⩽ 5}.

(b) State the co-ordinates of the vertices of the region A ∩ B.

*12 On axes x from −3 to 3, f(x) from −20 to 20, draw the graphs f(x) = 2x² and f(x) = −2x².

*13 (a) The area of a circle is given by the formula A = πR². By considering values of A for values of R from 0 to 5 at half-unit intervals, draw a graph of A against R. Take π as 3.14.

(b) Read from your graph, as accurately as possible:
   (i) the area of a circle of radius 3.2 cm
   (ii) the radius of a circle of area 20 cm².

14 By drawing the following pairs of graphs on axes from −6 to 6, solve the two equations simultaneously.
   (a) y = x; y = −⅓x + 4
   (b) y = x + 2; y + 2x + 4 = 0

15 On axes from −6 to 6 each, shade the region:
   {(x, y) : 0 ⩽ x < 3; −⅓x + 2 < y < ⅔x + 3}.

16 Figure 8:3 shows the parabola y = x² + x − 1.

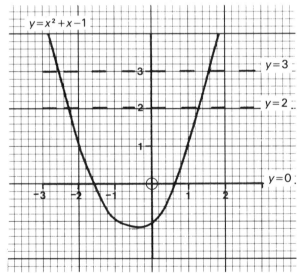

**Fig. 8:3**

The line y = 0 crosses this parabola at about x = 0.6 and x = −1.6. These are the solutions of x² + x − 1 = 0.

(a) Read the values of x where y = 3 crosses the parabola. Show that these are the solutions of x² + x − 4 = 0.

(b) Read the values of x where y = 2 crosses the parabola. Show that these are the solutions of x² + x − 3 = 0.

**17 Example** To find the equation solved where $y = x^2 + 4x - 1$ crosses $y = 2$.

Where the graphs cross they share the same value of $y$, hence the equation solved is $x^2 + 4x - 1 = 2$. By subtracting 2 from each side this will simplify to $x^2 + 4x - 3 = 0$.

Find the equation solved where the following pairs of graphs cross.
(a) $y = x^2 + 2x + 2$; $y = 1$   (b) $y = x^2 + 2x + 1$; $y = 2$
(c) $y = x^2 + 2x + 1$; $y = 3$   (d) $y = x^2 + 2x - 1$; $y = -1$
(e) $y = 2x^2 + 2x - 1$; $y = -2$

**18** (a) Copy and complete the table for the parabola $y = x^2 - 3x + 3$.

| $\cdot x$ | $-2$ | $-1$ | 0 | 1 | 2 | 3 | 4 |
|---|---|---|---|---|---|---|---|
| $x^2$ | 4 | | | 1 | | | |
| $-3x$ | 6 | | | $-3$ | | | |
| 3 | 3 | | | 3 | | | |
| $y$ | 13 | | | 1 | | | |

(b) At what value of $x$ will the smallest possible value of $y$ occur?

(c) Draw the parabola $y = x^2 - 3x + 3$, using scales:
$x$ from $-2$ to 4, 2 cm to 1 unit; $y$ from 0 to 14, 1 cm to 1 unit.

(d) The minimum value of $y$ is at $x = 1.5$ (see part (b)). What is this minimum value?

(e) What are the values of $x$ where $y = 1$ crosses your parabola? What equation is solved by these values of $x$?

(f) Repeat part (e) for:
(i) $y = 3$   (ii) $y = 7$   (iii) $y = 2$   (iv) $y = 5$   (v) $y = 8$.

**19** (a) Copy and complete the table for $y = 2x^2 + 4x - 5$.

| $x$ | $-4$ | $-3$ | $-2$ | $-1$ | 0 | 1 | 2 |
|---|---|---|---|---|---|---|---|
| $2x^2$ | 32 | | | | | | |
| $4x$ | $-16$ | | | | | | |
| $-5$ | $-5$ | | | | | | |
| $y$ | 11 | | | | | | |

(b) Draw the graph of $y = 2x^2 + 4x - 5$ using scales:
$x$ from $-4$ to 2, 2 cm to 1 unit; $y$ from $-7$ to 11, 1 cm to 1 unit.

(c) What is the minimum value of $2x^2 + 4x - 5$? At what value of $x$ does this minimum value occur?

(d) Read the values of *x* where the following lines cross your parabola, and state the equations solved by these values.
(i) $y = -5$    (ii) $y = 1$    (iii) $y = 11$    (iv) $y = 5$    (v) $y = -1$
(vi) $y = -4$    (vii) $y = 3$.

(e) By drawing a suitable line on your graph find the values of *x* that make $2x^2 + 4x - 5 = 0$.

**20** If you had drawn the parabola $y = x^2 - 3x - 6$, how would you solve $x^2 - 3x - 6 = 0$?

**21** The slope of the tangent to a curve at a point A gives the slope of the curve at A.

In Figure 8:4 the slope of the curve at A is $-\dfrac{u}{b}$.

**Fig. 8:4**

Note that *u* and *b* are the distances given by the axes' scales, not necessarily the distances measured in squares.

What connection can you see between the tangent to a curve and the tangent ratio used in right-angled triangles?

Tangents to curves can be drawn 'by eye', but for a parabola the method given below enables an exact slope to be found.

In Figure 8:5,
ST is the axis of symmetry of the parabola,
PM is the tangent to the parabola at point P.
Note that TM = MF. This fact means that you can draw accurate tangents to parabolas and calculate their slopes.

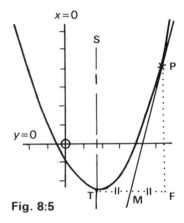

**Fig. 8:5**

Draw another copy of the graph of $y = 2x^2 + 4x - 5$ (see question 19). Find the slope of the tangent to your parabola at:
(a) $x = 1$    (Note: the tangent touches the parabola at (1, 1).)
(b) $x = -4$    (Note: the tangent touches the parabola at (-4, 11).)
(c) $x = -2$.

**22** Draw another copy of the graph of $y = x^2 - 3x + 3$ (see question 18). Find the slope of the tangent to your parabola at:
(a) $x = 4$    (b) $x = -2$    (c) $x = 0$    (d) $x = 1$    (e) $x = 1.5$

**23** (a) Draw up a table of values for $y = 2x^2 + 3x - 4$, taking *x* from $-4$ to $2$ at half-unit intervals (you may use a calculator).

(b) Plot the graph from your table, using scales: *x*, 2 cm to 1 unit; *y*, 1 cm to 1 unit. Note that the table is not symmetrical, so the turning point is not plotted but will have to be deduced by you from the shape of the rest of the curve. Do this by remembering that for a parabola the turning point lies on the axis of symmetry.

(c) Find as accurately as possible the slope of the curve at: (i) $x = -3$    (ii) $x = 1$.

**24** On your graph for question 23:

(a) Draw the line $y = 3$. Read the values of $x$ where your line crosses the parabola, and state the equation solved by these two values of $x$.

(b) Draw on the same grid the line $y = 2x + 2$. (If you use the slope/crossing method be careful to use the scale distances, not the true distances.)

(c) Read the values of $x$ where your line crosses the parabola, and state the equation solved by these values of $x$. (Hint: Replace $y$ in $y = 2x^2 + 3x - 4$ by $2x + 2$.)

**25** State the equation solved where the following lines cross $y = 2x^2 - 3x - 1$. Do not draw graphs.
(a) $y = 3$    (b) $y = -1$    (c) $y = x$    (d) $y = x + 2$    (e) $y = -x + 3$
(f) $y = -2x + 1$

**26 Example**  To solve the equation $2x^2 - 3x - 1 = 0$ using the parabola $y = 2x^2 - 3x - 1$, simply read the solutions where $y = 0$.

To solve $2x^2 - 3x - 5 = 0$ using the same parabola $(2x^2 - 3x - 1)$, the given equation must be changed until one side of it is the same as the equation of the parabola. This is done by adding 4:

$$2x^2 - 3x - 5 = 0 \xrightarrow{\text{add } 4} 2x^2 - 3x - 1 = 4$$

Now it is clear that the solutions will be found on the line $y = 4$.

**Example**  Having drawn the parabola $y = x^2 - 2x + 1$, to solve the equation $x^2 + 4x + 3 = 0$.

The equation must be changed so that the $+4x$ becomes $-2x$, and the $+3$ becomes $+1$:

$$x^2 + 4x + 3 = 0 \xrightarrow{\text{subtract } 6x} x^2 - 2x + 3 = -6x \xrightarrow{\text{subtract } 2} x^2 - 2x + 1 = -6x - 2$$

The solution will be found where the line $y = -6x - 2$ crosses the parabola. This is shown in Figure 8:6.

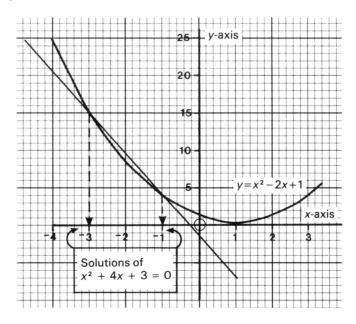

**Fig. 8:6**

Imagine that you have drawn the parabola $y = x^2 - 2x + 1$. What line should be drawn to solve:
(a) $x^2 + 2x - 3 = 0$   (b) $x^2 + 3x - 1 = 0$   (c) $x^2 - 3x + 1 = 0$
(d) $x^2 + x + 2 = 0$   (e) $x^2 - x - 4 = 0$?

---

**27** Draw the graph of:
  (a) $x = y^2 - 3$ for values of $y$ from $-3$ to 3
  (b) $y = 10/x^2$ for values of $x$ from $-10$ to 10
  (c) $y^2 = 9 - x^2$ for values of $x$ from $-3$ to 3
  (d) $y = x^3 - x^2 - x - 1$ for values of $x$ from $-2$ to 3.

**28** (a)  Draw the graph of $y = \dfrac{3 - x^2}{4 + x}$. Take $x$ from $-3$ to 6, 2 cm to 1 unit; $y$ from $-6$ to 1, 4 cm to 1 unit. Use A4 paper.

Calculate $y$ correct to 2 d.p. (You will find it helpful to find the value of $y$ when $x = -2\frac{1}{2}$.)

  (b)  Read the values of $x$ where $y = \frac{1}{2}$ crosses your graph, and show that these values are the solutions of $2x^2 + x - 2 = 0$.

  (c)  Find the equation solved where $y = -1$ crosses your graph.

  (d)  What is $y$ when $x = -4$?

**Practical graphs:**
   conversion, travel

**(Speed/time graphs:**
   area giving distance)

● # You need to know:

## Ratio 7

---

**1**   You will meet graphs in nearly all areas of school work and everyday life. Figures 9:1 to 9:9 are just a few examples for you to think about and discuss.

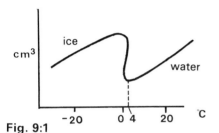

Fig. 9:1

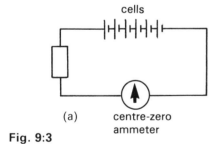

Fig. 9:3

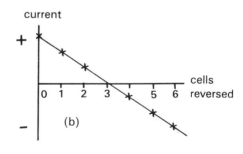

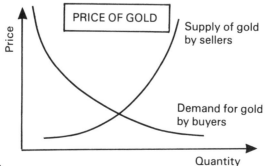

Fig. 9:4

43

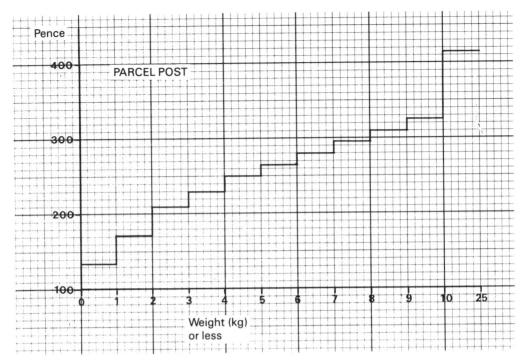

**Fig. 9:5**

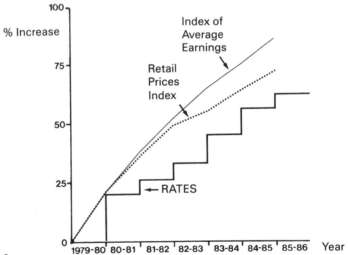

**Fig. 9:6**

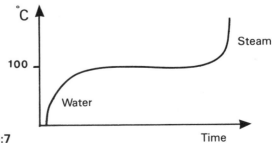

**Fig. 9:7**

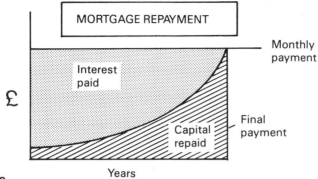

Fig. 9:8

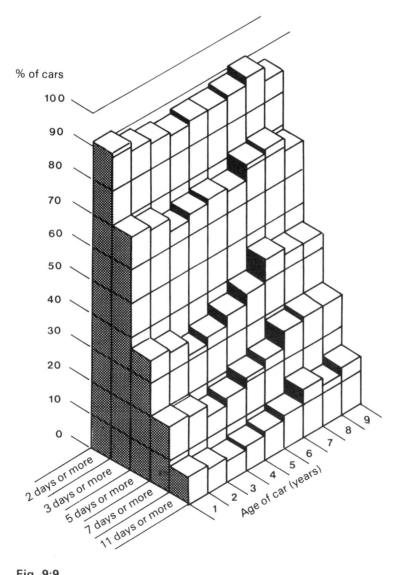

Fig. 9:9

**2** A percentage conversion graph provides a quick way to read off percentage amounts without calculation.

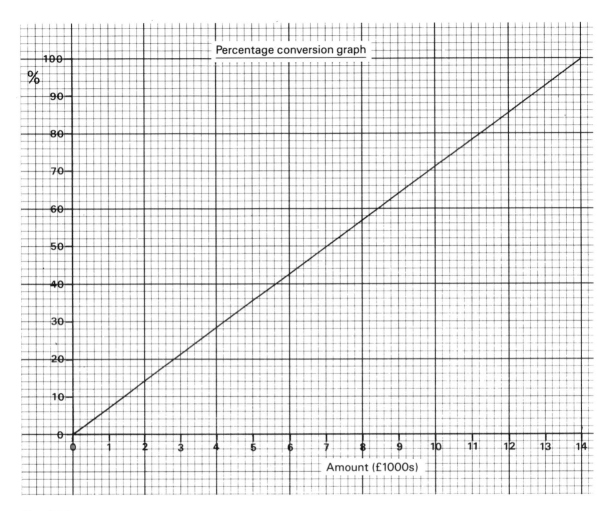

**Fig. 9:10**

Figure 9:10 shows Sharon's total income for a year.

(a) What is her salary (income per year)?

(b) Her electricity bills total £500 in a year. What percentage of her salary is this?

(c) Her mortgage repayments are £450 a month. What percentage of her salary is this?

(d) Sharon aims to give 15% of her income to charity. How much should she give each year?

**3** Figure 9:11 shows a graph to find the cost of producing a leaflet.

(a) What is the price per leaflet if 300 are ordered?

(b) Will the conversion line ever cross either axis? Explain your answer.

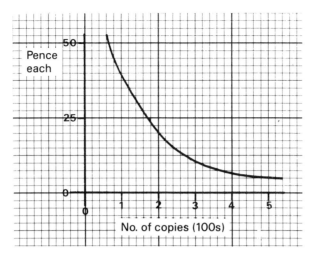

**Fig. 9:11**

4   Figure 9:12 represents the journeys made by a bus and a car starting at Sheffield, travelling to Leicester and returning to Sheffield.

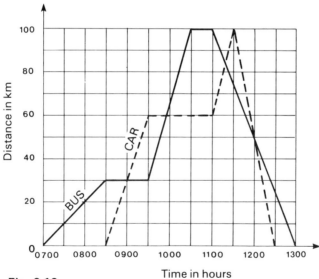

**Fig. 9:12**

(a)  How much longer, including stops, did it take the bus to complete the journey from Sheffield to Leicester than it did the car?

(b)  At approximately what time, between 0900 and 1000, did the bus overtake the car?

(c)  What was the greatest speed attained by the car during the entire journey?

(d)  What was the average speed attained by the car during the entire journey?

*(MEG)*

*5 A computer-company salesman receives a basic wage of £100 a week. For every computer system he sells in a week he receives a commission. The mapping diagram in Figure 9:13 shows how this increases his pay.

(a) Copy and complete the ordered pairs:
   (0, 100); (1000, 150); (2000, ); (3000, ); (4000, ); (5000; )

(b) Draw axes, vertical 100 to 600 to represent pay, horizontal 0 to 5000 to represent the sales. Plot your ordered pairs, then join them with a smooth curve.

(c) Estimate how many pounds' worth of equipment he must sell to bring in £400 a week.

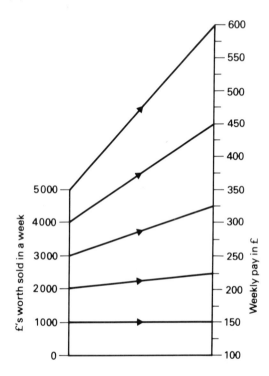

**Fig. 9:13**

*6 Taking 60 m.p.h. = 88 ft/s draw a graph to convert between these units. Use a vertical scale of 1 cm to 5 m.p.h. and a horizontal scale of 1 cm to 10 ft/s.

Use your graph to convert:
(a) 45 m.p.h. to ft/s    (b) 50 ft/s to m.p.h.    (c) 15 m.p.h. to ft/s    (d) 50 m.p.h. to ft/s.

*7 When a cassette recorder starts to rewind a cassette the counter reads 430. Counter readings ( y) after x seconds are shown in the table.

| x | 0 | 10 | 20 | 30 | 40 | 50 | 60 | 70 | 80 | 90 |
|---|---|----|----|----|----|----|----|----|----|----|
| y | 430 | 408 | 382 | 353 | 317 | 278 | 227 | 174 | 104 | 22 |

(a) Draw axes showing values of x from 0 to 100 and y from 0 to 450. On these axes draw a graph to show the readings in the table. Note that the graph will be a continuous curve.

(b) Estimate from your graph the time taken to rewind until the counter reads:
   (i) 300 (ii) 0.

(*MEG*)

*8 Describe the three journeys shown in Figures 9:14 to 9:16.

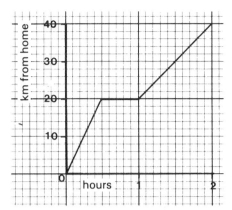

Fig. 9:14

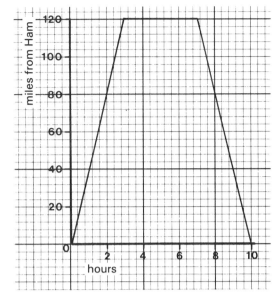

Fig. 9:15

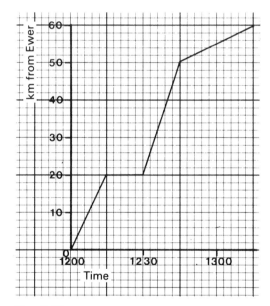

Fig. 9:16

*9 State the speeds for each part of each journey in Figures 9:14 to 9:16, then, by finding the total distance and the total time, find the average speed for the whole journey.

10 A passenger train leaves Motown at 1000 hours, averaging 40 m.p.h. on its journey to Nadir, 60 miles away. After a 30-minute halt it returns at 60 m.p.h. on average.

At 1100 a goods train leaves Nadir for Motown, travels at 40 m.p.h. for 30 minutes, then completes the journey at an average speed of 20 m.p.h.

Draw a graph to illustrate the journeys, taking the time axis from 1000 to 1300. Hence find when the trains pass and how far they then are from Motown.

**11** Figure 9:17 is a distance/time graph for a car journey. Tangents to the curve give the speed at various moments. One such tangent is shown 5 minutes from the start of the journey. What is the speed of the car at this moment?

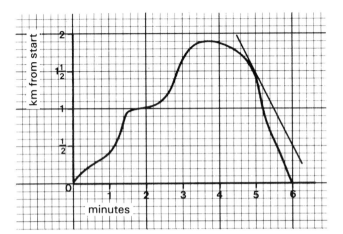

**Fig. 9:17**

**12** Figure 9:18 shows three straight roads, AB, CD and EF. The contour lines indicate the nature of the terrain. Figure 9:19 shows the speed/time graph for a cyclist on one of the roads. Which road do you think he is cycling along, AB, CD or EF?

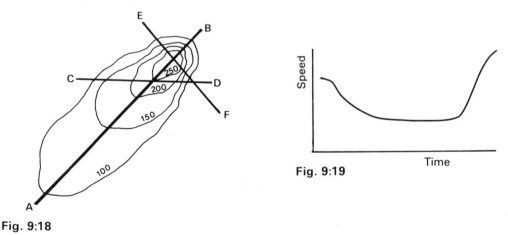

**Fig. 9:18**

**Fig. 9:19**

**13** Figure 9:20 shows a speed/time graph. From A to B a constant speed of 10 m/s is shown and during the next second, from B to C, there is an acceleration of 10 m/s² (10 metres per second per second). Describe what happens between C and F.

**14** Because speed multiplied by time gives distance, the area under a speed/time graph gives the distance travelled.

In Figure 9:20, area I represents a distance of $10 \times 2 = 20$ metres. Area II represents a distance of $\frac{1}{2}(10 + 20) \times 1 = 15$ metres (area of trapezium = half the sum of the parallel sides times the distance between them).

Find areas III, IV and V, and hence the total distance covered in the six seconds.

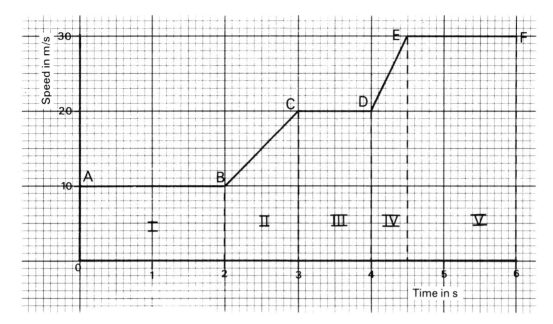

**Fig. 9:20**

**15** Figure 9:21 is the speed/time graph for a particle which moves with speed $v$ m/s at time $t$ seconds.

(a) Calculate the acceleration of the particle when $t = 10$.

(b) Calculate the total distance travelled in the 12 seconds, and hence the average speed of the particle for the whole journey.

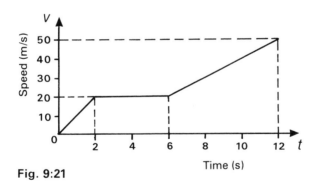

**Fig. 9:21**

**16** An aeroplane flying at a constant height of 320 m drops a load fitted with a parachute. During the time intervals stated the motion of the load is as follows:

0 s–2 s    free fall, negligible resistance, acceleration due to gravity of 10 m/s²

2 s–6 s    parachute opens, vertical speed decreases uniformly to 2 m/s

after 6 s   the load falls with a constant speed of 2 m/s.

(a) Sketch a speed–time graph for the first 8 s. (Speed, vertical, 0–20 m/s; Time, horizontal, 0–8 s.)

(b)  Determine the distance fallen in the first 6 s.

(c)  Determine the total time taken for the load to reach the ground.

(AEB Physics)

**17**  (a)  The speed of a car is observed at 10-second intervals over 1 minute. The readings are given in the table.

Time (s)        0   10   20   30   40   50   60
Speed (m/s)  0    5   14   26   34   38   40

Plot the points on axes, remembering that the time axis should be the horizontal one. Join the points with a smooth curve.

(b)  By drawing two tangents to your curve, estimate the acceleration of the car
(i)  after 30 seconds        (ii)  when its speed is 35 m/s.

(c)  The area under the curve cannot be found exactly, but by joining the plotted points with straight lines a reasonable approximation can be obtained from the resulting triangle and trapeziums.

Use this method (the 'trapezoidal method') to calculate the distance covered by the car during these 60 seconds.

**18**  The speed of a train at intervals of 1 minute during a journey of 8 minutes are 0, 11, 21, 28, 30, 30, 26, 15, 0 m.p.h. Draw the speed/time graph and from it estimate the total distance travelled.

**19**  Comment on the graph in Figure 9:22.

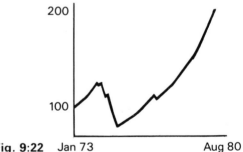

**Fig. 9:22**   Jan 73                                     Aug 80

**20**  When the tide is ebbing, water flows swiftly out of the harbour mouth at Lower Puddle-wick. The table shows the rate of flow in cubic kilometres per hour ($km^3/h$) for three hours on a day when high tide is at noon.

| Time | 12:00 | 12:30 | 1:00 | 1:30 | 2:00 | 2:30 | 3:00 |
|---|---|---|---|---|---|---|---|
| Hours after noon ($t$) | 0 | $\frac{1}{2}$ | 1 | $1\frac{1}{2}$ | 2 | $2\frac{1}{2}$ | 3 |
| Rate of flow ($f$) | 0 | 24 | 46 | 63 | 75 | 80 | 78 |

Using a scale of 2 cm to represent half an hour on the $t$-axis (horizontal), and 2 cm to represent 10 $km^3/h$ on the $f$-axis, plot ordered pairs ($t$, $f$) and join them with a smooth curve.

(a) It is dangerous for small boats to negotiate the harbour mouth if the flow exceeds $60\,km^3/h$. At what time does it become dangerous on this afternoon?

(b) Estimate the rate at which $f$ is increasing at 1:30p.m.

(c) Use the trapezoidal method, with intervals of half an hour, to estimate the total volume of water which flows out of the harbour during these three hours.

(*AEB* 1985)

**21** The position of a moving car with respect to an origin O is given by $r = \begin{pmatrix} 12 \\ 0 \end{pmatrix} + t \begin{pmatrix} -1 \\ 3 \end{pmatrix}$ where $t$ is the time in seconds and the distances are measured in metres.

Thus after 2 seconds the position of the car is given by $r = \begin{pmatrix} 12 \\ 0 \end{pmatrix} + 2 \begin{pmatrix} -1 \\ 3 \end{pmatrix} = \begin{pmatrix} 10 \\ 6 \end{pmatrix}$, giving the point (10, 6).

(a) Calculate the position of the car for $t = 0, 1, 2, 3, 4, 5$ and 6.

(b) Draw axes, $x$ from 0 to 15 metres, $y$ from 0 to 20 metres, and represent the path of the car on your diagram.

(c) The position of a second car is given by $r = t \begin{pmatrix} 1 \\ 2 \end{pmatrix}$ metres. On your diagram represent the path of this car.

(d) By measuring, estimate the distance between the two cars when $t = 5$.

(*MEI*)

**22** The petrol consumption ($y$ miles per gallon) of a car is related to its speed ($x$ m.p.h.) by the formula $y = 200 - \dfrac{3x}{2} - \dfrac{4200}{x}$.

Copy and complete the following table of values.

| $x$ | 40 | 45 | 50 | 55 | 60 | 70 | 80 |
|---|---|---|---|---|---|---|---|
| $3x/2$ $4200/x$ | | 67.5 93.3 | | 82.5 76.4 | | | |
| $y$ | | 39.2 | | 41.1 | | | |

Draw the graph of this relation, taking 1 cm to represent 5 m.p.h. on the $x$-axis and 1 cm to represent 1 mile per gallon on the $y$-axis. Label the $x$-axis from 40 to 80 and the $y$-axis from 27 to 42.

From your graph estimate:
(a) the petrol consumption at 75 m.p.h.
(b) the most economical speed at which to travel in order to conserve petrol.

**23** A cone of maximum volume is required from a circle of 10 cm radius. Using a graphical method find the radius, height and volume of the required cone, correct to 3 significant figures. (Volume of a cone is $\frac{1}{3}\pi r^2 h$, where $r$ is the base radius and $h$ is the vertical height.

| Substitution | (Change of subject— |
|---|---|
| Change of subject— | subject-letter more than |
| subject-letter once | once) |
| | (Functions) |

## ● You need to know:

**Algebra 1, 2, 7, 16**

---

**1**   For normal temperatures a rough way to change from degrees Celsius to degrees Fahrenheit is 'Double, then add 30'.

About how many degrees Fahrenheit is:
(a) 10 °C    (b) 0 °C    (c) −5 °C?

**2**   The surface area of a cube is $6s^2$, where $s$ is the length of one edge. Find the surface area if $s = 1$ m.

**3**   A car's stopping distance is reckoned to be $v + \dfrac{v^2}{20}$ feet at $v$ m.p.h. What would be the stopping distance at:
(a) 10 m.p.h.    (b) 50 m.p.h.?

**4**   When $x = 4$, $y = 2$ and $z = -3$, find the value of:

(a) $x + y + z$    (b) $x + y - z$    (c) $x - y + z$    (d) $x - (y - z)$    (e) $x^2$    (f) $\dfrac{x^2}{3y}$.

**5**   Write a simplified expression for the total length of the lines drawn in each of Figures 10:1 to 10:4.

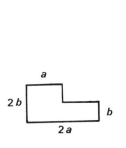

Fig. 10:1

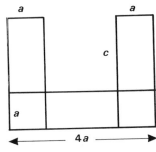

Fig. 10:2

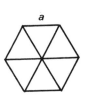

Fig. 10:3

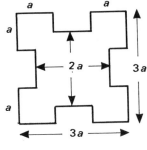

Fig. 10:4

54

**6**  Write a simplified expression for the total length of all the edges of each of the solids shown in Figures 10:5 to 10:8.

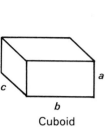

Cuboid

**Fig. 10:5**

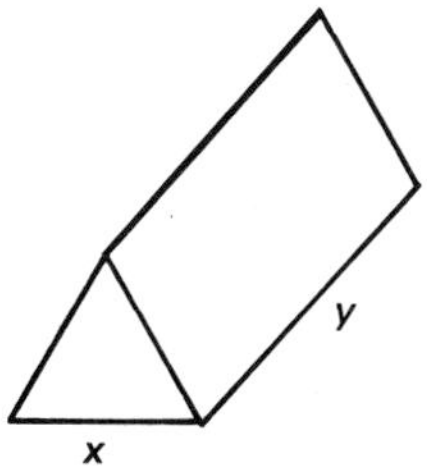

Equilateral
triangular
prism

**Fig. 10:6**

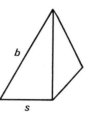

Square-based
pyramid

**Fig. 10:7**

Tetrahedron

**Fig. 10:8**

**7**  Jake has £$T$ to spend. He spends £$S$ and has £$L$ left. Write an expression to connect $T$, $S$ and $L$ starting:
(a)  $T =$      (b)  $L =$      (c)  $S =$      .

**8**  Anna buys $x$ apples at $y$ pence each. They cost her $z$ pence. Write an expression to connect $x$, $y$ and $z$ starting:
(a)  $z =$      (b)  $x =$      (c)  $y =$      .

**9**  Transpose the equation to make the term in square brackets the subject:
(a)  $V = wbh$   $[h]$      (b)  $A = \pi r^2$   $[r]$      (c)  $v^2 = u^2 + 2as$   $[s]$
(d)  $S = \frac{1}{2}(a + b + c)$   $[c]$      (e)  $a^2 + b^2 = 16$   $[a]$      (f)  $E = Mc^2$   $[c]$
(g)  $S = 2\pi rh + \pi r^2$   $[h]$.

**10**  A box is three times as long as it is deep and twice as wide as it is deep. Let it be $x$ cm deep.
(a)  How long is it?      (b)  How wide is it?
(c)  What is the sum of all its edges?
(d)  What is its surface area?
(e)  What is its volume?

**11**  The following formula gives a way of multiplying by 21:
'Double the number, then write a zero at the end, then add on the number.'

**Example**   38 × 21

$$38 \xrightarrow{\ 38 \times 2\ } 76 \xrightarrow{\ \text{write 0}\ } 760 \xrightarrow{\ \text{add 38}\ } 798$$

Use the formula to find:
(a)  23 × 21      (b)  47 × 21      (c)  102 × 21.

**12**  Make up a formula like the one in question 11 to multiply by 19.

**13**  A cookery book gives the formula: 'Number of pounds of jam obtained is found by multiplying the number of pounds of sugar used by five, then dividing by three.'

How many pounds of jam can be made from six pounds of sugar?

**\*14** A motoring organisation estimates that if a car has $x$ child passengers and $y$ adult passengers then the extra running cost is equivalent to adding $x + 2y$ pence to the price of a litre of petrol.

What is the equivalent extra cost per litre if the passengers are:
(a) 1 child, 1 adult   (b) 3 children, 0 adults   (c) 2 children, 1 adult?

**\*15** If $E = 2x^2 + x$ what is $E$ when $x$ is 4?

**\*16** When $x = 4$ and $y = -3$ find the value of :

(a) $2x + y$   (b) $3x - 6y$   (c) $(2x + y)(3x - 6y)$   (d) $\dfrac{3x - 6y}{2x + y}$.

(*LREB*)

**\*17** A stone is thrown upwards at 40 m/s. After $t$ seconds its height in metres is given by $h = 40t - 5t^2$. Find its height after 2 seconds.

(*SWEB*)

**\*18** A box weighs 1 kg when empty. What is the total weight of 6 boxes each containing $p$ kg of apples?

**\*19** How long will it take to travel $k$ km at $v$ km h$^{-1}$?

**\*20** For Figure 10:9 write an expression for:
(a) the perimeter of the figure
(b) the area of one square
(c) the area of the whole shape.

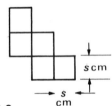

**Fig. 10:9**

**\*21** Figure 10:10 shows a cuboid, or 'brick shape'. The volume of a cuboid is length times width times height. Write a simplified expression for the volume of the cuboid in Figure 10:10.

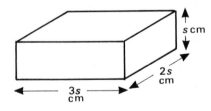

**Fig. 10:10**

**\*22** If Figure 10:10 represents the 'nominal size' (that is, including an allowance for mortar) of a building brick, and the wall it is used for contains 100 bricks, write an expression for the volume of the wall in terms of $s$.

**\*23** A wall is made with the bricks shown in Figure 10:10. It is 300$s$ cm long, 2$s$ cm wide and 5$s$ cm high.

(a) How many bricks wide is the wall?
(b) How many bricks high is the wall?
(c) How many bricks long is the wall?
(d) How many bricks are used altogether?

*24 Figures 10:11 to 10:13 show solids made from wire. Write an expression for the length of wire used for each.

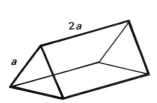

Equilateral
triangular
prism

**Fig. 10:11**

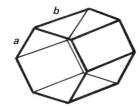

Regular
hexagonal
prism

**Fig. 10:12**

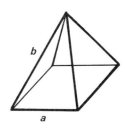

Square-based
pyramid

**Fig. 10:13**

*25 A man is paid £5 an hour for normal time and £8 for an hour's overtime. Write a formula to be used by the wages clerk for the total pay due to the man, using $x$ for his hours of normal time and $y$ for his hours of overtime.

*26 Given that $p = 2nx - y$, express:
(a) $y$ in terms of $n$, $x$ and $p$    (b) $n$ in terms of $p$, $x$ and $y$.

*27 Transpose the equation to make the term in square brackets the subject:
(a) $p = mv$  $[v]$    (b) $v = s^3$  $[s]$    (c) $a = m^2 - 3f$  $[f]$
(d) $g = \frac{1}{2}(x + y + z)$  $[y]$    (e) $x^2 + y^2 = 4$  $[x]$

28 If f:$x \rightarrow 2x$, g:$x \rightarrow x - 1$, and h:$x \rightarrow x^2$, find:
(a) f(2)    (b) g($-2$)    (c) h($-3$)    (d) fg(1)    (e) gf(1)
(f) gh($-1$)    (g) hf($-2$)    (h) fgh(1)    (i) $f^{-1}$    (j) $g^{-1}$.

29 Given that $a(bx + c) = c(x + 3a)$, express $x$ in terms of $a$, $b$ and $c$.

30 Given that $5a + 3b = c(4 - b)$, express:
(a) $c$ in terms of $a$ and $b$    (b) $b$ in terms of $a$ and $c$.

31 Given that $a + b = \dfrac{3a + 7}{b}$, express $a$ in terms of $b$.

32 Make $b$ the subject of $a = \dfrac{b}{b - 2}$.

33 The mean of $n$ items is $q$ and the mean of $m$ other items is $p$. Which of the following expressions gives the mean of all the items?

A  $\dfrac{p + q}{m + n}$    B  $\dfrac{mq + np}{(n + m)}$    C  $\dfrac{m + n}{p + q}$    D  $\dfrac{nq + mp}{(n + m)}$

(*AEB*)

**34** $T = 2\pi \sqrt{\dfrac{l}{g}}$, so $g =$

    **A** $\dfrac{2\pi\sqrt{l}}{T}$    **B** $\dfrac{T^2 l}{4\pi^2}$    **C** $\dfrac{l}{(T - 2\pi)^2}$    **D** $\dfrac{4\pi^2 l}{T^2}$.

**35** Alex cycles $k$ km in $t$ hours. What is his average speed in $m\,min^{-1}$?

**36** Find the inverse of the function:

    (a) $f: x \rightarrow 3 + \dfrac{1}{2x}$    (b) $f: x \rightarrow \dfrac{x + 2}{x - 4}$    (c) $f: x \rightarrow 2x^3$.

**37** $f(x)$ denotes the sum of the digits of $x$. For example, $f(75) = 12$.

Given that, in each of the following cases, $x$ is an integer with four digits, find:
(a) $x$ such that $f(x) = 1$
(b) the smallest $x$ such that $f(x) = 10$
(c) the largest $x$ such that $f(x) = 28$.

**38** The functions f, g and h are defined as follows:

    $f: x \rightarrow 2x$    $g: x \rightarrow x + 3$    $h: x \rightarrow \dfrac{1}{x}$

(a) Write down, in the form $x \rightarrow \ldots$, the composite functions fg and gf, and the inverse functions $f^{-1}$ and $h^{-1}$.

(b) Show that there is no value of $x$ for which $fg(x) = gf(x)$.

(c) Find a value for $x$ for which $fg(x) = f^{-1}g(x)$.

(d) Show that the values of $x$ for which $fh(x) = gf(x)$ are the roots of the equation $2x^2 + 3x - 2 = 0$ and hence find these values.

                                                                  *(EAEB)*

# 11 Algebra (ii)

Arithmetic with letters
Brackets and common
   factors
+ and − of integral indices
(Four-term common
   factors)

(Difference of two
   squares)
(Quadratic factors)
(Fractional indices)

## ● You need to know:

**Algebra 3, 8, 9, 10, 11**

---

**1** Simplify:
  (a) $c + c + 2c$   (b) $c \times c$   (c) $2c \times c$   (d) $c + c - 2c$   (e) $3c \times 2c$.

**2** Simplify:
  (a) $c + 3 + 4$   (b) $c + 2c - 2$   (c) $c - 2 + 2c$   (d) $3c + a + 2c$
  (e) $3 + 2c - 1$   (f) $c + 5c - 3 - 4c$.

**3** Simplify if possible:
  (a) $a + a + a$   (b) $a \times c$   (c) $a + c$   (d) $2a \times 2a$   (e) $2a + 2a$   (f) $2a + 2c$.

**4** Remove the brackets, then simplify if possible:
  (a) $2(a + b)$   (b) $2a(c - 3b)$   (c) $-3(2a - 3b + 2c)$
  (d) $6(a - b) + 4(a + b)$   (e) $4(a - 4) - 3(a - 5)$
  (f) $3(2t - 5) - 2(2t + 3)$   (g) $a - 2b + (3a - b) - (2a + 3b)$.

**5** Factorise by taking out a common factor:
  (a) $ax + bx$   (b) $4pq - 8p$   (c) $2a + 4p - 6c$   (d) $2ab - 4bc - 6cd$.

**6** Simplify:
  (a) $h \times h \times h$   (b) $h \times h^2$   (c) $(h^2)^2$   (d) $h^3 \times h^2$   (e) $h^4 \times h$   (f) $(h^3)^2$.

**7** Simplify:
  (a) $3a \times b$   (b) $4a^2 \times a$   (c) $2a \times 3a^2$   (d) $4ab \times a$   (e) $3b \times 2ab$.

**8** Simplify:
  (a) $2ab \times ab$   (b) $pq \times pq$   (c) $4p^2 \times 2c$   (d) $3mn^2 \times m^2n$.

59

**9** Simplify:

(a) $\dfrac{4a^2b}{6ab^3}$ (b) $\dfrac{3ab^2}{6a^2b}$ (c) $\dfrac{a^3b^2}{a^2b^3}$ (d) $\dfrac{2ab}{2a^2b^2}$ (e) $\dfrac{4km}{km}$.

**10** Simplify:

(a) $a^5 \div a^2$ (b) $a^4 \div a$ (c) $a^3 \div a^5$ (d) $2a^2b \div 6a$ (e) $4ab^2 \div 2ab$.

**11** Simplify if possible:

(a) $2a^2b + 3a^2b$ (b) $2a^2b + 3ab^2$ (c) $3a^2 - 2a + 2a$ (d) $3a^2 - 2a + 2a^2$

(e) $3a^3 - 2a + 2a^2$ (f) $3ab^2 + 2ab^2 - ab^2$.

**12** Simplify:

(a) $2x^3 \times 4x^2$ (b) $\dfrac{2x + 12}{2}$ (c) $\dfrac{4x + 14}{2}$ (d) $7x - y - 3x - 5y$

(e) $2a \times 3b \times 4a$ (f) $\dfrac{30x^5y^2}{16x^2y}$ (g) $\dfrac{10abc}{5ab}$ (h) $\dfrac{8x^2y}{16y^2}$ (i) $\sqrt{25a^4b^2}$.

**\*13** Simplify:

(a) $2d + d + 2d$ (b) $d \times 3d$ (c) $d \times d \times d$ (d) $c + 4c - 2c$ (e) $4f \times 2f$.

**\*14** Simplify:

(a) $5 + a - 2$ (b) $2a + 5a - 1$ (c) $3c - 2c - c$ (d) $4 + 2c - 3 + c$.

**\*15** Remove the brackets, then simplify if possible:

(a) $5(x - 2y)$ (b) $2c(c + 1)$ (c) $-2(1 - 4r + t^2)$ (d) $2(a + b) + 3(a - 2b)$

(e) $3(q + t) - (q - t)$ (f) $2a - a(1 + a) + 2a(a - 1)$.

**\*16** Factorise by taking out common factors:

(a) $4b - 2c$ (b) $3rt - 4r$ (c) $2mn - 4m^2$ (d) $ab - a^2b$ (e) $4x^2 - 4xy$.

**\*17** Simplify:

(a) $4c \times 3$ (b) $2a^2 \times a$ (c) $4c^2 \times 2c$ (d) $5bc \times b$ (e) $a^2b \times ab$.

**\*18** Simplify:

(a) $x^5 \div x^2$ (b) $5x^2r^3 \div x^2r^2$ (c) $12ab^3 \div 15a^2b$ (d) $a^5 \div a^8$.

**\*19** Find $n$ if:

(a) $3^4 \times 3^n = 3^7$ (b) $3^6 \div 3^2 = 3^n$. (SREB)

**\*20** What expression must be added to $3x + y$ to make it $7x + 4y$? (LREB)

**21** Factorise where possible:

(a) $a(c + d) - b(c + d)$ (b) $x(a + b) - y(a - b)$ (c) $3(a + c) - c(a + c)$

(d) $2(a - b) + c(a + b)$ (e) $-d(a - c) + b(a - c)$.

**22 Example** Factorise $xy + xz - ay - az$

$$xy + xz - ay - az \rightarrow x(y + z) - a(y + z)$$
$$\rightarrow (y + z)(x - a) \qquad \text{Note: } (y + z) \text{ is a common factor.}$$

Factorise:
(a) $ac + ad - bc - bd$    (b) $mn + mt + pn + pt$    (c) $2b + ab + 2c + ac$
(d) $ax - bx - 2ay + 2by$    (e) $6x + 4y - 9cx - 6cy$    (f) $3x - 3y - x^2 + xy$
(g) $2p^2 + ps - 4pt - 2st$.

**23** Factorise by taking out any common factors, then using the difference of two squares:
(a) $a^2 - 25$    (b) $a^2 - 25b^2$    (c) $4 - 36x^2$    (d) $3c^2 - 12d^2$    (e) $5x^2 - 5y^2$
(f) $3y^2 - 12$.

**24** Expand:
(a) $(x + 2)(x + 1)$    (b) $(x + 2)(x - 1)$    (c) $(x - 2)(x + 1)$    (d) $(x - 2)(x - 1)$
(e) $(2x - 3)(3x - 2)$    (f) $(2w - 1)^2$.

**25** Find all possible integral values of the ordered pair $(x, y)$ if $(x - 3)(y - 3) = 6$.

**26** Factorise:
(a) $t^2 - 4t + 3$    (b) $x^2 - x - 6$    (c) $x^2 - 6x + 5$    (d) $n^2 - 13n + 42$
(e) $a^2 - 6a - 16$    (f) $2a^2 - a - 10$    (g) $2x^2 + x - 6$    (h) $3a^2 - 22a - 16$
(i) $6a^2 - 5ab + b^2$    (j) $3x^2 + 10x - 8$.

**27** Find the value of $k$ if $x^2 + 4x + k$ is a perfect square.

**28** Find the value of $k$ if $4x^2 - 8x + k$ is a perfect square.

**29** Simplify:
(a) $a^{-2}$    (b) $b^{-3}$    (c) $6^{-2}$    (d) $2^{-3}$.

**30** Simplify:
(a) $100^{\frac{1}{2}}$    (b) $8^{\frac{1}{3}}$    (c) $16^{\frac{1}{4}}$    (d) $64^{\frac{1}{6}}$    (e) $(4d^4)^{\frac{1}{2}}$    (f) $(9d^6)^{\frac{1}{2}}$    (g) $(8c^3)^{\frac{1}{3}}$
(h) $(4a^3)^{\frac{1}{2}}$.

**31** Simplify:
(a) $8^{\frac{2}{3}}$    (b) $16^{\frac{3}{4}}$    (c) $32^{\frac{3}{5}}$    (d) $4^{\frac{3}{2}}$    (e) $81^{\frac{3}{4}}$.

**32** Simplify:
(a) $4^{-\frac{1}{2}}$    (b) $16^{-\frac{1}{4}}$    (c) $8^{-\frac{1}{3}}$    (d) $8^{-\frac{2}{3}}$    (e) $(\frac{1}{4})^{-2}$.

**33** Simplify:
(a) $27^{\frac{1}{3}}$    (b) $8^0$    (c) $81^{-\frac{3}{4}}$    (d) $9^{\frac{3}{2}}$    (e) $16^{1\frac{1}{2}}$    (f) $4^{2\frac{1}{2}}$    (g) $4^{-1}$
(h) $(\frac{1}{5})^{-1}$    (i) $(\frac{1}{2})^3$    (j) $(\frac{2}{3})^{-2}$.

**34** Assuming the denominator is not zero, factorise then simplify:
(a) $\dfrac{a^2 - 1}{a - 1}$    (b) $\dfrac{2m + 3n}{4m^2 - 9n^2}$    (c) $\dfrac{x^2 + 2x - 8}{x^2 - 2x}$    (d) $\dfrac{a + 4}{a^2 + 3a - 4}$
(e) $\dfrac{3a^2 + 8a + 4}{a^2 - a - 6}$    (f) $\dfrac{a^2 - 9}{a^2 - a - 12}$.

**35** Given that $n - 4\sqrt{3} = 6\sqrt{3}$, find $n$.

**36** Express as a single fraction in its lowest terms:

    (a) $\dfrac{a}{4} + \dfrac{a}{5}$   (b) $\dfrac{3a}{5} + \dfrac{2}{3}$   (c) $\dfrac{a-1}{2} - \dfrac{a-2}{3}$

    (d) $\dfrac{a-2b}{4} - \dfrac{a-3b}{8}$   (e) $\dfrac{2a+3}{5} - \dfrac{a+3}{6}$.

**37** Simplify:

    (a) $\dfrac{6a}{5a} \times \dfrac{15ac}{2}$   (b) $\dfrac{3a^2}{4} \times \dfrac{b}{9a}$   (c) $\dfrac{3a}{4} \div \dfrac{9a}{16}$   (d) $\dfrac{mnp}{6d} \div \dfrac{dnp}{3m}$

    (e) $6a^2b \div \dfrac{3a}{4c}$   (f) $\dfrac{12a^2c}{5d} \div \dfrac{9ac}{10d^2}$.

**38** Express as a single fraction in its lowest terms:

    (a) $\dfrac{x}{y} + \dfrac{y}{x}$   (b) $\dfrac{x}{y} - \dfrac{y}{x}$   (c) $\dfrac{3}{x} + \dfrac{4}{2x}$   (d) $\dfrac{3a}{b} - \dfrac{b}{3a}$   (e) $\dfrac{3a}{b} + \dfrac{a}{b^2}$

    (f) $\dfrac{4a-1}{2a} - \dfrac{2a-1}{3a} - \dfrac{1}{6a}$.

**39 Example**  Express as a single fraction in its lowest terms $\dfrac{5}{a-1} - \dfrac{2}{a+3}$.

          The L.C.M. of the denominators is $(a-1)(a+3)$.

$$\frac{5}{a-1} - \frac{2}{a+3} \rightarrow \frac{5(a+3)}{(a-1)(a+3)} - \frac{2(a-1)}{(a-1)(a+3)}$$

$$\rightarrow \frac{5a+15-2a+2}{(a-1)(a+3)} \rightarrow \frac{3a+17}{(a-1)(a+3)}$$

Express as a single fraction in its lowest terms:

    (a) $\dfrac{a}{a-b} - \dfrac{b}{a+b}$   (b) $\dfrac{1}{a+1} - \dfrac{1}{a+4}$   (c) $\dfrac{5}{a-1} - \dfrac{2}{a+3}$

    (d) $\dfrac{5}{3a-1} - \dfrac{3}{2a+3}$   (e) $\dfrac{a}{a-y} + \dfrac{y}{y-a}$   Note: $a - y = -(y - a)$

**40 Example**  Find the product of $(b+2)(b^2 - b + 2)$.

          Each term in the second bracket is multiplied by each term in the first bracket. Multiplying the second bracket by $b$ gives $b^3 - b^2 + 2b$, and multiplying it by 2 gives $2b^2 - 2b + 4$.

          Hence $(b+2)(b^2 - b + 2) \rightarrow b^3 - b^2 + 2b + 2b^2 - 2b + 4 \rightarrow b^3 + b^2 + 4$.

Find the product of:
    (a) $(b+1)(b^2 + 2b - 2)$   (b) $(3a-4)(2a^2 + 2a - 6)$
    (c) $(2x^2 - 3x + 4)(x^2 - 3x - 4)$.

**41** If $(x + a)$ is a factor of $f(x)$ then when $x = -a$, $f(x) = 0$.

*Reason:*  Let $Q$ be the result of dividing $f(x)$ by $(x + a)$.
Then $(x + a) \times Q = f(x)$.
If $x = -a$, then $(x + a) = 0$, so $(x + a) \times Q = 0$, so $f(x) = 0$.

**Example**  To find a factor of $x^3 + 5x^2 + 7x + 2$.

$f(1) = 1 + 5 + 7 + 2 \neq 0$
$f(-1) = -1 + 5 - 7 + 2 \neq 0$
$f(2) = 8 + 20 + 14 + 2 \neq 0$
$f(-2) = -8 + 20 - 14 + 2 = 0$, therefore $(x + 2)$ is a factor. The quotient may be found by inspection.

$(x + 2)(x^2 + 3x + 1) = x^3 + 5x^2 + 7x + 2$

Factorise:
(a)  $x^3 + 2x^2 - x - 2$     (b)  $x^3 - 3x + 2$     (c)  $x^3 - 6x^2 + 12x - 8$
(d)  $2x^3 + 5x^2 - 4x - 12$.

# 12 Algebra (iii)

Simple linear equations and inequalities (Fractional equations) (Linear simultaneous equations)

Quadratic equations by factors/formula) (Problems)

## ● You need to know:

Algebra 4, 5, 6, 12, 13, 14

---

**1** Find the value of the letter if:

(a) $a - 4 = 3$    (b) $a + 4 = 3$    (c) $4 - x = 7$    (d) $2a - 1 = 8$

(e) $3 - 2a = 7$    (f) $\dfrac{a}{2} + 1 = 9$.

**2** Find the value of the letter if:

(a) $3(a + 1) = 12$    (b) $4(2 - a) = 20$    (c) $\dfrac{2}{a + 1} = 1$    (d) $\dfrac{a + 1}{4} + 5 = 0$

(e) $\frac{1}{2}(2a - 3) = 6$    (f) $\dfrac{a}{3} + \dfrac{a}{2} = \dfrac{5}{6}$.

**3 Example**  Find the range of values of $x$ if $2x + 1 > 3$ and $x - 2 \leqslant 5$.

$2x + 1 > 3 \Rightarrow 2x > 2 \Rightarrow x > 1$
$x - 2 \leqslant 5 \Rightarrow x \leqslant 7$

*Answer*:  $1 < x \leqslant 7$  ($x$ is more than 1 but not more than 7.)

Find the range of values of the letter if:
(a) $x + 1 > 6$    (b) $x - 1 \leqslant 5$    (c) $2x - 1 > 5$    (d) $1 - 3x < 4$
(e) $x + 7 \geqslant 6$ and $2x - 1 < 5$.

**\*4** The relative density of a solid (that is, its density compared to water) is given by the formula

$$\text{Relative density} = \frac{\text{Mass of the solid}}{\text{Mass of water with the same volume as the solid}}$$

Figure 12:1 shows the two stages in an experiment to find the relative density of a solid. From the masses given calculate the relative density of the solid.

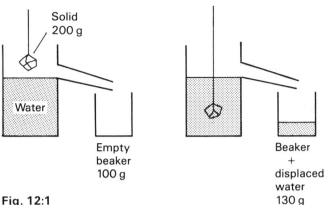

Solid
200 g

Water

Empty
beaker
100 g

Beaker
+
displaced
water
130 g

**Fig. 12:1**

*5   Find the value of the letter if:
(a)  $4 + x = 1$   (b)  $2x - 7 = 6$   (c)  $5(x - 3) = 15$   (d)  $\frac{1}{2}(2x + 1) = 9$
(e)  $\frac{3}{x} = 6$   (f)  $\frac{5}{x} = 15$.

*6   The coefficient of linear expansion of a substance is found from the formula

$$\text{Coefficient of linear expansion} = \frac{\text{expansion}}{\text{original length} \times \text{difference in temperature (}^\circ\text{C)}}$$

Thirty metres of copper pipe expands to 30.0357 metres when the temperature rises from 8 °C to 78 °C. What is the coefficient of linear expansion of copper?

*7   Figure 12:2 shows two squares.
(a)  Show that the perimeter $P$ of the shaded region is given by $P = 4x + 4y$.
(b)  Show that the area of the shaded region $A$ is given by $A = x^2 - y^2$.
(c)  When $x = 3$ cm and $y = 2$ cm calculate (i) $P$ and (ii) $A$.
(d)  Factorise (i) $4x + 4y$ and (ii) $x^2 - y^2$.
(e)  When $y = 7$ cm and $P = 100$ cm calculate (i) $x$ and (ii) $A$.
(f)  When $y = 1$ obtain a formula for (i) $x$ in terms of $P$ and (ii) $x$ in terms of $A$.

(*SWEB*)

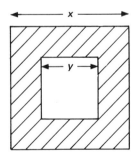

$x$

$y$

**Fig. 12:2**

8   Solve:
(a)  $2(x + 1) = x + 4$   (b)  $3a = 2(4 + a)$   (c)  $2a - 5 = 5a - 17$   (d)  $\frac{1}{2}(a - 4) = 3$
(e)  $\frac{3}{a} = 4$   (f)  $5 - 3(2 - a) = 1$   (g)  $2 + 2(4y + 11) = 21$
(h)  $p(p - 1) - p(p + 4) + 15 = 0$   (i)  $3(p - 2) - 2(3 - p) = 3p - 2$.

**9** Solve simultaneously:
   (a) $4x - 3y = 15$ and $2x + 3y = 3$
   (b) $2x - 3y = 13$ and $4x + 5y = 4$
   (c) $3x - 4y = 10$ and $5x + 7y = 3$
   (d) $9y = 9 - 4x$ and $3x = 11 + 6y$.

**10** Solve:
   (a) $t^2 + 3t = 0$    (b) $2x^2 = 7x$    (c) $2x^2 + 3x = 0$    (d) $4a^2 = 16a$
   (e) $3b^2 - 9b = 0$    (f) $3x^2 = 12x$.

**11** Solve by factorisation:
   (a) $x^2 - 3x + 2 = 0$    (b) $x^2 + 2x = 3$    (c) $x^2 + 6x + 9 = 0$    (d) $x^2 - 7x - 60 = 0$
   (e) $2x^2 + 6 = 7x$    (f) $8t^2 - 6 = 13t$.

**12** Solve:
   (a) $(x - 2)(x - 3) = 20$    (b) $(x + 2)(x + 3) = 12$    (c) $(x + 4)(x - 1) = 36$
   (d) $x(x - 5) = 6$    (e) $x(x + 4) = 32$    (f) $2(x + 1)(x - 3) = 24$.

**13** Solve by the formula, or by completing the square:
   (a) $x^2 - 4x + 2 = 0$    (b) $x^2 + 2x = 5$    (c) $x^2 - 3 = 6x$    (d) $2x^2 - 7x - 4 = 0$
   (e) $3d^2 + 2d = 4$.

**14** Find the range of values of $x$ for which $9 - (x - 3) \leqslant 2x$.

**15** The e.m.f. ($E$) and internal resistance ($r$) of a cell may be found by measuring the current flowing ($I$) for different external resistances ($R$).

The formula connecting these variables is $I = \dfrac{E}{R + r}$.

$I$ is in amps, $E$ in volts, and $R$ and $r$ in ohms.

Find the e.m.f. and the internal resistance of a cell which produces 0.25 amps when the external resistance is 5 ohms and 0.15 amps when the external resistance is 9 ohms.

**16** Given that $w = 3y$, $x = 4y$, and $x = z$, express $z$ in terms of $w$.

**17** Given that $f : x \rightarrow (x + 1)^2$ and $g : x \rightarrow (x - 2)^2$
   (a) find the values of $x$ that satisfy $f(x) = 4$
   (b) find the value of $x$ that satisfies $f(x) = g(x)$
   (c) solve $f(x) = 4x$.

**18** Given that $f : x \rightarrow (x - 1)^2$ and $g : x \rightarrow x^2 + 3x - 2$, solve $f(x) = g(x)$.

**19** Given that $f : x \rightarrow (x + 1)^2$ and $g : x \rightarrow 2x$, show that $f(x) = g(x)$ has no real solution.

**20** Three functions f, g and h are defined so that $f(x) = 3x$, $g(x) = 2x - 7$, and $h(x) = \dfrac{4}{x}$.

   (a) Find the values of $f(-2)$, $g(-2)$ and $h(-2)$.

   (b) Find the value of $x$ if $g(x) = 8$.

(c) (i) Write down and simplify an expression, in terms of $x$, for $g(f(x))$.
(ii) Find the value of $x$ for which $f(g(x)) = 12$.

(d) Find expressions, in terms of $x$, for $f^{-1}(x)$, $g^{-1}(x)$, and $h^{-1}(x)$.

(e) Find the values of $x$ for which $g(x) = h(x)$.

(f) Given that $k = h \circ g$ (that is $k(x) = h(g(x))$), find an expression for $k^{-1}(x)$ in terms of $x$.
(AEB)

**21** (a) Given that $y = \dfrac{x}{a - x}$

 (i) find $y$ when $x = \frac{2}{3}$ and $a = 3$
 (ii) express $x$ in terms of $a$ and $y$.

(b) Solve the equation $\dfrac{4}{2x + 3} = \dfrac{3}{x - 1}$.

(c) Simplify the expression $\dfrac{2x^2 - 3x - 9}{x^2 - 9}$. (MEG)

**22** A function $f(x)$ is defined as $f(x) = 2x^2 - x - 3$.
(a) Evaluate: (i) $f(-1)$     (ii) $f(\frac{1}{2})$.
(b) Find the values of $x$ for which: (i) $f(x) = 0$      (ii) $f(x) = -3$.

**23 Example** Find the range of values of $x$ for which $2x^2 - 5x - 3 \geqslant 0$.

$$2x^2 - 5x - 3 \equiv (2x + 1)(x - 3)$$
$$\therefore (2x + 1)(x - 3) \geqslant 0$$

Sketch $f(x) = (2x + 1)(x - 3)$, knowing that $f(x) = 0$ when $x = -\frac{1}{2}$ and when $x = 3$, and that $f(x)$ is a 'cup way up' parabola. See Figure 12:3.

From the diagram it is clear that $f(x) \geqslant 0$ when $x \leqslant -\frac{1}{2}$ and when $x \geqslant 3$, or $-\frac{1}{2} \geqslant x \geqslant 3$.

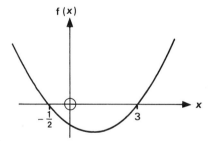

**Fig. 12:3**

Find the range of values of $x$ for which:
(a) $3x^2 + 5x - 2 \geqslant 0$     (b) $2x^2 - 7x - 15 < 0$     (c) $(2 + x)(4 - x) \geqslant 0$.

**24 Example** Solve $\dfrac{c}{2} - \dfrac{c}{3} = \dfrac{7}{5}$.

First remove the fractions by multiplying each term by the common denominator, 30.
Then $15c - 10c = 42 \rightarrow c = 8\frac{2}{5}$.

Solve:

(a) $\dfrac{a}{3} - \dfrac{a}{4} = \dfrac{1}{6}$    (b) $y + \dfrac{3y}{2} = 1$    (c) $\dfrac{3a}{2} - \dfrac{2a - 1}{4} = \dfrac{1}{8}$    (d) $\dfrac{2y - 4}{3} + 2 = \dfrac{3y + 3}{2}$

(e) $\dfrac{3(2y - 1)}{4} - \dfrac{2(y + 2)}{3} = 1.$

**25** Solve:

(a) $\dfrac{4}{a - 2} = 8$    (b) $\dfrac{9}{y} = \dfrac{4}{3}$    (c) $\dfrac{2a + 7}{a - 4} = 5$    (d) $\dfrac{4}{a} = \dfrac{5}{a + 2}$    (e) $\dfrac{a + 4}{a - 3} = \dfrac{a + 2}{a - 4}.$

**26** Given that $p = \dfrac{2y - 1}{y - 2}$ and $q = \dfrac{y + 2}{y - 1}$, show that $p - q = \dfrac{y^2 - 3y + 5}{y^2 - 3y + 2}$, then calculate the values of $y$, if any, which satisfy the equation:

(a) $q = 0$    (b) $p = 1$    (c) $p - q = 1$    (d) $p + q = 7\frac{1}{2}$.

**27** Find the solution set of integers if:

(a) $2 < x + 5 \leqslant 12$    (b) $-6 < 2x + 4 \leqslant 6$    (c) $3 < -3x < 9 - 4x.$

**28** Find the equation whose roots are:

(a) $2$ and $-3$    (b) $0$ and $4$    (c) $2\frac{1}{2}$ and $-2$.

**29** Given that $\dfrac{y}{x} - \dfrac{y - 2}{x - 3} = \dfrac{1}{x + 5}$, find the two values of $x$ for which $y = 3$.

---

**30** An allotment which is in the shape of a square of side $b$ metres has a neighbouring allotment which is in the shape of a rectangle $b$ metres long and $(b - 3)$ metres wide. The rectangular allotment is smaller than the square allotment by $24\,\text{m}^2$. Find the dimensions of each allotment.

**31** In an examination, the lowest and highest marks were 36 and 61 respectively. In order to change any mark $y$ into a mark $N$ on a new scale the formula $N = 4(y - 36)$ was used. Calculate the lowest and the highest mark on the new scale and the mark which would remain unchanged.

**32** In a factory a chargehand earns £40 per week more than a packer, and three packers and two chargehands together earn £430. Find the weekly wage of a packer.

**33** Given that $y = 2x^2 - 3x$
   (a) calculate, correct to 2 decimal places, the two values of $x$ for which $y = 1$
   (b) show that there is one value of $x$ for which $y = -\frac{9}{8}$ and find this value
   (c) find the set of values of $x$ for which $y < 0$.

**34** The formula $h = 12t - t^2$ gives the height $h$ metres of a ball above the ground, $t$ seconds after it is thrown into the air.
   (a) Find $h$ when $t = 1.2$.
   (b) Find when the ball subsequently hits the ground.
   (c) Find at what times the height of the ball is 4 metres.

**35** A rectangle has sides of length $(2x + 1)$ and $(x + 4)$ cm. Write down simplified expressions in $x$ for the perimeter and for the area.

Given that the area of this rectangle is $63 \text{ cm}^2$, form an equation in $x$ and solve it to find the positive value of $x$. Hence find the perimeter of the rectangle.

**36** Achmed bought some calculators for £200. Two were stolen, but, by selling each of the remaining ones for £1 more than he paid for it, he made an overall profit of £40.

(a) If he sold each calculator for £$x$, how many did he sell?

(b) How many did he buy?

(c) Show that $x$ must satisfy the equation $x^2 + 19x - 120 = 0$, and hence find the price at which he sold each calculator.

**37** A solid rectangular block has a square base of side $x$ cm and a height of $y$ cm. Given that the total length of the edges of the block is 28 cm and the total surface area of the block is $32 \text{ cm}^2$, write down two equations in $x$ and $y$, and by elimination prove that $3x^2 - 14x + 16 = 0$. Hence find the values of $x$ and $y$ and the two possible values for the volume of the block.

**38** (a) Show that $x = \dfrac{1}{x^2} + 2$ is equivalent to $x^3 - 2x^2 - 1 = 0$.

(b) Starting with $x_0 = 2$, use the iterative formula

$$x_{n+1} = \frac{1}{x_n^2} + 2$$

to calculate $x_1$, $x_2$, ... etc. correct to 4 decimal places, continuing the process until two successive values agree. Hence find an approximate root of the equation $x^3 - 2x^2 - 1 = 0$.

(c) Construct a flow-chart or computer program to carry out the above iterative process, which will stop when two successive values of $x_n$ agree to 4 decimal places, and which will print out that value.

**39** If $f(x)$ is a continuous function, then a change in value of $f(x)$ from +ve to −ve, or vice versa, means that $f(x)$ must become zero during the change.

Using this fact an equation may be solved by trial and error. A programmable calculator or a computer will be useful.

**Example** $f(x) = x^3 - 5x + 1$. Find the solutions of $f(x) = 0$.

| $x$ | $-3$ | $-2$ | $-1$ | $0$ | $1$ | $2$ | $3$ |
|------|------|------|------|-----|-----|-----|-----|
| $f(x)$ | $-11$ | $3$ | $5$ | $1$ | $-3$ | $-1$ | $13$ |

From the table, solutions will be found
   (i) between $-3$ and $-2$
  (ii) between $0$ and $1$
 (iii) between $2$ and $3$.

(i) f($-2.5$) is $-$ve ∴ solution is between $-2.5$ and $-2$
f($-2.3$) is $+$ve ∴ solution is between $-2.3$ and $-2.5$
f($-2.4$) is $-$ve ∴ solution is between $-2.3$ and $-2.4$
f($-2.35$) is $-$ve ∴ solution is between $-2.35$ and $-2.3$
f($-2.32$) is $+$ve ∴ solution is between $-2.32$ and $-2.35$
f($-2.33$) $= 0.000\,663$, which means it is very close to a solution.
The process can be continued to any degree of accuracy.

Find the other two solutions to the given function.

**40** Find the three solutions of f($x$) $= 0$ where f($x$) $= 2x^3 - x^2 - 13x - 4$, given that they all lie between $-3$ and $3$.

**41** There was an old man, much revered,
Who said, 'What's the length of my beard?
If I double it, then
Add its square minus ten
I get minus two feet.' How weird!

# 13 Algebra (iv)

## Variation

## ● You need to know:

**Ratio 10**
**Algebra 17**

---

**1**  **Example**  The volume ($V$) of a sphere of radius $r$ is given by $V = \dfrac{4\pi r^3}{3}$.

$\dfrac{4\pi}{3}$ is a constant; call this $k$.

Then $V = kr^3$
$V \propto r^3$
*V varies directly as the cube of r*
*V is directly proportional to r cubed*.

Write in $k$ form, in $\propto$ form, and in words, the following.

(a)  The cost ($c$ pence) of sending $n$ first-class letters is given by the formula $c = 17n$.

(b)  The surface area ($A$) of a sphere, radius $r$, is given by $A = 4\pi r^2$.

(c)  $y = \dfrac{2}{x}$

(d)  $y = \dfrac{3x}{z^2}$

(e)  The cost (£$C$) per person for an outing is given by $C = \dfrac{£120}{n}$ where $n$ is the number of people going.

**2**  1 m$^2$ of carpet costs £$k$. If $s$ square metres cost £$y$ write an equation and an expression connecting $y$ and $s$.

**3**  Painters are paid £$k$ per hour. If Jethro earns £$E$ in $h$ hours write an equation and an expression connecting $E$ with $h$.

**4**  The volume ($V$) of a prism varies directly as its cross-section area ($A$) and its height ($H$). Write an expression connecting $V$ with $A$ and $H$.

**5**  The height ($H$) of a cone varies directly as its volume ($V$) and inversely as the square of its radius ($R$). Write an expression connecting $H$ with $V$ and $R$.

**6** The acceleration ($A$) of a body is proportional to the force ($F$) and inversely proportional to the mass ($M$). Write an expression connecting $A$ with $F$ and $M$.

**7** The volume of a cylinder, radius $r$ and height $h$, is $\pi r^2 h$. What change will be made in the volume if:
(a) the radius is halved      (b) the height is halved
(c) both the radius and the height are halved
(d) the radius is doubled and the height is halved
(e) the radius is halved and the height is doubled?

**8** The variables $x$, $y$ and $z$ are connected by the equation $y = \dfrac{kx^2}{z}$ where $k$ is a constant.
(a) State in words how $y$ varies with $x$ and $z$.
(b) Given that $y = 8.1$ when $x = 9$ and $z = 3$ find the value of $k$.
(c) Find $x$ when $y = 6$ and $z = 5$.

**9** $y \propto x^n$ where $n \in \{-2, -1, 1, 2\}$.

When $n = -2$,

$$y \propto x^{-2} \rightarrow y \propto \frac{1}{x^2} \rightarrow y = \frac{k}{x^2}.$$

(a) Write similar statements about $y$ and $x$ when
  (i) $n = -1$      (ii) $n = 1$      (iii) $n = 2$.

(b) Find $k$ if:
  (i)   $n = -2$ and $y = 4$ when $x = 2$
  (ii)  $n = -1$ and $y = 8$ when $x = 8$
  (iii) $n = 1$ and $y = 6$ when $x = 9$
  (iv)  $n = 2$ and $y = 16$ when $x = -8$.

**10** $y \propto x^2$ yields a family of graphs, e.g. $y = x^2$, $y = 2x^2$, $y = 3x^2$, etc. They are all of the same basic shape (a parabola).

Sketch one example of each of the four graphs represented by $y \propto x^n$ where $n = -2$, $n = -1$, $n = 1$, $n = 2$.

**11** The volume ($V$) of a cone is directly proportional to the square of its base radius ($R$) and its height ($H$).

(a) Write an expression connecting $V$ with $R$ and $H$.

(b) If $H$ is constant, then $V \propto R^2$. If $R$ becomes four times as long, how many times will $V$ increase?

(c) How will $V$ change if $H$ is doubled and $R$ is trebled?

(d) How will $V$ change if both $H$ and $R$ are trebled?

**12** A variable $s$ is inversely proportional to a second variable $t$. If $t$ is increased by 25% find the percentage change in $s$.

(*AEB 1984*)

**13** The heat ($H$) in calories developed in an electrically heated wire varies directly as the square of the voltage ($V$), directly as the time ($T$) and inversely as the resistance ($R$ ohms).

(a) Write an expression connecting $H$ with $V$, $T$ and $R$.

(b) Using constant $k$, write an equation developed from your answer to part (a).

(c) Given that 4 calories are produced by 20 volts in 1 second for a wire of resistance 25 ohms, find the value of $k$.

(d) A longer length of the same wire has a resistance of 50 ohms. How many calories will be produced in 10 seconds by 5 volts?

**14** The square of the orbital period ($T$ years) of a planet varies as the cube of its mean distance ($D$ km) from the sun.

For Earth, $T$ is 1 year and $D$ is $1.5 \times 10^8$ km. Calculate the orbital period of Jupiter, $7.82 \times 10^8$ km from the sun.

**15** Charles' Law: Under conditions of constant pressure the volume of a fixed mass of an ideal gas is directly proportional to its kelvin temperature.

Boyle's Law: The pressure of a fixed mass of an ideal gas is inversely proportional to its volume provided that the temperature remains constant.

A certain mass of dry air is enclosed in a graduated vessel, with arrangements to vary and measure the temperature, the pressure, and the volume occupied by the air. Volumes are expressed in terms of the units in which the vessel is graduated.

The volume occupied by the air is 600 units when the temperature is 300 K and the pressure is $10^5$ N/m$^2$.

(a) If the pressure remains constant find the volume occupied by the air when the temperature is 362 K.

(b) At what pressure will the volume be 500 units when the temperature is 300 K?

*(Oxford Physics)*

**16** When scout bees find food they return to the hive and perform a 'waggle dance'. One theory suggests that during one circuit of the dance the average number of pulses of sound, $n$, emitted by the bee is the sum of two terms. The first term is a constant $a$; the second term is directly proportional to the distance, $x$ km, of the food from the hive, with constant of proportionality $b$.

(a) Write an equation relating $n$, $x$ and the two constants $a$ and $b$.

(b) Given that $n = 28$ when $x = 0.5$ and that $n = 88$ when $x = 2$ find $a$ and $b$ and hence calculate the predicted distance in metres of a food source from the hive if the scout bee emits an average of 44 pulses of sound during one circuit of the dance.

*(AEB 1982)*

# 14 Geometry (i)

| | |
|---|---|
| **Basic terms** | **Straight-line angles** |
| **Plane symmetry** | **Bearings** |
| **Measuring lines and angles** | **Polygons** |

## ● You need to know:

**Geometry 1, 3, 7**
**Symmetry 1, 2, 3**

---

**1** Name the shapes used for the road signs in Figure 14:1.

$60° \times 3 = 180° / 3 = 6°$

(a)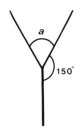

(b)

(c)

**Fig. 14:1**

**2** Calculate the sum of the interior angles of each shape used in Figure 14:1.

**3** ABCD is an isosceles trapezium. AB is parallel to DC with DC longer than AB.
 (a) Sketch the trapezium.
 (b) The acute angles are 50°. Calculate the size of the obtuse angles.
 (c) From vertex A draw AX perpendicular to DC, meeting DC in X.
 (d) Calculate angle DAX.

**4** (a) Figure 14:2 has a vertical line of symmetry. Calculate angle *a*.
 (b) Figure 14:3 has a horizontal line of symmetry. Calculate angle *b*.
 (c) Figure 14:4 has a vertical line of symmetry. Calculate angle *c*.

**Fig. 14:2**     **Fig. 14:3**     **Fig. 14:4**

**5** The bisectors of the angles of any triangle are concurrent. Draw a sketch to illustrate this.

**6** State the order of rotational symmetry for:
(a) an equilateral triangle  (b) a rhombus  (c) a regular pentagon.

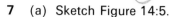

**7** (a) Sketch Figure 14:5.

(b) Has your sketch line symmetry? If so, draw the lines of symmetry.

(c) Has your sketch point symmetry? If so, mark the point about which it is symmetrical.

**Fig. 14:5**

**8** Figure 14:6 shows an observation post O on a coast line, and a dinghy A out at sea. The coast line runs north–south. The bearing of A from O is 030° and the distance OA is 900 m.

(a) Using a scale of 1 cm to 100 m make a scale drawing to show the positions of O and A.

(b) A second dinghy B is due east of A and AB is 500 m. Mark the position of B on your diagram. Measure angle OBA.

(c) A third dinghy C is due south of A and its bearing from O is 120°. Mark the position of C on your diagram.

(d) Measure and state the size of angle ABC.

(e) Give the three-figure bearing of C from B.
(*SWEB*)

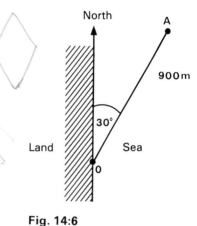

**Fig. 14:6**

**\*9** Figure 14:7 shows part of a tessellation made up from three tile shapes.
(a) Name the three shapes used.
(b) Calculate the size of the angle $\alpha$.

**\*10** Describe the symmetry of Figure 14:8.

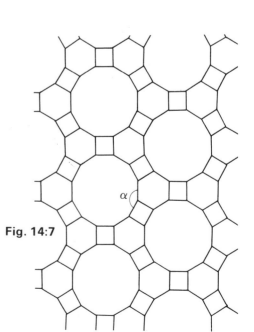

**Fig. 14:7**

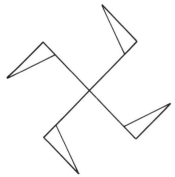

**Fig. 14:8**

**\*11** (a) Sketch Figure 14:9.

(b) Add two straight lines to your diagram to give it one vertical line of symmetry.

(c) Name the quadrilateral you have drawn.

(d) If angle HXY was 65°, what would be the size of angle HYX?

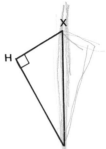

**Fig. 14:9**

**\*12** (a) Copy Figure 14:10 onto 1 cm-squared paper. Be careful to mark A, B, C, D and the harbour entrance correctly.

(b) In a speedboat race the boats leave port A, head for buoy B, then turn and head for buoy C, then buoy D. The race finishes as the boat passes through the harbour entrance, E. Draw on your sketch four straight lines to show the shortest possible course.

(c) What bearings should the boats take at each of the points A, B, C and D?

(d) About how many kilometres is the whole race?

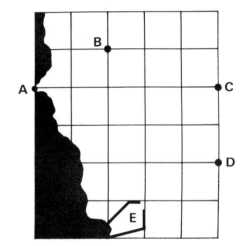

Scale   1 : 50 000
1 cm to 500 m

**Fig. 14:10**

**\*13** Triangle ABC is isosceles. XA is the bisector of angle A with X lying on BC. Calculate the size of angle AXC if:
(a) angle B is 100°     (b) angle B is 20°.

**\*14** What is strange about a 3 cm-, 6 cm-, 9 cm-sided triangle?

**15** (a) Sketch a diagram to show a point A on a bearing of 060° from a point B. State and illustrate the bearing of B from A.

(b) Sketch a diagram to show a point C on a bearing of 250° from a point D. State and illustrate the bearing of D from C.

(c) In parts (a) and (b) your answers are called back-bearings. Back-bearings may easily be calculated without drawing a diagram. Find the rule.

**16** The angles of a pentagon are in the ratio 2 : 3 : 4 : 5 : 6. Calculate the largest angle.

**17** A rhombus has diagonals of length $a$ cm and $b$ cm. A rectangle has sides of lengths $a$ cm and $b$ cm. State the ratio of the area of the rhombus to the area of the rectangle.

**18** In Figure 14:11, FHBD is a parallelogram. Calculate angle HBD.

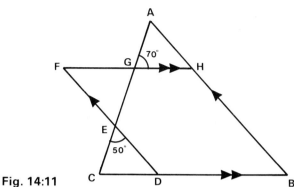

**Fig. 14:11**

**19** Calculate angle $\theta$ in Figure 14:12.

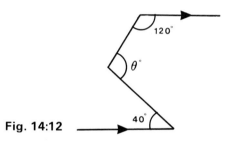

**Fig. 14:12**

**20** A regular polygon X has twice as many sides as polygon Y. The interior angle sum of Y is 540°. What is the interior angle sum of X?

*(AEB 1985)*

**21** In triangle XYZ, angle X is 100° and angle Z is 35°. P is the foot of the perpendicular from X to YZ. Show that triangle XPY is isosceles.

**22** The pilot of an aircraft flying over the Indian Ocean spotted a yacht which was anchored at a point on a bearing of 335° and 110 km from a port in the Seychelles Islands. The pilot signalled to the port, and a ship set off from there to investigate. However, due to a misunderstanding, the ship set off on a bearing of 355°, at a speed of 25 km/h.

(a) Draw a scale diagram showing the position of the port, the position of the yacht, and the course of the ship, showing clearly the direction of north.

(b) Measure the shortest distance between the yacht and the ship as the ship sailed in a straight line from the port.

Five hours after leaving the port the captain of the ship realised his mistake and altered course to sail directly to the yacht.

(c) Measure the distance of the ship from the yacht when the captain altered course.

(d) Measure and state the new bearing of the ship.

*(AEB 1985)*

**23** To trisect angle AOB.

Draw a circle centre O, to cut OB at C. Produce AO.
Draw line CDE such that D lies on the circle, E lies on AO produced, and DE = OC.

Prove that angle DOE is a third of angle AOB.

**24** Prove that the bisector of one angle of a triangle divides the opposite side in the ratio of the sides enclosing the angle.

# 15 Geometry (ii)

| Similarity | Areas and volumes of |
|---|---|
| Enlargement | similar shapes |
| Congruence | |

## ● You need to know:

**Geometry 4, 5**
**Ratio 8, 9**

---

**1** Which of the following must be mathematically similar?
   (a) A negative of a photo and an enlarged print made using it.
   (b) A large painting and a reproduction of the painting in a book.
   (c) Two brothers.   (d) Two spheres.   (e) Two mugs.
   (f) Equilateral triangles.   (g) Isosceles trapeziums.   (h) Cones.

**2** (a) The squares in Figure 15:1 have 0.5 cm sides.
       Using 1 cm-squared paper, draw a similar shape
       to that shown, with sides twice as long.

   (b) State the ratio of the area of the shape in Figure
       15:1 to the area of the shape that you have
       drawn.

**Fig. 15:1**

**3** Figure 15:2 represents a scientific experiment in which a lens casts an image of a match on a
   screen.

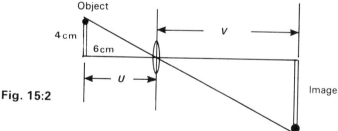

**Fig. 15:2**

The magnification of the lens is defined as

$$\frac{\text{height of image}}{\text{height of object}}$$

The lens shown has a magnification of $\times 2\frac{1}{2}$.

Calculate:
(a) the height of the image   (b) the distance $v$.

**4** Figure 15:3 shows two similar triangles.
   (a) Their sides are in the ratio 12:8. Simplify this ratio.
   (b) Calculate the value of (i) $x$ (ii) $y$.

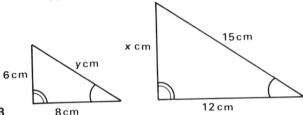

Fig. 15:3

**5** Figure 15:4 shows triangle ABC enlarged by various scale factors from centre O.

   (a) Which triangle is the result of an enlargement of triangle ABC by:
      (i) scale factor 3    (ii) scale factor $-\frac{1}{2}$    (iii) scale factor $-1$?

   (b) If triangle A″B″C″ is taken as the object triangle, what is the enlargement scale factor of:
      (i) $\triangle A'''B'''C'''$    (ii) $\triangle ABC$    (iii) $\triangle A'B'C'$?

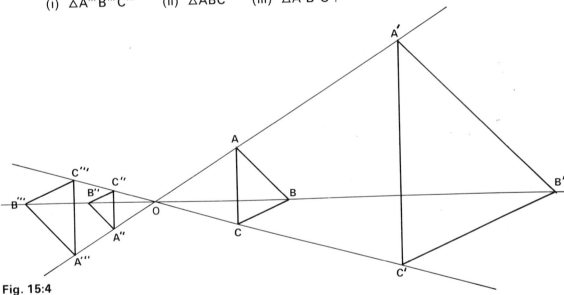

Fig. 15:4

**6** Congruent shapes are exactly the same in size and shape, although one shape may be a reflection of another ('turned over'). Which two shapes in Figure 15:5 are congruent?

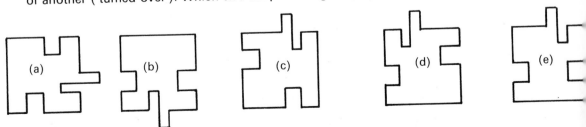

Fig. 15:5

**7** A model of a car is to a scale of 1 : 50. The model has five doors and a total length of 8 cm. How long is the real car, and how many doors has it?

**\*8** The three rectangles in Figure 15:6 are not drawn to scale.

(a) Calculate the area of rectangle ABCD.

(b) Find the perimeter of ABCD.

(c) Rectangles EFGH and IJKL are similar to rectangle ABCD.
   (i) Find the length of the side EF.
   (ii) Find the length of the side IL.

(d) Express as fractions in their lowest terms:
   (i) $\dfrac{IJ}{AB}$   (ii) $\dfrac{\text{area IJKL}}{\text{area ABCD}}$   (iii) $\dfrac{\text{perimeter EFGH}}{\text{perimeter ABCD}}$.

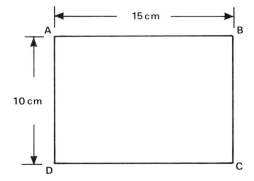 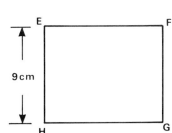 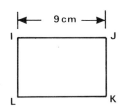

**Fig. 15:6**

(e) A rectangular carpet 4 metres long and 3 metres wide costs £246.00. A second carpet of the same material is similar in shape, is 2 metres long, and costs the same per square metre. Calculate:
   (i) the width   (ii) the cost of the second carpet.

(*SWEB*)

**\*9** A child has a set of wooden bricks. Each brick is a cube of side 5 cm. The bricks are to be put together to make larger cubes.

(a) How many bricks are needed to make a cube of side:
   (i) 10 cm   (ii) 15 cm   (iii) 20 cm?

(b) What is the surface area of each cube in part (a)?

(c) What is the volume of each cube in part (a)?

(d) Find the ratio of surface area to volume for each cube in the form 1 : $n$ (use a calculator).

**10** Refer to Figure 15:8.

   (a) By measurement check that the rectangles are similar.

   (b) State the ratio of their lengths.

   (c) State the ratio of the areas of the two rectangles.

**Fig. 15:8**

**11** In Figure 15:9 RQ is parallel to BC and QP is parallel to AB. AQ = 2 cm, QC = 6 cm, RQ = 4 cm and RB = 9 cm.

   (a) Name a triangle congruent to triangle PQR.

   (b) Name two triangles, each of which is similar to triangle ARQ.

   (c) Calculate (i) PC, (ii) AR, and (iii) $\dfrac{\text{area } \triangle ARQ}{\text{area } \triangle ABC}$.

   (d) Given that area $\triangle ARQ = k$ cm$^2$, express area $\triangle PRQ$ in terms of $k$.

                                                   (*MEG*)

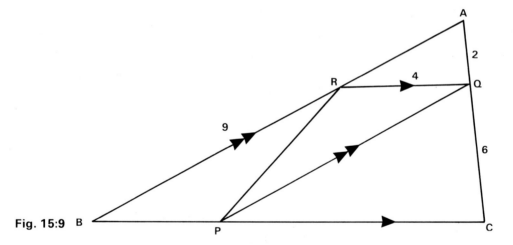

**Fig. 15:9**

**12** In Figure 15:10, angle A is 90°, and AC is an altitude.

   (a) Name an angle equal to the angle marked $\theta$.

   (b) Name an angle equal to the angle marked $\alpha$.

   (c) Write equal angles over each other to complete the statements:

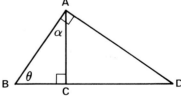

**Fig. 15:10**

   (i)    $\triangle$s $\dfrac{\text{A B C}}{\underline{\ } \text{ A } \underline{\ }}$ are similar

   (ii)   $\triangle$s $\dfrac{\text{A B D}}{\underline{\ } \text{ B } \underline{\ }}$ are similar

   (iii) $\triangle$s $\dfrac{\text{A C D}}{\underline{\ } \ \underline{\ } \text{ D}}$ are similar.

(d)  Using your answers to part (c) copy and complete:

(i)  $\dfrac{AB}{DC} = \underline{\quad} = \dfrac{BC}{\underline{\quad}}$     (ii)  $\dfrac{\underline{\quad}}{CB} = \dfrac{AD}{\underline{\quad}} = \dfrac{\underline{\quad}}{BA}$     (iii)  $\dfrac{AC}{\underline{\quad}} = \dfrac{\underline{\quad}}{BD} = \dfrac{\underline{\quad}}{AD}$.

**13**  In Figure 15:11, AX : XY = AP : PQ.
Calculate XY if AY is 12 cm, AP is 5 cm and PQ is 4 cm.

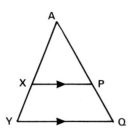

**Fig. 15:11**

**14**  For Figures 15:12 to 15:16 state if the pair of triangles is congruent, giving your reason.

**Fig. 15:12**

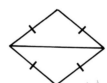

**Fig. 15:13**

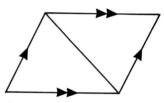

**Fig. 15:14**

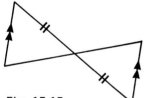

**Fig. 15:15**

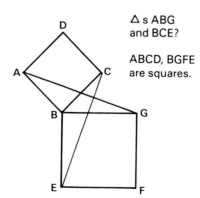

△ s ABG
and BCE?

ABCD, BGFE
are squares.

**Fig. 15:16**

**15**  Two cans are mathematically similar. One holds 0.125 litres, the other holds a full litre. The smaller can is 3 cm high. How tall is the larger can?

**16**  Two cuboids are mathematically similar. One is 12 cm long by 10 cm wide by 8 cm high. The other is 9 cm long. State as simply as possible the ratio of:
(a)  their heights     (b)  their surface areas     (c)  their volumes.

**17** Figure 15:17 shows a six-pointed star which is formed by drawing an equilateral triangle on each side of the regular hexagon PQRSTU. The centre of the hexagon is O.

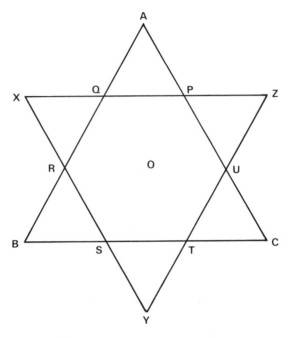

**Fig. 15:17**

(a) Prove that △XYZ is congruent to △ABC.

(b) Show that the area of the six-pointed star is twice the area of the hexagon PQRSTU.

(c) If ON is drawn from O perpendicular to QP to meet QP at N, find the value of the ratio ON : OA.

(d) Find the value of the ratio

Area of circle AXBYCZ : Area of the circle inscribed in hexagon PQRSTU.

(*EAEB*)

**18** Two cylinders X and Y are such that the height of X is six times the height of Y and the radius of the base of X is a third of the radius of the base of Y. What is the ratio of the volume of X to the volume of Y?

(*AEB 1985*)

**19** A cone of height 18 cm and base radius 9 cm is cut by a plane parallel to the base circle and 9 cm from it. Find the ratio of the volumes of the two resulting pieces.

**20** Figure 15:18 shows a triangle, right-angled at B, with BD perpendicular to AC. BD is of length 2 cm and CD is of length $x$ cm.

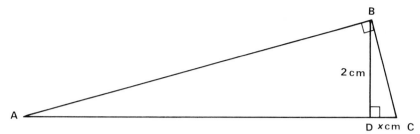

Fig. 15:18

Using similar triangles, show that the length of AD is $\frac{4}{x}$ cm and hence that the area, in cm², of triangle ABC is $x + \frac{4}{x}$.

Find, correct to 3 significant figures, the value of $x$ when the area of triangle ABC is 7 cm².

(*Scottish*)

21 An important application of the effect of enlargement is the ratio of surface area to volume for various sizes of animals and plants. Heat loss depends on surface area (of the skin); heat production depends on muscle volume. An idea of the effect can be found in comparing the surface area and volume of cubes:

1 cm cube: area 6 cm²; volume 1 cm³; ratio 6 : 1.

10 cm cube: area 600 cm²; volume 1000 cm³; ratio 3 : 5.

Clearly a large animal is in far less danger of hypothermia (excessive loss of body heat) than a similar-shaped small one.

Compare the surface area to weight ratio of a man of 25 weighing 68 kg with a skin area of 1.8 m², and a baby of one year weighing 10 kg with a skin area of 0.47 m². Discuss the implications of your answer.

# 16 Geometry (iii)

Parts of a circle
Perpendicular bisector
of a chord
Tangent and radius

Angles in a circle
(Alternative Segment)
Theorem)
(Intersecting chords)

## ● You need to know:

### Geometry 8

Note: In the diagrams in this chapter the centre of a circle is called O and is marked with a large dot.

**1** Link Figures 16:1 to 16:5 with the following facts:

**A** ⌐ bisector of a chord is a diameter

**B** ∠ at centre = 2∠ at circumference

**C** ∠s in same segment are equal

**D** ∠ in semicircle = 90°

**E** Opposite ∠s of cyclic quad. are supplementary.

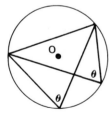
Fig. 16:1

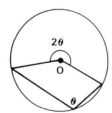
Fig. 16:2

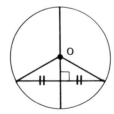
Fig. 16:3

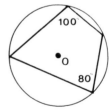
Fig. 16:4

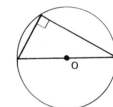
Fig. 16:5

**2** Copy Figure 16:6 and show how to complete it to find the centre of the circle.

**3** Calculate the shortest distance from the centre of a 10 cm-radius circle to a 16 cm chord. (Use Pythagoras' Theorem.)

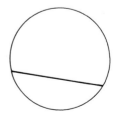
Fig. 16:6

**4** In Figure 16:7, AB and CD are straight lines. E may, or may not, be the centre.

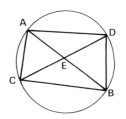

**Fig. 16:7**

(a) If E *is* the centre and ∠DEB = 80°, state the size of ∠BAD.

(b) If ∠BDC = 48°, state the size of ∠BAC.

(c) If AB is a diameter and ∠BAD = 42°, state the size of angle ABD.

(d) If ∠ACB = 100°, state the size of ∠ADB.

(e) If AD//CB and ∠BCD = 40°, state the size of ∠ABC.

**5** Calculate the value of x in Figure 16:8.

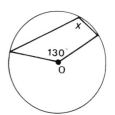

**Fig. 16:8**

**6** For Figure 16:9

(a) name two radii

(b) name two tangents

(c) state the size of:
   (i) angle ASO    (ii) angle OTX
   (iii) angle SOT   (iv) angle SOT reflex.

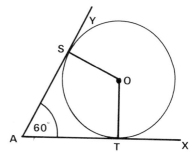

**Fig. 16:9**

**\*7** (a) Name an angle in Figure 16:10 equal to ∠BAC because they are 'angles in the same segment'.

(b) Repeat part (a) for ∠DAE.

(c) **Example** Angles CAD and CED are equal angles in the same segment, standing on chord CD.

Name three equal angles in the same segment standing on chord AE.

(d) If ∠ACD = 90°, which line would be a diameter?

(e) Name three cyclic quads which have A as one corner.

(f) If ∠BCD = 160°, calculate ∠BED.

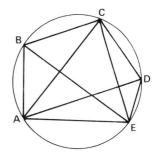

**Fig. 16:10**

**\*8** (a) Why is △OAB in Figure 16:11 isosceles?

(b) If ∠C = 25°, calculate the three angles of △OAB.

(c) If △OAB is equilateral and CA bisects ∠OAB, show that AB = BC.

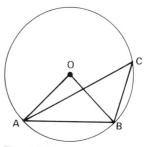

**Fig. 16:11**

*9 (a) If in Figure 16:12 ∠K = 60°, calculate ∠N.
(b) If ∠MOL = 130°, calculate ∠K and ∠N.
(c) If ∠N = 100°, calculate ∠MOL.
(d) Why is MOLN *not* a cyclic quadrilateral?

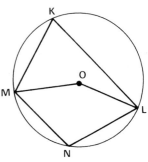

**Fig. 16:12**

*10 For Figure 16:13

(a) name two angles equal to ∠P and say why they are equal

(b) name one angle equal to:
(i) ∠PTQ (ii) ∠PSR (iii) ∠QSR.

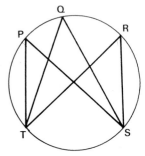

**Fig. 16:13**

11 (a) If in Figure 16:14 ∠RST = 110°, calculate the four angles of the cyclic quad.

(b) If ∠P = ∠R, calculate ∠RST.

(c) If PQ//SR (as well as PS//QR) explain why parallelogram PQRS must be a square or a rectangle.

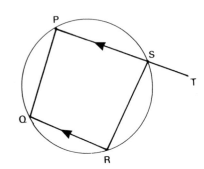

**Fig. 16:14**

12 Two chords AB and CD cross at E. If AE = AC, prove that DE = DB.

13 PR is a diameter of a circle and PQRS is a cyclic quadrilateral with ∠QPR = ∠RPS. Prove that ∠QRP = ∠SRP.

14 ABC is an equilateral triangle with its vertices on a circle. The bisector of ∠A meets the circle at D. Prove that AD is a diameter.

15 In cyclic quadrilateral ABCD, BA = BC and ∠ADB = 40°. Calculate ∠ABC.

16 Calculate the angle formed on a clock-face by joining the point representing 6 hours to the points representing 4 and 9 hours. (Use '∠s at centre and circumference'.)

**17** In Figure 16:15, AX, BY and CZ are the altitudes of △ABC.

(a) Why must B, Z, Y and C be concyclic points (that is, points on the circumference of the same circle)?

(b) Why must B, Z, P and X be concyclic points?

(c) Name four other sets of concyclic points.

(d) Draw a large copy of Figure 16:15 and draw the six circles.

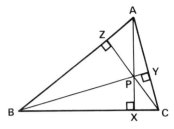

**Fig. 16:15**

**18** For Figure 16:16

(a) state the size of
(i) ∠ATC (ii) ∠CBT.

(b) calculate
(i) ∠BTC (ii) ∠BCT (iii) ∠BDT.

Angle ATB will always equal angle BDT. This is called the Alternate Segment Theorem. See Figure 16:17.

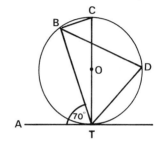

**Fig. 16:16**

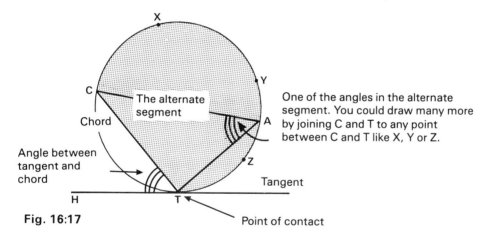

The alternate segment

Chord

Angle between tangent and chord

Tangent

**Fig. 16:17**

Point of contact

One of the angles in the alternate segment. You could draw many more by joining C and T to any point between C and T like X, Y or Z.

**19** In Figure 16:18

p = t (Alternate Segment Theorem, tangent TAM, chord AC.)

Write in a similar way the angle-pairs starting with:
(a) v (b) r (c) u.

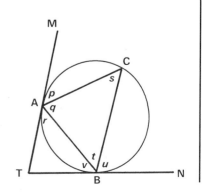

**Fig. 16:18**

**20** Prove that angle QPT in Figure 16:19 is a right angle for all values of ∠VTU. (Hints: Let ∠VTU = $\theta°$; then find angles TPV, PVT, PTV, PQV and QPV in terms of $\theta$.)

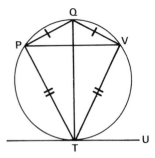

**Fig. 16:19**

**21** In Figure 16:20, ADE is straight, CBT is a tangent, but EB is not. Prove AC//BE.

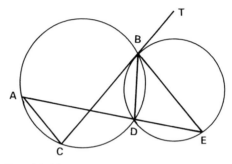

**Fig. 16:20**

**22** In Figure 16:21, XZ is parallel to RS. Prove that YT bisects ∠RTS.

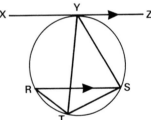

**Fig. 16:21**

**23** TC is a tangent to a circle at C. CB is a chord such that CB = CT. Line BT crosses the circle at A. Prove that △CAT is isosceles.

**24** TA and TB are tangents touching a circle at A and B. Chord BC is drawn parallel to TA. Prove that △ABC is isosceles.

**25** AB and CD are two chords of a circle, intersecting at P, which is not the centre of the circle. Explain why △APC must be similar to △DPB and show that AP × PB = CP × PD.

This is called the Intersecting Chord Theorem. The product AP × PB is sometimes called 'the rectangle contained by the two parts (AP and PB) of the line AB'. Can you see why?

**26** If, for the circle given in question 25, AB = 8 cm, AP : PB = 1 : 3, and CP = 3 cm, calculate PD.

**27** PQ is the diameter of a 19 cm-radius circle. ABC is a chord cutting PQ at B. PB = 32 cm and CB = 24 cm. Calculate the length of chord AC, verifying your answer with a scale drawing.

**28** Two circles intersect at M and N. P is a point on MN. APB and CPD are straight lines, A and B being points on the circumference of one circle, C and D being points on the other. Prove that ACBD is a cyclic quadrilateral.

# 17 Geometry (iv)

**Representation of solids**     **Solid symmetry**
**Nets**

## ● You need to know:

**Symmetry 4, 5, 6**

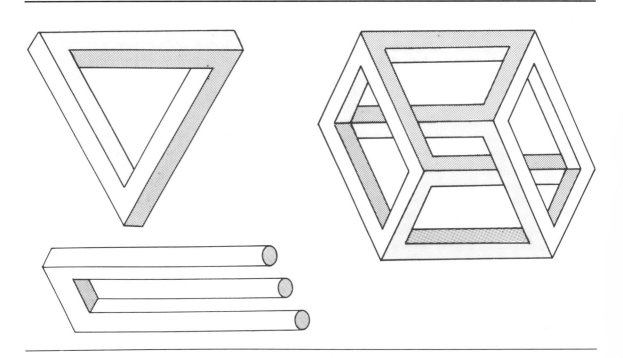

**1** Select from the following list the correct mathematical name for each solid shown in Figure 17:1.

Cone   Cube   Cuboid   Cylinder   Pyramid

Sphere   Square   Circle   Tetrahedron

(a) OXO     (b) Polycell
(c) Nestlé     (d) golf ball

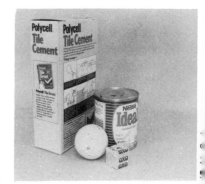

**Fig. 17:1**

**2** Figure 17:2 shows the net of a cube of edge 10 cm. The net is folded to make the cube.

(a) How many edges has the cube?

(b) Which line will come together with the line AK?

(c) Which points will come together with the point B?

(d) State the shortest distance from P to E on the cube.

(e) State the shortest distance from A to M along the edges of the cube.

(*MEG*)

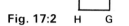

**Fig. 17:2**

**3** In Figure 17:3, one net will not make a cube. Which one?

(*EAEB*)

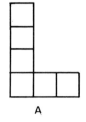

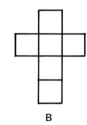

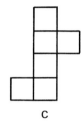

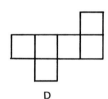

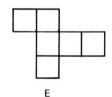

A            B            C            D            E

**Fig. 17:3**

**4** (a) Draw full size a net for a cuboid which is to be 4 cm long, 3 cm wide and 2 cm deep. You must be able to cut the net from a rectangle of card 13 cm long and 8 cm wide.

(b) State the dimensions of the minimum-area rectangle of card from which two such nets could be cut.

**5** Figure 17:4 shows the net of a solid with one face missing.

(a) By measuring Figure 17:4, state the size and the shape of the missing face.

(b) Name the solid.

(c) Sketch the solid in three dimensions.

(d) If the solid is laid on a table with face AJED downwards, what is the height of point I above the table?

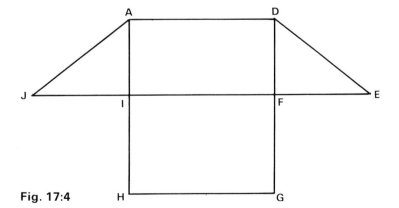

**Fig. 17:4**

**6** Figures 17:5 to 17:9 show the five regular Platonic solids. They are, in increasing order of number of faces:

tetrahedron, cube, octahedron, dodecahedron, icosahedron.

(a) Write the name of the solid shown in each figure.

(b) State the number of faces ($F$), the number of vertices ($V$), and the number of edges ($E$) for each solid. Show that in each case $F + V = E + 2$.

(c) Sketch a net for a tetrahedron.

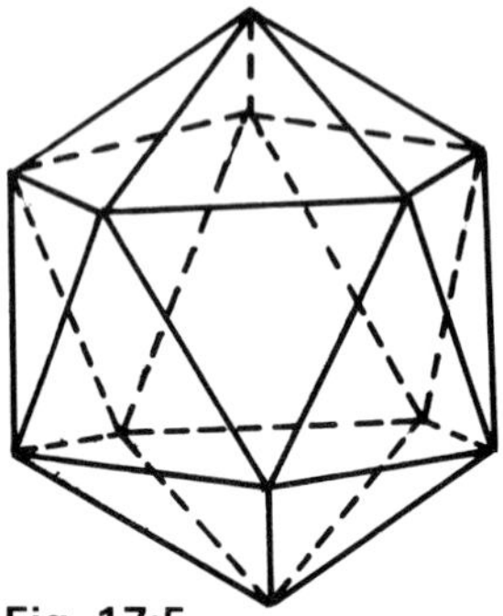

**Fig. 17:5**

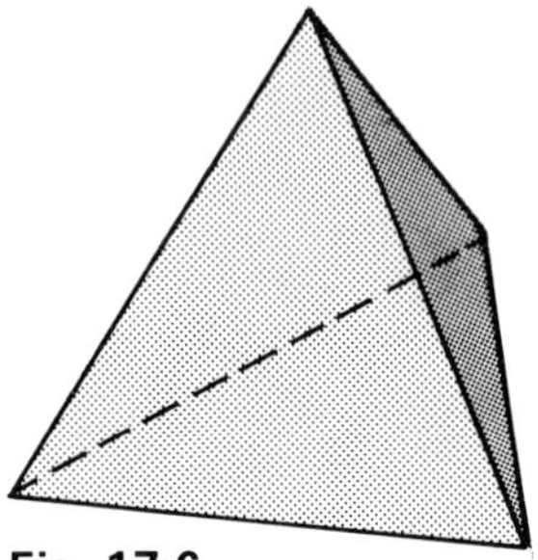

**Fig. 17:6**

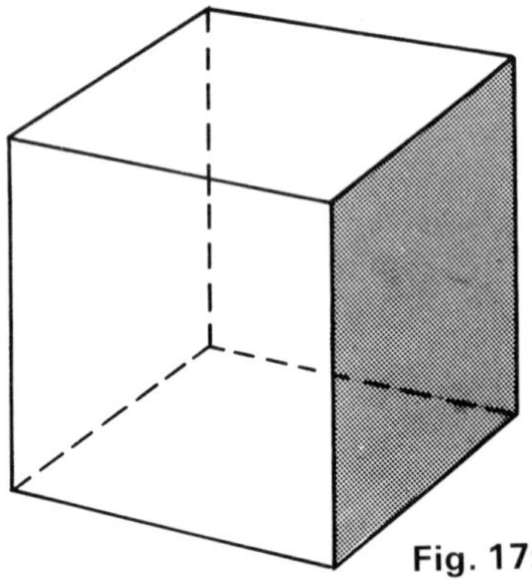

**Fig. 17:7**

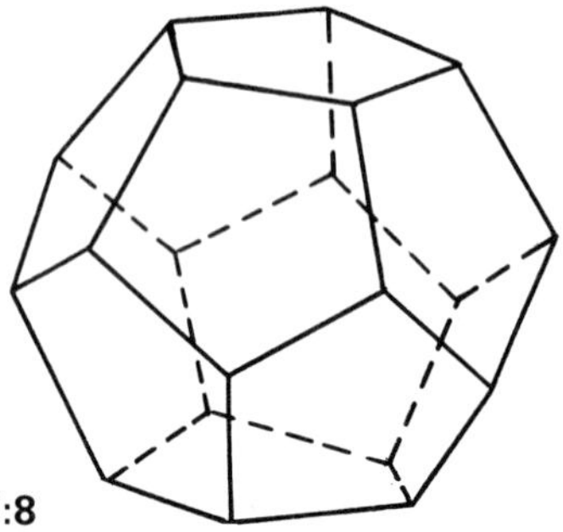

**Fig. 17:8**

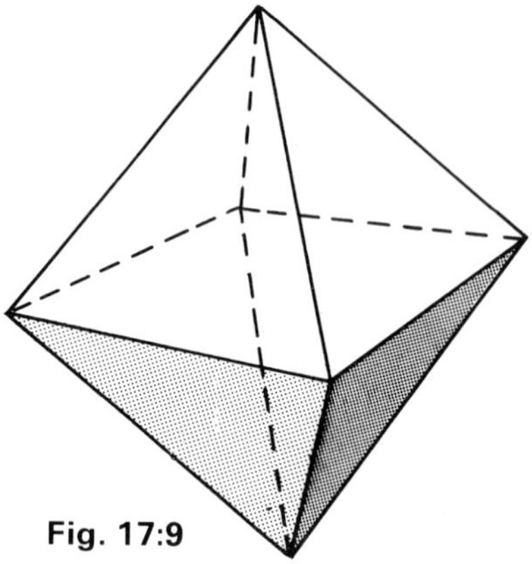

**Fig. 17:9**

***7** Figure 17:10 shows a cylindrical water tank. There are six marks on the tank; these are equally spaced from the bottom.

(a) When the water level is at mark 4, fifteen litres are poured in, and the water level rises to mark 5.
  (i) How much water was in the tank originally?
  (ii) How much water is there in the tank now?
  (iii) How much water will be in the tank when it is at mark 6?

(b) Water is now drawn off so that the level falls from mark 5 to exactly half-way between mark 1 and mark 2. How much water has been drawn off?

*(MEG)*

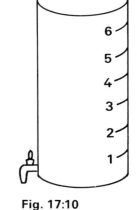

**Fig. 17:10**

**8** Figures 17:11 to 17:17 show the plans and elevations of some solids.

(a) Name the solids.

(b) Sketch a 3D view of each solid.

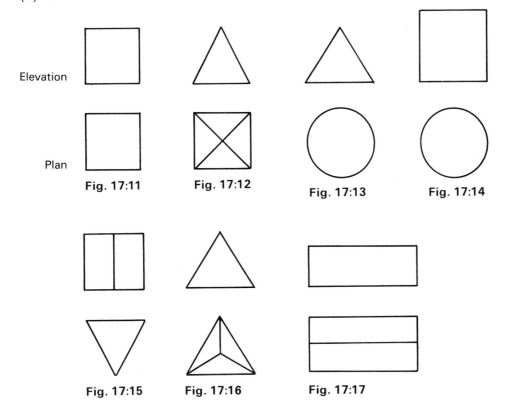

Elevation

Plan

**Fig. 17:11**   **Fig. 17:12**   **Fig. 17:13**   **Fig. 17:14**

**Fig. 17:15**   **Fig. 17:16**   **Fig. 17:17**

**9** Figure 17:18 shows a cuboid ABCDEFGH. Which of the following angles are right angles in the actual cuboid?

(a)  ∠ABC    (b)  ∠AEH    (c)  ∠ACG
(d)  ∠AHC    (e)  ∠AHG    (f)  ∠BAH
(g)  ∠ACG    (h)  ∠ACH

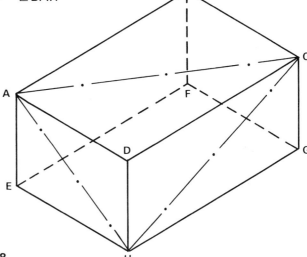

**Fig. 17:18**

**10** For each of Figures 17:19 to 17:23 state:
  (a) the number of axes of symmetry
  (b) the number of planes of symmetry
  (c) the symmetry number (that is, the number of different ways the solid can be placed in a mould of itself).

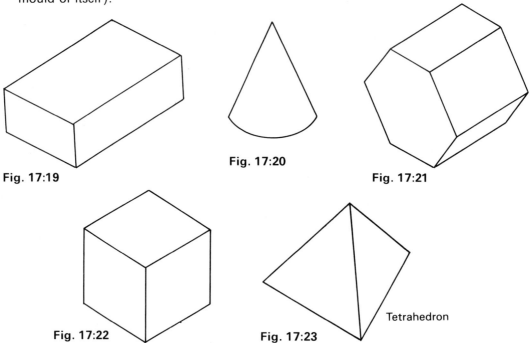

**Fig. 17:19**

**Fig. 17:20**

**Fig. 17:21**

**Fig. 17:22**

**Fig. 17:23**

Tetrahedron

**11** Draw a plan and elevation, as in question 8, for the solids shown in Figure 17:24.

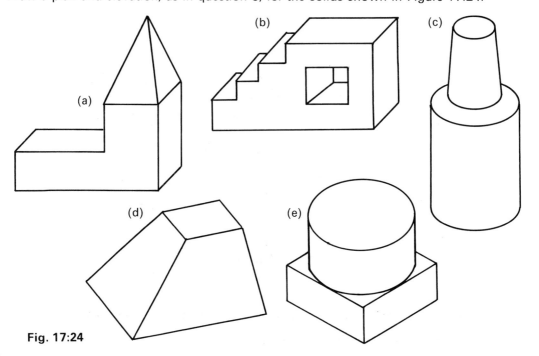

(a)

(b)

(c)

(d)

(e)

**Fig. 17:24**

**12** Figure 17:25 shows a stereogram, which represents the axes of symmetry for a cube.

To draw it, the cube is first surrounded by a sphere. The thirteen axes of symmetry are then extended until they meet the sphere at the points marked with squares, triangles and circles. A conical projection is then drawn looking down on the sphere, points above or on the equator being marked solid, and points below the equator left open.

Squares are the axes through the centres of faces, with order-4 rotational symmetry.

Triangles are the axes through the vertices, with order-3 rotational symmetry.

Circles are the axes through the centres of edges, with order-2 rotational symmetry.

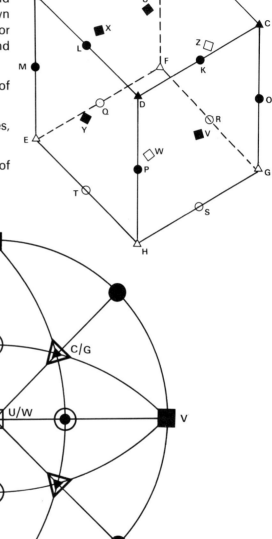

**Fig. 17:25**

(a) Copy the diagrams and complete the letter labels on the stereogram.

(b) Draw a stereogram for a tetrahedron.

**13** Figures 17:26 and 17:27 show Schlegel diagrams for a cube and an octahedron. A Schlegel diagram enables us to see all the faces of a solid at the same time. One face is removed and the rest of the solid is topologically stretched outwards. The removed face then becomes the outside of the diagram.

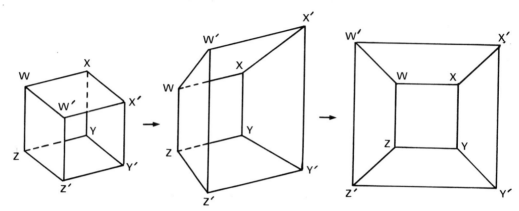

**Fig. 17:26**

Face W'X'Y'Z' removed

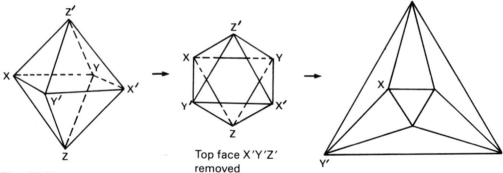

**Fig. 17:27**

Top face X'Y'Z' removed

(a) Copy Figures 17:26 and 17:27. Complete the letter labels on Figure 17:27.

(b) Draw a Schlegel diagram for a tetrahedron, and, if you are feeling really inspired, for a dodecahedron.

**Construction of angles based on 60°**

**Construction of triangles**

**Scale drawings**

**Loci**

# ● **You need to know:**

## Geometry 2

---

Note:  Your examination syllabus may require you to use compass constructions for angles based on 60° and its bisection, e.g. 120°, 30°, 90°, 45°. Alternatively, you may be permitted to use a protractor for all angles. Check with your teacher.

**1**  If you have to construct angles using ruler and compasses only, practise drawing the angles given in the Reference Notes: Geometry 2.

**2**  Two marker buoys, X and Y, are 100 metres apart. A boat is 150 metres from both buoys. Construct a scale diagram to show the course of the boat if it is to pass midway between the buoys.

**3**  (a)  Construct a triangle, sides 9 cm, 7.5 cm and 6 cm.

(b)  By bisecting two angles of your triangle, find the centre of the incircle of the triangle and draw this circle.

**4**  A road sign is to consist of an equilateral triangle of side 40 cm, surrounded by a circle which passes through the three vertices of the triangle. Draw the sign to a scale of 1 : 5.

**5**  Figure 18:1 represents part of a rugby pitch. XY is the goal. A player touches down at P; he may then try to 'convert' by kicking the ball between the goalposts from anywhere on the line PA. Copy the diagram, the same size, then use instructions (1) to (4) to find the best position from which to attempt the conversion.

(1)  Draw the perpendicular bisector of XY, crossing XY at M.

(2)  Draw an arc, centre Y, to cross the perpendicular bisector at O, where YO = PM.

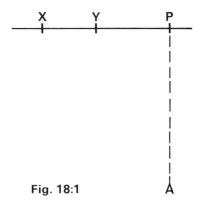

**Fig. 18:1**

(3) Draw a circle, centre O, passing through X and Y, and touching PA at C.

(4) Point C is the best position from which to attempt the conversion, as angle YCX is then a maximum. Measure angle YCX. Mark a point D and a point E, each 1 cm from C on PA, and check that both angle YDX and angle YEX are smaller than angle YCX.

**6** Figure 18:2 shows a square KLMN with sides of 20 mm. A 100 mm thread is attached to K and pulled to P so that PKN is a straight line. The thread is kept tight and wound round the square in a clockwise direction.

(a) Copy the diagram and draw the locus of P as the thread is wound.

(b) Calculate the length of this locus (circumference of a circle ≃3.14 × diameter).

*(EAEB)*

**Fig. 18:2**

***7** A rugby player is 8 yards from the touchline. Construct his shortest route to the touchline, using a scale of 1 cm to 2 yards.

***8** Angela walks 8 km from A in a direction of 040°, then turns and walks 3 km in a direction of 290°. Use a scale diagram, scale 1 : 100 000, to find how far she then is from her starting point.

***9** Construct a rhombus, side 4 cm and acute angle 45°. Measure the longest diagonal of your rhombus.

***10** A dinghy race is organised to sail round a triangular course XYZ. The race starts at X. A buoy Z is positioned 1.4 km due north of X. A buoy Y is positioned 2 km from X on a bearing of 045° from X.

(a) Using a scale of 1 cm to 200 metres, draw a plan of the course.

(b) Measure the length of YZ on your diagram and write down the distance in km which this length represents.

(c) The race starts at X, then passes round the marker buoys as follows: X, Y, Z, X, Y, X, Y. The race finishes at buoy Y. What is the minimum length of the race in km?

(d) A safety-boat patrols between north of Z and a bearing of 270° from Z, so that it is always 1 km from Z and at times passes through the course of the race. Plot the course of the safety-boat.

(e) A second safety-boat motors so that it is always 1 km from the line YX, and on the north side of the line YX. Plot its course with a dotted line.

*(SREB)*

*11 A plane takes off from Aberdeen. It develops a fault while over the North Sea and the pilot ejects. A search is made over an area from 350 km to 500 km from Aberdeen, and between the bearings 020° and 060° from Aberdeen.

(a) Using a scale of 2 cm to 100 km make an accurate scale drawing of the area to be searched. Indicate clearly the position of Aberdeen and the direction of north from Aberdeen.

The pilot actually comes down 400 km from Aberdeen on a bearing of 040° and his life-raft drifts east at a rate of 5 km/h.

(b) Show the position of the pilot when he lands on the sea.

(c) (i) Draw in a line to show how the raft drifts across the search area.
   (ii) Use this line to calculate how long it will be after the crash before the raft drifts out of the search area. Answer to the nearest hour.

(ALSEB)

*12 (Note: 1 knot = 1 nautical mile per hour.)

Four ships, A, B, C and D, receive a distress signal from a ship at point S. Ship A is 40 nautical miles due east of point S, and B is 9 nautical miles due south of S.

(a) Using 1 cm to represent 5 nautical miles, draw a scale diagram showing the positions of S, A and B.

(b) The ship C is 21 nautical miles due west of S, and the ship D is 45 nautical miles from S on a bearing of 300°.
   Mark the positions of C and D on your diagram.

(c) Measure the angle DCS.

(d) What is the bearing of ship D from ship C?

(e) Ships A and C answer a distress signal from ship S. Ship A travels at a speed of 12 knots and ship C travels at 6 knots.
   (i) Which ship arrives first at S?
   (ii) How many minutes earlier does it arrive than the second ship?     (SREB)

13 Construct triangle ABC, with AB = 12 cm, AC = 8 cm and ∠CAB = 60°.

(a) From your triangle measure as accurately as you can
   (i) the length of the side BC
   (ii) the size of angle ABC.

(b) Construct the perpendicular from C to meet AB at D.
   (i) Measure the length of CD.
   (ii) Calculate the area of triangle ABC.

(c) Bisect ∠ABC. Let this bisector meet the side AC at E.
   Measure the length AE.     (EAEB)

14 Draw a line PQ, 8 cm long. Construct and label clearly:
(a) the locus of points R equidistant from P and Q
(b) a point S, equidistant from P and Q and such that angle SPQ = 45°
(c) the locus of points T which are 4 cm from S.

(Leave all your construction lines and arcs clearly visible.)     (LREB)

**15** Using a scale of 1 cm to 10 m, draw a plan of a rectangular field ABCD, with AB = 100 m, and BC = 40 m. On your plan draw accurately the path of a man who walks over the field in the following way:

(a) He starts at A and walks, keeping always 40 m from D, until he reaches a point which is 40 m from A.

(b) He then walks towards CB, keeping always the same distance from C as he is from B, until he reaches a point where he is equally far from the boundary BC as he is from the boundary CD.

(c) He then walks to C, keeping as far from BC as he is from CD.

(*MEG*)

**16** Figure 18:3 shows a bicycle. When it stands on horizontal ground CB is also horizontal and D is 26 cm above the ground. Angle BCD = 72° and BA is parallel to CD. AB = 5 cm, BC = 58 cm, and CD = 50 cm.

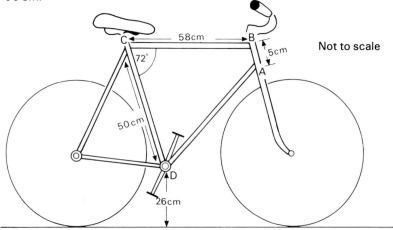

**Fig. 18:3**

(a) Make an accurate scale drawing of ABCD, one-fifth of full size.

(b) Using your drawing, find the total length of tubing needed to construct ABCD.

(c) A tall man requires a cycle with its saddle 1 m above the ground. The saddle of this cycle can be raised to be 22 cm vertically above BC. Is it big enough for him? Show the measurement which you take from your drawing to answer this.

(*MEG*)

**17** Figure 18:4 shows the design for a vase. Construct the diagram to the sizes given. Arc centres are marked with large dots.

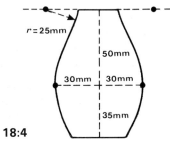

**Fig. 18:4**

**18** Figure 18:5 shows a view looking down on a door, hinged at B to the door-post BC. XP and YP are the arms of a spring-loaded door closer, fixed to the door at X and to the door-post at Y.

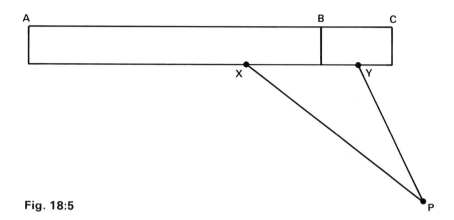

**Fig. 18:5**

Copy the diagram to the size drawn, leaving 8 cm above ABC, then draw about six different positions of bar PX as the door opens.

Find the angle ABC when the door is as wide open as the closer will allow.

**19** A boat at S is 400 m due west of a marker-buoy at B. A second marker-buoy at C is 500 m due north of B. The boat steers a course along SX so as to pass between the marker buoys with angle BSX = 30°.

  (a) Illustrate S, B and C in a diagram using a scale of 1 cm to represent 50 m.

  (b) Construct the line SX.

  (c) Locate and mark the point P on SX at which the boat is closest to C.

By measurement, find the distance CP, giving your answer in metres correct to the nearest 10 m. State also the bearing of P from C.

*(AEB 1981)*

**20** A civil engineer wishes to build a bridge over a river. To find the width AD of the river he stands on one bank at a point A, and measures the angle of elevation of a tree CD on the opposite bank, finding it to be 60°. He then walks 8 m away from the river to another point B and measures the angle of elevation of the tree again, finding it to be 30°. Using a scale of 1 cm to represent 1 m, draw an accurate diagram of ABCD, leaving at least 10 cm below line BD. Measure and state the height of the tree and the width of the river.

The bridge is a footbridge from A to D, which is to be an arc of a circle of radius 5 m. Construct this arc, showing clearly the centre of the circle. Measure as accurately as you can the height of the bridge above the line AD at its highest point.

*(AEB 1984)*

**21** An architect is given the job of designing a site in a shopping precinct of a new town. The site is semicircular, and there are three trees on the boundary at points A, B and C, where C is due north of A, B is due east of A, and AB = 80 metres. The diameter of the semicircle is BC, and angle ABC = 30°. A fountain is planned at point F on AB, such that BF = CF. There is a gate at G on the boundary, where CFG is a straight line.

(a) Draw a rough sketch of the site, showing the approximate positions of A, B, C, F and G.

(b) Using a scale of 1 cm to represent 10 m, construct, showing all your construction lines clearly:
  (i) the triangle ABC
  (ii) the locus of points P such that BP = PC, marking clearly the point F
  (iii) the semicircular boundary of the site
  (iv) the line CG, marking G clearly.

(c) Measure and state the distance BG, giving your answer in metres to the nearest metre.

*(AEB 1983)*

**22** Figure 18:6 shows James Watt's link-motion, by which he attempted to keep a point P moving in a straight line as rods AC and BD pivot about A and B.

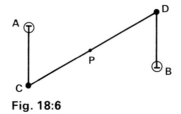

**Fig. 18:6**

(a) Let AC = BD = 5 cm, CD = 1 cm, and AB = 9 cm. Find the locus of P, the midpoint of CD.

(b) Let AB = CD = 10 cm, and AC = BD = 7 cm. Construct the locus of P.

**23** Design and make some rod-linkages.

# 19 Mensuration (i)

### Pythagoras' Theorem

## ● You need to know:

### Geometry 6

---

**1** Calculate the unknown side in each triangle in Figure 19:1, giving each answer correct to 2 d.p.

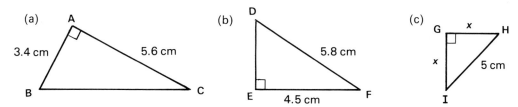

**Fig. 19:1**

**2** Some of the triangles with the following sides have three acute angles, some have an obtuse angle, some have a right angle, and some do not exist. Use Pythagoras' Theorem to calculate which is true for each.
(a) 5 cm, 6 cm, 7 cm    (b) 3 cm, 5 cm, 7 cm    (c) 5 cm, 9 cm, 10 cm
(d) 2 cm, 3 cm, 6 cm    (e) 8 cm, 15 cm, 17 cm    (f) 2 cm, 9 cm, 11 cm
(g) 6 cm, 6 cm, 6 cm    (h) 4 cm, 4 cm, 5 cm

**3** At a school, pupils have to walk on the path round the perimeter of a rectangular lawn, 16 metres long and 12 metres wide. Teachers are allowed to walk across the lawn! How much farther than a pupil does a teacher do to get from the gate at one corner to the main door at the opposite corner?

**4** (a) Copy Figure 19:2 exactly.
(b) Join the points to make kite ABCD.
(c) Measure AB and BD.
(d) Check the accuracy of your construction by calculating AB and BD.

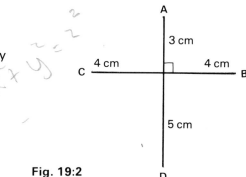

**Fig. 19:2**

105

**5** A rhombus has diagonals of length 18 cm and 13 cm. Calculate the length of its sides.

**6** A circle, centre O and radius 13 cm, has two parallel chords of lengths 10 cm and 24 cm. Calculate the two possible perpendicular distances between the chords.

**7** Figure 19:3 shows a cuboid measuring 6 cm by 3 cm by 2 cm. Calculate the length of:
(a) AF    (b) DF.

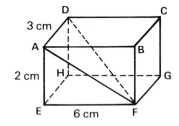

Fig. 19:3

**8** Figure 19:4 represents a frame made from 15 cm, 12 cm, and 8 cm lengths. It is to be strengthened with a strut from corner A to corner B. Calculate the length of the strut.

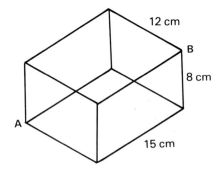

Fig. 19:4

**9** Figure 19:5 shows a section through the Earth. A and B are points on the Tropic of Cancer; C and D are points on the Tropic of Capricorn. O is the centre of the Earth.

The straight line joining A to B is 11 690 km long and the radius of the Earth is 6370 km.

Calculate the length of the straight line joining A to C.

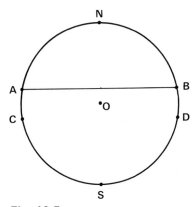

Fig. 19:5

**10** Show that the altitude of an equilateral triangle of side 2 units is $\sqrt{3}$ units.

**11** In Figure 19:6, O is the centre of the circle and AB is a tangent. AO is to be 30 cm when AB is twice the radius of the circle. Find this radius.

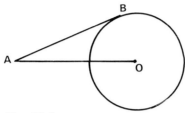

**Fig. 19:6**

**12** (a) Calculate the shortest distance between the points whose co-ordinates are $(2, -3)$ and $(-5, 2)$.

   (b) Find a formula to give the shortest distance between two points $(X, Y)$ and $(x, y)$.

**13** A right-angled triangle has to have sides of lengths $x$ cm, $x + 2$ cm, and $x + 4$ cm. Calculate the value of $x$.

**14** In Figure 19:7 AOB and COD are two straight lines intersecting at right angles at the point O. The area of the triangle AOD is 15 cm², that of the triangle COB is 75 cm², and the length of the line AOB is 20 cm. Taking the length of AO as $x$ cm show that the length of OD is $30/x$ cm and that the length of OC is $150/(20 - x)$ cm. Given also that the length of COD is 16 cm, obtain an equation in $x$ and solve it to find two possible values of $x$.

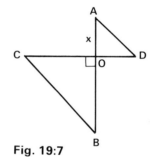

**Fig. 19:7**

*(O & C)*

**15** (a) Write any fraction.

   (b) Invert the fraction, then double the result.

   (c) Add 2.

   (d) Multiply by the L.C.M. of the two numbers used to make the original fraction. Call the answer $x$.

   (e) Add 2 to the fraction you started with, converting your answer to a top-heavy fraction.

   (f) Multiply by the L.C.M. of the two numbers used to make the original fraction. Call the answer $y$.

Let $x$ and $y$ be the shorter sides of a right-angled triangle. Calculate the hypotenuse. It should be integral. Can you prove why this must be so?

**16** If $n$ is one side of a right-angled triangle and $n + 1$ is the hypotenuse, then $\sqrt{2n + 1}$ is the third side. Show that this is so.

If $n$ is an integer then $2n + 1$ must be an odd number. If $\sqrt{2n + 1}$ is rational then it too must be odd. Letting $\sqrt{2n + 1}$ be any odd number, there must then be a right-angled triangle with integral sides having that odd number as the length of one side.

Find the integral right-angled triangles with one side:
(a) 3    (b) 5    (c) 7    (d) 9    (e) 11    (f) 13.

# 20 Mensuration (ii)

| | |
|---|---|
| Triangle | (Arc) |
| Parallelogram | (Sector) |
| Circle | (Sphere) |
| Cuboid | (Pyramid) |
| Prism | (Cone) |
| Cylinder | |

## ● You need to know:

### Mensuration 1 to 4

Find out from your teacher which formulae you need to know and learn them!

1 (a) Figure 20:1 shows a running track. Taking $\pi$ as 3.14 calculate the length of one lap.  *257*

(b) A runner completes one lap in 42 seconds. What is his average speed in m/s correct to 2 d.p.?  *6·12(2dp)*

(c) What is the area of the running track, if it has 5 one-metre wide lanes and Figure 20:1 shows the inside edge?

(d) How much stagger is needed between the outside and inside tracks if runners are assumed to run on the inside of their lane and to have covered the same distance after one lap?

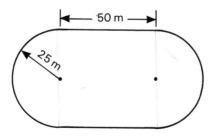

**Fig. 20:1**

2 A circular tree-trunk has a circumference of 1.8 metres. What is its diameter in cm? (Take $\pi$ as 3.14; give your answer correct to 1 d.p.)

**3** Mr Coates needs to do some repair work on his garage, which is shown in Figure 20:2. He draws a series of views of the garage to help him with his calculations. These are shown in Figures 20:3 to 20:5. Figures 20:4 and 20:5 are drawn to an exact scale.

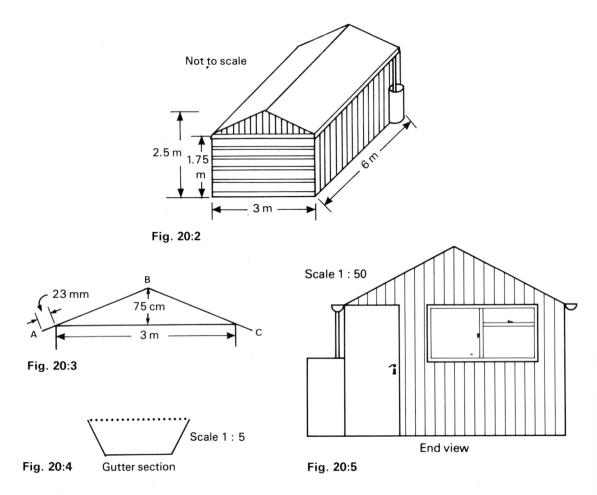

Fig. 20:2

Not to scale

2.5 m  1.75 m  3 m  6 m

B
23 mm
75 cm
A      3 m      C

Fig. 20:3

Scale 1 : 5

Fig. 20:4     Gutter section

Scale 1 : 50

End view

Fig. 20:5

(a) Mr Coates is going to re-felt the roof. Calculate from Figure 20:3 the distance ABC, from one side of the roof to the other.

(b) Roofing felt is supplied in rolls 1 m wide and 20 m long. The strips need to overlap each other by at least 3 cm. They are laid from front to back, along the length of the garage.
   (i) How many strips will Mr Coates need?
   (ii) How many strips can he cut from one roll?
   (iii) How many rolls of felt should he buy?

(c) The wood is to be preserved with two coats of red-cedar preservative at £2 per litre. One litre should cover $8\,m^2$.
   (i) Use Figure 20:2 to calculate the area of wood forming the sides of the garage.
   (ii) Use Figure 20:2 to calculate the area of the triangle of wood above the door.
   (iii) Use Figure 20:5, which is drawn to scale 1 : 50, to find the area of wood (not including the painted door) on the rear wall.
   (iv) Find the number of litres of preservative needed for two coats, and state their cost.

(d) The main door is made of 1 mm-thick metal sheet, corrugated as shown for strength. The density of the metal is 4.5 g/cm³. Allowing 20% extra on the area for corrugation and the edge flanges, calculate the weight of the door in kg.

(e) A gutter drains both sides of the roof with a connecting section above the main door. Use Figure 20:4, which is drawn to a scale of 1 : 5, to find the cross-section area of the gutter, and hence the volume of water in a 6 m length of gutter when it is full, giving your answer in cm³.

(f) The gutter drains into a butt. Taking measurements from Figure 20:5 calculate the capacity of the butt to the nearest litre, using either the calculator value of pi, or taking it as 3.1415.

(g) Calculate the area of the roof in m².

(h) How many mm of rain will need to fall on the roof to fill the butt from empty?

**4** Figure 20:6 shows a cycle milometer. The eight-toothed wheel is turned one tooth each time the cycle wheel rotates. The cycle wheel is 26 inches in diameter. How many turns must the toothed wheel make to record 1 mile? (1 mile = 1760 yards; 1 yard = 36 inches. Take $\pi$ as 3.142.)

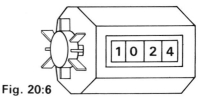

**Fig. 20:6**

**5** Pots of jam, each of 500 g gross weight, are to be packed in boxes of 24. Figure 20:7 shows a plan of a full box. Figure 20:8 shows an elevation of one jar.

(a) Calculate the weight of a full box in kg, allowing 500 g for the packing material.

(b) The box top is formed of four flaps, ACDB, GEFH, AIJG and BIJH, as shown in Figure 20:7. The base of the box is formed in the same way. Calculate the area of card used in making the box, allowing 100 cm² for the vertical join.

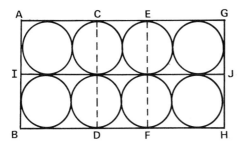

**Fig. 20:7**

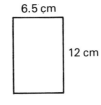

6.5 cm

12 cm

**Fig. 20:8**

**\*6** Figure 20:9 shows the design for a metal block. The density of the metal is 8.6 g/cm³. Calculate the weight of the block.

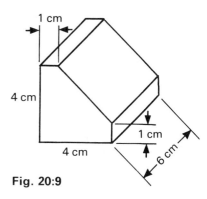

1 cm

4 cm

4 cm

1 cm

6 cm

**Fig. 20:9**

**\*7** A wall 3.6 m long and 2.4 m high is to be tiled with 10 cm square tiles. How many tiles are needed, and what is their total cost at 15p each?

An alternative is to use 15 cm square tiles at 24p each. Would this be cheaper?

**\*8** A rectangular flower-bed, 15 m by 9 m, is to be surrounded by a 1.5 m-wide path, made from paving slabs 30 cm square costing £1.25 each. Find the cost of paving the path.

**\*9** Figure 20:10 shows how a well rope is wound round a cylindrical axle of 7 cm radius. How many times must the handle be turned to lower the bucket 22 metres? (Take $\pi = 3\frac{1}{7}$.)

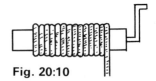

**Fig. 20:10**

**\*10** A shed floor, 2.5 m long and 2 m wide, is to be concreted to a depth of 10 cm. One cubic metre of concrete mix requires one cubic metre of ballast and 3 bags of cement. Ballast costs £6.50 per cubic metre and cement is £6.50 a bag.

(a) Write down the cost of 1 $m^3$ of concrete mix.

(b) Find the area of the shed floor in $m^2$.

(c) Find, in cubic metres, the volume of concrete mix required for the floor.

(d) Find the cost of concrete used for the floor.

(e) If ballast may be bought by the $\frac{1}{2}$ cubic metre, but cement has to be bought by the bag, find the total cost of material for the floor.

*(EAEB)*

**11** Figure 20:11 shows the plan and elevation of a cone to be made from a sector of card as shown in Figure 20:12. A 5° sector is allowed as a joining tab. Take $\pi$ as 3.14. Calculate:
(a) the slant height of the cone
(b) the volume of the cone
(c) the circumference of the base of the cone
(d) the radius of the sector
(e) the length of arc ABC
(f) the angle $\theta$
(g) the total area of card used in making the cone.

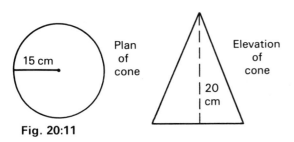

**Fig. 20:11**

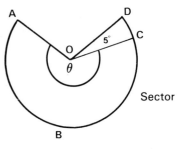

**Fig. 20:12**

**12** A metal ball 7 cm in diameter is placed in a cylindrical can of 9 cm diameter. Water is poured in until it is 10 cm deep.
(a) What volume of water has been poured into the can?
(b) If the ball is removed, how deep will the water be?

**13** An ice-cream cornet is in the form of a cone of diameter 6 cm and vertical depth 12 cm. Figure 20:13 shows the cross-section through a plane of symmetry of the cornet when it is partly filled with ice-cream (shaded) to a depth of 4 cm.

The ice-cream above the cornet forms a hemisphere and that within the cornet forms a frustum of a cone.

Assuming that the cornet is of negligible thickness, calculate the value of:
(i)   $k$, if the volume of ice-cream above the cornet is $k\pi$ cm$^3$
(ii)  $x$, the radius of the circular cross-section of the ice-cream at a depth of 4 cm
(iii) $p$, if the total volume of the ice-cream is $p\pi$ cm$^3$.

Evaluate the percentage of the ice-cream which is above the cornet, giving your answer correct to two significant figures.
(Volume of sphere $= \frac{4}{3}\pi r^3$.
 Volume of cone $= \frac{1}{3}\pi r^2 h$).

*(AEB 1981)*

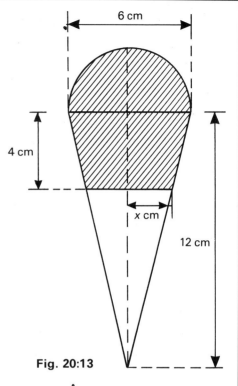

**Fig. 20:13**

**14** Figure 20:14 represents a solid tetrahedron ABCD, where BC = BD = 8 cm, and AB = 7 cm.

Given that angle ABC = angle CBD = angle ABD = 90°, calculate:
(a)  the length of the perpendicular from B to CD
(b)  the length of the perpendicular from A to CD
(c)  the volume of the tetrahedron
(d)  the area of the triangle ACD.
(e)  Use your answers to (c) and (d) to find the length of the perpendicular from B to face ACD, to 3 significant figures.

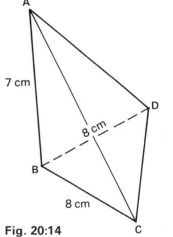

**Fig. 20:14**

**15** A base for a table lamp is to be made by cutting tetrahedrons from each of the corners of a 15 cm-sided cube of wood, leaving faces that are regular octahedrons. Figure 20:15 shows one corner.

Calculate:
(a)  the length of one side of the octahedron
(b)  the volume of one tetrahedron
(c)  the percentage of the original cube that remains.

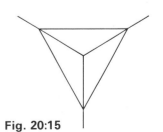

**Fig. 20:15**

**16** An emergency reservoir in a forest is in the shape of a frustum of a cone, as shown in Figure 20:16. The reservoir has a radius of 12 m at the top and a radius of 9 m at the bottom. It is 4 m deep.

(a) Use similar triangles to find the length FE correct to 3 d.p.

(b) Calculate:
   (i) the volume of the cone DCE
   (ii) the volume of the cone ABE, and hence the volume of the frustum ABCD.

(c) Calculate the capacity of the reservoir in litres.

(d) Calculate the lengths:
   (i) AE    (ii) AD.

(e) The sides and the base of the reservoir are to be coated with a paint containing a herbicide. One litre of the paint will cover 6 m² to the nearest m². Calculate:
   (i) the surface area of the walls
   (ii) the area of the base
   (iii) the number of litres of paint needed to coat the reservoir.

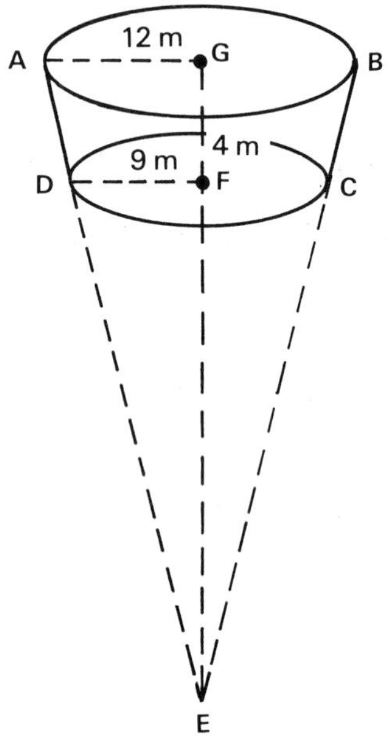

Volume of cone = $\frac{1}{3}\pi r^2 h$;
curved surface area of cone = $\pi r l$, where $l$ is the slant height.

**Fig. 20:16**

**17** An open-air theatre is being constructed as follows:
The stage area is a circle of radius 12 m, and the seating is all round the stage on the inside of the frustum of a cone. The radius of the top of the seating area is 24 m and the seating area rises 5 m vertically from the stage area. A cross-section is shown in Figure 20:17.

Calculate the seating area of this theatre.

*(O & C)*

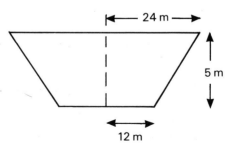

**Fig. 20:17**

**18** A 20 mm-diameter water pipe delivers 5 litres in 30 seconds. Calculate the speed of the water in the pipe, in cm/min, assuming that the water completely fills the pipe.

# 21 Trigonometry

Right-angled triangles    (Area of a triangle)
(Sine and cosine rules)

## ● You need to know:

### Trigonometry 1 to 6

1  Calculate side $x$ or angle $\theta$ in the triangles in Figure 21:1.

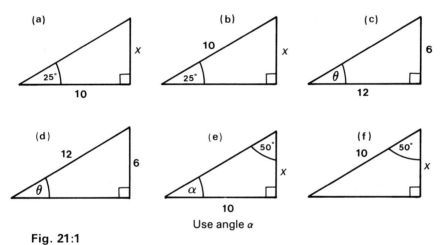

Fig. 21:1

2  Three different triangles are all right-angled, have one angle of 67°, and one side of length 4 cm. Sketch the three triangles, then calculate the lengths of the other two sides for each.

3  Two different triangles are both right-angled and have one 5 cm side and one 3 cm side. Sketch both triangles, then calculate the other angles in each.

4  The top of a tree has an angle of elevation of 25° from an observer 25 metres from its foot. How high is the tree?

5  Looking down from her prison window in a tower, Rapunzel sees a prince 100 metres from the foot of the tower on level ground, at an angle of depression of 15°. About how long does her hair have to be if the prince is to climb up it to rescue her?

6  At noon one day a post 6 metres high has a shadow 3 metres long. What is the altitude of the sun at this moment?

**7** A hill has a gradient of 20% (1 in 5). What is its inclination to the horizontal in degrees?

**8** An isosceles triangle has two sides of 8 cm and one of 6 cm. Calculate its vertical angle.

**9** A ship is 3 km from a 150 m-high cliff. What is its angle of depression from the top of the cliff?

**10** A rocket travels 5 km at an inclination of 80° to the horizontal, then a further 10 km at an angle of 32.6° with the vertical. How far down-range is it then?

**11** A ship sails at 8 knots (8 nautical miles per hour) for 2 hours on a bearing of 135° from a buoy A. It then turns to a bearing of 200° and continues at the same speed for 30 minutes. How far south and how far east of A is it then?

*****12** Find side $x$ or angle $\theta$ in the triangles in Figure 21:2.

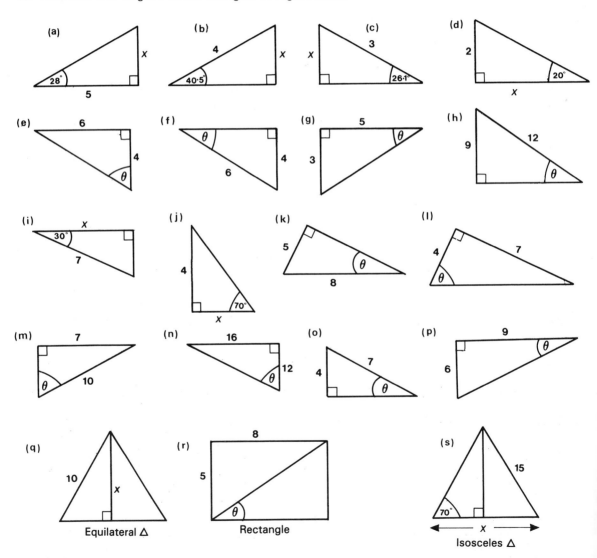

**Fig. 21:2**

**\*13** Figure 21:3 shows a cuboid ABCDEFGH. AB = 4 cm, BC = 5 cm and AE = 3 cm. Calculate angle BHC.

(*Scottish*)

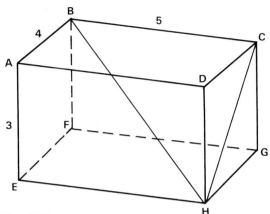

**Fig. 21:3**

**\*14** Figure 21:4 shows a rectangle ABCD. The point X on AB is such that DX = XB = 10 cm and angle CXB = 37°. The point Y is on XC such that angle BYX = 90°.

Calculate:
(a) XY     (b) BC     (c) sin ∠AXD.                              (*Cambridge*)

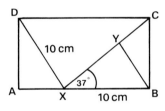

**Fig. 21:4**

**\*15** ABCD is a quadrilateral with ∠B = ∠D = 90°. AB = 39 cm, CD = 25 cm, AD = 60 cm.

Calculate:
(a) AC     (b) BC     (c) sin ∠CAD     (d) cos ∠CAD.          (*Welsh*)

**16** Calculate the semi-vertical angle of a cone of height 6 cm and base radius 6 cm.

**17** Calculate the length $x$ for each triangle in Figure 21:5.

(a)
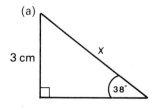

(b)
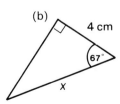

(c)
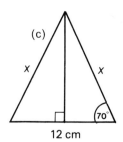

**Fig. 21:5**

**18** Use first the cosine rule then the sine rule to solve fully triangle ABC where:
   (a)  AB = 7 cm, AC = 3 cm, ∠A = 25° (Remember to use the cosine rule to find the *bigger* of the two unknown angles.)
   (b)  AB = 6 cm, AC = 4 cm, ∠A = 50°
   (c)  AB = 7 cm, BC = 8 cm, AC = 6 cm
   (d)  AB = 5 cm, BC = 6 cm, AC = 7 cm
   (e)  ∠B = 71.3°, AB = 2.7 cm, BC = 3.1 cm
   (f)  AB = 2.75 cm, AC = 4.6 m, BC = 3.9 m
   (g)  AB : BC : CA = 2 : 4 : 5, perimeter = 25.3 m.

**19** A ship's navigator observes two landmarks 5 km apart with one due east of the other. They bear 045° and 330° from his ship. Calculate how far he is from each landmark and from the straight line joining them.

**20** A surveyor needs to find the height of a watch-tower on the other side of a mined border strip, as shown in Figure 21:6. The angles of elevation from two points 50 metres apart, level and in line with the base of the tower, are 7.2° and 10.1°. Calculate the height of the tower, to the nearest tenth of a metre.

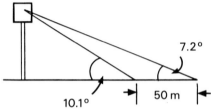

**Fig. 21:6**

**21** In Figure 21:7, ABCD is the circumcircle of △ABC with its centre at O. Show, by angles in the same segment, angle in a semicircle, and the sine ratio, that BD, the diameter of the circumcircle of △ABC, is $a/\sin A$.

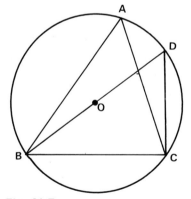

**Fig. 21:7**

**22** Calculate the area of the triangle in Figure 21:8.

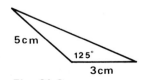

**Fig. 21:8**

**23** By first calculating angle A, find the area of the triangle in Figure 21:9.

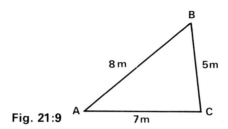

**Fig. 21:9**

**24** Two ships set out at 0630 from ports A and B, 50 nautical miles apart, A being due west of B. The ship leaving A is on a course of 037°, travelling at 12 knots. The other ship is travelling at 15 knots on a course of 330°.

Calculate the distance between the ships at:
(a) 0730     (b) 0830     (c) 0930     (d) 1030.

**25** Refer to Figure 21:10. Three survivors of a sea disaster are stationary at A, B and C in a calm, flat sea. A helicoper X is hovering 100 m vertically above A, angle ACX is 32° and AB is 200 m.

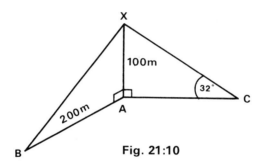

**Fig. 21:10**

(a) Show that AC is about 160 metres.

(b) If A is due north of B and the bearing of C from A is 060°, calculate:
   (i) the distance between the survivors at C and B correct to the nearest metre
   (ii) the value of angle ABC correct to the nearest degree.

(c) Deduce the bearing that the helicopter should follow when travelling directly from survivor C to survivor B.

*(AEB 1981)*

**26** A, B and C are three observation posts in the same horizontal plane. B is 800 m due east of A, and C is south of the line AB such that AC = 300 m and BC = 700 m. Calculate the bearing of C from A.

P is the foot of a vertical radio mast on the line AB, 100 m from A. The angle of elevation of the top of the mast is 12°. Calculate the height of the mast.

Q is a point on the line AC and lies due south of P. Calculate:
(a) the angle of elevation of the top of the mast from Q
(b) the distance BQ.

*(JMB)*

**27** Figure 21:11 shows the roof of a building. The base ABCD is a horizontal rectangle, the face QDC is vertical and the remaining faces are inclined to the horizontal. M and N are the mid-points of AB and DC respectively, and the ridge PQ is parallel to, and vertically above, MN. The point V lies in the plane ABCD and is vertically below P.

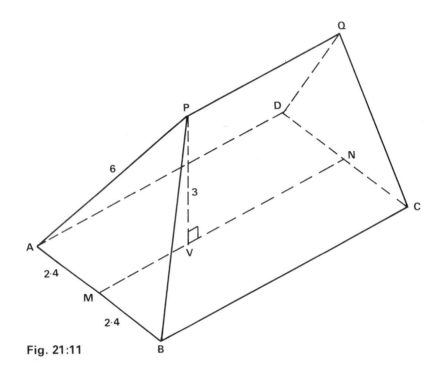

**Fig. 21:11**

It is given that AM = MB = 2.4 m, PV = 3 m and AP = PB = 6 m.

(a) Calculate PM.

(b) Calculate the inclination to the horizontal of the edge PA.

(c) Name, and calculate, the angle between the sloping face PQCB and the horizontal.

(d) Name, and calculate, the angle between the two sloping faces PQCB and PQDA.

(*Cambridge*)

**28** In Figure 21:12, A, B and C are three points on a horizontal plane, forming an isosceles triangle in which AB = AC = 6 m and BC = 4 m. D is the midpoint of BC. A vertical rod PO stands with its foot at the point O on the line AD, where OD = 1 m. PB and PC are rods each of length 5 m and PA is a rod of a different length.

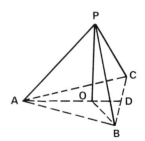

**Fig. 21:12**

Calculate:
(a) the lengths of BO and AO
(b) the length of the rod PO
(c) the angle which the rod PA makes with the horizontal
(d) the angle between the rods PB and PC.

(*O & C*)

**29** (a) Copy the table, then use your calculator to help you complete it, giving values correct to 2 significant figures.

| $\theta$ | 0° | 10° | 20° | 30° | 40° | 50° | 60° | 70° | 80° | 90° | 100° | etc. to 360° |
|---|---|---|---|---|---|---|---|---|---|---|---|---|
| sin $\theta$ | | 0.17 | | | | | | | | | 0.98 | |
| cos $\theta$ | | 0.98 | | | | | | | | | −0.17 | |
| tan $\theta$ | | 0.18 | | | | | | | | $\infty$ | −5.7 | |

(b) Setting degrees along the horizontal axis, draw the graphs of $y = \sin\theta$, $y = \cos\theta$, and $y = \tan\theta$. For the first two graphs, take $y$ from −1 to 1 with a scale of 2 mm to 0.1. For the third, take $y$ from −10 to 10 with a scale of 1 mm to 0.1. Figure 21:13 shows you how to plot the tangent graph as the curve approaches $\infty$ (infinity) at 90° (and at 270°).

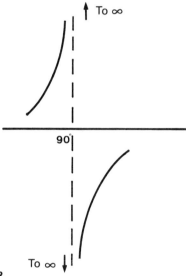

**Fig. 21:13**

**30** Draw graphs of:
(a) $y = \sin\theta + \cos\theta$ for $\theta$ from 0° to 360°
(b) $y = 3\sin\theta - 1$ for $\theta$ from 0° to 360°.

# 22 Statistics (i)

**Pictogram**
**Bar-chart**
**Frequency polygon**

**Pie-chart**
**Interpretation**

---

**1** (a) Study Figure 22:1. How well do you think it illustrates the information given in the table?

|                              | 1982 | 1983 | 1984 | 1985 | 1986 |
|------------------------------|------|------|------|------|------|
|                              | £    | £    | £    | £    | £    |
| Value of car                 | 5000 | 3400 | 2800 | 2500 | 1800 |
| Loss of value (depreciation) | 0    | 1600 | 600  | 300  | 700  |
| Loss of interest (at 10 per cent) | 0 | 500  | 550  | 605  | 666  |
| Repairs                      | 0    | 37   | 158  | 331  | 274  |

**Depreciation**

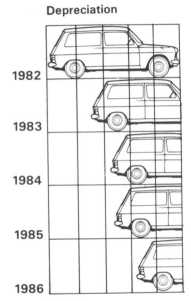

1982
1983
1984
1985
1986

**Fig. 22:1**

(b) Design a pictogram to illustrate the increasing cost of repairs, using a spanner symbol to represent £50.

• **2** Figure 22:2 shows a hospital patient's record sheet.
   (a) What is the average human body temperature in °C?
   (b) What units are used to measure pulse and respiration?
   (c) What is the average human pulse rate?
   (d) What is the average human respiration rate?
   (e) Was the patient ill on the 15th February? If so, describe the symptoms. If not, say how you know.
   (f) On what date did the patient's condition return to normal?

Name *John Murphy* ............... Age *56* Reg. No. *007* Ward *7B*

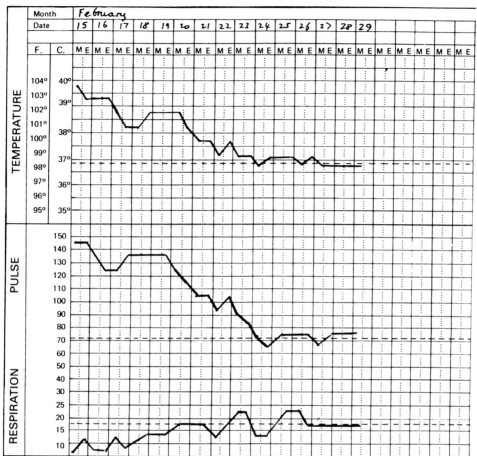

**Fig. 22:2**

**3** Study Figure 22:3.

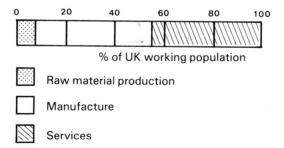

% of UK working population

Raw material production

Manufacture

Services

(a) What percentage of the U.K. working population are working in each of the three categories?

(b) Redraw the chart
  (i) as a bar-chart with three separate bars
  (ii) as a pie-chart.

*4   The pie-chart in Figure 22:4 represents a town with a population of 720 000. The number of people over 60 is half the number of people under 16.

(a)  Calculate the angle of the sector representing the remaining population.

(b)  How many people in the town are aged over 60? Give your answer in standard form.

(*AEB Arithmetic 1982*)

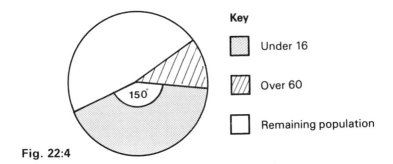

**Key**

☐ Under 16

▨ Over 60

☐ Remaining population

**Fig. 22:4**

*5   Figure 22:5, which is drawn accurately, shows the breakdown of the selling price of items from a small firm.

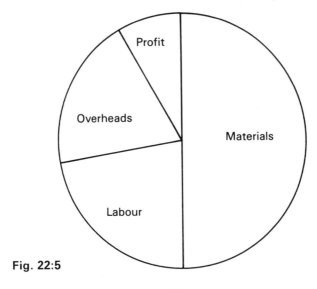

**Fig. 22:5**

(a)  The selling price for item A was £18. What was the cost of materials for this item?

(b)  The cost for labour to make item B was £6. What was the total selling price for this item?

(c)  To make a third type of item the firm found that the cost of the materials was £10 more than the labour cost. What was the selling price for this item?

(d)  Another firm wishes to draw a pie-chart to represent the cost of the items it sells. An item with a selling price of £72 costs £30 for materials, £24 for labour, £12 for overheads, and gave £6 profit. What would be the size of the angle of the sector representing the cost of materials for this item?

(*EAEB*)

*6   In 1983 Britain's teenagers spent £71 million on soft drinks, £57 million on crisps and snack-foods, and £25 million on ice-cream. Illustrate this with a bar-chart.

*7   A salesman can choose one of three ways to be paid his weekly wage:

Method A   $10\frac{1}{5}$% commission on the value of the goods he sells.

Method B   A basic wage of £20 a week plus 5% commission on the value of the goods he sells.

Method C   $7\frac{1}{2}$% commission on the value of goods sold up to £200, and 20% on the value of goods sold above £200.

Figure 22:6 shows the three methods illustrated graphically.

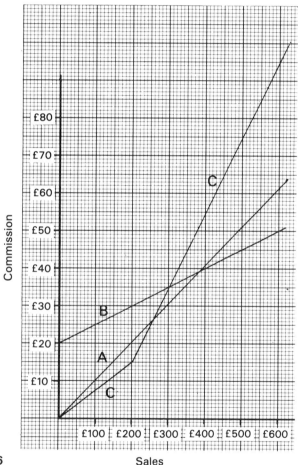

**Fig. 22:6**

(a)  Which method earns him the most money when goods to the value of £250 are sold?
(b)  To earn £40 a week by Method B what is the value of the goods he must sell?
(c)  Above what amount has he to sell before Method C produces the best earnings?
(d)  When the salesman sells £500 worth of goods how much more does he earn by Method C than Method A?
(e)  Which method is never as good as one or the other of the remaining two?

(*SREB*)

**\*8** Draw a bar-chart to illustrate the following marks obtained by a year-group in an examination.

| Mark % | 0–9 | 10–19 | 20–29 | 30–39 | 40–49 | 50–59 | 60–69 | 70–79 | 80–89 | 90–100 |
|---|---|---|---|---|---|---|---|---|---|---|
| No. of pupils | 5 | 17 | 26 | 42 | 58 | 60 | 36 | 21 | 8 | 5 |

**9** (a) In 1985 an apprentice electricians's 'take-home' pay was £60 a week. His weekly budget was as follows:

Rent, food, heat and light    £18
Clothes    £12
Entertainment    £16
Travel    £8
Savings and other items    £6

Draw a pie-chart to represent his weekly budget.

(b) Figure 22:7 represents the 'average family' budget in 1985. The 'average family's' net income in 1985 was £6480.

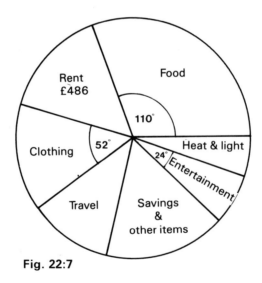

**Fig. 22:7**

Calculate:
(i)   how much was spent on food
(ii)   what angle is represented by rent
(iii)   what percentage of the family's net income was spent on entertainment.

(c) By comparing the two pie-charts, comment briefly on the major differences between the two budgets.

(*AEB*)

**10** The prices of 500 houses offered for sale on the south side of Manchester during a certain week in 1980 are summarised in the following table.

| Price (£) | 0– | 5000– | 15 000– | 20 000– | 25 000– | 30 000– |
|---|---|---|---|---|---|---|
| Frequency | 0 | 11 | 51 | 130 | 90 | 55 |

| Price (£) | 35 000– | 40 000– | 45 000– | 50 000– | 60 000–90 000 |
|---|---|---|---|---|---|
| Frequency | 52 | 40 | 30 | 21 | 20 |

Represent this information in a histogram.

*(JMB)*

**11** As a test of general knowledge, 200 pupils from a city school had to mark the names of as many streets as they could on a map of the area. The results are given in the following table.

| No. of streets correct ($x$) | 46 | 47 | 48 | 49 | 50 | 51 | 52 | 53 |
|---|---|---|---|---|---|---|---|---|
| No. of pupils ($f$) | | 12 | 25 | 46 | 44 | 30 | 17 | 16 | 10 |

Draw the frequency polygon of this distribution.

*(UoC)*

**12** Collect examples of statistical data graphs from magazines and newspapers. Display them with critical comments.

# 23 Statistics (ii)

| Mean | (Cumulative frequency |
|------|----------------------|
| Mode | curve) |
| Median | (Quartiles) |
| Grouped data | |

## ● You need to know:

### Statistics

---

**1** Calculate the mode, the median, and the mean of:
(a) 6, 7, 7, 8, 8, 8, 10, 10      (b) 3, 8, 8, 11, 15, 15, 17
(c) 8, 3, 2, 6, 9, 11, 9, 8, 1, 10      (d) 4, 10, 3, 10, 6, 5, 11, 12.

**2** A survey of the number of children living in the houses of pupils in class 3W resulted in the following data:

| No. of children in house | 1 | 2 | 3 | 4 | 5 | 6 |
|---|---|---|---|---|---|---|
| No. of pupils | 3 | 12 | 8 | 6 | 0 | 1 |

Find:
(a) the number of pupils in class 3W      (b) the modal number of children in the house
(c) the mean average number of children in the house.

**3** A teacher keeps records of the marks for a year-group in a mathematics tests as shown in the table.

| Class (marks) | Assumed mark | Frequency (no. of pupils) | Total score |
|---|---|---|---|
| 0–9 | 4.5 | 15 | 67.5 |
| 10–19 | | 30 | |
| 20–29 | | 55 | |
| 30–39 | | 46 | |
| 40–50 | 45 | 24 | |
| | TOTALS | | |

(a) State the modal class.

(b) State the class in which the median lies.

(c) By assuming the mark of each pupil in each mark-range is the mean of that range, calculate an approximation for the mean mark of the class.

**4** By grouping the following marks in a similar manner to that of question 3, calculate an approximation to their mean average.

28, 11, 19, 36, 27, 3, 30, 25, 31, 40, 26, 27, 37, 41, 13, 38, 22, 24, 23, 6, 30, 31, 29, 35, 30, 31, 16, 35, 45, 20, 36, 45, 20, 18, 21, 39, 30, 26, 15, 39, 30, 46, 47, 31, 48, 28, 20, 8, 38, 48, 17, 31, 25, 15, 36, 10, 32, 21, 9, 11, 34, 37, 49, 25, 36, 20, 19, 40, 26, 15

**5** Calculate the mode, the median, and the mean of:

(a) 9, 9, 1, 3, 6, 7, 7, 9, 1, 7, 3    (b) 12, 11, 13, 12, 11, 10, 15, 9, 12, 8.

**6** (a) Copy and complete the table for the answers given by a class to the number of cats and dogs they had at home.

Replies: 1, 0, 1, 3, 0, 2, 3, 1, 1, 6, 1, 7, 2, 1, 1, 2, 3, 0, 1, 2, 6, 2, 0, 3

| No. of pets | 0 | 1 | 2 | 3 | 4 | 5 | 6 | 7 |
|---|---|---|---|---|---|---|---|---|
| No. of pupils | | | | | | | | |

(b) Find:

(i)   the number of pupils in the class

(ii)   the total number of cats and dogs in their homes

(iii)   the modal number of pets

(iv)   the mean average number of pets per pupil

(v)   the median number of pets.

**7** A new pupil joins the class in question 6. She has 4 pets at home. What is the effect on:

(a) the modal number of pets    (b) the mean average number of pets per pupil

(c) the median number of pets?

**\*8** A shop conducts a survey to find how often its customers used the shop in a month. The results were recorded in the following table.

| No. of times | 1 | 2–4 | 5–7 | 8–10 | 11–15 | 16–20 | 21–25 | 26–30 |
|---|---|---|---|---|---|---|---|---|
| Frequency | 32 | 27 | 43 | 21 | 29 | 16 | 8 | 15 |

Find:

(a) the number of customers who answered the survey

(b) the modal class

(c) the class in which the median lies

(d) the mean number of times, correct to the nearest whole number, taking each frequency as that for the middle of the class.

*9  A police speed-check records the following speeds in m.p.h. for a hundred vehicles. By grouping the speeds in classes of 10 m.p.h., that is 0–9 m.p.h.; 10–19 m.p.h.; 20–29 m.p.h.; etc. up to 90–100 m.p.h., calculate the mean average speed.

60, 29, 30, 40, 35, 19, 8, 23, 30, 48, 52, 68, 49, 69, 68, 48, 35, 50, 57, 43, 49, 55, 60, 67, 45, 36, 46, 60, 68, 58, 12, 35, 57, 46, 56, 30, 28, 39, 55, 40, 63, 45, 62, 66, 58, 37, 36, 20, 15, 38, 39, 49, 53, 47, 26, 37, 46, 65, 70, 65, 36, 20, 11, 45, 41, 58, 24, 18, 48, 46, 56, 50, 48, 39, 72, 56, 40, 53, 67, 45, 30, 38, 37, 41, 38, 49, 60, 62, 79, 59, 85, 80, 56, 98, 58, 35, 65, 63, 50, 38

*10  Use a calculator to find the exact mean average speed for the cars surveyed in question 9.

*11  Joe Mendit buys a cheap batch of 240 radios, some of which are known to be faulty. The number of faults in each radio is given by the following table:

| No. of faults | 0 | 1 | 2 | 3 | 4 | 5 | 6 |
|---|---|---|---|---|---|---|---|
| No. of radios | 40 | 70 | 50 | 30 | 10 | 20 | 20 |

(a)  How many radios had five or more faults?

(b)  State the modal number of faults.

(c)  Using a radius of 5 cm for the circle, draw an accurate, clearly labelled pie-chart to show the information given in the table.

(d)  Calculate the mean number of faults per radio, giving your answer as a fraction in its lowest terms.

(e)  Joe Mendit paid £1200 for the radios and it cost him £1 to repair each fault. He scraps the radios with five or more faults and repairs and sells the rest for £10 each. Calculate: (i) the number of radios sold, and (ii) the total profit made.

(SWEB)

12  Calculate the mean 6 a.m. temperature for January, given that the readings in °C at 6 a.m. each day were:

0, 2, 3, 5, 2, 0, −1, −1, −5, −4, 0, −1, 0, 1, 1, 3, 4, 5, 5, 6, 5, 4, 4, −1, −6, −7, −9, −10, −6, −4, −1.

13  Six employees earn a mean average wage of £270 each a week. What is their total weekly earnings?

14  Class 5A calculates their mean average income is £2.75 a week. Class 5B calculates theirs as £3.25 a week. Class 5A has 25 pupils and class 5B has 35 pupils. What is the mean average income of the combined classes?

15  A shop pays 10 part-time assistants £45 a week, 4 check-out operators £70 a week, 9 full-time assistants £50 a week, 2 supervisors £80 a week, and the manager £136 a week. Calculate:
(a)  the modal wage
(b)  the median wage
(c)  the mean average wage.

**16** The mean of five numbers is 18. Three of the numbers are equal and the other two have a mean of 10. Find the equal numbers.

**17** A die was thrown 40 times and the frequency of each score was as follows:

| Score | 1 | 2 | 3 | 4 | 5 | 6 |
|-----------|---|---|---|---|---|---|
| Frequency | 5 | 4 | 9 | 8 | 8 | 6 |

(a) Write down the modal score.
(b) Find the median score.
(c) Calculate the mean of these scores.
(d) The die was then thrown another 20 times. The mean of these 20 throws was 3.4. Calculate the overall mean for all 60 throws.

(*AEB 1981*)

**18** Write three different positive integers with a mean of 3 and a median of 2.

**19** Find the four positive integers with a mean of 11, a mode of 10, and a range of 20.

**20** Figure 23:1 shows the cumulative frequency curve for the results of a test given to a group of children. The top mark was 70. Use the curve to find:
(a) how many pupils took the test
(b) how many children have 50 marks or less
(c) the pass mark if 35% of the children failed
(d) the median mark
(e) the interquartile range.

(*SREB*)

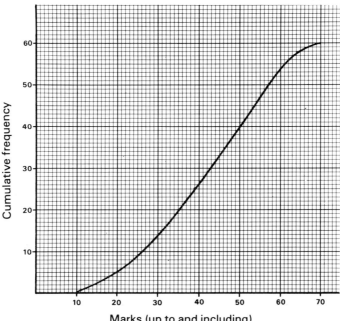

**Fig. 23:1**

Marks (up to and including)

**21** Figure 23:2 shows the cumulative frequency curve for the percentage of people liable to surtax in 1934.
(a) What percentage received not more than £15 000?
(b) What was the median income?
(c) What was the upper quartile?

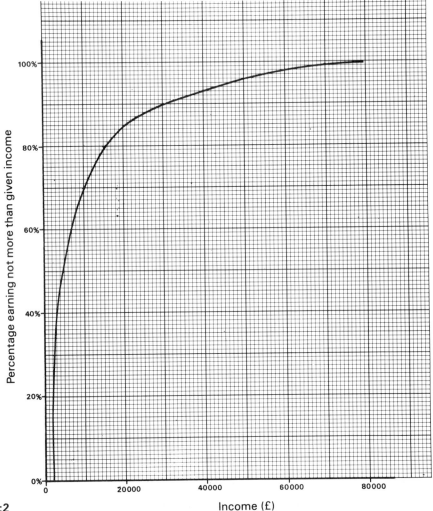

**Fig. 23:2**    Income (£)

**22** Two hundred oranges were weighed to the nearest 5 g. The weights were as shown in the table.

| Weight (g) | 70/75 | 80/85 | 90/95 | 100/105 | 110/115 | 120/125 | 130/135 |
|---|---|---|---|---|---|---|---|
| Frequency | 9 | 21 | 31 | 37 | 44 | 39 | 19 |

(a) Draw up a cumulative frequency table and draw the cumulative frequency curve.
(b) Use your curve to estimate the median weight.
(c) Approximately how many oranges weigh more than 105 g?

**23** Draw a cumulative frequency curve for the data of question 9, using the suggested class intervals.

**24** The cumulative frequencies for the ages of the brides and bridegrooms at 100 weddings are given in the table.

| Age | Under 20 | Under 25 | Under 30 | Under 35 | Under 40 | Under 45 |
|---|---|---|---|---|---|---|
| Brides | 33 | 79 | 93 | 98 | 100 | 100 |
| Grooms | 7 | 42 | 81 | 91 | 96 | 100 |

(a) How many brides were under 25 years of age?

(b) How many grooms were not under 25 years of age?

(c) How many of these persons were under 20 years of age?

(d) How many more brides than grooms were under 30 years of age?

(e) On one set of axes draw the cumulative frequency curves for both the ages of the brides and for the ages of the grooms.

(f) Estimate from your graph (i) the median age for the brides, and (ii) how many more bridegrooms than brides were at least 27 years of age.

(*SWEB*)

**25** A sample of 120 people in a West Country city was selected for a survey in 1937. The ages of the people in the sample are given in the following cumulative frequency table.

| Age in years LESS THAN | 10 | 20 | 30 | 40 | 50 | 60 | 70 | 80 | 90 |
|---|---|---|---|---|---|---|---|---|---|
| Number of people | 15 | 34 | 55 | 74 | 90 | 103 | 113 | 118 | 120 |

(a) Using a scale of 2 cm to represent 10 years on the horizontal axis, and 2 cm to represent 10 people on the vertical axis, draw the cumulative frequency curve of this sample.

(b) Use your curve to estimate the median age.

(c) Estimate how many people were aged between 16 and 65 years old.

(d) Copy and complete the following frequency table, obtained from the given cumulative frequency table.

| Age range (years) | 0–10 | 10–20 | 20–30 | 30–40 | 40–50 | 50–60 | 60–70 | 70–80 | 80–90 |
|---|---|---|---|---|---|---|---|---|---|
| No. of people | 15 | 19 | 21 | | | | | | |

(e) Use your table to calculate an approximation for the mean age of people in the sample.

(*AEB 1985*)

**26** Draw up bar-charts for the following four sets of marks.

| Pupil code | a | b | c | d | e | f | g | h | i | j | k | l | m | n | o | p |
|---|---|---|---|---|---|---|---|---|---|---|---|---|---|---|---|---|
| Test 1 | 0 | 1 | 1 | 2 | 2 | 2 | 3 | 3 | 3 | 3 | 4 | 4 | 4 | 5 | 5 | 6 |
| Test 2 | 0 | 3 | 3 | 3 | 3 | 3 | 3 | 3 | 3 | 3 | 3 | 3 | 3 | 3 | 3 | 6 |
| Test 3 | 0 | 0 | 1 | 1 | 2 | 2 | 3 | 3 | 3 | 3 | 4 | 4 | 5 | 5 | 6 | 6 |
| Test 4 | 0 | 0 | 0 | 0 | 2 | 3 | 3 | 3 | 3 | 3 | 3 | 4 | 6 | 6 | 6 | 6 |

Calculate the mean, the mode, the median and the range for each test.

**27** Question 26 shows you that it is possible to have the same three statistical averages for a set of data, and the same range, yet for the data to be very different. We also need a measure of how the marks are spread out. This measure is called the **standard deviation**. It is found as follows:
(a) Find the mean.
(b) Find the deviation from the mean for each score.
(c) Square the deviations and sum them.
(d) Find the mean of this sum.
(e) Find the square root of this mean.

Calculate the standard deviation for each of the four tests. Does this measure give you a better idea of the spread of the data?

**28** Calculate the standard deviation for the marks given in question 4. Use the approximate mean of 28.

A 'normal' curve is the frequency curve you would expect from a large sample of unbiased data. Its shape is shown in Figure 23:3.

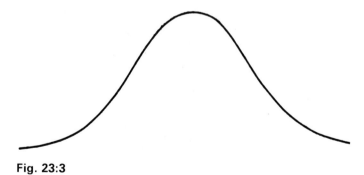

**Fig. 23:3**

The symbol for standard deviation is $\sigma$ (small sigma). For a normal curve we expect that about 68% of the scores will be within $1\sigma$ of the mean, about 95% within $2\sigma$ of the mean, and nearly 100% within $3\sigma$ of the mean. How true is this of the marks in question 4?

# 24 Probability

**One event**             **(Exclusive events)**
**Independent events**

## ● You need to know:

### Probability

---

**1** From a full pack of 52 playing cards, one card is drawn. What is the probability that the card is:
(a) a black suit      (b) a diamond      (c) a king      (d) the Ace of Spades?

**2** In one inner city the police calculate that householders have a 1 in 4 chance of being burgled during any one year. What is the probability that a householder will not be burgled during any one year?

**3** Copy and complete the tree diagram. You will need 16 lines of your book for the final column. When you have completed the diagram, use it to find the probability of an equal number of heads and tails in four throws of a coin.

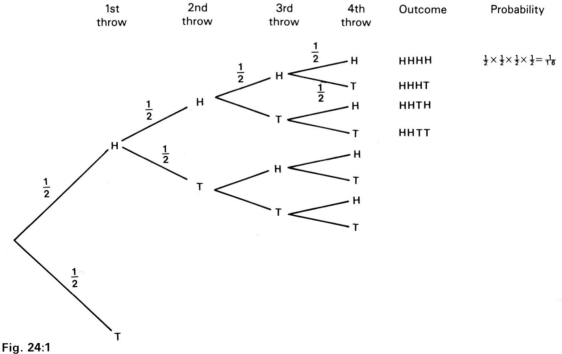

**Fig. 24:1**

**4** By observing a certain set of traffic lights each time that I am 25 metres from them during the course of a year I have calculated the following probabilities:

$P(\text{red}) = \frac{1}{2};$   $P(\text{red and amber}) = \frac{1}{8};$   $P(\text{amber}) = \frac{1}{6}.$

What is $P(\text{green})$?

**5** (a) Copy and complete the following table, using the tree-diagram in question 3 or otherwise. Note that, for example, 2H1T means the number of different ways you can have 2 heads and 1 tail in the outcome, e.g. HHT, THH.

| No. of throws | 1 | | 2 | | | 3 | | | |
|---|---|---|---|---|---|---|---|---|---|
| Results | 1H | 1T | 2H | 1H1T | 2T | 3H | 2H1T | 1H2T | 3T |
| No. of ways | 1 | 1 | 1 | 2 | 1 | | | | |

| No. of throws | 4 | | | | |
|---|---|---|---|---|---|
| Results | 4H | 3H1T | 2H2T | 1H3T | 4T |
| No. of ways | | | | | |

(b) The results are lines of Pascal's triangle:

```
1 throw              1     1
2 throws          1     2     1
3 throws       1     3     3     1
4 throws    1     4     6     4     1
```

By continuing Pascal's triangle calculate the probability in six tosses of a coin of:
(i) 6 heads   (ii) 3 heads and 3 tails   (iii) HHTTTT   (iv) more heads than tails.

**6** Three cards, marked with the numbers 7, 8 and 3 respectively, are placed in a box. Two cards are picked at random.

(a) Write down all possible numbers that result, e.g. a 7 and then a 3 gives 73.

(b) What is:
(i) $P(78 \text{ is drawn})$   (ii) $P(\text{an odd number is drawn})$?

**7** A small ferry can carry a maximum of 6 cars and a maximum of 2 coaches. Figure 24:2 is the possibility space-diagram showing all combinations of up to 6 cars and up to 2 coaches. However, there are the constraints that if 1 coach is aboard then only 4 cars can be fitted in, and if 2 coaches are aboard only 2 cars can be fitted in.

Copy the diagram and ring the dots that represent possible ferry loads. (The ferry does not sail if there is no vehicle aboard.)

Ferries are inspected at random. Assuming that all possible loads are equally likely, what is the probability of the ferry holding:
(a) 2 coaches   (b) 3 or more cars   (c) more cars than coaches?

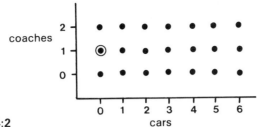

**Fig. 24:2**

**8** After a national series of spot checks, traffic police consider that on checking a car the probability of finding a car with an illegally worn tyre is $\frac{1}{10}$, of a faulty light $\frac{1}{12}$, and of a leaky exhaust $\frac{1}{8}$.

What is the probability on a random check of a car having:
(a) a worn tyre and a faulty light    (b) a worn tyre and a leaky exhaust
(c) all three faults    (d) no faulty lights?

**9** In a laboratory making computer 'chips', 1 in 5 chips on average are imperfect. What is the probability that three chips selected at random will be:
(a) all faulty    (b) all perfect?

**10** Three cards are dealt from a shuffled pack of 52 cards. What is the probability of:
(a) the first card being a spade
(b) the second card being the Queen of Clubs, assuming this card is not dealt first
(c) the third card being a red suit, assuming the first two cards are black suits
(d) the first card being a spade, the second being the Queen of Clubs, and the third being a red card?

**11** A coin is biased so that it is twice as likely to fall heads as tails. What is the probability of:
(a) three heads in a row    (b) two tails followed by a head?

**12** A lucky dip contains 30 prizes worth under 10p, 20 prizes worth between 10p and 25p, and 10 prizes worth over 25p. I have two dips, one after the other. What is the probability of:
(a) picking two prizes worth over 25p each
(b) picking two prizes worth under 10p each
(c) picking a prize worth between 10p and 25p, followed by a prize worth over 25p
(d) picking a prize worth over 25p followed by a prize worth between 10p and 25p?

**13** In a game of chance, four sets of ten cards are turned face down on a table. The backs are identical, but the fronts are sets of ten cars (C), ten planes (P), ten ships (S), and ten horses (H).

Calculate:
(a) $P(C)$   (that is, the probability of a car card on the first pick)
(b) $P(C, H)$   (that is, first a car card then a horse)
(c) $P(P, P)$
(d) $P(S, C, P)$   (in that order)
(e) $P(H)$   if five cards have already been turned over and one of them was a horse
(f) $P(S, S)$   if 20 cards have been turned over, three of them being ships.

**\*14** There are 4 white marbles, 3 black marbles and 3 red marbles in a bag. Find the probability of picking, each time from a full bag:
  (a) a white marble
  (b) a black marble, which is replaced, then a white marble
  (c) a black marble, which is not replaced, then a red marble
  (d) two black marbles if the first one is
      (i) replaced     (ii) not replaced
  (e) either a white or a red marble.

**\*15** Two dice are thrown. Copy and complete the table to show all possible scores.

2nd die

|        |   | 1 | 2 | 3 | 4 | 5 | 6 |
|--------|---|---|---|---|---|---|---|
|        | 1 |   |   |   |   |   |   |
|        | 2 |   |   |   |   |   |   |
| 1st die| 3 |   |   |   |   |   |   |
|        | 4 |   |   |   |   |   |   |
|        | 5 |   |   |   |   |   |   |
|        | 6 |   |   |   |   |   |   |

What is the probability of the total score being:
(a) 3     (b) 7     (c) 16     (d) more than 8     (e) less than 10?

**\*16** Figure 24:3 represents a spinner at a fete, consisting of a wheel coloured in sections as shown.

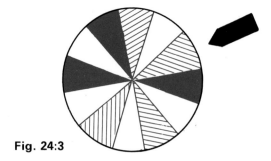

**Fig. 24:3**

What is the chance of the spinner stopping at:

(a) ◼     (b) ▨     (c) ▧   or   ☐     (d) ◼ three times in a row

(e) ☐ then ▨ ?

**\*17** Three cards are dealt from a full pack. What is the probability of dealing:
  (a) first an ace     (b) first an ace, then a jack     (c) first a heart, then a spade
  (d) two aces, then a five of diamonds     (e) three black cards
  (f) all picture cards (Ace, King, Queen, or Jack)?

**\*18** A rat is trained to negotiate a maze set out in a series of blocks. The maze is represented in Figure 24:4.

At each junction the rat can turn left (L), right (R), or go straight ahead (S). From past experience it is reckoned that the rat is more likely to go straight ahead than turn, the probabilities being assessed as:

$P(S) = \frac{3}{5}, P(R) = \frac{3}{10}, P(L) = \frac{1}{10}.$

Copy and complete the tree-diagram, Figure 24:5, to show all the possible routes at three consecutive junctions.

(a) The rat is in the maze as shown in Figure 24:4, heading towards A. If it takes the shortest route, what is the probability that it will emerge at:
    (i) A    (ii) B    (iii) C    (iv) D?

(b) What is the probability of the rat taking (exactly) two left turns at three consecutive junctions?

(c) What is the probability that if the rat starts at E it will go straight to A?

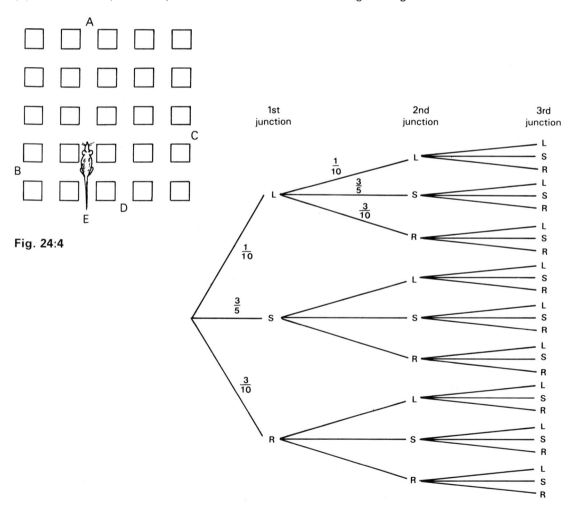

Fig. 24:4

Fig. 24:5

**19** A computer is programmed to play chess. After each game that it wins it is a better player. Against an average player it is reckoned to have a 1 in 10 chance of winning if it has not won any previous games, a 1 in 5 chance of winning if it has won one game previously, and a 1 in 3 chance of winning if it has won two games previously.

Copy and complete the tree-diagram to show all the possible outcomes of the first three games the computer plays. Hence, or otherwise, calculate the probability of the computer winning:
(a) the first three games    (b) the first game, but losing the other two
(c) one of the first two games    (d) two of the first three games.

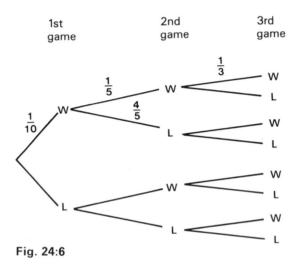

**Fig. 24:6**

**20** Assuming that babies of either sex are equally likely, calculate the chance of a family of four children:
(a) being all boys    (b) having two boys and two girls    (c) having at least one girl.

**21** A bag contains 5 red, 1 green, 2 white, and 2 blue balls. Calculate the chance of picking from the bag, each time without replacement:
(a) two white balls    (b) a white and a red ball    (c) two red balls and one white ball
(d) a green ball and two white balls    (e) two balls of the same colour in two picks
(f) exactly two balls of the same colour out of three picked.

**22** Two cards are dealt from a shuffled pack. What is the probability of them being:
(a) both hearts    (b) one an ace and the other a heart
(c) the first a black card and the second an ace    (d) one a spade but the other not a spade?

**23** A manufacturer checks every bolt made for flaws. Out of a batch of 10 000 bolts, 30 are found to have a flaw. What was the probability that two consecutive bolts tested would both be flawed?

**24** Before an election the Conservative party asks a fifth of the residents of a housing estate who they will vote for. The Labour party ask a third of the residents of the same housing estate who they will vote for. What is the probability that a certain resident will be asked by:
(a) both parties    (b) only one party    (c) neither party?

If there are 195 residents on the estate, find the least possible number who would not be asked.

**25** In a game of Bingo, Jeff has a card with the numbers 1, 7, 11, 23 and 24 on it, whilst Jane's card has 1, 7, 10, 15 and 22. The numbers are selected by drawing balls from a drum, the thirty balls being numbered from 1 to 30.

(a) What is the probability that on the first draw Jeff will have one of his numbers called?

(b) What is the probability that on the first draw neither Jeff nor Jane will have a number called?

(c) What is the probability that Jane will have one of her numbers called in both of the first two draws?

(d) Find the probability that Jane has a number called in the first draw but Jeff does not.

(e) Find the probability that on the first draw Jeff has a number called, but Jane does not, then on the second draw Jane has a number called but Jeff does not.

---

**26** At the start of a game, six ships are represented on a 6 × 6 grid by shading in any six different squares. An example is shown in Figure 24:7.

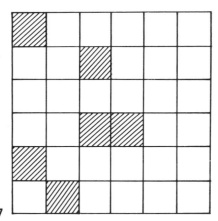

**Fig.24:7**

In the first round of the game, a player tries to locate the position of a ship without seeing the grid. He does this by selecting a square at random. In each succeeding round he selects a square at random from those he has not already selected.

State the probability that:

(a) a ship is located in the first round

(b) a ship is located in the second round if:
   (i) one was also located in the first round
   (ii) one was not located in the first round.

Calculate the probability that in the first two rounds

(c) two ships are located

(d) just one ship is located.

In a particular game, after $n$ rounds the player has located no ships. Find the value of $n$ if the probability that a ship is located in the next round is $\frac{2}{9}$.

(*AEB 1982*)

**27** Algernon, Bertrand and Cuthbert spend many of their evenings in coffee bars. In order to decide who pays for the next round of drinks they have invented a game using 16 playing cards: the jacks, queens, kings and aces. The cards are shuffled, and one is dealt to each of them in alphabetical order: Algernon, Bertrand, Cuthbert. They then look at the cards to see who has been dealt an ace, or not. The possibility tree is shown in Figure 24:8. Copy and complete it.

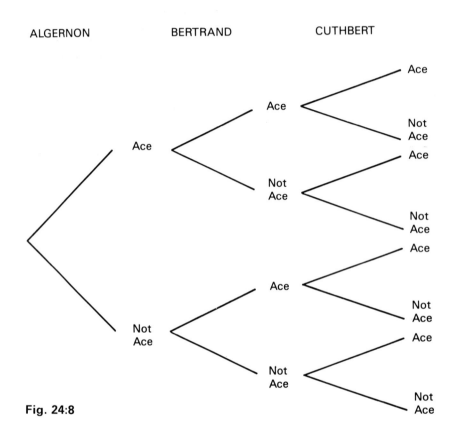

ALGERNON        BERTRAND        CUTHBERT

**Fig. 24:8**

In one deal of the cards what is the probability that:
(a) three aces are dealt
(b) no aces are dealt
(c) just one of them is dealt an ace?

If they are all dealt aces, or none of them is dealt an ace, then each of them pays for his own cup of coffee. If only two are dealt aces, then the one who is not dealt an ace pays for all three cups of coffee. If only one is dealt an ace, then he pays for all three cups of coffee.

What is the probability that Algernon will not have to pay for the next cup of coffee he drinks?

*(AEB 1983)*

**28** The River Gurgle is deep and dangerous. It has no bridge and one-quarter of those who try to cross it fail in the attempt.

   (a)  If Tom tries to cross the river, what is the probability that he will succeed?

   (b)  If both Tom and Dick try to cross the river, what is the probability that:
      (i)  both succeed     (ii)  both fail     (iii)  one succeeds but the other fails
      (iv)  at least one of them succeeds?

   (c)  Tom, Dick, Harriet, Gill and Gwen are a band of five explorers who arrived at the river one day. If two of the band could cross the river taking a rope with them, then the rest could cross safely. To decide which two should try to cross, the names of the five were drawn at random from a hat. The first two drawn made the attempt. What is the probability that:
      (i)   the first name taken out was Tom
      (ii)  the two selected to make the attempt were Tom and Dick
      (iii)  the two selected to make the attempt were Tom and Dick, and they succeeded?

*(AEB 1985)*

# 25 Vectors

**(Simple geometrical applications)**

## ● You need to know:

### Vectors

---

**1** Referring to Figure 25:1, describe the following vectors as column matrices, e.g. $\overrightarrow{AB} = \begin{pmatrix} 1 \\ 1 \end{pmatrix}$.

(a) $\overrightarrow{BC}$    (b) $\overrightarrow{CD}$    (c) $\overrightarrow{DE}$    (d) $\overrightarrow{EF}$    (e) $\overrightarrow{FG}$

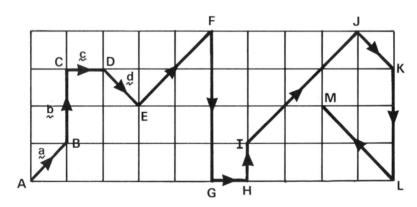

Fig. 25:1

**2** Referring to Figure 25:1, state the following vectors in terms of $\underset{\sim}{a}$, $\underset{\sim}{b}$, $\underset{\sim}{c}$, or $\underset{\sim}{d}$.

(a) $\overrightarrow{EF}$    (b) $\overrightarrow{FG}$    (c) $\overrightarrow{GH}$    (d) $\overrightarrow{HI}$    (e) $\overrightarrow{IJ}$    (f) $\overrightarrow{JK}$    (g) $\overrightarrow{KL}$    (h) $\overrightarrow{LM}$

**3** The magnitude, or length, of a vector is called its **modulus**. The symbol used is $|\overrightarrow{AB}|$ or $|\underset{\sim}{a}|$.

When the vector is not parallel to a grid line its modulus is found using Pythagoras' Theorem.

Referring to Figure 25:1 find the length of:

(a) $\overrightarrow{BC}$    (b) $\overrightarrow{EF}$    (c) $\overrightarrow{IJ}$.

**4** Calculate:

(a) $|\underset{\sim}{v}|$ where $\underset{\sim}{v} = \begin{pmatrix} 3 \\ 4 \end{pmatrix}$    (b) $|\underset{\sim}{w}|$ where $\underset{\sim}{w} = \begin{pmatrix} -2 \\ 5 \end{pmatrix}$.

**5** Calculate the resultant of the following vectors, then check your answer by drawing.

(a) $\begin{pmatrix} 3 \\ 0 \end{pmatrix} + \begin{pmatrix} 2 \\ 0 \end{pmatrix}$    (b) $\begin{pmatrix} 1 \\ 0 \end{pmatrix} + \begin{pmatrix} 0 \\ 1 \end{pmatrix}$    (c) $\begin{pmatrix} 4 \\ -2 \end{pmatrix} + \begin{pmatrix} -3 \\ 1 \end{pmatrix}$    (d) $\begin{pmatrix} -2 \\ -1 \end{pmatrix} + \begin{pmatrix} -1 \\ -2 \end{pmatrix}$

**\*6** (a) Copy Figure 25:2.

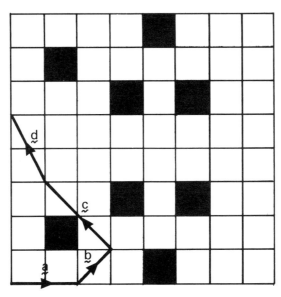

**Fig. 25:2**

(b) Continue the vectors from the end of $\underset{\sim}{d}$ as follows, marking an arrow on each one to show its direction.

$\begin{pmatrix} 2 \\ 0 \end{pmatrix} \begin{pmatrix} 2 \\ 2 \end{pmatrix} \begin{pmatrix} 1 \\ -2 \end{pmatrix} \begin{pmatrix} -1 \\ -1 \end{pmatrix} \begin{pmatrix} 2 \\ -4 \end{pmatrix} \begin{pmatrix} 2 \\ 0 \end{pmatrix} \begin{pmatrix} -2 \\ 4 \end{pmatrix} \begin{pmatrix} 2 \\ 0 \end{pmatrix} \begin{pmatrix} -3 \\ 3 \end{pmatrix} \begin{pmatrix} 3 \\ 0 \end{pmatrix} \begin{pmatrix} -1 \\ -1 \end{pmatrix} \begin{pmatrix} 1 \\ 0 \end{pmatrix}$

Note: If you hit a black square you have made a mistake!

(c) Write on each of the vectors you have drawn its relationship to $\underset{\sim}{a}$, $\underset{\sim}{b}$, $\underset{\sim}{c}$, or $\underset{\sim}{d}$.

**\*7** $\overrightarrow{AB} = \underset{\sim}{a}$,   $\overrightarrow{BC} = 2\underset{\sim}{a}$,   $\overrightarrow{CA} = -\underset{\sim}{a}$,   $\overrightarrow{CE} = \underset{\sim}{b}$.

$\overrightarrow{AB} = \begin{pmatrix} 2 \\ 0 \end{pmatrix}$ and $|\overrightarrow{AB}| = 2\,\text{cm}$,   $\overrightarrow{CE} = \begin{pmatrix} 0 \\ -2 \end{pmatrix}$ and $|\overrightarrow{AB}| = |\overrightarrow{CE}|$.

Sketch the following pairs of vectors (not on squared paper).

(a) $\overrightarrow{AB}$ and $\overrightarrow{BC}$    (b) $\overrightarrow{AB}$ and $\overrightarrow{CD}$    (c) $\overrightarrow{AB}$ and $\overrightarrow{CA}$

(d) $\overrightarrow{AB}$ and $\overrightarrow{CE}$    (e) $\overrightarrow{BC}$ and $\overrightarrow{CE}$    (f) $\overrightarrow{CA}$ and $\overrightarrow{CE}$

**\*8** If $\underset{\sim}{a} = \begin{pmatrix} 2 \\ 3 \end{pmatrix}$ and $\underset{\sim}{b} = \begin{pmatrix} -5 \\ 1 \end{pmatrix}$ find $\underset{\sim}{p}$ and $\underset{\sim}{q}$ when:

(a) $\underset{\sim}{p} = 2\underset{\sim}{a} + \underset{\sim}{b}$    (b) $\underset{\sim}{q} + \underset{\sim}{b} = 4\underset{\sim}{a}$.

                                                              *(SWEB)*

**\*9** p is the vector which translates the point (1, 4) to the point (5, 7). Express p as column vector.

(*EAEB*)

**10** Refer to Figure 25:3. Vector $\overrightarrow{AD}$ can be expressed in terms of a and b by finding a way of getting from A to D by only travelling along vectors parallel to a and b.

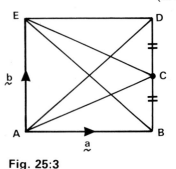

We could go along to B, then on to D, so $\overrightarrow{AD} = \overrightarrow{AB} + \overrightarrow{BD} = a + b$.

Similarly $\overrightarrow{BE} = \overrightarrow{BA} + \overrightarrow{AE} = -a + b$.

**Fig. 25:3**

(a) In terms of b what is:

    (i) $\overrightarrow{BD}$   (ii) $\overrightarrow{DB}$   (iii) $\overrightarrow{BC}$   (iv) $\overrightarrow{CB}$   (v) $\overrightarrow{CD}$   (vi) $\overrightarrow{DC}$?

(b) Express in terms of a and b:

    (i) $\overrightarrow{DA}$   (ii) $\overrightarrow{EB}$   (iii) $\overrightarrow{AC}$   (iv) $\overrightarrow{CA}$   (v) $\overrightarrow{CE}$   (vi) $\overrightarrow{EC}$.

**11** In Figure 25:4, ABCD is a parallelogram and L and M are the midpoints of AC and CB.

Write in terms of a and d:

(a) $\overrightarrow{CD}$   (b) $\overrightarrow{AC}$   (c) $\overrightarrow{LM}$   (d) $\overrightarrow{BL}$.

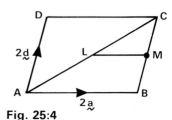

**Fig. 25:4**

**12** Refer to Figure 25:5.

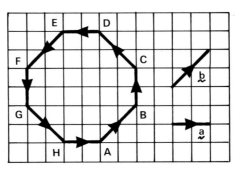

**Fig. 25:5**

(a) Write in terms of a and b:

    (i) $\overrightarrow{DE}$   (ii) $\overrightarrow{BC}$   (iii) $\overrightarrow{CD}$   (iv) $\overrightarrow{AD}$.

(b) Which side or diagonals could be represented as:

    (i) $-b$   (ii) $a - b$   (iii) $3a$   (iv) $2a - 3b$?

**13** In Figure 25:6, ABCDEF is a regular hexagon. Q is the midpoint of ED. Find in terms of $\underset{\sim}{x}$ and $\underset{\sim}{y}$:

(a) $\overrightarrow{DE}$   (b) $\overrightarrow{FD}$   (c) $\overrightarrow{QF}$   (d) $\overrightarrow{CD}$.

(*SWEB*)

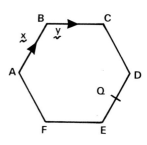

**Fig. 25:6**

**14** (a) You are given that $\underset{\sim}{i} = \begin{pmatrix} 1 \\ 0 \end{pmatrix}$ and that $\underset{\sim}{j} = \begin{pmatrix} 0 \\ 1 \end{pmatrix}$.
Express as a column matrix:
(i) $2\underset{\sim}{i}$   (ii) $2\underset{\sim}{i} + \underset{\sim}{j}$   (iii) $3\underset{\sim}{i} - 2\underset{\sim}{j}$.

(b) In Figure 25:7:
(i) State two ways in which AB and DC are related.
(ii) What is the size of angle DCB?
(iii) Find $\overrightarrow{AC}$ in terms of $\underset{\sim}{a}$ and $\underset{\sim}{b}$.
(iv) Find $\overrightarrow{DE}$ in terms of $\underset{\sim}{a}$ and $\underset{\sim}{b}$.
(v) State fully the relationship between $\overrightarrow{DE}$ and $\overrightarrow{CA}$.

(*SWEB*)

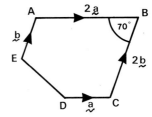

**Fig. 25:7**

**15** (a) Simplify $\begin{pmatrix} 2 \\ 3 \end{pmatrix} - \begin{pmatrix} -1 \\ 4 \end{pmatrix}$.

(b) In Figure 25:8, D is the midpoint of BC, E is the midpoint of AC, and F is the midpoint of AB. G is on AD such that $AG = \frac{2}{3}AD$. If $\overrightarrow{AB} = \underset{\sim}{a}$ and $\overrightarrow{AC} = \underset{\sim}{c}$ express in terms of $\underset{\sim}{a}$ and $\underset{\sim}{c}$:
(i) $\overrightarrow{BC}$   (ii) $\overrightarrow{BD}$   (iii) $\overrightarrow{AD}$   (iv) $\overrightarrow{AG}$
(v) $\overrightarrow{DG}$   (vi) $\overrightarrow{BG}$   (vii) $\overrightarrow{BE}$.

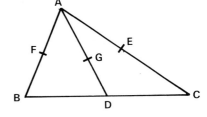

**Fig. 25:8**

(c) From your answers to (b), (vi) and (vii), show that G is on BE and that $BG = \frac{2}{3}BE$.

(*ALSEB*)

**16** In Figure 25:9, T is the midpoint of PS. W and V are the midpoints of SR and RT. QVW and TVR are straight.
$\overrightarrow{QR} = \underset{\sim}{a}$, $\overrightarrow{QP} = \underset{\sim}{b}$, and $\overrightarrow{RS} = 2\underset{\sim}{b}$.

(a) Find in terms of $\underset{\sim}{a}$ and $\underset{\sim}{b}$:
(i) $\overrightarrow{PS}$   (ii) $\overrightarrow{PT}$   (iii) $\overrightarrow{RT}$   (iv) $\overrightarrow{RV}$
(v) $\overrightarrow{QV}$   (vi) $\overrightarrow{VW}$.

(b) By using your answers to (i) and (v) what can you deduce about the lines PS and QV?

(c) Write down the ratio QV : VW.

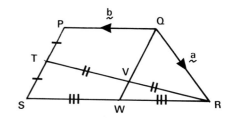

**Fig. 25:9**

(*SREB*)

**17** In Figure 25:10, ABCD is a parallelogram, E is the midpoint of BC, and CF = 2FD.

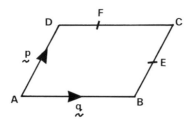

**Fig. 25:10**

(a) · Find in terms of p and q:

   (i) $\overrightarrow{BE}$  (ii) $\overrightarrow{AE}$  (iii) $\overrightarrow{DF}$  (iv) $\overrightarrow{AF}$  (v) $\overrightarrow{BF}$  (vi) $\overrightarrow{FE}$.

(b) Given that AE and BF meet at X and that $BX = \frac{3}{8}BF$, find $\overrightarrow{AX}$ in terms of p and q, and simplify your answer.

(c) If $\overrightarrow{AX} = k\overrightarrow{AE}$ find the value of $k$.                    (*SWEB*)

**18** (a) In Figure 25:11, T is the midpoint of AB and M is the midpoint of AT.

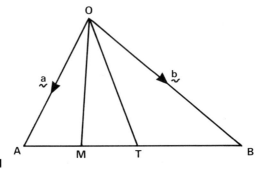

**Fig. 25:11**

   Given that $\overrightarrow{OA} = $ a and $\overrightarrow{OB} = $ b, express as simply as possible in terms of a and b:

   (i) $\overrightarrow{AB}$   (ii) $\overrightarrow{AM}$   (iii) $\overrightarrow{OM}$.

(b) Two points P and Q have position vectors p and q respectively, relative to the origin O.

   Given that $p = \begin{pmatrix} 5 \\ 3 \end{pmatrix}$ and that $\overrightarrow{PQ} = \begin{pmatrix} -2 \\ 1 \end{pmatrix}$ find:

   (i) q    (ii) $|\overrightarrow{PQ}|$

   (iii)  the co-ordinates of the point R which is such that $\overrightarrow{OR} = \overrightarrow{QP}$.

(c) Given also that $s = \begin{pmatrix} 1 \\ 1 \end{pmatrix}$, that $t = \begin{pmatrix} 8 \\ 2 \end{pmatrix}$, and that $l p + m s = t$, write down two simultaneous equations in $l$ and $m$ and solve them.

                    (*UoC*)

**19** Figure 25:12 shows a regular hexagon where $\overrightarrow{OA}$ = p and $\overrightarrow{OE}$ = q.

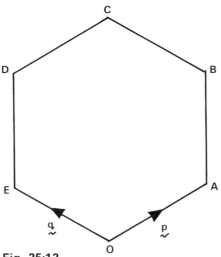

**Fig. 25:12**

(a) Express in terms of p and q:
   (i) $\overrightarrow{OD}$   (ii) $\overrightarrow{OB}$   (iii) $\overrightarrow{EA}$.

(b) Using your answer to (a) (i) and (ii) express the journey D to O to B in terms of p and q.

(c) What does this tell you about EA and DB?

(d) T is a point such that $\overrightarrow{OT}$ = 2p, and R is a point such that $\overrightarrow{OR}$ = 2q. Express $\overrightarrow{RT}$ in terms of p and q.

(e) What does your answer to (d) tell you about RT and DB?

(f) O is the point (0, 0), A is the point ($\sqrt{3}$, 1), and E is the point ($-\sqrt{3}$, 1). Write down $\overrightarrow{OA}$ and $\overrightarrow{OE}$ as column vectors.

(g) Calculate the co-ordinates of T, B, D and R.

(h) Calculate the length of RT.

(SEG)

**20** (a) OABC is a quadrilateral and the vectors $\overrightarrow{OA}$ and $\overrightarrow{OB}$ are equal to a and b respectively. OPQR is the image of OABC under an enlargement with centre O and scale factor 2. Give the vectors $\overrightarrow{AB}$, $\overrightarrow{OP}$ and $\overrightarrow{PQ}$ in terms of a and b.

(b) XPYZ is the image of OPQR under the enlargement with centre P and scale factor 2. Give the vectors $\overrightarrow{PY}$, $\overrightarrow{OY}$ and $\overrightarrow{YB}$ in terms of a and b.

(c) By treating XPYZ as an enlargement of OABC, or otherwise, show that YB and ZC meet on OA. If they meet at T, use the fact that $\overrightarrow{OT}$ = $\overrightarrow{OY}$ + $k\overrightarrow{YB}$ where $k$ is a number, to find $\overrightarrow{OT}$ in terms of a.

(EEG)

**21** In Figure 25:13, OAB is a triangle, where OA is produced to L. It is given that OL = 2OA, M is the midpoint of AB, and the point N lies on OB such that ON : NB = 2 : 1.

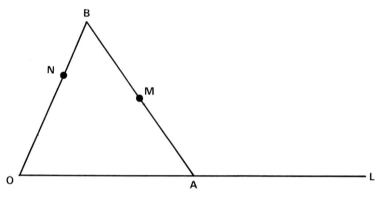

**Fig. 25:13**

If $\overrightarrow{OA}$ = a and $\overrightarrow{OB}$ = b write down in terms of a and b the vectors:

(a) $\overrightarrow{OL}$    (b) $\overrightarrow{OM}$    (c) $\overrightarrow{ON}$    (d) $\overrightarrow{NM}$    (e) $\overrightarrow{ML}$.

Use your answers to (d) and (e) to write down two facts about the points L, M and N.

Two points not shown on the diagram are Q and R. The vector $\overrightarrow{OQ} = \frac{4}{5}\overrightarrow{OM}$. The point R lies on AN such that AR : RN = 3 : 2. Write down, in terms of a and b, the vectors $\overrightarrow{OQ}$ and $\overrightarrow{OR}$. What do these answers tell you about the points Q and R?

(*AEB 1985*)

| Reflection | Translation |
|---|---|
| Rotation | (Shear) |
| Enlargement | (Stretch) |

## ● You need to know:

Transformations

Matrices 2

---

**1** In Figure 26:1, squares A3 and B2 have been shaded. Which squares should be shaded to give Figure 26:1

(a) reflection symmetry in:
  (i) line q    (ii) line p    (iii) line r

(b) rotational symmetry of order:
  (i) 2    (ii) 4?

**2** In Figure 26:1, square B2 is to be translated by the vector $\begin{pmatrix} 2 \\ -1 \end{pmatrix}$. What is its transformed position?

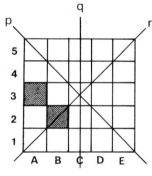

Fig. 26:1

**3** (a) Draw axes, both from −8 to 12. Plot the triangle whose vertices are at (2, 2), (2, 4) and (4, 2).

(b) By drawing, or otherwise, state the co-ordinates of the vertices of the triangle when it is enlarged, centre the origin, by scale factor:
  (i) 3    (ii) −1    (iii) $\frac{1}{2}$    (iv) −2.

**4** Repeat question 3(a), then draw the triangle when it is enlarged as follows, stating the co-ordinates of the new vertices.
(a) Scale factor 2, centre (2, 2).
(b) Scale factor −1, centre (3, 1).
(c) Scale factor −$\frac{1}{2}$, centre (4, 4).

**5** Which numbers from 1001 to 8008 inclusive have rotational symmetry of order 2?

**6** How many lines of symmetry has each of the following capital letters?
(a) H    (b) T    (c) S    (d) C    (e) O

**\*7** PQRS is a rectangle with PQ = 3 cm and QR = 2 cm.

(a) Draw the rectangle, then enlarge it:
(i) by scale factor $1\frac{1}{2}$ from centre P   (ii) by scale factor $-\frac{1}{2}$ from centre P.

(b) Calculate the area of both transformed rectangles, and state how many times as large as the original rectangle they are.

**8** (a) Draw three sets of axes, $x$ from $-2$ to 4, $y$ from 0 to 10. Plot the kite with vertices at A (0, 2), B ($-1$, 3), C (0, 6), and D (1, 3) on each grid. Answer (b) to (d), one on each grid.

(b) Draw the image of the kite after a shear from AD invariant such that $(-1, 3) \rightarrow (1, 5)$.

(c) Draw the image of the kite after a shear from AC invariant such that $(-1, 3) \rightarrow (-1, 1)$.

(d) Draw the image of the kite after a stretch of stretch factor 2 from $y = 4$.

---

**9** Refer to Figure 26:2.

(a) $A_1B_1C_1D_1$ is the image of ABCD under a single transformation. Write down the column vector which effects this transformation.

(b) $A_2B_2C_2D_2$ is the image of ABCD under an anticlockwise rotation. Write down: (i) the angle of the rotation, and (ii) the co-ordinates of the centre of the rotation.

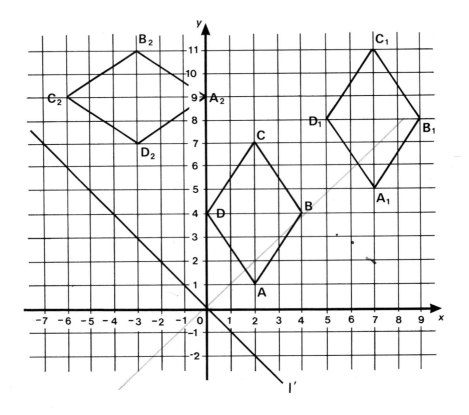

**Fig. 26:2**

(c) The rhombus $A_3B_3C_3D_3$ (not shown in the figure) is the image of ABCD under a reflection in the line ll'. Write down: (i) the equation of line ll', and (ii) the co-ordinates of the point $C_3$.

(d) The quadrilateral $A_4B_4C_4D_4$ (not shown in the figure) is the image of ABCD under a shear with invariant line $y = 0$. Given that $A_4$ is the point (4, 1) write down the co-ordinates of the point $D_4$.

(MEG)

**10** Name all possible special quadrilaterals if they have the following properties:
  (a) two lines of symmetry and rotational symmetry of order 2
  (b) one line of symmetry and no rotational symmetry (that is, only order 1)
  (c) no lines of symmetry and order 2 rotational symmetry
  (d) four lines of symmetry and rotational symmetry of order 4.

**11** (a) On squared paper draw rectangular axes $0_x$ and $0_y$, using a scale of 1 cm to 1 unit. On these axes draw the graph of the line $y = 2x$.

  (b) P is the point (5, 0). The operation of reflection in the line $y = 2x$ is denoted by **M**, and **R** is the operation of rotation anticlockwise through 90° about the origin. On your diagram mark the points **M**(P), **RM**(P), **MRM**(P), **RMRM**(P), together with their co-ordinates. Join these four points and name the figure formed.

(MEI)

**12** (a) Under a shear with the $x$-axis invariant, the point (1, 2) is mapped onto the point (3, 2). Find the co-ordinates of the image, under this shear, of:
  (i) the point (1, 3),     (ii) the point (−2, −1).

  (b) In Figure 26:3, triangle ABC is isosceles, with AB = AC and $\angle$BAC = 100°. The side AB is produced to D so that AD = BC.
  Triangle A'B'C is the image of triangle ABC under an anticlockwise rotation about C.
  (i)   Calculate the angle of rotation.
  (ii)  Write down the size of $\angle$B'A'C.
  (iii) Prove that A'B = BD, clearly stating your reasons.

(UoC)

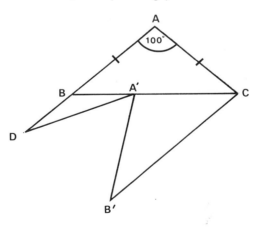

**Fig. 26:3**

**13** Using a scale of 1 cm to represent 1 unit on each axis, draw the axes for $-3 \leqslant x \leqslant 9$, and $-3 \leqslant y \leqslant 9$. Also draw the line $y = x$.

The trapezium Q has vertices (3, 0), (4, 2), (6, 2) and (7, 0). Draw this trapezium on your diagram and label it Q.

Three transformations are defined:

M is reflection in the line $y = 0$,

T is translation with vector $\begin{pmatrix} 2 \\ 4 \end{pmatrix}$,

D is reflection in the line $y = x$.

On your diagram draw and label M(Q), TM(Q), and DTM(Q). The point P has co-ordinates (1, 3). Mark it on your diagram. Also label the point DTM(P). Hence describe the single transformation which maps Q onto DTM(Q).

*(AEB 1984)*

# 27 Matrices

## ● You need to know:

### Matrices

---

**1** $A = \begin{pmatrix} 3 \\ 2 \end{pmatrix}$   $B = (4 \quad 1)$   $C = \begin{pmatrix} -1 \\ -3 \end{pmatrix}$   $D = (-2 \quad 1)$   $E = \begin{pmatrix} 1 & 3 \\ 2 & 4 \end{pmatrix}$   $F = \begin{pmatrix} 0 & 1 \\ 2 & 0 \end{pmatrix}$

$G = \begin{pmatrix} -1 & 3 \\ 0 & -2 \end{pmatrix}$

Calculate where possible:

(a) A + C   (b) B + D   (c) C + D   (d) 3A   (e) $\frac{1}{2}$D   (f) 2G   (g) BC
(h) CE   (i) DE   (j) DG   (k) FC   (l) EF   (m) FE   (n) FG   (o) GF.

**\*2** $H = \begin{pmatrix} 2 \\ 1 \end{pmatrix}$   $I = \begin{pmatrix} -3 \\ -1 \end{pmatrix}$   $J = (-1 \quad 0)$   $K = \begin{pmatrix} 1 & 0 \\ -1 & 0 \end{pmatrix}$   $L = \begin{pmatrix} -2 & 1 \\ 3 & -4 \end{pmatrix}$

$M = \begin{pmatrix} -1 & 5 \\ 0 & -1 \end{pmatrix}$

Calculate where possible:

(a) 2I   (b) $\frac{1}{2}$H   (c) H + I   (d) I + J   (e) JI   (f) IK   (g) JK   (h) JL
(i) KL   (j) LK   (k) LM   (l) ML   (m) KM   (n) MK.

**3** (a) On squared paper draw eight sets of axes, each from −6 to 6.

(b) On each grid plot the triangle represented by the matrix $\begin{pmatrix} 1 & 4 & 5 \\ 1 & 2 & 4 \end{pmatrix}$.

(c) Write the eight possible matrices $\begin{pmatrix} a & b \\ c & d \end{pmatrix}$ where either $a = d = 0$, and $b, c \in \{1, -1\}$; or $b = c = 0$, and $a, d \in \{1, -1\}$.

(d) Apply each matrix in turn to the triangle's matrix and plot the resulting transformation, one on each pair of axes. Describe each transformation.

**4** By investigating its effect on the triangle given in question 3, or otherwise, find the transformation effected by the matrix:

(a) $\begin{pmatrix} 1 & 2 \\ 0 & 1 \end{pmatrix}$ 　(b) $\begin{pmatrix} 1 & 0 \\ -2 & 1 \end{pmatrix}$ 　(c) $\begin{pmatrix} 2 & 0 \\ 0 & 2 \end{pmatrix}$ 　(d) $\begin{pmatrix} -2 & 0 \\ 0 & -2 \end{pmatrix}$ 　(e) $\begin{pmatrix} 2 & 0 \\ 0 & 1 \end{pmatrix}$

(f) $\begin{pmatrix} 1 & 0 \\ 0 & 2 \end{pmatrix}$.

**5** Find the multiplicative inverse of:

(a) $\begin{pmatrix} 5 & -3 \\ -3 & 2 \end{pmatrix}$ 　(b) $\begin{pmatrix} 6 & 1 \\ 0 & -1 \end{pmatrix}$ 　(c) $\begin{pmatrix} 1 & 2 \\ 3 & 4 \end{pmatrix}$ 　(d) $\begin{pmatrix} -4 & 2 \\ -1 & 1 \end{pmatrix}$.

**6** Use the inverse matrix to find $x$ and $y$ where:

(a) $\begin{pmatrix} 2 & 1 \\ 3 & 4 \end{pmatrix}\begin{pmatrix} x \\ y \end{pmatrix} = \begin{pmatrix} 7 \\ 18 \end{pmatrix}$ 　(b) $\begin{pmatrix} 2 & 0 \\ -2 & 3 \end{pmatrix}\begin{pmatrix} x \\ y \end{pmatrix} = \begin{pmatrix} 5 \\ -2 \end{pmatrix}$.

**7** Find matrix A where:

(a) $\begin{pmatrix} 2 & 1 \\ 1 & -2 \end{pmatrix} A = \begin{pmatrix} 1 & 3 \\ 3 & -1 \end{pmatrix}$ 　(b) $\begin{pmatrix} -1 & 3 \\ 0 & 2 \end{pmatrix} A = \begin{pmatrix} -3 & 4 \\ 1 & 2 \end{pmatrix}$.

**8** Solve by a matrix method:
   (a) $x - y = -4$ and $2x + y = -5$
   (b) $10x + 3y = 4$ and $4x - 9y = 5$
   (c) $3x + 2y = 5x + 18y = -11$.

---

**9** The **determinant** of matrix $\begin{pmatrix} a & b \\ c & d \end{pmatrix}$ is $ad - bc$. This determinant gives the change in area when matrix $\begin{pmatrix} a & b \\ c & d \end{pmatrix}$ is used to transform a shape.

**Example** $\begin{pmatrix} 2 & 1 \\ 1 & 2 \end{pmatrix}$ has a determinant of $4 - 1 = 3$.

So $\begin{pmatrix} 2 & 1 \\ 1 & 2 \end{pmatrix}$ increases the area of a shape three times.

Plot the rectangle $\begin{pmatrix} 0 & 3 & 3 & 0 \\ 2 & 2 & 0 & 0 \end{pmatrix}$. Transform it using the matrix $\begin{pmatrix} 2 & 1 \\ 1 & 2 \end{pmatrix}$ and plot the resulting quadrilateral. Check the area of the quadrilateral is three times that of the rectangle.

**10** State the effect on the area when a shape is transformed by using the matrix:

(a) $\begin{pmatrix} 3 & 1 \\ 2 & 1 \end{pmatrix}$ 　(b) $\begin{pmatrix} 2 & 1 \\ 1 & 3 \end{pmatrix}$ 　(c) $\begin{pmatrix} 1 & 2 \\ 2 & 2 \end{pmatrix}$ 　(d) $\begin{pmatrix} 0 & 1 \\ -1 & 0 \end{pmatrix}$.

**11** In Figure 27:1, O is the origin, A is the point (2, 0) and B is (2, 1). OAD and OCE are triangles onto which the triangle OAB is mapped by certain transformations.

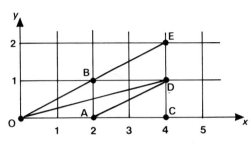

**Fig. 27:1**

(a) Name the type of transformation $T_1$ which maps OAB onto OAD.

(b) State the transformation $T_2$ which maps OAB onto OCE.

(c) Find the matrix which determines transformation $T_1$ and write it down.

(d) Find the matrix which determines transformation $T_2$ and write it down.

(e) What is the area of the triangle onto which OAB is mapped by the transformation $T_2T_1$? Find the matrix of this transformation.

*(Welsh)*

**12** On squared paper, using a scale of 1 cm to represent 1 unit on each axis, draw axes to show values of $x$ from 0 to 10 and values of $y$ from $-10$ to 10.

Draw and label the rectangle with vertices at O (0, 0), A (10, 0), B (10, 5) and C (0, 5).

(a) The points O, P, Q and R are the images of O, A, B and C respectively under the transformation represented by the matrix $\frac{1}{5}\begin{pmatrix} 3 & 4 \\ -1 & 7 \end{pmatrix}$.

Find, draw, and label the quadrilateral OPQR on your diagram. Draw, and label, the line $s$ which is invariant under this transformation and write down the equation of the line.

(b) Find the matrix representing the transformation which maps the points O, P, Q and R onto O, A, B and C respectively. Hence deduce the $2 \times 2$ matrix representing the single transformation which maps the points O, P, Q and R onto O, L (2, 0), M (2, 1) and N (0, 1) respectively.

*(AEB 1981)*

**13** Draw $x$- and $y$-axes on graph paper with values on the $x$-axis from $-8$ to 8 and on the $y$-axis from $-12$ to 8, with a scale of 1 cm to 1 unit on each axis.

The triangle $T_0$ has vertices O (0, 0), P (2, 0) and Q (2, 1). This triangle is to be transformed to triangle $T_1$ by the matrix A where A $= \begin{pmatrix} 1 & -1 \\ 1 & 1 \end{pmatrix}$. Similarly, A will transform $T_1$ to $T_2$, and so on.

(a) Draw $T_0$ on your diagram. Calculate the co-ordinates of the vertices of $T_1$ and $T_2$, and draw these two triangles on your diagram.

(b) Either by noticing the geometric effect of A on these triangles, or by calculation, draw triangles $T_3$, $T_4$ and $T_5$ on your diagram.

(c) The transformation represented by A is a combination of a rotation and another transformation. State the angle of rotation, and describe precisely the other transformation.

(d) The matrix $A^n$ will transform $T_0$ to $T_n$. What is the smallest value of $n$ (excluding $n = 0$) for which $A^n$ represents a simple enlargement with a positive scale factor? For your value of $n$, give the co-ordinates of the vertices of $T_n$, and also express $A^n$ as a $2 \times 2$ matrix.

$(O \& C)$

**14** (a) Using a scale of 2 cm to represent 1 unit on each axis, draw axes for $0 \leqslant x \leqslant 6$ and $-3 \geqslant y \geqslant 3$. Draw the parallelogram P with vertices $(2, -1)$, $(\frac{1}{2}, \frac{1}{2})$, $(2\frac{3}{4}, -\frac{1}{4})$, $(4\frac{1}{4}, -1\frac{3}{4})$.

(b) The transformation T is represented by the matrix $\begin{pmatrix} 2 & 2 \\ 1 & 3 \end{pmatrix}$. Find the co-ordinates of the image T(P) of the parallelogram P under the transformation T, and draw the image on your diagram.

(c) Find the area of T(P). Hence, or otherwise, calculate the exact area of P.

(d) Find the images under T of the points $(2a, -a)$ and $(b, b)$. What do you deduce about the images of points on the lines (i) $x + 2y = 0$, and (ii) $x - y = 0$?

$(AEB\ 1984)$

**15** The position vectors of the points O, A and B are $\begin{pmatrix} 0 \\ 0 \end{pmatrix}$, $\begin{pmatrix} 1 \\ -1 \end{pmatrix}$, $\begin{pmatrix} 3 \\ 1 \end{pmatrix}$ respectively. The triangle OAB is denoted by R. Show the triangle R in a diagram on squared paper, using a scale of 2 cm to 1 unit on each axis, and placing the origin near the middle of the left-hand margin of the paper.

X is the transformation represented by the matrix $\begin{pmatrix} 1 & 1 \\ 0 & 1 \end{pmatrix}$.

Y is the transformation represented by the matrix $\begin{pmatrix} 1 & 0 \\ -0.5 & 1 \end{pmatrix}$.

The image of triangle R under the transformation X is a triangle S; the image of triangle S (*not* R) under the transformation Y is a triangle T.

(a) Calculate the co-ordinates of the vertices of the triangle S and draw the triangle on your diagram, labelling it clearly.

(b) Repeat the process for the triangle T.

(c) Describe as fully as possible in geometric terms each of the transformations X and Y.

(d) Explain briefly why R, S and T all have the same area, and calculate this area.

(e) Calculate the matrix representing the single transformation which maps R directly onto T.

$(O \& C)$

**16** The rectangle R has vertices (0, 1), (1, 1), (1, −1) and (0, −1).

(a) Using a scale of 2 cm to represent 1 unit, draw axes on squared paper, taking values of $x$ from −3 to 4, and values of $y$ from −4 to 5. Draw and label the rectangle R and write down its area in square units.

(b) S is the shear, with invariant line $y = 0$, which maps (0. 1) onto (2, 1). Draw and label S(R).

(c) T is the shear, with invariant line $x = 0$, which maps (1, 0) onto (1, 1). Draw and label TS(R) and write down its area in square units.

(d) The matrix representing S is $\begin{pmatrix} 1 & 2 \\ 0 & 1 \end{pmatrix}$ and that representing T is $\begin{pmatrix} 1 & 0 \\ 1 & 1 \end{pmatrix}$. What is the matrix representing TS?

(e) What is the matrix of the transformation which maps TS(R) onto R?

(f) Is TS the same transformation as ST? Give a reason for your answer.

(*AEB 1983*)

| Notation | Regions |
|---|---|
| Venn diagrams | |

# ● You need to know:

## Sets
## Graphs 3

---

**1** Say whether each of the following statements is true or false for the sets in Figure 28:1. Where false, make it true by changing the right-hand side of the statement.

   (a) $n(A) = 1$    (b) $n(B) = \{b, c\}$    (c) $f \in D$    (d) $D \supset E$    (e) $F \subset D$
   (f) $F \cap C = \varnothing$    (g) $A \cup B = \{b\}$    (h) $A \cap B = \{b\}$    (i) $D \cup F = \{k, j, i, f, e\}$
   (j) $D \cap F = \{k\}$    (k) $H' = \{m, n, s, l\}$    (l) $d \notin D$    (m) $n(G) = \{4\}$

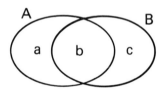 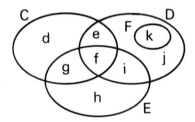 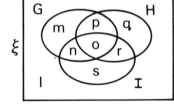

**Fig. 28:1**

**2** For the sets in Figure 28:1 list:
   (a) A    (b) C    (c) D    (d) $C \cup D$    (e) $G'$    (f) $D \cap F'$    (g) $(H \cup G)'$
   (h) $(H \cup G \cup I)'$    (i) $(G \cap H) \cup I$    (j) $G \cap H \cap I$.

**3**  $\xi = \{$integers from 1 to 12$\}$    $A = \{1, 2, 3, 4, 6, 12\}$    $B = \{1, 3, 6, 10\}$    $C = \{3, 6, 9, 12\}$

   (a) Which set is:
      (i) {triangular numbers}    (ii) {factors of 12}    (iii) {multiples of 3}?

   (b) Draw a Venn diagram to illustrate the four sets, and write the numbers 1 to 12 on your diagram in the correct sections.

   (c) Copy the Venn diagram in Figure 28:2, then fill in the sections to show the number of elements in each section.

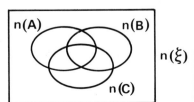

**Fig. 28:2**

**4** $\xi$ = {recipes in a book}     P = {recipes using pepper}     F = {recipes using flour}

There are 43 recipes, of which 4 use both pepper and flour, 7 use pepper, and 11 use flour.

Copy the Venn diagram in Figure 28:3, writing the correct number of recipes in each section.

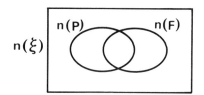

**Fig. 28:3**

**\*5** Say whether each of the following statements is true or false for the sets in Figure 28:4. Where false, write a correct statement by changing the right-hand side of the statement.
(a) $n(K) = 2$     (b) $K \cap L \cap N = \{6\}$     (c) $M = \{0, 9, 12\}$     (d) $1 \in N$
(e) $n(M \cup N \cup K) = \{11\}$     (f) $M \cup K = \varnothing$     (g) $P = \{1\}$     (h) $n(P \cup Q \cup R)' = 9$
(i) $(P \cup Q) \cap R = \{2, 6, 7\}$     (j) $n(R') = 3$

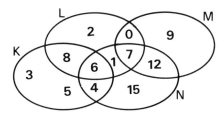
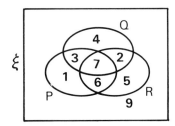

**Fig. 28:4**

**\*6** For the sets in Figure 28:4 list:
(a) N     (b) $P \cap Q$     (c) $P \cup R$     (d) $P'$

**\*7** $\xi$ = {all shoes}     X = {leather shoes}     Y = {black shoes}     Z = {lace-up shoes}

Copy Figure 28:5 and shade the set of leather lace-up shoes which are not black.

(*SREB*)

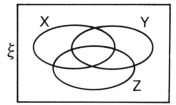

**Fig. 28:5**

**\*8** For this question, $\xi$ is the set of natural numbers greater than three. Four subsets are:
W = {$w : w$ is an even number}     X = {$x : x$ is prime}     Y = {$y : y$ is a factor of 90}
Z = {$z : z$ is a square number}

(a) Which of the given sets is finite?
(b) List all the pairs of disjoint subsets.
(c) Given that $w \in W$ and that $10 < w \leqslant 20$ list all possible values of $w$.
(d) Given that $x \in X$ and that $30 < x < 50$ list four possible values of $x$.

(*EAEB*)

161

*9 Fifty boys were asked whether they owned a bicycle or a motorcycle. Thirty-six had a bicycle and twenty-one had a motorcycle. Of these, twelve had both. By drawing a Venn diagram find how many boys had neither kind of transport.

(*EAEB*)

*10 Draw a Venn diagram to illustrate sets A, B and C if A ⊃ C, C ∩ B = ∅ and A ∩ B = ∅.

(*LREB*)

11 Of 30 ladies on a coach tour, all carried at least one of the following: a pair of spectacles (S); a headscarf (H); a bag (B). 16 carried spectacles, 22 carried bags, and 10 carried headscarves. 6 not only carried spectacles and a headscarf but a bag as well. 2 carried spectacles and headscarves but not a bag. 2 carried a bag and a headscarf but not spectacles. Twice as many carried only a bag as only spectacles.

By using the Venn diagram shown in Figure 28:6 find:

(a) how many carried spectacles and a bag but not a headscarf

(b) how many carried a bag but neither spectacles nor a headscarf.

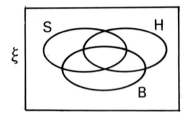

**Fig. 28:6**

(*LREB*)

12 ξ = {a, b, d, f, g}     X = {a, b, g}     Y = {d, g}

List the elements of:
(i) X' ∪ Y     (ii) (X ∩ Y)'.

13 n(ξ) = 200     n(A) = 75     n(B) = 35

(a) Find the smallest and largest possible value of n(A ∩ B). Illustrate your two answers on a suitable Venn diagram.

(b) If n(A ∪ B) = 90 find n(B ∩ A').

14 (a) Copy Figure 28:7 and outline clearly the boundary of the set A ∩ (B ∪ C)'.

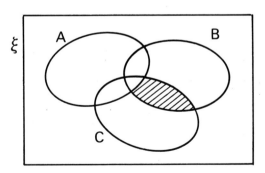

**Fig. 28:7**

(b) Using similar notation identify the set which is shaded.

(c) P, Q, R and S are subsets of the universal set ξ. Write each of the equations (i) P ∩ Q' = ∅

162

and (ii) R ∪ S′ = ξ in a form involving only some of the sets P, Q, R and S and the inclusion sign ⊂.

(d) What can you deduce about sets P, Q, R and S in part (c) if it is also known that S′ ⊂ Q′?

(*MEI*)

**15** ξ = positive integers     P = {$x : 7 \leqslant 3x \leqslant 15$}     Q = {$x : 9 \leqslant 2x + 1 \leqslant 14$}

List the set P ∪ Q.

---

**16** A number of travellers were questioned about the transport that they used on a particular day. Each of them used one or more of the methods shown in the Venn diagram, Figure 28:8.

Of those questioned, 6 said that they travelled by bus and train only, 2 by train and car only, and 7 by bus, train and car.

The number, $x$, who travelled by bus only was equal to the number who travelled by bus and car only.

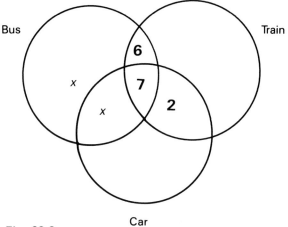

Fig. 28:8

(a) Given that 35 people used buses and 25 people used trains, find:
   (i)   the value of $x$
   (ii)  the number who travelled by train only
   (iii) the number who travelled by at least two methods of transport.

(b) Given also that 85 people were questioned altogether calculate the number who travelled by car only.

(*MEG*)

**17** Let ξ be the set of points in a plane in space. The motion of all spacecraft in this question takes place in this plane.

The locus of the spaceship Helena is given by {$(x, y) : y = 1 - \frac{1}{2}x^2$}.

The locus of a space shuttle, which is launched from the point (0, 0) in such a way as

to be able to rendezvous with the Helena, is a subset of L, where
L = {(x, y) : y = −x, x ⩽ 0}.

On squared paper, using a scale of 2 cm to represent 1 unit, draw on a single diagram the locus of the Helena for −3 ⩽ x ⩽ 3, and the set L for −3 ⩽ x ⩽ 0.

(a) Show that the rendezvous occurs when $x$ satisfies the equation $x^2 - 2x - 2 = 0$ and hence *calculate* this value of $x$ correct to 2 decimal places.

(b) The locus of the starship Avenger is given by {(x, y) : xy = k, x < 0} where $k$ is a constant. Given that this locus passes through the rendezvous point of the Helena with the shuttle, use your answer to part (a) to estimate the value of $k$ correct to 1 significant figure.

*(AEB 1982)*

**18** The British Ambassador is giving a party for 40 guests. Let ξ = {guests at the party}, P = {politicians}, B = {businessmen}, A = {Americans}.

The Venn diagram in Figure 28:9 shows the number of guests in the various sets. There are 20 Americans and 17 businessmen at the party.

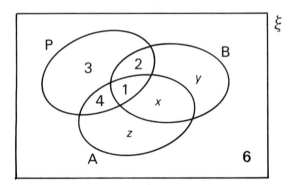

**Fig. 28:9**

(a) Find the values of $x$ and $y$.

(b) Given that a guest who is neither a politician nor a businessman is a diplomat find the least number of guests who are diplomats.

(c) The Ambassador circulates randomly amongst his guests, speaking to each guest just once. Calculate the probability that:
    (i) the first guest he speaks to is an American politician
    (ii) the first two guests he speaks to are both politicians.

*(AEB 1981)*

# Papers

**Paper One**

**1** Calculate, using a calculator and giving your answers correct to two decimal places:

(a) $348 - 6.3(3.46 - 8.03)$    (b) $\dfrac{236 \times 14.8}{6.4 \times 5.09}$    (c) $\dfrac{(7.34 + 6.74)}{(4.89 - 2.93)}$

**2** A drawing is made to a scale of 1 cm to 5 m. Find the actual distances represented by a line on the drawing of length:
(a) 6 cm     (b) 4.7 cm     (c) 32 mm.

**3** Find the time taken in hours and minutes for a car to travel 180 miles at 50 m.p.h.

**4** (a) Copy and complete the table of values for $y = 2x^2$.

| $x$ | $-3$ | $-2$ | $-1$ | 0 | 1 | 2 | 3 |
|---|---|---|---|---|---|---|---|
| $y$ | 18 | | | 0 | 2 | | |

(b) Draw a graph of the results using a horizontal scale of 2 cm to 1 unit ($x$-axis) and a vertical scale of 1 cm to 1 unit ($y$-axis).

(c) On the same set of axes draw the graph of $y = -x + 6$.

(d) From the graph read off the values of $x$ where the lines $y = 2x^2$ and $y = -x + 6$ cross.

**\*5** A family is going to buy a new television set. They have a choice of two methods of payment:

CASH                A single payment of £180.

HIRE PURCHASE   A deposit of £36 followed by 24 monthly payments of £8.

(a) If they choose hire purchase:
    (i)   After paying their deposit how much more will they have left to pay?
    (ii)  How much more do they have to pay above the cash price?
    (iii) Express the extra amount as a percentage of the cash price.

(b) The family could also rent the set at £6.95 per month. How much would this method cost over:
    (i) 2 years     (ii) 3 years?

**6** Figure P1:1 shows part of an ornament formed from a cylinder 10 mm in diameter and 30 mm long. One end is surmounted by a hemisphere. The other end has a right cone-shaped piece removed. The height of the cone is 12 mm and it has a 10 mm-diameter base.

Calculate:
(a) the slant height of the cone

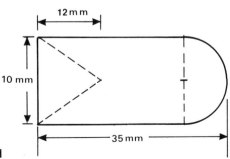

**Fig. P1:1**

165

(b) the volume of the ornament correct to four significant figures

(c) the total surface area of the ornament to the nearest $10\,mm^2$

(d) the weight of 40 pieces, correct to the nearest gram, given that the weight of the material is 8.4 grams per $cm^3$.

(Use the calculator value of $\pi$.)

*Volumes*: sphere $= \frac{4}{3}\pi r^3$, cylinder $= \pi r^2 h$, cone $= \frac{1}{3}\pi r^2 h$.
*Surface areas*: sphere $= 4\pi r^2$, cylinder $= 2\pi rh$, cone $= \pi rl$ where *l* is the slant height.

## Paper Two

**1** Evaluate:
   (a) $(2\frac{1}{2} - 1\frac{1}{3}) \times 3\frac{1}{2}$    (b) $(\frac{1}{2} \times \frac{1}{3}) \div (\frac{1}{2} - \frac{1}{3})$    (c) $(2\frac{3}{4} \div 2\frac{1}{5}) \div 3\frac{1}{2}$.

**2** A coat costing £85 and a jacket costing £56 are offered in a sale at a reduction of 25%.

   (a) Find the sale price of each item.

   (b) The sale price is then reduced by a further 15%. Find the new price of each item, correct to the nearest penny.

   (c) Express the final price as a percentage of the original price, correct to two decimal places.

**3** Solve:
   (a) $5a - 3(a - 1) = 17$    (b) $2(5 - 3a) + 7(2a - 1) = 19$.

**4** Eva is 2 years older than Mark who is 1 year older than Saskia. The sum of their ages is 49 years. How old are they?

**5** A distribution service charges the following rates for the number of leaflets delivered:

| No. of leaflets | 100 | 200 | 400 | 600 | 800 |
|---|---|---|---|---|---|
| Cost | £13.50 | £15 | £18 | £21 | £24 |

On a piece of A4 graph paper draw a graph of these charges. Use a vertical scale (Cost) of 1 cm to £1 and a horizontal scale (No. of leaflets) of 2 cm to 100 leaflets.

Use the graph to find:
(a) the fixed charge
(b) the cost of delivering 280 leaflets
(c) approximately how many leaflets you can have delivered for £20.

A rival company has no fixed charge but simply a rate of £3.50 per 100 leaflets delivered. On the grid you have already drawn plot a graph of their rates. Use this new line to determine:
(d) the cost of delivering 280 leaflets
(e) approximately how many leaflets you can have delivered for £20.

   (f) Find the number of leaflets at which the charge is the same for both firms.

**\*6** The charges made by British Gas in 1986 were 30p per unit plus a standing charge of £9.90 per quarter.

166

At the end of the autumn quarter my meter reading was 8437. At the end of the previous quarter it was 8251.

(a) Find the total cost of the bill for the autumn quarter.
(b) A neighbour paid a bill of £70.80. How many units had he used?

At the beginning of the winter quarter the standing charge was increased by 50p and the cost per unit by 6%. During the quarter I used 304 units.

(c) Find the new cost per unit and the new standing charge.
(d) Find the cost of my winter bill.

7   During a week in July, 21.4 mm of rain fell on a flat roof measuring 6 m by 1.2 m. The rain was collected in a cylindrical butt of 70 cm diameter and height 1.2 m.

Calculate:
(a) the area, in $cm^2$, of the roof
(b) the volume, in $cm^3$, of the rain which fell onto the roof
(c) the base area of the butt, in $cm^2$ (use the calculator value of $\pi$)
(d) the height to which the water in the butt rose, to the nearest cm
(e) how many litres of rain, to the nearest litre, fell on the roof.

## Paper Three

1   Evaluate, using a calculator and giving your answer correct to 2 decimal places:
(a) $\frac{3}{4} + \frac{2}{3}$     (b) $\frac{5}{6} - 0.34$     (c) $(\frac{3}{5} - \frac{1}{4}) \div 1.4$

2   A bicycle which cost £160 is sold for £120. What is the percentage loss?

3   Change 72 km/h to m/s.

4   The world record in 1986 for the 5000 metres was slightly under 13 minutes. Assuming a steady pace, how long did it take to cover 100 metres?

5   In 1985 a firm gave its employees a pay increase of 5%. In 1986 it gave an increase of 4%.

(a) In 1984 Michael Jones earned £8600. Calculate his salary in:
(i) 1985     (ii) 1986.

(b) In 1985 Diana Parker received an increase of £400 on her 1984 salary. What did she earn in 1984?

(c) In 1986 Mervin Bradner earned £13 311.48. How much did he earn in:
(i) 1985     (ii) 1984?

*6   The length of a rectangular field is 84 metres and the ratio of its length to its breadth is 8 : 5. Find:
(a) its breadth     (b) its area in $m^2$
(c) the cost of fencing the field at £1.26 per metre.

A similar-shaped field has a length of 144 metres. Find:
(d) its breadth     (e) its area in hectares (1 hectare = 10 000 $m^2$).

**7** (a) A British woman took a holiday, partly in France and partly in Canada. She spent a total of £1650 made up of 5445 francs in France and 1776 dollars in Canada. Assuming that the rate of exchange in France was 12.1 francs to the £, find the rate of exchange in Canada, giving your answer in dollars to the £.

(b) In each of these two countries, the total cost of her visit consisted of fares, hotel bills and all other expenses. In France, her fares, hotel bills and all other expenses were in the ratios $5:7:h$. In Canada, the corresponding ratios were $9:k:3$. (The letters $h$ and $k$ stand for whole numbers.)

Use the information already given and that appearing in the table below to answer the questions under it.

| | FRANCE | CANADA |
|---|---|---|
| Fares | 1815 francs | $y$ dollars |
| Average daily hotel bill | 423.5 francs | $z$ dollars |
| Number of days in the country | $n$ days | 8 days |
| All other expenses | $x$ francs | 333 dollars |
| TOTAL AMOUNT SPENT | 5445 francs | 1776 dollars |

(i) Express the woman's fares in France as a fraction (in its lowest terms) of the total amount she spent there. Hence find the value of $h$.

(ii) Find the values of $n$ and $x$.

(iii) Express her 'all other expenses' in Canada as a fraction of the total amount she spent there. Give the working which shows that this fraction, in its lowest terms, is $\frac{3}{16}$. Hence find the value of $k$.

(iv) Find the values of $y$ and $z$.

(*AEB*)

**Paper Four**

**1** Estimate, giving your answer correct to 2 significant figures:

(a) $47.6 \times 69.37$  (b) $\dfrac{683 \times 2.14}{392}$  (c) $\dfrac{4812}{0.042}$

**2** Using ruler and compasses construct a triangle ABC such that AC = 8 cm, AB = 9 cm and CB = 7 cm.

(a) Measure the perpendicular distance of B from the line AC.

(b) Calculate the area of the triangle ABC.

(c) Bisect perpendicularly the sides of the triangle to find the centre of the circumcircle. Draw the circumcircle and measure its radius.

**3** (a) Taking 5 miles as being equivalent to 8 kilometres, calculate the kilometre equivalent of:
   (i) 70 m.p.h.     (ii) 30 m.p.h.

(b) Travelling on a motorway Vera Palmer averaged 68 m.p.h. for $2\frac{1}{2}$ hours. Find the distance she travelled in:
   (i) miles     (ii) kilometres.

(c) How long would it have taken Vera to do the same journey at 50 m.p.h.?

(d) What is the difference in minutes between the times taken in (b) and (c)?

(e) If Vera's car did 36 miles per gallon and petrol cost £1.98 per gallon, how much did the journey cost her?


**\*4** The Wells family received bills for gas, electricity and telephone during the same week! Gas is subject to a standing charge of £9.90 and each unit used costs 31.4p; electricity is subject to a standing charge of £14.25 and each unit used costs 8.6p; telephones are subject to a standing charge of £15.15 and each unit used costs 4.7p. Each bill has V.A.T. at 15% added to it.

Find the bill for using:
(a) 136 units of gas     (b) 210 units of electricity     (c) 432 telephone units.

(d) What is the sum of the bills presented?


**5** Using a scale of 2 cm to represent 1 unit on the x-axis and 1 cm to represent 1 unit on the y-axis draw an x-axis from 0 to 6 and a y-axis from 0 to 16.

Copy and complete the table below which gives the values of the function $y = 16 - \dfrac{9}{x}$.

| $x$ | $\frac{3}{4}$ | 1 | 2 | 3 | 4 | 5 | 6 |
|---|---|---|---|---|---|---|---|
| $y$ | 4 | | | | | 14.2 | |

On the axes draw the graph of $y = 16 - \dfrac{9}{x}$.

Using the same axes draw the graph of $y = 3x + 4$.

At the points of intersection of the two lines the equations are equal. Write down the equation in x which satisfies these two points and show that it simplifies to $x^2 - 4x + 3 = 0$.

Use your graph to solve the equation $x^2 - 4x + 3 = 0$.


**6** The area of a circle may be calculated by the formulae $A = \pi r^2$ or $A = \frac{1}{4}\pi d^2$, where r is the radius and d the diameter.

(a) Show that the second formula may be obtained from the first.

(b) Calculate the area of a 4 cm-radius circle, taking $\pi$ as 3.14.

(c) Draw a 4 cm-radius circle on 5 mm-squared paper, and verify your answer to part (b) by counting squares.

169

Paper Five

**1** Evaluate, giving your answer in standard form:
(a) $(3.4 \times 10^2) \times (2.1 \times 10^3)$     (b) $(34.6 \times 10^2) \times (16.4 \times 10^{-3})$.

**2** Change 240 km/h to m/s.

**3** Solve:
(a) $7a - (4 + a) = 0$     (b) $7 - 3a = 5 - 2a$     (c) $10x - (2x + 3) = 21$.

**4** A school clothing shop has as part of its stock 150 jumpers, 65 skirts and 180 pairs of training shoes.

(a) The jumpers are bought for £5.50 each and are sold for £7.59 each. Find the profit and express it as a percentage of the cost price.

(b) The skirts, dependent upon their size, are sold for 35% profit. What is the selling price of a skirt which cost the shop £8.40?

(c) The training shoes are sold for £9.00 thus earning the shop 25% profit. Find the cost to the shop.

(d) Find the total cost of all the items to the shop.

(e) Find the total amount of money received if all the items are sold.

(f) Express the profit as a percentage of the cost price.

Last year the shop bought jumpers at £5.20 and skirts at £8.20. These became shop-soiled.

(g) The jumpers were sold for £3.90. What was the percentage loss on each jumper?

(h) The skirts were sold at a 35% loss. What was the selling price?

**\*5** A family of four travelled to France, exchanging £400 into francs at a rate of exchange of £1 = 11.20 francs. They spent their first night in an hotel, which charged 140 francs per person, before travelling to Strasbourg which was to be their centre for the holiday.

While there they bought a jacket for 420 francs, presents for 375 francs, petrol for 660 francs and food for 1842 francs.

On the return journey they stayed for one night at the same hotel as on the outward journey.

(a) How many francs did they receive when they changed their £400?

(b) What was the pound sterling equivalent of:
(i) the hotel bill on the outward journey     (ii) the jacket which they bought
(iii) the petrol they used     (iv) the food they bought?

(c) Calculate the number of francs they had left when they boarded the boat for the return journey.

(d) On the boat they exchanged their remaining francs for pounds at a rate of exchange of £1 = 11.40 francs. How much did they receive?

**6** (a) Figure P5:1 shows a speed–time graph for the motion of a car lasting 30 seconds.

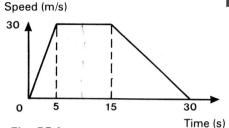

Speed (m/s)

**Fig. P5:1**

    (i)   Find the rate of acceleration in the first five seconds.

    (ii)  Find the rate of deceleration during the last 15 seconds.

    (iii) Find the rate of acceleration 10 seconds from the start.

    (iv) Find the total distance travelled.

(b) The table gives the motion of a particle undergoing acceleration in a straight line:

| Time (s) | 0 | 1 | 2 | 3 | 4 | 5 |
|---|---|---|---|---|---|---|
| Speed (m/s) | 0 | 4.5 | 8 | 10.5 | 12 | 12.5 |

    (i)   Draw a speed–time graph to represent this motion using a time scale of 2 cm to 1 unit and a speed scale of 1 cm to 1 unit.

    (ii)  Using the points you have plotted draw straight lines between them and use the trapezoidal method to estimate the distance travelled by the particle in 5 seconds.

    (iii) By drawing a tangent to your graph, estimate the acceleration of the particle after 2 seconds.

**7** (a) Draw the graph of $y = \dfrac{6}{x}$ for values of $x$ between 1 and 6 inclusive, taking a scale of 2 cm to 1 unit on each axis.

(b) On the same axes draw the graph of $y = \frac{3}{2}(5 - x)$.

(c) Write down the equation in $x$ which is solved where the graphs cross and show that it simplifies to $x^2 - 5x + 4 = 0$.

(d) Use your graph to solve the equation $x^2 - 5x + 4 = 0$.

## Paper Six

**1**   Two partners in a firm shared their profits of £30 000 in the ratio 3 : 2. How much did they each receive?

**2**   Find the average speed in km/h of a car which covers 408 km in 4 h 15 min.

**3**   A group of 34 people travelled by train from Birmingham to Weston-Super-Mare for the day. The train times were:

    Birmingham New Street   0915 | 2111↑
    Weston-Super-Mare      1119↓ 1856 |

The cost per person for a group return ticket was £6.40. A normal day-return ticket cost £8.56. For the journey find:

(a)  how long the morning train took    (b)  how long the evening train took

(c)  the total cost for the group at the cheap rate

(d)  the total amount saved by not buying normal day-return tickets.

171

*4 In 1985 the total rateable value of a town was £2 800 000 and a rate of £1.19 in the £ was levied.

(a) Calculate the expected total income from the rates.

(b) In 1985 Mr Fairhurst's house had a rateable value of £360. How much did he have to pay in rates?

(c) A neighbour paid rates of £452.20. What was the rateable value of his house?

In 1986 the rateable value of Mr Fairhurst's house was re-assessed and was increased by £24. The rate in the £ to be levied in 1986 was increased to £1.21.

(d) How much did Mr Fairhurst have to pay in rates in 1986?

(e) Express his increase in rates as a percentage of the amount he paid in 1985, correct to one decimal place.

5 Two parts of a child's toy are made from a piece of wood with a square cross-section. One piece is a cube, the other is a cuboid, Figure P6:1. The volume of the cuboid is 75 cm$^3$ greater than the cube.

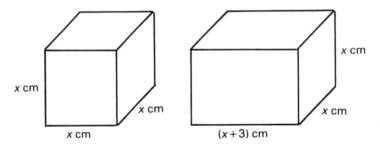

**Fig. P6:1**

(a) Write down an expression in $x$ for:
(i) the volume of the cube    (ii) the volume of the cuboid.

(b) Use these expressions and the difference in volume to write down an equation in $x$ and show that this simplifies to $x^2 - 25 = 0$.

(c) Find the dimensions of the blocks.

(d) Write down an expression, in terms of $x$, for the total surface area of the two blocks.

(e) Hence, or otherwise, find the total surface area of the two blocks.

(f) How many pairs of blocks could be painted from 1 litre of paint if one litre covers 8 m$^2$?

(g) How many metres of wood, cross-section $x^2$, would be needed to make the blocks in part (f)? Give your answer correct to the nearest centimetre.

6 Design a flow-chart that could be used as the instructions to find and repair a suspected puncture in a cycle tyre (or any other process which you are familiar with). Include at least one question box (to which the answer must be YES or NO).

**Paper Seven**

**1**  A club buys 46 jumpers for £391. How much would they have to pay for 70 jumpers?

**2**  A car travels between London and Birmingham, a distance of 110 miles, at an average speed of 65 m.p.h .

(a)  Find the time taken to the nearest second.

A second car does the journey at an average speed of 50 m.p.h.

(b)  How long does this car take? Give your answer to the nearest second.
(c)  How much time, in minutes and seconds, does the first car save?

**3**  Refer to Figure P7:1.

(a)  If AB = 6 cm, AM = 3 cm, and AC = 5 cm, find AN.
(b)  If  AB = 9 cm,  AM = 6 cm,  AN = 4 cm,  and BC = 6 cm, find:
(i)  AC      (ii)  MN.

(It is sometimes easier to understand this sort of question if you separate the diagram into two triangles i.e. ABC and AMN.)

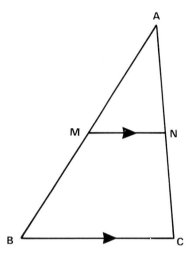

**Fig. P7:1**

**4**

| Width (cm) | TRIUMPH WORK SURFACES Price List (£) | | | | | | |
|---|---|---|---|---|---|---|---|
| | Length (cm) | | | | | | |
| | 50 | 75 | 100 | 125 | 140 | 165 | 180 |
| 30 | 1.20 | 1.80 | 2.40 | 3.00 | 3.40 | 3.90 | 4.40 |
| 45 | 1.80 | 2.70 | 3.60 | 4.50 | 5.10 | 5.80 | 6.40 |
| 60 | 2.40 | 3.60 | 4.80 | 6.00 | 6.80 | 7.20 | 8.80 |

(a)  Using the table, find the cost of a piece 125 cm by 45 cm.

(b)  Find the cost per square metre of a piece 30 cm wide and one metre long.

(c)  A bench measures 135 cm by 50 cm.
(i)  What size surface would be needed if the bench was to be covered in one piece?
(ii)  What per cent of the sheet would be wasted?
(iii)  If the bench was to be covered exactly without waste what size pieces would you buy?
(iv)  How much would you save using this method rather than covering the bench in one piece?

173

**P**

**\*5** (a) Calculate 4.89 × 34.2, giving your answer correct to:
     (i) 2 significant figures    (ii) 2 decimal places    (iii) to the nearest 10.

    (b) Write your answer to part (i) in standard form.

**\*6** A map is drawn to a scale of 1 : 25 000.
    (a) What distance, in metres, does 1 cm on the map represent?
    (b) What distance, in km, does 8.7 cm on the map represent?
    (c) A wood measures 3 cm by 1.5 cm on the map. What is its true area in hectares? (1 hectare = 10 000 m$^2$).

**\*7** (a) Add 12 hours 48 minutes 36 seconds to 18 hours 31 minutes 29 seconds.
    (b) Subtract 12 hours 48 minutes 36 seconds from 18 hours 31 minutes 29 seconds.

**\*8** If $a = \frac{2}{3}$ and $b = \frac{3}{4}$ find:
    (a) $a + b$    (b) $b - a$    (c) $b \div a$    (d) $ab$.

**9** (a) Figure P7:2 shows a picture frame. The length of the picture is 2 cm longer than the width ($x$ cm). The surround is 2 cm wide. The total area of the picture and its surround is 168 cm$^2$. Find the dimensions of the picture.

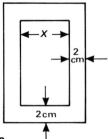

**Fig. P7:2**

    (b) Factorise:
       (i) $ax + ay + bx + by$    (ii) $am - an - bm + bn$    (iii) $6a + 4b - 9ac - 6bc$.

**10** Four functions, e, f, g and h are defined so that
$$e(x) = 2x, \qquad f(x) = 3x - 3, \qquad g(x) = x^2, \qquad h(x) = \frac{6}{x}.$$

    (a) Find the values of:
       (i) e(3)    (ii) f(−3)    (iii) g(3)    (iv) h(−3).

    (b) Find the value of $x$ if f($x$) = 18.

    (c) Write down and simplify the expression f(e($x$)) = 9.

    (d) Find the values of $x$ for which:
       (i) e($x$) = f($x$)    (ii) g($x$) = e($x$).

    (e) Find expressions for the inverse for each of the functions of $x$, i.e. find: $e^{-1}(x), f^{-1}(x), g^{-1}(x), h^{-1}(x)$.

## Paper Eight

**1** Divide 800 in the ratio 3 : 5 : 8.

**2** A lamp costing £24.60 has V.A.T. added at 15%. What is the selling price?

174

**3** Find the average speed of a cyclist who covers 31.5 miles in 1 hour 45 minutes.

**4** Refer to Figure P8:1.

    (a) Write down the equations of lines a, b and c.

    (b) Write down the values of $x$ and $y$ where:
       (i) line a intersects line b
       (ii) line b intersects line c
       (iii) line a intersects line c.

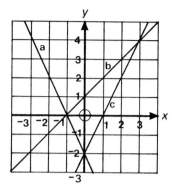

Fig. P8:1

**5** Using axes from $-1$ to 5 draw the graphs of $y = x - 1$ and $y = -2x + 5$. What are the values of $x$ and $y$ at the crossing point of the lines?

**\*6** (a) Taking values of $x$ from $-3$ to $+3$ make a table of values for $y = 2x^2$.

    (b) Taking 2 cm to 1 unit on the $x$-axis and 1 cm to 1 unit on the $y$-axis draw the graph of $y = 2x^2$.

    (c) Using the same axes draw the graph of the straight line $y = -x + 3$.

    (d) From your graph read off and write down the values of $x$ where the graphs cross.

    (e) Factorise $2x^2 + x - 3 = 0$.

**7** ABCO is a rhombus and OCD is an equilateral triangle. $\overrightarrow{OC} = \mathbf{p}$, $\overrightarrow{DO} = \mathbf{q}$.

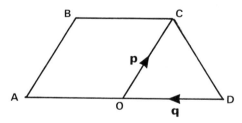

Fig. P8:2

    (a) Express in terms of $\mathbf{p}$ and $\mathbf{q}$:
       (i) $\overrightarrow{OB}$    (ii) $\overrightarrow{DC}$    (iii) $\overrightarrow{AC}$.

    (b) Show that the journey D to O to A to B to C is equivalent to $\overrightarrow{DC}$.

    (c) F is the point such that $\overrightarrow{OF} = -\mathbf{p}$ and E is the point such that $\overrightarrow{OE} = -(\mathbf{p} + \mathbf{q})$. Express $\overrightarrow{EF}$ in terms of $\mathbf{p}$ and $\mathbf{q}$, as simply as possible.

    (d) If O is the origin and D $= (2, 0)$ write down the co-ordinates of:
       (i) C    (ii) B.

**8** (a) A shop sold $x$ bottles of lemonade at 30p each and $y$ packets of nuts at 42p each. The total number of bottles and packets sold was 36 and the amount received from their sale was £13.20. Write down one equation in $x$ and $y$ to find the total number sold and another equation to find the total cost. Hence find the number of bottles sold and the number of packets sold.

(b) Solve the equation $4x^2 - 3x - 5 = 0$ correct to 2 decimal places.

**Paper Nine**

**1** A family bought the following items in a West German shop:

| | | |
|---|---|---|
| 200 g | Dutch cheese | 2.58DM |
| 1000 g | frozen chips | 0.99DM |
| 500 g | tomato ketchup | 2.29DM |
| 250 ml | vegetable oil | 2.48DM |
| 10 | eggs | 2.75DM |
| 1000 g | peaches | 1.49DM |

(a) How much was their bill?
(b) How much change did they receive from a DM20 note?
(c) Using an exchange rate of £1 = DM3.92 calculate the equivalent sterling price for each item.

**2** Calculate the gradient of the line joining
(a) (3, 0) to (4, 3)   (b) (1, 6) to (−1, 2).

**3** Taking values of $x$ from 1 to 8 make a table of values for the equation $y = \dfrac{8}{x}$.

On axes from −3 to +8, using 1 cm to 1 unit on both axes, plot the graph of $y = \dfrac{8}{x}$.

On the same axes draw the graph of $y = 3x - 2$.

Write down the value of $x$ where the lines intersect.

**\*4** A motorway is 115 miles long and runs from north to south. A lorry with a heavy load joins the southern end of the motorway at noon and travels at an average speed of 30 m.p.h. After 2 hours the driver stops at a service station for 40 minutes before continuing at the same speed as before to the end of the motorway.

A car joins the motorway at 2p.m. and travels the whole length of the motorway from south to north at an average speed of 69 m.p.h.

A motorbike joins the motorway 35 miles from the northern end at 1p.m. and travels south at an average speed of 60 m.p.h.

Draw on the same axes graphical representations of these journeys, taking 3 cm to 1 hour on the horizontal axis and 2 cm to 10 miles on the vertical axis.

At what time does:
(a) the car reach the end of the motorway
(b) the lorry reach the end of the motorway
(c) the motorbike reach the end of the motorway
(d) the motorbike pass the car (approximately), and about how far is it then from the souther end of the motorway?

5  Using a scale of 1 cm to represent 1 unit on each axis, draw $x$- and $y$-axes, taking values of $x$ from $-7$ to $+10$ and values of $y$ from $-9$ to $+13$.

Draw and label the triangle T with vertices at (3, 1), (3, 4) and (1, 4).

(a)  Draw the single transformation A which maps the triangle T onto the triangle A(T) with vertices at (9, 3), (9, 12) and (3, 12). Label the triangle A(T). What is this transformation?

(b)  Draw the single transformation B which maps the triangle T onto the triangle B(T) with vertices at $(-6, -2)$, $(-6, -8)$ and $(-2, -8)$. Label the triangle B(T). What is this transformation?

(c)  The transformation R is an anticlockwise rotation of 90° about the origin. Draw and label the triangle R(T).

(d)  The transformation C is the translation $\begin{pmatrix} -4 \\ -5 \end{pmatrix}$. Draw and label the triangle C(T).

(e)  Draw the translation RC(T). Label the triangle RC(T).

(f)  The single transformation D is represented by the matrix $\begin{pmatrix} 0 & 1 \\ 1 & 0 \end{pmatrix}$. Draw and label the triangle D(T). Describe fully the transformation D.

**Paper Ten**

1  The distance between Gloucester and Birmingham is 82 kilometres. How far apart will they be, in cm, on a map of scale 1 : 500 000?

2  The total cost of a holiday in France is 2744 francs when there are 11.2 francs to the pound. How much does the holiday cost in pounds?

3  A regular octagon has sides 4 cm long. What is the length of a side of the regular hexagon which has the same perimeter as the octagon?

4  Write in algebraic form each of the following.

(a)  Three times the sum of $b$ and $c$.

(b)  Three times the product of $b$ and $c$.

(c)  The square of $c$ added to the square of $d$.

(d)  The total cost of 10 bananas at $b$ pence each and 6 pears at $p$ pence each.

(e)  Your answer to part (d) expressed in £.

(f)  The number of pupils in a school if $f$ pupils are absent and $p$ pupils are present.

5  Make $y$ the subject of the following:
(a)  $p = y - c$    (b)  $Ty + b = R$    (c)  $q = py - 4$.

*6  Simplify:
(a)  $y^2 \times y^3$    (b)  $a^4 \times a^{-3}$    (c)  $a^6 \div a^3$    (d)  $a^6 \div a^{-3}$    (e)  $3a^3 \times 4a^{-1}$
(f)  $24a^4 \div 6a^{-1}$.

**\*7** (a) (i) $-4 + (-6)$    (ii) $-8 \div (-2)$    (iii) $+12 - (-6)$    (iv) $-6 \times (-2)$

(b) If $a = -2$, $b = 3$ and $c = 4$ evaluate:
  (i) $3a - b$    (ii) $4bc - 3a$    (iii) $a - b + 2c$    (iv) $c - a - b$
  (v) $a^2 - 3c$    (vi) $2b^2 - a^2$.

(c) Remove the brackets and simplify:
  (i) $2y + 2(y - 4)$    (ii) $3y(y - 4) - 2(y - 3)$    (iii) $3(y - 2) - (y - 2)$.

**8** Simplify:

(a) $\dfrac{4x - 2}{3} - \dfrac{2x + 3}{2}$    (b) $\dfrac{5}{x - 1} + \dfrac{3}{x + 2}$.

**9** Solve:

(a) $\dfrac{x + 3}{2} = \dfrac{x - 4}{5}$    (b) $\dfrac{3}{x + 2} - \dfrac{2}{x - 1} = 0$    (c) $\dfrac{x - 4}{3x} = \dfrac{x + 3}{3x + 7}$.

**10** A social club offers three sports: angling, boxing and cricket. All boxers fish, but the cricket section has members who do not fish or box. Some members do none of these sports.

Draw a Venn diagram to illustrate these relationships and add numbers to show that: 12 members fish and play cricket, 18 members play cricket only, 4 members fish, box and play cricket, 90 members do not take part in any of the three sports, 16 members box, 27 members fish but do not play cricket.

(a) How many members:
  (i) fish    (ii) fish and play cricket but do not box    (iii) take part in one sport only?

(b) How many members are there in the club?

(c) Which is the biggest sports section, and how many members has it?

**Paper Eleven**

**1** Work out, using a calculator and giving your answer correct to 2 decimal places:

(a) $\dfrac{120}{6.4 + 18.3}$    (b) $\dfrac{14.3}{5.6} + \dfrac{6.42}{3.5}$    (c) $\dfrac{1}{6.4} - \dfrac{1}{14.3}$    (d) $\dfrac{1}{3.48} \times \dfrac{1}{0.37}$

(e) $\dfrac{1}{4} + \dfrac{3}{5} - \dfrac{3}{8}$.

**2** Solve:
(a) $2(x + 5) - 3(2x - 4) = 2(2 - 3x)$.

**3** The sum of three consecutive numbers is 27. Write down an equation to show this, using $x$ to represent the smallest number. Solve your equation to find the three numbers.

**4** One number is five times bigger than another. The sum of the numbers is 162. Find the numbers.

**\*5** Three boys weigh themselves. Mike is 8 kg less than John who is 6 kg less than Philip.

(a) By using $x$ to represent Mike's weight write down expressions for John's and Philip's weight.

(b) If their total weight is 202 kg find the weight of each of them.

*6 (a) If the perimeter of the triangle in Figure P11:1 is 58 cm find the lengths of the sides.

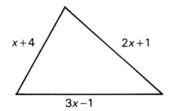

Fig. P11:1

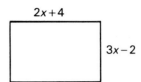

Fig. P11:2

(b) If the perimeter of the rectangle in Figure P11:2 is 124 cm find the lengths of the sides.

(c) The result of multiplying a number by 3 is the same as adding 12 to it. What is the number?

7 (a) The distance a boulder falls from rest is proportional to the square of the time taken. If the boulder falls 125 metres in 5 seconds how far will it fall in 10 seconds? How long will it take to fall 64 metres?

(b) Two variables $A$ and $B$ are such that $\dfrac{a}{A} + \dfrac{b}{B} = 2$, where $a$ and $b$ are constants.

If $A = 2$ when $B = 14$ and $A = -9$ when $B = 3$ calculate:
(i) the values of $a$ and $b$ (ii) the value of $A$ when $B = -2$.

8 (a) Factorise $2x^2 - 7x - 4$.

(b) Solve the inequality $2x^2 - 7x - 4 \geqslant 0$.

9 A, B, C and D are four points such that A = $(-3, 2)$, C = $(6, -3)$, $\overrightarrow{AB} = \begin{pmatrix} 5 \\ 4 \end{pmatrix}$ and $\overrightarrow{CD} = \begin{pmatrix} -5 \\ -4 \end{pmatrix}$.

Calculate:
(a) the co-ordinates of B and D (b) the vectors $\overrightarrow{BC}$ and $\overrightarrow{AD}$.

What can you conclude about:
(c) vectors $\overrightarrow{BC}$ and $\overrightarrow{AD}$ (d) vectors $\overrightarrow{AB}$ and $\overrightarrow{DC}$ (e) quadrilateral ABCD?

## Paper Twelve

1 A prize of £900 is shared so that Colin receives three times as much as Sarah, who receives twice as much as Liz. How much do they each receive?

2 A record is sold for £5.04, thereby making a profit of 40%. What was the cost price?

3 A car costing £6800 depreciates in value by 26% during the first year and then by 15% of its value at the beginning of the year each year thereafter. Calculate:
(a) its value after 3 years
(b) the percentage loss after 3 years, to 2 significant figures.
(c) the average annual depreciation over the first 3 years
(d) the number of complete years which will elapse before the value of the car is less than £2700.

**P**

**4** Find the angles marked with letters in Figure P12:1.

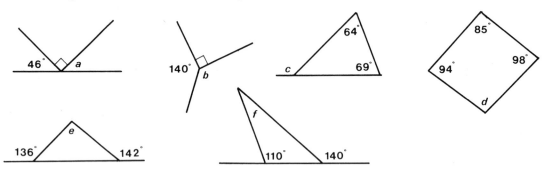

**Fig. P12:1**

**5** In the pairs of similar figures shown in Figure P12:2 find the sides marked with letters.

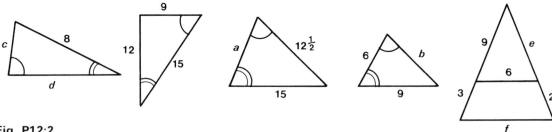

**Fig. P12:2**

*6 Decide which of the pairs of triangles in Figure P12:3 are congruent and which conditions of congruence they satisfy.

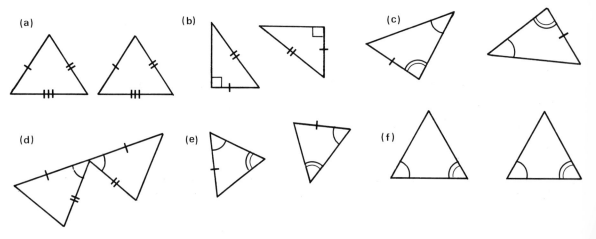

**Fig. P12:3**

**7** $P$ is proportional to $y^2$. If $P = 9$ when $y = 7\frac{1}{2}$, calculate:
   (a) the value of $P$ when $y = 10$    (b) the value of $y$ when $P = 4$.

**8** A horticulturalist wishes to compare the areas of leaves from different species of plants. Explain, with at least one example, how he could use a 'counting squares' method to find the areas of the leaves.

180

**Paper Thirteen**

**1**   While on a 12-day holiday in France a family spent a total of £768.

   (a)  What was their average spending per day?

   (b)  Using an exchange rate of £1 = 11.62 francs find how many francs they spent during their holiday.

**2**   An adult train fare is £12 more than a child's fare. If the combined fare is £40 find the cost of each fare.

**3**   Find the angles marked with letters in Figure P13:1.

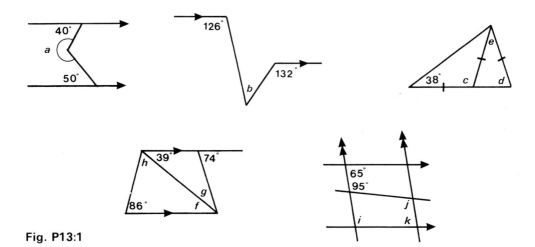

**Fig. P13:1**

**4**   (a)  Calculate the number of sides of a regular polygon:
   (i)  whose exterior angles are each 40°    (ii)  whose interior angles are each 156°.

   (b)  ABCD is a quadrilateral in which ∠A = 96°, ∠B = 94°, ∠C = 48° and ∠DBC = 79°. Calculate ∠BDC and ∠BDA.

   (c)  A pentagon has angles $m°$, $(m + 10)°$, $(m + 22)°$, $(m + 48)°$ and $(m - 5)°$. Find $m$.

**\*5**   Mary has some square patches and some regular hexagonal patches, each with sides of 10 cm. She wants to use them to make a patchwork quilt. Make a sketch of each shape.

   (a)  What is the size of each interior angle of:
   (i)  a square patch    (ii)  a hexagonal patch?

   (b)  Mary finds that she cannot fit the pieces together to make a quilt. Why not?

   (c)  (i)   What other single regular-shaped patch would she need to enable her to make the quilt?
   (ii)  What is the size of each interior angle of the new patch?

**6**   A wooden post consists of a cylinder, 20 cm in diameter and 274 cm long, with the last 24 cm being tapered to a point. It is shown in Figure P13:2.

**P**

(a) Calculate:
    (i)  the slant height of the conical point
    (ii) the cost of painting the post to the nearest
        penny if it costs 1p to paint $35\,cm^2$.

(b) Calculate the weight of the post, in kg, if $1\,cm^3$
    of wood weighs 1.4 grams.

(c) A similar post has a diameter of 15 cm. Calculate
    (i)   its length (use the properties of similar
        figures)
    (ii)  the cost of painting it
    (iii) its weight in kg.

(The volume of a cone $= \frac{1}{3}\pi r^2 h$, curved surface
area of a cone $= \pi r l$. Use the calculator value
of $\pi$.)

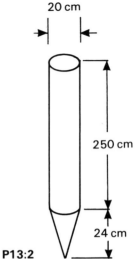

**Fig. P13:2**

---

**Paper Fourteen**

**1**  Work out, using a calculator and giving your answer correct to two decimal places:

  (a)  $\sqrt{\dfrac{4.374}{2.18}}$    (b)  $\sqrt{\dfrac{3.74}{18.4}}$    (c)  $\sqrt{\dfrac{16.47 + 11.34}{15.67}}$.

**2**  Draw an example of each of the following quadrilaterals: square, rectangle, parallelogram, rhombus, kite, isosceles trapezium, trapezium. Mark all lines of equal length and all parallel lines. Under each figure list the number of lines of symmetry and the order of rotational symmetry.

**3**  Copy Figure P14:1 and write in the missing angles for the quadrilateral OATB.

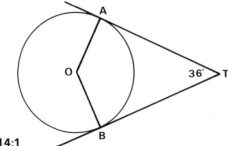

**Fig. P14:1**

**4**  Draw the net of the square-based pyramid in Figure P14:2. Find, by measuring, the perpendicular distance between the square and the apex of one of the triangular faces.

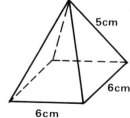

**Fig. P14:2**

**\*5**  A model of a building is made to a scale of 1 : 50. The dimensions of the building are: length 22 m, width 12 m and height 34 m. Find the dimensions of the model, in cm. If the total area of the windows in the model is 6500 cm², find in m² the total area of the windows in the actual building.

**\*6**  A pilot takes a family on a pleasure flight. He sets out to fly the following route: to Alcester 70 miles N 30° E, then to Breen 50 miles on a bearing of 150°, then to Cappel 50 miles due south, and then back to the airfield. Taking a scale of 1 cm to 1 mile make a plan of the route.

Use your drawing to find:
(a)  the distance and bearing of the airfield from Breen
(b)  the distance and bearing of the airfield from Cappel.

**7**  Calculate the sizes of the lettered angles in Figure P14:3. O indicates the centre of the circle.

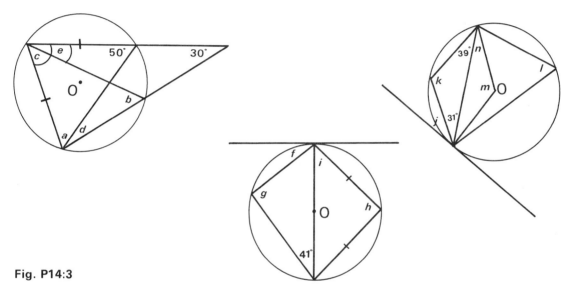

**Fig. P14:3**

## Paper Fifteen

**1**  A motorist travelled 1500 miles in a month at an average of 33 miles per gallon. How much did he spend on petrol if one gallon cost £1.98?

**2**  Figure P15:1 represents the plan of a garden. Find its area in m².

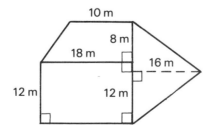

**Fig. P15:1**

183

**3** Figure P15:2 represents a template cut out of a piece of card. Calculate:

(a) its area

(b) its perimeter.

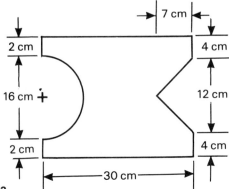

**Fig. P15:2**

**4** A cylindrical barrel has a radius of 25 cm and a height of 115 cm.

(a) Calculate its volume in $cm^3$ to the nearest whole number.

(b) A cylindrical tin has a radius of 6 cm and a height of 14 cm. Calculate its volume in $cm^3$ to 2 decimal places

(c) If the contents of a full barrel is poured into tins how many tins will be needed?

(d) Calculate the total area of metal used to make all of the tins, in $m^2$ to 4 significant figures. (Ignore the seams.)

**\*5** (a) Construct the triangle ABC in which BC = 12 cm, AB = 10 cm and the angle BAC = 60°.

(b) Construct the bisector of the angle ABC and let this bisector meet AC at D.

(c) Construct the bisector of the angle ACB and let this bisector meet AB at E.

(d) Mark the point where BD meets CE and call this point O.

(e) From O construct a line perpendicular to BC to meet BC at F.

(f) Using OF as a radius, centre O, draw a circle.

(g) Extend OT to P so that OP = 10 cm. From P construct a tangent to the circle, marking the point of contact as T.

(h) Measure and write down the distances:
(i) CD   (ii) AE   (iii) OF   (iv) PT.

**6** Draw up the route matrices for the networks shown in Figures P15:3(a) and (b).

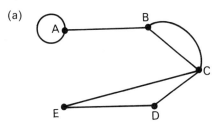

**Fig. P15:3**

# Paper Sixteen

**1** Find the value of $3x^2$ if:
(a) $x = 3$    (b) $x = -2$    (c) $x = \frac{1}{3}$.

**2** Factorise:
(a) $2x^2 - 8x + 8$    (b) $4x^2 - 16$    (c) $2x^2 - 6x$.

**3** Solve the equation:
$3(2 + x) - (x - 2) - 20 = 0$.

**4** Figure P16:1 shows a corner of a sheet of metal measuring 50 cm by 70 cm with $3\frac{1}{2}$ cm-radius discs cut from it so that each disc touches the next. (Take $\pi = \frac{22}{7}$.)

(a) What is the area of the sheet, in cm²?

(b) How many discs can be cut along its length?

(c) How many discs can be cut across its width?

(d) What is the total area of all the discs that can be cut from one sheet?

(e) Express the amount of metal left over as a percentage of the area of a complete sheet.

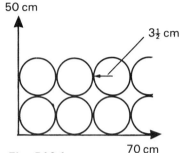

**Fig. P16:1**

**5** Find the lengths of $p$ and $q$ in Figure P16:2 and hence the area of the triangle ABC.

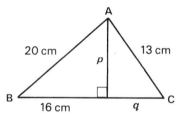

**Fig. P16:2**

**\*6** Construct a triangle ABC in which AB = 8 cm, BC = 10 cm and angle ABC = 60°.

(a) Construct the perpendicular bisector of AC.

(b) Construct the locus of the point P such that PB = PC.

(c) Mark O, the point at which the perpendicular bisector of AC meets the locus of the point P.

(d) Using O as the centre construct a circle radius OC.

(e) Produce OC to X so that OX = 12 cm. From X draw a tangent to touch the circle at T.

(f) Measure:
  (i) AC    (ii) OC    (iii) XT.

**7** In Figure P16:3 AD is a diameter and AD bisects the angle BAC. Calculate:
(a) BC    (b) BD    (c) CD.

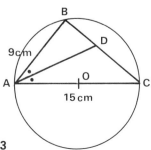

**Fig. P16:3**

185

**8** (a) In Figure P16:4 OA and OB are radii of concentric circles. Calculate:
  (i) the area ABCD correct to 2 decimal places
  (ii) the difference in lengths of arcs BC and AD correct to 3 decimal places.

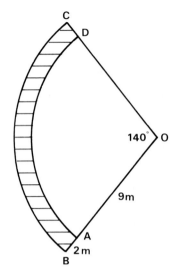

Fig. P16:4

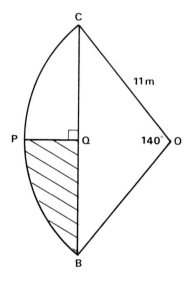

Fig. P16:5

(b) In Figure P16:5 OB is the radius of a circle and PQ is the perpendicular bisector of chord BC. Giving all your answers correct to 2 decimal places calculate:
  (i) BC   (ii) the area of sector OBPC   (iii) the area of triangle OBC
  (iv) the shaded area BPQ.

**Paper Seventeen**

**1** Work out, using a calculator and giving your answer correct to 2 decimal places:

  (a) $\left(\dfrac{2.46}{1.64}\right)^4$   (b) $6.47 - 1.64^2$   (c) $\dfrac{1}{3.4^2} - \dfrac{1}{4.7^2}$   (d) $\left(\dfrac{49.87^2 - 17.36^2}{3.7}\right)^2$.

**2** Using one set of axes from 0 to 5 sketch the lines:
  (a) $x = 0$   (b) $y = 0$   (c) $x + y = 5$   (d) $y + x = 3$.

**3** In Figure P17:1 CBE is a straight line.
  Calculate:
  (a) BC   (b) AE   (C) BE.

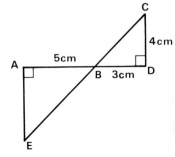

Fig. P17:1

186

**4** (a) Solve:

(i) $3p - 6 - 2p + 8 + 4p = 0$    (ii) $4(p - 6) = 2p - 9$.

(b) Peter is $x$ years of age and his mother is 24 years older. If the sum of their ages is 56 find Peter's age.

(c) $A = 4y^2 - x^2$ and $B = 4(2y + x)$.

(i) If $y = 5$ and $x = 3$ calculate $A$ and $B$.

(ii) If $x = 4$ and $B = 48$ calculate $y$ and $A$.

**\*5** In Figure P17:2 the faces EFGH, DHGC, ABCD and AEFB are rectangles of length 3.2 m.

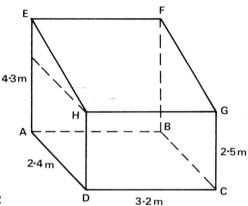

**Fig. P17:2**

Using Pythagoras' Theorem calculate the length of:

(a) the diagonal CH    (b) the diagonal AC    (c) the diagonal EC    (d) the length EH

(e) the total surface area of the figure    (f) the volume of the figure.

Using a scale of 1 cm to 1 m draw a net of the solid.

**6** (a) In Figure P17:3, AB is a chord 8 cm long with a perpendicular distance of 3 cm from the centre of the circle O. Sector OCD has angle COD = 60°. Calculate:

(i)   the radius of the circle

(ii)  the length CD

(iii) the length of arc CD

(iv) the area of sector OCD.

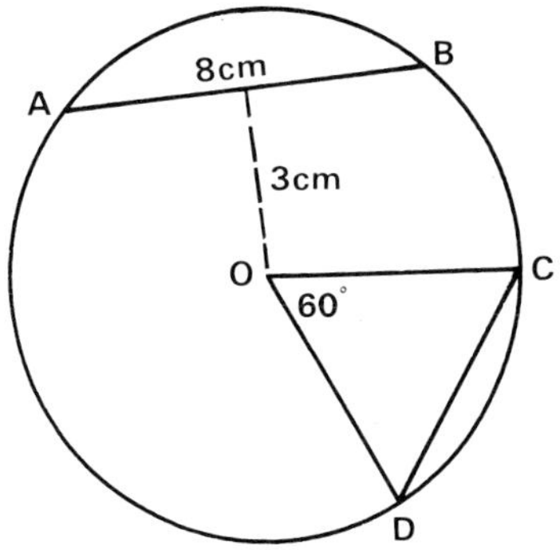

(b) In Figure P17:4 calculate:

(i)  $x$ to 4 significant figures

(ii) $h$ to 2 decimal places.

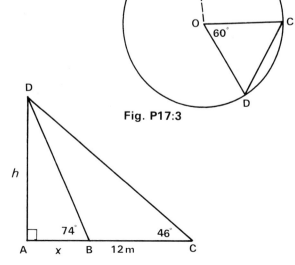

**Fig. P17:3**

**Fig. P17:4**

187

**7** Simplify:

(a) $8^{\frac{1}{3}}$     (b) $27^{\frac{2}{3}}$     (c) $4^{-1}$     (d) $8^{-\frac{2}{3}}$.

**8** (a) If $\mathbf{p} = \begin{pmatrix} 2 \\ 3 \end{pmatrix}$ and $\mathbf{q} = \begin{pmatrix} 4 \\ -2 \end{pmatrix}$ find:

    (i) $2\mathbf{p} + \mathbf{q}$     (ii) $\mathbf{p} - 3\mathbf{q}$.

(b) If A is (3, 2) and B is (6, 6):

    (i) write $\overrightarrow{AB}$ as a vector     (ii) find $|\overrightarrow{AB}|$.

**9** $m$ varies directly as $p^2$ and inversely as $n$.
$m = 3$ when $p = 3$ and $n = 6$.

Find $n$ when $m = 10$ and $p = 5$.

**10** Solve the equation $2x^2 - 3x - 4 = 0$ correct to 2 decimal places.

## Paper Eighteen

For questions 1–20 you are asked to select the correct answer from the four given. Be careful, as the three wrong answers are worked out by making common mistakes; try to ignore the given answers until you have done your own working.

**1** $4 \times (8 - 3) =$            **A** 8   **B** 20   **C** 44   **D** 25

**2** $72.37 + 4.9 =$           **A** 72.46   **B** 72.86   **C** 77.27   **D** 121.37

**3** $-8 - 3 =$            **A** 11   **B** −5   **C** −11   **D** 5

**4** 4% of £3.50 is         **A** 14p   **B** £1.40   **C** £1.25   **D** 13p

**5** The next two numbers in the sequence 2, 3, 5, 8, 13
are         **A** 18, 24   **B** 20, 29   **C** 20, 27
        **D** 21, 34

**6** 50% of people asked said they ate brown bread.
Which of the following must be true?        **A** 100 people were asked
        **B** Half the people ate brown bread
        **C** 50% ate white bread
        **D** 50 people ate brown bread

**7** If $x = \sqrt{8}$ then $x^2 =$       **A** 8   **B** 64   **C** 16   **D** 4

**8** The mean of 4, 7, 10, 5, 4 is      **A** 5   **B** 4   **C** 6   **D** 30

**9** The median of 4, 7, 10, 5, 4 is     **A** 5   **B** 4   **C** 6   **D** 30

**10** The mode of 4, 7, 10, 5, 4 is      **A** 5   **B** 4   **C** 6   **D** 30

**11** Which of the letters of STOP have line symmetry?    **A** S, T   **B** S, T, O   **C** O, P   **D** T, O

**12** $46 - 9 - 8 =$    **A** 45   **B** 29   **C** 63   **D** 47

**13** Which is the nearest approximate value of $\sqrt{160}$?    **A** 17   **B** 13   **C** 40   **D** 4

**14** 0.034 km expressed in metres is    **A** 34   **B** 3.4   **C** 340   **D** 0.34

**15** If $4x - 3 = 9$ then $x$ is    **A** 1.5   **B** 6   **C** 12   **D** 3

**16** If $a = 3$ and $b = 2$ then $2a^2b$ equals    **A** 24   **B** 72   **C** 36   **D** 32

**17** The sum of 1.5 kg, 250 g, $2\frac{1}{2}$ kg and 0.75 kg is    **A** 5 kg   **B** 4.25 kg   **C** 277.25 kg   **D** 7.25 kg

**18** The area of triangle ABC in Figure P18:1 is    **A** 12 cm²   **B** 40 cm²   **C** 24 cm²   **D** 25 cm²

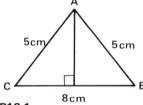

**Fig. P18:1**

**19** Length AB in Figure P18:2 is    **A** 10 cm   **B** 13 cm   **C** 169 cm   **D** 17 cm

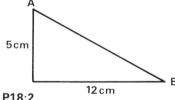

**Fig. P18:2**

**20** Angle $x$ in Figure P18:3 is    **A** 115°   **B** 180°   **C** 65°   **D** 125°

**Fig. P18:3**

**21** (a) A family's budget for a month was as follows:

| Mortgage | £180 | Heat, light, rates | £120 | Food | £140 |
|---|---|---|---|---|---|
| Savings | £80 | Travel, car | £160 | Clothes etc. | £40 |

Using a 4 cm-radius circle draw a pie-chart to represent their budget.

(b) Figure P18:4 represents a survey of a group of 5th Years' plans for the following year. 28 pupils didn't know what they were going to do.

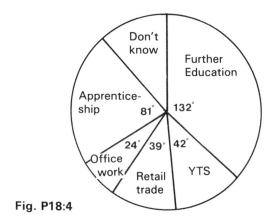

**Fig. P18:4**

Calculate:
(i) the number of pupils in each sector      (ii) how many pupils were questioned.

**22** A motorist buys 5 gallons of petrol and 2 pints of oil for £12.66. A second motorist buys 3 gallons of the same grade petrol and 1 pint of oil for £7.32. Find the prices of petrol per gallon and of oil per pint.

**23** Figure P18:5 represents a field. Calculate:
(a) the lengths AB and BC in metres, to the nearest metre
(b) angles BAD, BCD and ABC in degrees to the nearest 0.1°
(c) the area of the quadrilateral ABCD in hectares correct to 4 significant figures (1 hectare = 10 000 m²).

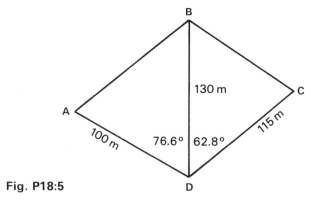

**Fig. P18:5**

**Paper Nineteen**

Questions 1–20 are multiple-choice, as in Paper Eighteen.

**1** A rectangle measures 50 cm by 18 cm. A square of equal area has sides of      **A** 25 cm   **B** 45 cm   **C** 90 cm   **D** 30 cm

**2** In Figure P19:1 the value of $x$ is ⠀⠀⠀**A** 85° ⠀**B** 136° ⠀**C** 125° ⠀**D** 75°

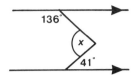

**Fig. P19:1**

**3** In Figure P19:2 angle $x$ is ⠀⠀⠀⠀⠀**A** 72° ⠀**B** 64° ⠀**C** 128° ⠀**D** 98°

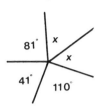

**Fig. P19:2**

**4** Given that $ac + d = p$ then $c =$ ⠀⠀⠀**A** $\dfrac{p-d}{a}$ ⠀**B** $p - d - a$ ⠀**C** $\dfrac{p}{ad}$ ⠀**D** $\dfrac{p}{d} - a$

**5** In Figure P19:3 the value of $x$ is ⠀⠀⠀**A** 43° ⠀**B** 32° ⠀**C** 46° ⠀**D** 51°

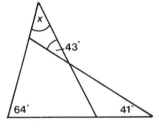

**Fig. P19:3**

**6** The exterior angle of a 12-sided regular polygon is ⠀**A** 36° ⠀**B** 45° ⠀**C** 30° ⠀**D** 42°

**7** The factors of $x^2 + 4x - 12$ are ⠀⠀⠀**A** $(x + 12)(x - 1)$ ⠀**B** $(x + 6)(x - 2)$
⠀⠀⠀⠀⠀⠀⠀⠀⠀⠀⠀⠀⠀⠀⠀⠀⠀⠀⠀⠀⠀**C** $(x - 6)(x + 2)$ ⠀**D** $(x - 4)(x + 8)$

**8** In Figure P19:4, $\sin x =$ ⠀⠀⠀**A** $\dfrac{3}{\sqrt{34}}$ ⠀**B** $\dfrac{3}{4}$ ⠀**C** $\dfrac{5}{3}$ ⠀**D** $\dfrac{4}{3}$

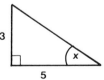

**Fig. P19:4**

**9** The area, in cm², of a circle with diameter 19 cm is
approximately ⠀⠀⠀⠀⠀⠀⠀⠀**A** 300 ⠀**B** 1200 ⠀**C** 120 ⠀**D** 60

**10** $(0.08)^2 =$ ⠀⠀⠀⠀⠀⠀⠀⠀⠀⠀**A** 0.16 ⠀**B** 0.64 ⠀**C** 0.016 ⠀**D** 0.0064

**11** The ratio of the heights of two similar cylinders is 1 : 3. The ratio of their volumes is

**A** 1:6 **B** 1:9 **C** 1:27 **D** 4:9

**12** Given that $x = 4$, $y = 2$, $a = 2$ and $b = -1$, then the value of $x^a + y^b$ is

**A** 6 **B** 16.5 **C** 7.5 **D** 14

**13** In Figure P19:5 the equation of the line is

**A** $y = -3x + 3$ **B** $y = -x + 3$
**C** $y = x + 3$ **D** $y = -3x - 3$

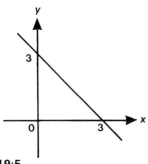

**Fig. P19:5**

**14** Which of the following has the greatest value?

**A** $\frac{2}{3} + \frac{1}{4}$ **B** $\frac{2}{3} \times \frac{1}{4}$ **C** $\frac{2}{3} - \frac{1}{4}$ **D** $\frac{2}{3} \div \frac{1}{4}$

**15** In Figure P19:6 the height AB is

**A** $\sqrt{153}$ cm **B** 5 cm **C** 4 cm **D** 9 cm

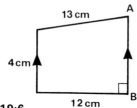

**Fig. P19:6**

**16** A cylinder has a radius of 7 cm and a height of 10 cm. Its volume is (take $\pi = \frac{22}{7}$)

**A** 385 cm³ **B** 440 cm³ **C** 1540 cm³
**D** 880 cm³

**17** If $x = 4.0 \times 10^{-2}$ and $y = 6.0 \times 10^4$ then $xy$ equals

**A** $2.4 \times 10^2$ **B** $2.4 \times 10^3$
**C** $2.4 \times 10^{-8}$ **D** $2.4 \times 10^{-9}$

**18** £500 increased by 100% is

**A** £500 **B** £1000 **C** £600 **D** £550

**19** The mean of 4, 3, 9, 3, 1 is

**A** 3 **B** 4 **C** 5 **D** 9

**20** A rhombus has sides of length 13 cm and a diagonal of length 24 cm. The area of the rhombus in cm² is

**A** 240 **B** 169 **C** 156 **D** 120

**21** Using a circle of 5 cm radius make a copy of Figure P19:7 and mark on it the sizes of all angles.

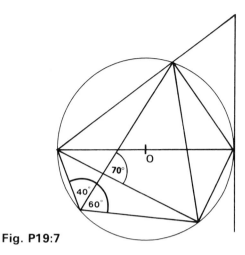

**Fig. P19:7**

Paper Twenty

**1** Telephone charges are 4.7p per unit plus a standing charge of £15.15 per quarter. V.A.T. at 15% is added to this total. Find the payment due if the number of units used is:
(a) 432     (b) 744.

**2** The hour-hand of a clock is 12.8 cm long and the minute-hand 17.4 cm long. Calculate the distance between the tips of the hands at 9 o'clock.

**3** For Figure P20:1 calculate:
(a) the angles BAC, BCA and ABC
(b) the length AC.

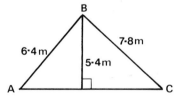

**Fig. P20:1**

**4** Find the angles *a*, *b* and *c* in Figure P20:2.

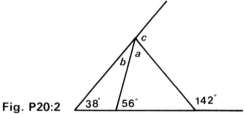

**Fig. P20:2**

**5**

| Marks | 3 | 4 | 5 | 6 | 7 | 8 | 9 | 10 |
|---|---|---|---|---|---|---|---|---|
| No. of pupils | 2 | 4 | 5 | 10 | 14 | 8 | 5 | 2 |

The table shows the result of a test. Find:
(a) the mean mark     (b) the modal mark     (c) the median mark.

**\*6** A class set out to find the speed of vehicles on a road. When a vehicle passed a lamp-post a signal was given to pupils 100 yards away to start their stop-watches to time the vehicles over the distance. They had worked out that the formula they needed to make a conversion graph was:

$$\text{time over 100 yards} = \frac{60 \times 60 \times 100}{1760 \times \text{speed in m.p.h.}} \text{ seconds}$$

Cancel the fraction, reducing its denominator to 11.

Copy the table and complete it for speeds between 10 and 120 m.p.h.

Speed over 100 yards

| Speed (m.p.h.) | 10 | 12 | 15 | 20 | 30 | 40 | 60 | 80 | 100 | 120 |
|---|---|---|---|---|---|---|---|---|---|---|
| Time (s) | 20.5 | | | | 6.8 | | | | | |

Using a scale of 1 cm to 1 second on the x-axis and 1 cm to 10 m.p.h. on the y-axis draw a graph of your results. Use your graph to convert the following times over 100 yards to m.p.h.:
(a) 7 s    (b) 12 s    (c) 3 s.

**7** A function, f, is defined by $f: x \rightarrow x^2 - 5$.

(a) Evaluate:
(i) $f(3)$    (ii) $f(2)$    (iii) $f(3^{-1})$    (iv) $f(7^{\frac{1}{2}})$.

(b) If $f(p) = \frac{4}{9}$ find the two possible values of $p$.

**8** Simplify: $\dfrac{3a - 2}{5} - \dfrac{2a - 3}{4}$.

**9** Solve: $\dfrac{1}{x + 2} - \dfrac{1}{x} = \dfrac{2}{x - 4}$.

**10** A group of explorers above a ravine want to measure its width and depth. They stand at a point (A) directly opposite a tree (T) on the other side of the ravine. From where they stand the angle of depression of a rock (R) at the bottom of the ravine, directly beneath the tree, is 53°. They measure out 100 metres at right angles to line RA to a point (B), from where they find that the angle to the tree is now 33°. Find:
(a) the width of the ravine
(b) the depth of the ravine.

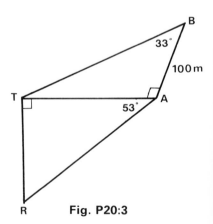

Fig. P20:3

**11** A garden contains 50 trees and shrubs. Their heights were measured, in metres to the nearest 10 cm, to be:

12.1, 3.6, 6.2, 6.6, 8.9, 6.1, 4.8, 4.9, 7.5, 11.2, 5.1, 6.3, 9.2, 4.2, 5.8, 7.2, 6.5, 4.3, 5.1, 8.4, 8.1, 9.0, 7.9, 9.2, 7.1, 0.5, 4.9, 5.7, 2.8, 5.1, 8.3, 8.0, 6.1, 9.1, 4.1, 8.4, 10.2, 8.1, 8.3, 4.7, 6.4, 7.8, 6.1, 7.8, 5.1, 7.3, 1.1, 6.5, 4.4, 5.9

(a) Make a grouped frequency distribution table of their heights using classes of 0.0–, 2.0–, 4.0– etc.

(b) Use the table to construct a cumulative frequency curve, using a scale of 2 cm to 2 m on one axis, and 2 cm to represent 10 trees/shrubs on the other axis.

(c) By using your diagram, or otherwise, estimate the median and the quartiles.

(d) Estimate the percentage of trees and shrubs less than 6.5 m high.

# Aural Test Reference Sheets

## SHEET A

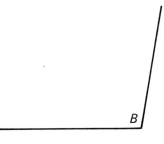

**Fig. A1**

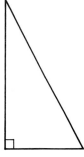

**Fig. A2**

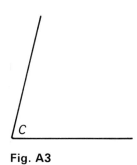

**Fig. A3**

### EXHAUSTS AT THE BEST PRICES YOU CAN GET

| | | | |
|---|---|---|---|
| ALLEGRO | £21.70 | MAXI (SSP) (NOT HL) | £19.95 |
| ALPINE | £41.70 | MARINA 1.3 | £19.95 |
| PRINCESS 1800 | £27.80 | MINI | £14.90 |
| CAPRI 1.6/2.0 | £26.04 | RENAULT 12 TL | £41.69 |
| CAVALIER 1.6/1.9 (RWD) | £30.39 | ROVER 2.3/2.6 (NOT S) | £51.74 |
| CHEVETTE | £28.65 | SIERRA 1.3/1.6 | £52.13 |
| CORTINA 1.6/2.0 | £19.96 | SOLARA/HORIZON | £41.70 |
| ESCORT MK 1&2 | £19.96 | VAUXHALL ASTRA 1.3 (NFP) | £28.65 |
| ESCORT MK 3 | £31.26 | VOLVO 343 (NFP) (76/81) | £39.00 |
| FIESTA 1.1 | £19.96 | | |

**Fig. A4**

### CABINS—*SINGLE JOURNEY*

| | DAY | NIGHT |
|---|---|---|
| LUXURY CABIN, shower/WC For up to 4 persons per cabin | £27.00 | £48.00 |
| SINGLE OUTER, shower/WC per cabin | £16.00 | £29.00 |
| SINGLE INNER, shower/WC | £12.00 | £19.00 |
| DOUBLE OUTER, shower/WC per berth | £8.00 | £12.00 |
| DOUBLE INNER, shower/WC per berth | £6.00 | £11.00 |
| 4 BERTH OUTER, shower/WC per berth | £6.00 | £9.00 |
| 4 BERTH INNER, shower/WC per berth | £4.00 | £7.00 |
| 4 BERTH INNER, without shower/WC per berth | £3.00 | £5.00 |

**Fig. A5**

### *BBC1* TODAY AT A GLANCE *BBC2*

| BBC1 | | BBC2 | |
|---|---|---|---|
| 6.0 | Ceefax AM | | |
| 6.50 | Breakfast Time | | |
| | | 6.55 | Open University |
| | | 7.20 | Closedown |
| | | 9.0 | Pages from Ceefax |
| 9.20 | Pages from Ceefax | | |
| | | 9.38 | Daytime on Two— a mix of education programmes for school, college and home, including: |
| 10.30 | Play School | | |
| 10.50 | Gharbar | | |
| 11.15 | Pages from Ceefax | | 10.0 You and Me |
| 12.30 | News After Noon | | 2.0 Watch |
| 12.55 | Regional News | | |
| 1.0 | Pebble Mill at One | | |
| 1.45 | Bagpuss | | |
| 2.0 | Racing | | |
| | | 3.0 | Bowls and Racing |
| 3.25 | Pages from Ceefax | | |
| 3.52 | Regional News | | |
| 3.55 | Henry's Cat | | |
| 4.10 | Jimbo and the Jet Set | | |
| 4.15 | Jackanory | | |
| 4.30 | Laurel and Hardy | | |
| 4.35 | Wizbit | | |
| 5.0 | Newsround | | |
| 5.10 | Running Scared | | |
| | | 5.30 | News and Weather |
| 5.35 | First Class | 5.35 | Bridge Club |
| 6.0 | Six O'Clock News | 6.0 | Film: The Ghost Goes West |
| 6.35 | Regional magazines | | |
| 7.0 | Wogan | 7.20 | 100 Great Sporting Moments |
| | | 7.30 | Out of Court |
| 7.40 | No Place Like Home | | |
| | | 8.0 | All Our Working Lives |
| 8.10 | Dynasty II: The Colbys | | |
| 9.0 | Nine O'Clock News Regional News | 9.0 | M.A.S.H. |
| | | 9.25 | Dead Head |
| 9.30 | The Marriage | | |
| 10.15 | Sportsnight | 10.15 | Tonight in Person |
| | | 11.0 | Newsnight |
| | | 11.45–11.55 | Weather |
| 12.10–12.15 | Weather | | |

**Fig. A6**

197

## SHEET B

### London→Reading→Westbury→Taunton→Exeter→Torbay→Plymouth

Mondays to Fridays

| | | 🛏 | | 125 | 125 | 125 | | 125 | | 125 | 125 | | 125 | 125 | | 125 | 125 | 125 | | 125 | 125 |
|---|---|---|---|---|---|---|---|---|---|---|---|---|---|---|---|---|---|---|---|---|---|
| | | | | | | | | | | | | | | | FO | | | | FO | FO | FX |
| | | | | ■ | ■ | X ■ | X ■ | ■ | ■ | X ■ | X ■ | X ■ | ■ | ■ | | X ■ | X ■ | X ■ | ■ | X ■ | X ■ |
| Paddington | d | 23 59 | — | 07 25 | 08 45 | 09 05 | 09 40 | 10 05 | 10 25 | 11 40 | 12 40 | 13 40 | 14 05 | 14 45 | 14 47 | 15 45 | 16 45 | 17 45 | 17 47 | 18 57 | 19 00 |
| Reading E | d | 00 40 | — | 07 53 | 09 09 | 09 30 | 10 14 | 10 29 | 10 58 | — | 13 04 | 14 14 | 14 30 | 15 09 | 15 17 | 16 09 | 17 09 | 18 10 | 18 19 | 19 21 | 19 24 |
| Newbury | d | — | — | — | 09 24 | — | — | — | 11 18 | — | 13 23 | — | — | 15 24 | 15 34 | — | — | — | 18 41 | — | — |
| Pewsey | d | — | — | — | — | — | — | — | 11 41 | — | — | — | — | — | — | — | 17 39 | — | 19 03 | — | 19 54 |
| Westbury | d | — | 06 30 | 08 04 | 10 00 | — | — | — | 12 01 | — | 13 59 | — | — | 16 00 | 16 13 | — | 18 00 | — | 19 24 | — | 20 13 |
| Castle Cary | d | — | — | — | 09 23 | — | — | — | — | — | 12 17 | — | — | 14 11 | — | — | 18 17 | — | — | — | 20 32 |
| Taunton | a | 03 06 | 08 32 | 09 44 | 10 40 | 11 22 | — | — | 12 45 | — | 14 39 | — | 16 23 | 16 40 | 16 56 | 17 31 | 18 40 | 19 32 | 20 08 | 20 43 | 20 55 |
| Tiverton Junction | a | — | 08 50 | — | — | — | — | — | — | — | — | — | — | — | 17 13 | — | 18 56 | — | — | — | — |
| Exeter St David's | a | 03 48 | 09 06 | 10 12 | 11 08 | 11 50 | 12 21 | 12 44 | 13 20 | 13 40 | 15 07 | 16 26 | 16 51 | 17 08 | 17 30 | 17 59 | 19 12 | 20 01 | 20 41 | 21 11 | 21 23 |
| Barnstaple | a | 05 07 | — | — | 12 28 | — | — | — | 14 36 | — | 16 27 | — | — | 18 35 | — | — | 20 49 | — | — | 22 38 | 22 38 |
| Exmouth | a | 06 55 | — | 10 52 | 11 46 | — | 13 00 | — | 14 10 | 15 25 | 16 00 | — | 17 41 | 18 11 | — | 18 41 | 19 49 | 20 41 | — | 22 14 | 22 14 |
| Dawlish | a | — | 09 22 | 11 10 | — | 12 04 | — | — | 13 38 | 14 49 | 15 30 | 16 58 | — | 17 22 | 17 57 | 18 29 | — | 20 32 | — | — | 22 09 |
| Teignmouth | a | — | 09 28 | 11 15 | — | 12 09 | — | — | 13 44 | 14 54 | 15 35 | 17 03 | — | 17 27 | 18 02 | 18 35 | — | 20 37 | — | — | 22 15 |
| Newton Abbot | a | 04 15 | 09 35 | 10 34 | 11 30 | 12 16 | — | — | 13 53 | 14 43 | 15 29 | 16 52 | 17 19 | 17 34 | 18 08 | 18 20 | 19 35 | 20 23 | 21 06 | 21 33 | 21 46 |
| Torquay | a | 05 56 | 10 19 | — | 11 46 | 12 48 | — | — | 14 04 | 15 15 | 16 14 | 17 25 | — | 18 13 | — | 18 55 | 19 54 | 20 58 | — | 22 02 | 22 02 |
| Paignton | a | 06 01 | 10 27 | — | 11 53 | 12 56 | — | — | 14 12 | 15 22 | 16 20 | 17 32 | — | 18 20 | — | 19 02 | 20 00 | 21 05 | — | 22 07 | 22 07 |
| Totnes | a | — | — | — | — | 12 30 | — | 13 16 | — | — | 15 56 | — | — | 17 48 | 18 24 | — | 19 49 | — | 21 21 | 22 16 | 22 00 |
| Plymouth | a | 05 05 | 10 17 | 11 13 | 12 09 | 12 58 | 13 26 | 13 44 | — | 14 40 | 16 08 | 17 37 | 17 58 | 18 16 | 18 55 | 18 59 | 20 17 | 21 01 | 21 52 | 22 12 | 22 28 |

Fig. B1

**SATURDAY**
***BBC1***

7.35 Open University
8.30 Hunters Gold
8.55 Bananaman
9.00 Saturday Superstore
12.15 Grandstand inc. News
5.05 News, Weather, Sport
5.20 The Muppet Show
5.45 Jim'll Fix It
6.20 The Late Late Breakfast Show
7.10 Every Second Counts
7.45 Les & Dustin's Laughter Show
8.20 Strike It Rich!
9.10 News, Sport, Weather
9.25 Film: Sleuth
11.40 Film: The Beast Must Die
1.10 Weather

Fig. B2

## REVENUE REQUIREMENT 1985/86

**HOW THE MONEY IS SPENT** **£106 million**

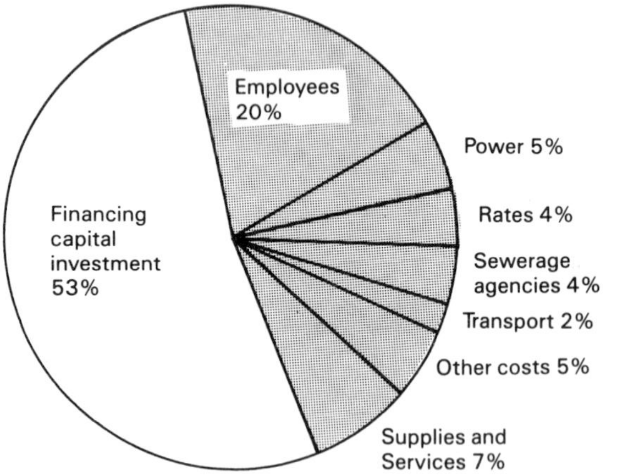


Fig. B3

Total operating costs 47%

## *TYRES!*

***JUST LOOK AT THIS RANGE OF BARGAINS!!***

**SPECIALS!**

185/60 (HR) × 13 £32.00
185/60 (HR) × 14 £33.90
195/60 (HR) × 14 £35.60
195/60 (HR) × 15 £39.95
205/60 (HR) × 15 £39.90
195/50 (HR) × 15 £76.50
225/50 (VR) × 15 £99.99

| | |
|---|---|
| 145 × 10 . . . £13.87 | 175(SR) × 14 . . . £21.70 |
| 135 × 12 . . . £14.75 | 165/70 × 10 . . . £18.22 |
| 145 × 12 . . . £13.50 | 155/70(SR) × 13 . . . £19.96 |
| 145 × 13 . . . £14.75 | 165/70 × 13 . . . £18.20 |
| 155 × 13 . . . £13.50 | 175/70 × 13 . . . £19.08 |
| 165 × 13 . . . £15.65 | 185/70 × 13 . . . £21.08 |
| 165 × 14 . . . £19.50 | 185/70 × 14 . . . £21.90 |

Fig. B4

| VEHICLES | Standard Season 1st Jan to 11th June 12th Sept to 31st Dec | | Peak Season 12th June to 11th Sept | |
|---|---|---|---|---|
| | DAY | NIGHT | DAY | NIGHT |
| **SINGLE JOURNEY FARES 1986** | | | | |
| **1. CARS AND OTHER VEHICLES** not exceeding 5.5 metres in length and 2.4 metres in height, inc. roof rack, etc. EACH: | £17.00 | £29.50 | £22.50 | £37.00 |
| **2. CARS, MINIBUSES & MOBILE HOMES** if not falling into the above category. PER METRE/OR PART THEREOF: | £6.50 | £12.50 | £8.00 | £15.00 |
| **3. CARAVANS.** Charged PER METRE/OR PART THEREOF: inc. towbar*. | £8.50 | £13.00 | £16.00 | £16.00 |
| **4. CAR TRAILERS.** Maximum length 5.5 metres, maximum height when loaded 2.4 metres. Charged PER METRE/OR PART THEREOF: inc. towbar. | £6.50 | £12.50 | £15.00 | £15.00 |
| **5. LIGHT COMMERCIAL VEHICLES** up to 6.5 metres in length, not falling into any of the above categories. PER METRE/OR PART THEREOF: | £12.50 | £12.50 | £14.50 | £14.50 |
| **6. MOTORCYCLES WITH SIDE CARS** EACH: | £9.00 | £18.00 | £11.50 | £22.00 |
| **7. MOTORCYCLES/SCOOTERS** EACH: | £6.50 | £12.50 | £8.00 | £15.00 |
| **8. BICYCLES/MOPEDS** EACH: | £2.00 | £5.00 | £3.00 | £7.00 |

**Fig. C1**

1.10 Insult to Injury
2.00 The Court Jester
3.55 This was Richard Tauber
5.05 Brookside
6.00 Family Ties
6.30 Unforgettable
7.00 News & Weather
7.30 Fragile Earth
8.30 Saturday Live
10.00 Hill Street Blues
11.00 Monster Horrors: The Mummy
12.20 The Mask of Fu Manchu

**Fig. C2**

| | | | |
|---|---|---|---|
| 1979 | **FORD ESCORT 1300 L 4-DOOR,** finished in red with black vinyl roof, well above average for year................................................. | **£1,750** |
| 1985 | **RENAULT 5 GTL 3-DOOR HATCH,** in turquoise, only 7,000 miles, a one-owner car, must be good value compared with new price............ | **£4,450** |
| 1983 | **FIESTA XR2 SALOON,** finished in signal red with grey trim, sunroof, only 21,000 miles .................................................. | **£4,795** |
| 1984 | **METRO 1.3 HLE 5-DOOR HATCH,** in silver only 9,500 miles; one owner from new .................................................... | **£4,450** |
| 1982 | **BMW 320 AUTOMATIC SALOON,** in smoke grey, only 21,000 miles, a fine example of this prestigious car ................................ | **£5,795** |
| 1981 | **METRO 1.3 S HATCH,** in dark blue with grey striped trim, 23,000, one owner, arriving shortly | |
| 1983 | **FORD ESCORT 1300 L ESTATE,** finished in dark brown, brown trim, 46,000 miles, hence price ...................................... | **£3,250** |
| 1979 | **CORTINA 1.6 GL SALOON,** in white, a one-owner car and only 41,000 miles | **£1,795** |
| 1981 | **VAUXHALL CAVALIER 1.6 LS AUTOMATIC,** in maroon, well above average for year (selling on behalf of customer) ...................... | **£1,995** |
| 1978 | **ESCORT ESTATE 1.3 L,** in beige, this car is good value at only ........ | **£1,450** |
| 1981 | **DATSUN 180 BLUEBIRD GL SALOON,** finished in blue with blue trim, well above average for year.......................................... | **£2,495** |

**Fig. C3**

## READY RECKONER FOR MONTHLY REPAYMENTS

| RATE | | 6% | | | 8% | | | 10% | | | 12% | | |
|---|---|---|---|---|---|---|---|---|---|---|---|---|---|
| **PERIOD** | | 2 yrs | 3 yrs | 4 yrs | 2 yrs | 3 yrs | 4 yrs | 2 yrs | 3 yrs | 4 yrs | 2 yrs | 3 yrs | 4 yrs |
| SUM BORROWED | £50 | £2.33 | £1.64 | £1.29 | £2.42 | £1.73 | £1.38 | £2.50 | £1.81 | £1.46 | £2.59 | £1.89 | £1.55 |
| | £100 | £4.67 | £3.28 | £2.58 | £4.84 | £3.45 | £2.75 | £5.00 | £3.62 | £2.92 | £5.17 | £3.78 | £3.09 |
| | £200 | £9.33 | £6.56 | £5.17 | £9.67 | £6.89 | £5.50 | £10.00 | £7.23 | £5.84 | £10.34 | £7.56 | £6.17 |
| | £500 | £23.33 | £16.39 | £12.92 | £24.17 | £17.23 | £13.75 | £25.00 | £18.06 | £14.59 | £25.84 | £18.89 | £15.42 |
| | £600 | £28.00 | £19.67 | £15.50 | £29.00 | £20.67 | £16.50 | £30.00 | £21.67 | £17.50 | £31.00 | £22.67 | £18.50 |
| | £800 | £37.33 | £26.22 | £20.67 | £38.67 | £27.56 | £22.00 | £40.00 | £28.89 | £23.34 | £41.34 | £30.23 | £24.67 |
| | £1000 | £46.67 | £32.78 | £25.83 | £48.34 | £34.45 | £27.50 | £50.00 | £36.12 | £29.17 | £51.67 | £37.78 | £30.84 |
| | £2000 | £93.34 | £65.56 | £51.66 | £96.68 | £68.90 | £55.00 | £100.00 | £72.24 | £58.34 | £103.34 | £75.56 | £61.68 |
| | £3000 | £140.01 | £98.34 | £77.49 | £145.02 | £103.35 | £82.50 | £150.00 | £108.36 | £87.51 | £155.01 | £113.34 | £92.52 |
| | £4000 | £186.68 | £131.12 | £103.32 | £193.36 | £137.80 | £110.00 | £200.00 | £144.48 | £116.68 | £206.68 | £151.12 | £123.36 |
| | £5000 | £233.35 | £163.90 | £129.15 | £241.70 | £172.25 | £137.50 | £250.00 | £180.60 | £145.85 | £258.35 | £188.90 | £154.20 |

**Fig. D1**

**SECOND CLASS FARES FROM LONDON**

| | Ordinary Single | Senior Citizen Single | Economy Fare Single | | European Saver (5-day Return) | Family Fare Single |
|---|---|---|---|---|---|---|
| | | | Day Sailing | Night Sailing | | |
| Aachen | £32.70 | £19.70 | — | — | £39.70 | £72.20 |
| Berlin | £66.60 | — | — | — | — | — |
| Bremen | £51 | £29.10 | £38.30 | £40 | £55.60 | £105.40 |
| Dortmund | £41 | £26.10 | £35.40 | £31.80 | £50.70 | £89.30 |
| Frankfurt | £46.90 | £30.40 | £39.70 | £36.20 | £57.80 | £101.20 |
| Hamburg | £52.40 | £33.20 | £39.20 | £45.40 | £62.60 | £112.80 |
| Hannover | £47.20 | £29.70 | £35.50 | £39.10 | £56.70 | £102.30 |
| Köln | £35 | £22 | £30.80 | £27.20 | £42 | £77.30 |
| Mainz | £44.50 | £28.80 | £37.80 | £34.30 | £55.60 | £96.50 |
| München | £66.40 | £50.70 | £54.30 | £43.90 | £81.50 | £140 |

**Fig. D2**

### COUNTY COUNCIL SPENDING

WHO PAYS → HOW SPENT → ON SERVICES

£

13p Clients
45p Taxpayers
22p Domestic ratepayers
19p Commercial & industrial ratepayers
41p
1p Reserves

54p Employees
35p Running expenses (premises, fuel, transport, materials, etc.)
4p Capital charges
7p Precepts & contingencies

63p Education
11p Social Services
8p Transportation
5p Police
2p Fire Brigade
4p Central services
7p Other

**Fig. D3**

**Au**

| MILEAGE FROM PORTS | Boulogne | Calais | Cherbourg | Dieppe | Dunkerque | Hoek van Holland | Oostende |
|---|---|---|---|---|---|---|---|
| Amsterdam | 245 | 224 | 489 | 300 | 209 | 48 | 172 |
| Barcelona | 833 | 854 | 804 | 786 | 859 | 938 | 869 |
| Basel | 475 | 478 | 572 | 473 | 473 | 449 | 439 |
| Biarritz | 619 | 640 | 508 | 527 | 645 | 752 | 656 |
| Bordeaux | 504 | 525 | 400 | 411 | 527 | 637 | 540 |
| Bruxelles | 146 | 127 | 362 | 195 | 112 | 107 | 71 |
| Esbjerg | 664 | 643 | 897 | 771 | 828 | 508 | 589 |
| Firenze | 878 | 867 | 950 | 834 | 852 | 890 | 841 |
| Frankfurt | 387 | 367 | 585 | 426 | 356 | 292 | 320 |
| Genève | 476 | 484 | 545 | 446 | 489 | 546 | 509 |
| Hannover | 446 | 425 | 647 | 500 | 410 | 297 | 368 |
| København | 886 | 664 | 918 | 781 | 649 | 528 | 611 |
| Köln | 268 | 253 | 488 | 312 | 239 | 187 | 202 |
| Lisboa | 1269 | 1285 | 1167 | 1179 | 1290 | 1417 | 1308 |
| Luxembourg | 252 | 256 | 433 | 280 | 250 | 231 | 211 |
| Lyon | 454 | 469 | 508 | 409 | 457 | 536 | 472 |
| Madrid | 942 | 963 | 843 | 855 | 964 | 1075 | 984 |
| Marseille | 653 | 664 | 703 | 604 | 669 | 735 | 678 |
| Milano | 666 | 679 | 751 | 645 | 668 | 682 | 649 |
| München | 598 | 607 | 725 | 594 | 594 | 529 | 563 |
| Napoli | 1190 | 1194 | 1251 | 1143 | 1179 | 1182 | 1157 |
| Nice | 732 | 747 | 801 | 702 | 749 | 804 | 764 |
| Paris | 151 | 172 | 221 | 122 | 182 | 284 | 186 |
| Roma | 1054 | 1059 | 1115 | 1007 | 1044 | 1046 | 1021 |
| St-Malo | 298 | 319 | 121 | 220 | 332 | 487 | 363 |
| Salzburg | 684 | 693 | 814 | 680 | 678 | 615 | 649 |
| Strasbourg | 386 | 393 | 518 | 372 | 388 | 381 | 348 |
| Trieste | 892 | 894 | 999 | 900 | 878 | 864 | 860 |
| Venezia | 837 | 836 | 929 | 809 | 831 | 818 | 824 |
| Wien | 864 | 858 | 992 | 860 | 843 | 769 | 797 |

**Fig. E1**

### Continental and British Clothing Sizes

SHOES

Children's
U.K.    1    2    3    4    5    6    7    8    9    10
Cont.  17  18  19  20  22  23  24  25  27  28
U.K.   11  12  13
Cont.  29  30  31

Women's
U.K.    1    2    3    4    5    6    7    8
Cont.  33  34  35  36  37  38  39  40

Men's
U.K.    1    2    3    4    5    6    7    8    9    10
Cont.  35  36  37  38  39  40  41  42  43  44
U.K.   11  12  13
Cont.  45  46  48

SHIRTS AND COLLARS
U.K.   14  $14\frac{1}{2}$  15  $15\frac{1}{2}$  16  $16\frac{1}{2}$  17
Cont.  36  37  38  39  41  42  43

SUITS AND OVERCOATS (Men's)
U.K.   36  38  40  42  44  46
Cont.  46  48  50  52  54  56

DRESSES AND SUITS (Women's)
U.K.    8  10  12  14  16  18
Cont.  34  36  38  40  42  44

HATS (Men's)
U.K.   $6\frac{1}{2}$  $6\frac{3}{8}$  $6\frac{3}{4}$  $6\frac{7}{8}$  7  $7\frac{1}{8}$  $7\frac{1}{4}$  $7\frac{3}{8}$  $7\frac{1}{2}$
Cont.  53  54  55  56  57  58  59  60  61

GLOVE sizes are usually the same as in U.K.

SOCKS, STOCKINGS, etc., where different, are measured in cms, not ins.

**Fig. E2**

### Distances—miles and kilometres

| miles | km | miles | km |
|---|---|---|---|
| 0.62 | 1 | 1 | 1.61 |
| 1.86 | 3 | 3 | 4.83 |
| 3.11 | 5 | 5 | 8.05 |
| 4.34 | 7 | 7 | 11.27 |
| 5.59 | 9 | 9 | 14.48 |
| 6.20 | 10 | 10 | 16.10 |
| 12.40 | 20 | 20 | 32.20 |
| 31.00 | 50 | 50 | 80.50 |
| 43.00 | 70 | 70 | 112.70 |
| 62.00 | 100 | 100 | 161.00 |

For a quick conversion, km to miles, divide the km distance by 8, then multiply the result by 5.

### Sample Distances

Ostend to:

| Berlin | 601 miles |
|---|---|
| Cologne | 212 miles |
| Frankfurt | 326 miles |
| Freiburg | 499 miles |
| Hamburg | 425 miles |
| Munich | 586 miles |
| Trier | 241 miles |

Boulogne to:

| Cologne | 276 miles |
|---|---|
| Frankfurt | 421 miles |
| Munich | 639 miles |

Hook of Holland to:

| Cologne | 205 miles |
|---|---|
| Frankfurt | 319 miles |
| Munich | 561 miles |

### Pounds into kilograms

| lb | kg | lb | kg |
|---|---|---|---|
| 1 | 0.45 | 20 | 9.07 |
| 2 | 0.91 | 30 | 13.61 |
| 3 | 1.36 | 40 | 18.14 |
| 5 | 2.27 | 60 | 27.22 |
| 10 | 4.54 | 112 | 50.80 |

### Kilograms into pounds

| kg | lb | kg | lb |
|---|---|---|---|
| 1 | 2.20 | 20 | 44.09 |
| 2 | 4.41 | 30 | 66.14 |
| 3 | 6.61 | 40 | 88.19 |
| 5 | 11.02 | 60 | 132.28 |
| 7 | 15.43 | 80 | 176.37 |
| 9 | 19.84 | 100 | 220.46 |
| 10 | 22.05 | 250 | 551.15 |

### Petrol and Oil—gallons and litres

| litres | gallons | litres | gallons |
|---|---|---|---|
| 4.55 | 1 | 1 | 0.22 |
| 13.65 | 3 | 3 | 0.66 |
| 22.75 | 5 | 5 | 1.10 |
| 31.82 | 7 | 7 | 1.54 |
| 40.92 | 9 | 9 | 1.98 |
| 45.46 | 10 | 10 | 2.20 |
| 90.92 | 20 | 20 | 4.40 |
| 227.30 | 50 | 50 | 11.01 |
| 454.60 | 100 | 100 | 22.00 |

### Temperatures

| °F | °C | °F | °C |
|---|---|---|---|
| 212 | 100 | 59 | 15 |
| 104 | 40 | 50 | 10 |
| 102 | 38.9 | 41 | 5 |
| 101 | 38.3 | 32 | 0 |
| 100 | 37.8 | 28 | −2 |
| 98.4 | 37 | 23 | −5 |
| 97 | 36.1 | 18 | −8 |
| 86 | 30 | 12 | −11 |
| 80 | 26.7 | 5 | −15 |
| 77 | 25 | 0 | −18 |
| 68 | 20 | −4 | −20 |
| 64 | 17.8 | | |

# REFERENCE SECTION

# Reference Notes

## Contents

See also: Trigonometry, pages 250 to 254; Percentages, notes 6 and 8, pages 216 and 217

206

## BASIC ARITHMETIC

The number in brackets after each heading indicates the exercise in Book 5 which contains questions on the topic.

### 1 Approximation methods (1)

Many amounts used in life are approximations to (not exactly) the true amount. This may be because there is no exact amount (e.g. the length of a line), or to make the number easier to read or remember (e.g. a football crowd of 21 000).

Approximations may be expressed in many ways, e.g. 15.79 is 16 **to the nearest whole number**; 31 215 is 31 200 **to the nearest hundred**; 7.68 cm is 7.7 cm **to the nearest mm**; £10 ÷ 3 is £3.33 **to the nearest penny**.

You will often need to approximate calculator answers. How approximate you should make them usually depends on the information supplied, e.g. if a question is based on an average speed correct to the nearest km/h, and a distance correct to the nearest km, then it is silly to give a time for the journey correct to the nearest second, and even sillier to give an answer like 1.245367 hours.

Two special approximations are used in mathematics:

#### (a) Decimal places (d.p.)

This states the number to a given number of figures after the decimal point. Clearly it is of no use when there are no figures after the point!

**Examples**   7.0145 → 7.015 to 3 d.p.
7.0145 → 7.01 to 2 d.p.
7.98 → 8.0 to 1 d.p. (the 'key' 8 makes 9 → 10)

#### (b) Significant figures (s.f.)

All figures are counted, except zeros between the decimal point and the first non-zero digit, and place-value zeros before the point.

**Examples**   126.87 → 130 to 2 s.f. (The zero is not a significant figure, but it is needed to show the empty units' column, otherwise 126.87 → 13, which is silly.)
0.001 34 → 0.0013 to 2 s.f.
0.0598 → 0.060 to 2 s.f.

**It is very important to check that your approximated answer *is* approximately the same size as the original number.** (Students have been known to state that 1236.8 is approximately 12 to 2 s.f.)

### 2 Standard form (1)

#### (a) Numbers above 1

$$1.2346 \quad 08$$

This shows the way most scientific calculators display the answer to 123 456 × 1000. Because the answer (123 456 000) is too long for the display it has been switched to standard form. (The calculator we used cuts off all figures after the first five, so the number has also been rounded to 5 s.f. Yours may show more, or less, figures.)

The 08 at the right is called the **exponent**. It tells you that 1.2346 is 8 columns too small. Moving the figures up the 8 columns gives the answer as 123 460 000, which is the most accurate this calculator can achieve. You may find it easier to think of the 08 as meaning that there are 8 figures between the first figure and the decimal point.

When we handwrite standard form we use the form $A \times 10^n$, where $A$ is between 1 and 10 and $n$ is an integer.

$$123\,456\,000 \to 1.234\,56 \times 10^8 \quad (\text{i.e. } 1.234\,56 \times 100\,000\,000)$$
$$318 \to 3.18 \times 10^2 \quad (\text{i.e. } 3.18 \times 100)$$

A calculator would not normally use standard form for numbers like 318, but using the $\boxed{\text{EXP}}$ or $\boxed{\text{EE}}$ key you can type in 318 as 3.18 $\boxed{\text{EXP}}$ 2 to give the display 3.18   02. When you type $\boxed{=}$ the calculator will probably switch it back to 318. If it does not, try typing $\boxed{\times}$ 1 $\boxed{=}$ instead.

Computers also use standard form for very large numbers (how large depends on your computer), but they show the exponent by an E, without leaving a gap, so that 1.234   06 becomes 1.234E6.

## (b) Numbers below 1

$$7.8 \quad -02$$

The calculator display here shows 0.078 in standard form. The $-02$ tells us that the 7.8 should be shifted two columns to the right to give the true value. You may think of the $-2$ as meaning there are two leading zeros, including the one before the decimal point.

This would be handwritten as $7.8 \times 10^{-2}$.

$10^{-2}$ is the index way of writing the fraction $\dfrac{1}{10^2} = \dfrac{1}{100}$.

## 3   Decimal fraction arithmetic (2)

When adding or subtracting be sure to keep the units' figures in a vertical line.

When multiplying, ignore zeros at the beginning or end of the numbers; multiply the resulting integers, then replace all omitted 'end' zeros; finally replace the decimal point so that there are as many figures after it as there were after the points in the original question.

**Example**   $0.381 \times 10700 \to 381 \times 107 \to 40\,767 \to 4\,076\,700 \to 4076.700 \to \underline{4076.7}$

When dividing, multiply both numbers by the power of 10 needed to change the divisor (the number you are dividing by) into an integer, then divide as usual. No further change in the position of the point is required.

**Example**   $18.324 \div 0.09 \to \dfrac{18.324}{0.09} \xrightarrow{\times \text{top and bottom by 100}} \dfrac{1832.4}{9} \to \underline{203.6}$

## 4   Common fraction arithmetic (2)

### (a) Common fraction to decimal fraction

**Example**   $\frac{3}{5} \to 3 \div 5 \to 5\,\overline{)3.0}\,{}^{0.6} \to \underline{0.6}$

### (b) Decimal fraction to common fraction

**Example**   $0.375 \xrightarrow[\substack{\text{last figure is in the} \\ \text{thousandths' column}}]{} \dfrac{375}{1000} \to \dfrac{\overset{75}{\overset{3}{\cancel{375}}}}{\underset{200}{\underset{8}{\cancel{1000}}}} \to \dfrac{3}{8}$

### (c) Addition and subtraction

It is best to deal with the whole numbers first.

**Examples** $6\frac{3}{8} + 1\frac{1}{4} \rightarrow 7\frac{3}{8} + \frac{2}{8} \rightarrow 7\frac{5}{8}$

$4\frac{1}{3} - 2\frac{2}{5} \rightarrow 2\frac{5}{15} - \frac{6}{15} \rightarrow 2 - \frac{1}{15} \rightarrow 1\frac{14}{15}$

### (d) Multiplication of a fraction by an integer

**Examples** $\frac{^2\cancel{8}}{_1\cancel{12}} \times \cancel{9}^3 \rightarrow \frac{6}{}$

$2\frac{1}{6} \times 3 \rightarrow \frac{13}{_2\cancel{6}} \times \cancel{3}^1 \rightarrow \frac{13}{2} \rightarrow 6\frac{1}{2}$

### (e) Fraction multiplied by fraction

Change all mixed numbers to improper (top-heavy) fractions first.

**Example** $3\frac{3}{4} \times 1\frac{1}{5} \rightarrow \frac{^3\cancel{15}}{_2\cancel{4}} \times \frac{\cancel{6}^3}{\cancel{5}_1} \rightarrow \frac{9}{2} \rightarrow 4\frac{1}{2}$

### (f) Fraction divided by integer

To divide by $n$, multiply instead by its reciprocal $\left(\frac{1}{n}\right)$.

**Example** $\frac{3}{4} \div 4 \rightarrow \frac{3}{4} \times \frac{1}{4} \rightarrow \frac{3}{16}$

### (g) Division by a fraction

'To divide by a fraction, multiply instead by its inverse.

**Examples** $3 \div \frac{1}{2} \rightarrow 3 \times \frac{2}{1} \rightarrow \frac{6}{}$

$2\frac{1}{2} \div 1\frac{2}{3} \rightarrow \frac{5}{2} \div \frac{5}{3} \rightarrow \frac{5}{2} \times \frac{3}{\cancel{5}_1} \rightarrow \frac{3}{2} \rightarrow 1\frac{1}{2}$

## 5 Divisibility (2)

| A number divides exactly by: | 2 | 3 | 5 | 6 | 9 | 10 |
|---|---|---|---|---|---|---|
| if its digit-sum is: | any | 3;6;9 | any | 3;6;9 | 9 | any |
| and its last digit is: | even | any | 0;5 | even | any | 0 |

A number divides exactly by 4 if its last two digits divide exactly by 4.

A number divides exactly by 8 if its last 3 digits divide exactly by 8.

## 6 Directed numbers (2)

Negative (−ve) numbers | Positive (+ve) numbers

$-3 \quad -2.5 \quad -2 \quad -1.5 \quad -1 \quad -0.5 \quad 0 \quad 0.5 \quad 1 \quad 1.5 \quad 2 \quad 2.5 \quad 3$

Positive (plus) numbers need no signs; negative (minus) numbers need − signs.

Like signs multiply to make a plus:

$$- \; -3 \rightarrow +3 \qquad -3 \times -2 \rightarrow +6$$

Unlike signs multiply to make a minus:

$$- \; +3 \rightarrow -3 \qquad + \; -3 \rightarrow -3 \qquad -3 \times +2 \rightarrow -6 \qquad +3 \times -2 \rightarrow -6$$

210

## 7 The metric system (SI) (6)

**Base units likely to be met in mathematics:**

Length: metre (m)
Mass (weight): kilogram (kg)
Time: second (s)

**Prefixes in common use:**

mega (M) = $10^6$    kilo (k) = $10^3$    centi (c) = $10^{-2}$ $(\frac{1}{100})$
milli (m) = $10^{-3}$ $(\frac{1}{1000})$    micro (μ) = $10^{-6}$ $(\frac{1}{1\,000\,000})$

**Other units which may be used with SI:**

litre (best not abbreviated) = $1000\,cm^3$
tonne (best not abbreviated) = $1000\,kg$
hectare (best not abbreviated) = $10\,000\,m^2$

Some metric prefixes are used with these, e.g. centilitre (cl) = $\frac{1}{100}$ litre = $10\,cm^3$, millilitre (ml) = $\frac{1}{1000}$ litre = $1\,cm^3$, megatonne.

**Changing from one metric unit to another:**

Never insert zeros between figures. The figure in the units' column is rewritten in the correct column of the new unit.

Examples    (a) 108.9 mm → metres
The 8 in the units' column is 8 mm = $\frac{8}{1000}$ metre, so the 8 is rewritten in the thousandths' column, giving 108.9 mm → 0.1089 metres.

(b) 3.06 cm → metres

$$3.06\,cm \xrightarrow{\quad 3\,cm\,=\,\frac{3}{100}\,m \quad} 0.0306\,m$$

(c) 0.00 306 m → km

$$0.00\,306\,m \xrightarrow{\quad 0\,m\,=\,\frac{0}{1000}\,km \quad} 0.000\,003\,06\,km$$

## 8 Prime numbers (1)

Primes have only two different factors, e.g. 19 is prime because its factors are 1 and 19; 9 is not prime because it has three factors, 1, 3 and 9.

Example    To write a number as a product of prime factors.

162 → **2** × 81 → **2** × **3** × 27 → **2** × **3** × **3** × 9 → **2** × **3** × **3** × **3** × **3**

This may be written: 2) 162
3)  81
3)  27
3)   9
3)   3
1

## 9 Highest common factor (HCF) (1)

A factor divides exactly into a number. The HCF is the highest factor that divides exactly into a set of numbers. For large numbers a prime factor method is useful.

**Examples**   The HCF of {12, 15, 18} is 3. (This can be done by just thinking about it.)

To find the HCF of 168 and 180:

$168 \to$ ② × ② × 2 × ③ × 7
$180 \to$ ② × ② × ③ × 3 × 5
HCF = 2 × 2 × 3 = <u>12</u>

## 10   Lowest common multiple (LCM) (1)

A multiple is made by multiplying by an integer. The LCM is the lowest number that is a multiple of each member of a given set of numbers.

**Example**   The LCM of {6, 8, 12} is 24. (This can be done by just thinking about it.)

To find the LCM of 18, 30 and 36:
As 36 is a multiple of 18, we need not think about the 18. All multiples of 30 end in a zero, therefore the answer is a multiple of 36 that ends in a zero and also divides exactly by 30. The answer is 180.

For large numbers a prime factor method is useful.

**Example**   To find the LCM of {18, 24, 64}.

$18 \to 2 \times 3 \times 3$
$24 \to 2 \times 2 \times 2 \times 3$
$64 \to 2 \times 2 \times 2 \times 2 \times 2 \times 2$
The prime factors of the LCM will consist of 2's and 3's. We need two 3's for 18 and six 2's for 64.
Hence the LCM is $2 \times 2 \times 2 \times 2 \times 2 \times 2 \times 3 \times 3 = 576$.

## RATIO

The number in brackets after each heading indicates the exercise in Book 5 which contains questions on the topic.

### 1   The meaning of a ratio (4)

A ratio states the connection between two quantities, e.g. the ratio of weight of cheese to number of eggs for a cheese omelette could be 20 g cheese to every one egg.

Ratios are often expressed with a colon (:), e.g. 2 : 3 (say '2 to 3'). In this case, both numbers must be in the same units, so we could not write the omelette example in this way, but we could say that the ratio of the weights of flour to margarine for plain scones is 4 : 1. That is, you use 4 times as much flour as margarine, e.g. 400 g flour and 100 g margarine.

### 2   Simplifying ratios (4)

Ratios may be simplified by dividing by a common factor, as we do with fractions.

**Example**   2 litres water to 12 cl Jeyes Fluid
$\xrightarrow{\text{becomes}}$ 200 : 12 (both units are now cl)
$\longrightarrow$ 50 : 3 (dividing both 200 and 12 by 4).

## 3 Expressing a ratio in the form $n:1$ and $1:n$ (4)

Ratios are easier to use if one of the quantities is 1, e.g. a ratio $1:2\frac{1}{4}$ clearly shows that the second amount is $2\frac{1}{4}$ times the first; this is not so obvious when the same ratio is written as $4:9$.

**Example**  Express $17:6$ in the ratio (a) $n:1$   (b) $1:n$.

(a) $17:6 \xrightarrow{\div \text{both by } 6} 2\frac{5}{6}:1$

(b) $17:6 \xrightarrow{\div \text{both by } 17} 1:\frac{6}{17}$

## 4 Given one amount, to find the other (4)

**Example**  A 200 g jar of coffee granules makes about 120 cups of coffee.
The ratio of coffee to cups is 200 to 120 → 5 to 3.
Therefore a 250 g jar should make about $250 \times \dfrac{3}{5}$ cups = 150 cups.

For 50 cups we need about $50 \times \dfrac{5}{3} \simeq 85$ g of coffee.

Note how the ratio $5:3$ became $\frac{3}{5}$ or $\frac{5}{3}$, depending on whether the required answer is to be bigger or smaller than the given amount.

## 5 Given the total, to find each (divide in a ratio) (4)

**Example**  Concrete for a path should consist of 1 part cement, 2 parts sand, and 3 parts coarse aggregate. If $3\,\text{m}^3$ of dry mix is required, what volume of each material should be purchased?

Cement : sand : aggregate = $1:2:3$
Total = $1 + 2 + 3 = 6$ parts
$3\,\text{m}^3$ in 6 parts → $\frac{1}{2}\,\text{m}^3$ per part
$\therefore$ use $1 \times \frac{1}{2} = \frac{1}{2}\,\text{m}^3$ cement:
$\qquad 2 \times \frac{1}{2} = 1\,\text{m}^3$ sand;
$\qquad 3 \times \frac{1}{2} = 1\frac{1}{2}\,\text{m}^3$ aggregate.

## 6 Changing in a ratio (4)

**Example**  Increase 16 in the ratio $11:6$.
An increase, so multiply by $\frac{11}{6}$.
$\dfrac{{}^{8}\cancel{16} \times 11}{\cancel{6}_3} = \dfrac{88}{3} = 29\frac{1}{3}$

**Example**  Decrease 35 in the ratio $6:11$.
A decrease, so multiply by $\frac{6}{11}$.
$\dfrac{35 \times 6}{11} = \dfrac{210}{11} = 19\frac{1}{11}$

**Example**  6 men can paint a school in 46 days. How long should 8 men take?
The number of men has increased in the ratio $8:6$.
The time taken should *decrease* in the ratio $6:8$.
$\dfrac{{}^{23}\cancel{46} \times \cancel{6}^{3}}{\cancel{8}_{{}_4{}_2}} = \dfrac{69}{2} = 34\frac{1}{2}$ days

## 7  Using a conversion graph (9)

When two quantities are in a constant ratio, a straight-line conversion graph may be used to convert one to the other. Figure R3 shows conversion from gallons to litres.

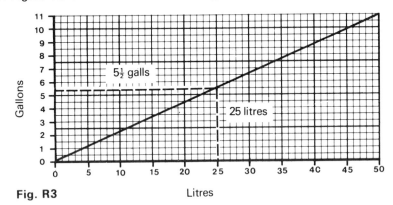

**Fig. R3**

## 8  Lengths and areas of similar shapes (15)

The two triangles in Figure R4 are similar.

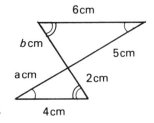

Looking at the positions of the sides we can see that
$4\,\text{cm} \xrightarrow{\text{becomes}} 6\,\text{cm}$, $a\,\text{cm} \rightarrow 5\,\text{cm}$, and $2\,\text{cm} \rightarrow b\,\text{cm}$.
Therefore their sides are in the ratio $4:6 = 2:3$.
$a$ is smaller than 5 so $a = \dfrac{2}{3} \times 5 = 3\frac{1}{3}\,\text{cm}$.

$b$ is larger than 2, so $b = \dfrac{3}{2} \times 2 = 3\,\text{cm}$.

**Fig. R4**

Note that the areas of the triangles are in the ratio $2^2 : 3^2 = 4:9$.
That is, the larger triangle has sides only half as big again as the smaller, but its area is $2\frac{1}{4}$ times as big.

**Remember:  Areas' ratio = Lengths' ratio squared**

## 9  Ratio of volumes (15)

**The ratio of the volumes of similar solids is the cube of the ratio of their corresponding lengths.**

**Example**  The two boxes in Figure R5 are similar solids.
The ratio of their lengths is $3:5$.
The ratio of their volumes is therefore $3^3 : 5^3 = 27 : 125$.
The larger is $\frac{125}{27} = 4\frac{17}{27}$ times as large in volume, but only $\frac{5}{3} = 1\frac{2}{3}$ times as large in lengths.

$$\text{Volume of smaller} = \frac{27}{125} \times \text{volume of larger}$$
$$= \frac{27}{125} \times 75\,\text{cm}^3 = 16.2\,\text{cm}^3.$$

**Summary**
Ratio of lengths $= x:y$
Ratio of areas $= x^2 : y^2$
Ratio of volumes $= x^3 : y^3$

Vol.
75 cm³

**Fig. R5**    3 cm        5 cm

214

## 10 Direct and inverse proportion (13)

Two quantities are in direct proportion when a multiplicative increase in one leads to the same increase in the other, e.g. if one quantity becomes four times bigger, then the other becomes four times bigger as well.

Two quantities are in inverse proportion when a multiplicative increase in one leads to the inverse multiplicative decrease in the other, e.g. if one quantity becomes four times bigger the other becomes a quarter of itself.

### Example of direct proportion
The number of turns made by a car wheel is directly proportional to the number of miles travelled.

### Example of inverse proportion
The time taken for a journey is inversely proportional to the average speed for the journey.


## PERCENTAGES

The number in brackets after each heading indicates the exercise in Book 5 which contains questions on the topic.

### 1 How to change a fraction to a percentage (3)

Multiply the fraction by 100%.

Note that because $100\% = \frac{100}{100} = 1$ we do not increase the fraction when we multiply it by 100%.

**Example** $\quad \frac{11}{15} \rightarrow \frac{11}{_3\cancel{15}} \times \overset{20}{\cancel{100}}\% \rightarrow \frac{220}{3}\% \rightarrow 73\frac{1}{3}\%$

### 2 How to find a percentage of an amount (3)

**Example** To find 35% of £45.

35% is another way of writing $\frac{35}{100}$.

Hence $35\%$ of £45 $\rightarrow \frac{35}{100} \times £45 \rightarrow \frac{^7\cancel{35}}{_{4}\cancel{_{20}\cancel{100}}} \times £\cancel{45}^9 \rightarrow £15.75$

### 3 How to find one amount as a percentage of another (3)

Write it as a fraction, then use the method of note 1.

**Example** To find 32 as a percentage of 128.

Write this as $\frac{32}{128}$, then $\frac{32}{128} \rightarrow \frac{32}{128} \times 100\% \rightarrow \frac{^1\cancel{^8\cancel{32}}}{_{4}\cancel{_{32}\cancel{128}}} \times 100\% \rightarrow 25\%$.

**Remember**: One amount as a percentage of another amount is the first over the second times 100%.

215

## 4 Percentage changes (3)

A change can be an increase, a decrease, a profit, a loss, etc.

Change % = change over original times 100%.

**Example**   To find the percentage loss if a book bought for £20 is re-sold for £18.
The change in the cost is £2.
The original cost was £20.

Hence the percentage loss is $\dfrac{2}{20} \times 100\% = 10\%$.

## 5  To increase or decrease by a percentage (3)

It is possible just to find the increase, then add it on, but a better method to use is:

To increase by $r\%$ multiply by $\dfrac{100 + r}{100}$.

To decrease by $r\%$ multiply by $\dfrac{100 - r}{100}$.

**Examples**   To increase by 12% you multiply by $\dfrac{100 + 12}{100} \rightarrow \dfrac{112}{100}$ or 1.12

To decrease by 12% you multiply by $\dfrac{100 - 12}{100} \rightarrow \dfrac{88}{100}$ or 0.88

## 6  Using a calculator percentage key (3)

Unfortunately different calculators do not always use the same method, but one of the following two methods will probably work:

To find 8% of £60.     Key: 60 $\boxed{\times}$ 8 $\boxed{\%}$ **or** 60 $\boxed{\times}$ 8 $\boxed{\%}$ $\boxed{=}$
To increase £60 by 8%.  Key: 60 $\boxed{+}$ 8 $\boxed{\%}$ **or** 60 $\boxed{+}$ 8 $\boxed{\%}$ $\boxed{=}$
To decrease £60 by 8%. Key: 60 $\boxed{-}$ 8 $\boxed{\%}$ **or** 60 $\boxed{-}$ 8 $\boxed{\%}$ $\boxed{=}$

## 7  Percentage changes (inverse calculations) (3)

Sometimes you know the amount resulting from a percentage change and have to find the amount before the change took place. This would occur in a shop where the price given includes 15% VAT and the customer wants to know what the price was before VAT.

A shopkeeper once told me that the VAT on a £100 television was £15, because 15% of £100 was £15. He was wrong, because the VAT was 15% of the 'before-VAT' price. This is what he should have done:

To increase by 15% multiply by 1.15,
so 1.15 × before-VAT price = £100
→ before-VAT price = £100 ÷ 1.15 = £86.96
The VAT was therefore £13.04.

**Example**   Selling price £28, profit 12%, find the cost price.

The temptation is to work out 12% of £28, then take this away from the £28, but this is not correct, for the 12% profit is reckoned on the cost price. The correct method is:

To increase by 12% multiply by $\dfrac{112}{100}$ or 1.12

Then 1.12 × cost price = £28 → cost price = £28 ÷ 1.12 = £25.

**Example**  Selling price £21, loss 40%, find the cost price.

To reduce by 40% multiply by $\dfrac{100-40}{100} \rightarrow \dfrac{60}{100}$ or 0.60

Then 0.60 × cost price = £21 → cost price = £21 ÷ 0.60 = £35.

# 8  Paying interest (7)

Interest is paid to someone who lends money. If you lend money to the Government through your Post Office Savings Bank then the Government will pay you interest.

If the interest rate is $5\frac{1}{2}$% per annum (p.a.) then the Government will pay you £5.50 a year for every £100 you lend them.

If the interest is *not* added to the loan it is called **simple interest**.

If the interest *is* added to the loan it is called **compound interest**. Most everyday-life interest is compound interest.

**Examples**  £100 loaned at 5% p.a. simple interest for 3 years gives £5 each year, making £15 interest altogether.

£100 loaned at 5% p.a. compound interest for 3 years gives £5 interest the first year, but 5% of £105 = £5.25 the second year, and 5% of £110.25 = £5.51 the third year, a total of £15.76 interest.

There are two formulae which you can use, but they are not essential:

Simple interest = $\dfrac{P \times R \times T}{100}$      Compound interest = $P\left(1 + \dfrac{R}{100}\right)^{T} - P$

where $P$ is the principal (the initial amount lent)
$\quad R$ is the interest rate p.a.
$\quad T$ is the number of years for which the principal is lent.

Using a calculator:

**(a) Simple interest**

To find the interest on £50 at 8%.

Key: 50 $\boxed{\times}$ 8 $\boxed{\%}$
**or**   50 $\boxed{\times}$ 8 $\boxed{\%}$ $\boxed{=}$
**or**   50 $\boxed{\times}$ 0.08 $\boxed{=}$

**(b) Compound interest**

The $\boxed{M+}$ key can be used to increase the principal gradually. Either a % key may be used, or the fact that, e.g., 8% is 0.08.

**Example**  To find the principal and interest paid each year on £100 saved at 8% compound interest.

$$\boxed{CM}\ 100\ \boxed{M+}\ \boxed{\times}\ \left\{ \begin{array}{l} 8\ \boxed{\%}\ \boxed{=} \\ 8\ \boxed{\%} \\ 0.08\ \boxed{=} \end{array} \right\}\ \boxed{M+}\ \boxed{RM}$$

repeat

Alternatively, using the fact that to increase by $r$% you multiply by $(100 + r)$% and to decrease by $r$% you multiply by $(100 - r)$%, the following sequence may be used.

Compound interest at 8% on £100:

100 $\boxed{\times}$ 1.08 $\boxed{\text{MS}}$ $\boxed{=}$ $\boxed{\times}$ $\boxed{\text{MR}}$ $\boxed{=}$

$\uparrow$ repeat $\uparrow$

Depreciation (reduction in value) at 8% per annum on £10 000:

10 000 $\boxed{\times}$ 0.92 $\boxed{\text{MS}}$ $\boxed{=}$ $\boxed{\times}$ $\boxed{\text{MR}}$ $\boxed{=}$

$\uparrow$ repeat $\uparrow$

Using the formula C.I. $= P\left(1 + \dfrac{R}{100}\right)^T$ to find the compound interest on £700 for 15 years at $8\frac{1}{2}$%:

$P = £700$; $1 + \dfrac{R}{100} = 1.085$; $T = 15$

Key: 700 $\boxed{\times}$ 1.085 $\boxed{y^x}$ 15 $\boxed{=}$

giving £2379.82 interest!

## CALCULATORS

The number in brackets after each heading indicates the exercise in Book 5 which contains questions on the topic.

### 1 How a calculator carries out calculations (5)

All calculators have two kinds of keys:

Digits and the decimal point 0 1 2 3 4 5 6 7 9 .

Function keys, e.g. $+$ $-$ $\times$ $\div$ $x^2$ $\sqrt{\phantom{x}}$ $\dfrac{1}{x}$ $+/-$ TAN

Most calculators also have an $=$ key and memory, or store, keys, e.g. MS STO MR M+

It is important to remember that all function keys operate on the number showing in the display at the moment that they are pressed (but see the note on 'BODMAS' below). This is why $\dfrac{12}{2 \times 3}$ will come to the wrong answer if you key in 12 $\boxed{\div}$ 2 $\boxed{\times}$ 3 $\boxed{=}$. The correct answer is 2, because $12 \div 6 = 2$.

| Key | 12 | $\boxed{\div}$ | 2 | $\boxed{\times}$ | 3 | $\boxed{=}$ |
|---|---|---|---|---|---|---|
| Display | 12 | 12 | 2 | 6 | 3 | 18 |

To get the right answer key in 12 $\boxed{\div}$ 2 $\boxed{\div}$ 3 $\boxed{=}$

Notice that the calculator does not appear to do anything when the first function key is pressed, but in fact it puts the display into a hidden memory called the $y$ register. When the next function key is pressed the calculator carries out the first operation, combining the number in the $y$ register with the number on display ($x$). It then displays the answer (new $x$) and also stores the answer in the $y$

register. ('BODMAS' calculations do not always follows this system; this is explained later.) This is what happens when you work out $\dfrac{12}{2 \times 3}$:

| Key | 12 | $\div$ | 2 | $\div$ | 3 | $=$ |
|---|---|---|---|---|---|---|
| Display ($x$) | 12 | 12 | 2 | 6 | 3 | →2 |
| Hidden ($y$) | – | 12 | 12 | 6 | 6 | 2 |

Most scientific calculators follow the BODMAS (Brackets; Of; Divide; Multiply; Add; Subtract) rule, in as much as they save up additions and subtractions until any multiplications and divisions have been carried out. Mathematicians consider that the correct answer to $4 + 3 \times 2$ is $4 + 6 = 10$, not $7 \times 2 = 14$.

Key in: 4 $+$ 3 $\times$

If your display is still 3, then your calculator is following the BODMAS rule; if it shows 7 it is not going to give the correct answer.

A BODMAS calculator stores up the pending operations in a 'stack', for which it has extra hidden memories. The example $4 + 3 \times 2$ only needs one extra memory ($z$):

| Key | 4 | $+$ | 3 | $\times$ | 2 | $=$ |
|---|---|---|---|---|---|---|
| Display ($x$) | 4 | 4 | 3 | 3 | 2 | → 6 →10 |
| Stack ($y$) | – | +4 | +4 | 3 | 3 | +4 |
| Stack ($z$) | – | – | – | +4 | +4 | |

A similar effect is obtained by using bracket keys, e.g. $(4 + 3) \times 2 = 14$:

| Key | $($ | 4 | $+$ | 3 | $)$ | $\times$ | 2 | $=$ |
|---|---|---|---|---|---|---|---|---|
| Display ($x$) | – | 4 | 4 | 3 | 3 | 3 | 2 | →14 |
| Stack ($y$) | – | – | +4 | +3 | 7 | 7 | 7 | |
| Stack ($z$) | – | – | – | +4 | – | – | – | |

## 2 Constant function (k) (5)

Most calculators will remember the last operation and keep repeating it. Some do this always, others need two presses of the function key or the use of a k key. Try the following. One of them, at least, will probably work out $2 \times 2 \times 2 = 8$.

2 $\times$ $=$ $=$     2 $\times$ $\times$ $=$ $=$     2 $\times$ k $=$ $=$

Now try:

4 $\div$ 2 $=$ 6 $=$     4 $\div$ 2 k $=$ 6 $=$     4 $\div$ $\div$ 2 $=$ 6 $=$

## 3 Memory keys (5)

There are two kinds of memory; one is called a 'store', the other is called an 'accumulator'.
Store keys are usually marked MS or STO or $x \to$ M.
Accumulator keys are usually marked M+ or M+= or M− or M−= or ACC.
The memory content is recalled by a key usually marked RM or MR or REC.

**Examples**

| Key | 6 | MS | 8 | MR | 9 | MS | MR |
|---|---|---|---|---|---|---|---|
| Display | 6 | 6 | 8 | 6 | 9 | 9 | 9 |
| Store | 0 | 6 | 6 | 6 | 6 | 9 | 9 |

| Key | 6 | M+ | 8 | M+ | 9 | MR |
|---|---|---|---|---|---|---|
| Display | **6** | **6** | **8** | **8** | **9** | **14** |
| Store | 0 | 6 | 6 | 14 | 14 | 14 |

You have to be careful to note whether or not the memory is empty when using the M+ key. Usually the display shows **M** to remind you that there is something in the memory. There is no problem with the MS store key, because the memory is automatically emptied as soon as this key is pressed. There are various ways of cancelling memories. Consult your handbook.

## 4 Powers (5)

Powers like $2^3$ can be worked out using the constant facility explained in point 2, but scientific calculators usually have a $y^x$ key†, which is quicker if you have a large index, like $2^9$.

| Key | 2 | $\boxed{y^x}$ | 9 | $\boxed{=}$ |
|---|---|---|---|---|
| Display ($x$) | **2** | **2** | **9** ⌐→**512** |
| Store ($y$) | – | 2 | 2 ⌐ – |

## 5 Roots (5)

Use the $\sqrt{\ }$ key for square roots (and the $\sqrt[3]{\ }$ key for cube roots if you have one). For further roots you need either a $y^{\frac{1}{x}}$ key (sometimes marked $\sqrt[x]{y}$) or a $y^x$ and $\dfrac{1}{x}$ key (although it is possible use a 'trial and error' method that only uses basic functions). On TEXAS use INV $y^x$.

Remember that $8^{\frac{1}{2}}$ is an alternative way of writing $\sqrt{8}$, $8^{\frac{1}{3}} \equiv \sqrt[3]{8}$, and $8^{\frac{1}{4}} \equiv \sqrt[4]{8}$, so $y^{\frac{1}{x}} \equiv \sqrt[x]{y}$.

**Example** To find $\sqrt[4]{2}$.

Key: 2 $\boxed{y^{\frac{1}{x}}}$ 4 $\boxed{=}$ **or** 2 $\boxed{y^x}$ 4 $\boxed{\frac{1}{x}}$ $\boxed{=}$ **or** 2 $\boxed{INV}$ $\boxed{y^x}$ 4 $\boxed{=}$

## 6 Reciprocals (5)

The $\dfrac{1}{x}$ (or 1/x) key is the **reciprocal** key. The reciprocal of $x$ is the fraction $\dfrac{1}{x}$, usually changed to a decimal. The reciprocal of 4 is 0.25.

Reciprocals of fractions sometimes cause trouble to students, e.g. the reciprocal of $\frac{3}{4}$ is $\dfrac{1}{\frac{3}{4}}$. Think of this as $1 \div \frac{3}{4} \rightarrow 1 \times \frac{4}{3} = 1.\dot{3}$. Your calculator would need the key sequence 3 $\boxed{\div}$ 4 $\boxed{=}$ $\boxed{\frac{1}{x}}$.

Remember that a function key operates on the number in the display. Function keys like $x^2$, $\sqrt{\ }$, TAN, etc. operate as soon as they are pressed. Others, like ×, +, $y^x$, etc. wait until another function key or = is pressed before operating; this is because they combine the $x$ and $y$ registers.

To find the reciprocal of $\frac{3}{4}$ it would be wrong to key in 3 $\boxed{\div}$ 4 $\boxed{\frac{1}{x}}$ $\boxed{=}$. Why?

Reciprocals are 'self-inverses'. Try 4 $\boxed{\frac{1}{x}}$ $\boxed{\frac{1}{x}}$ $\boxed{\frac{1}{x}}$ $\boxed{\frac{1}{x}}$.

**See also** the notes on Trigonometry, and Percentages notes 6 and 8.

---

†Labelled $x^y$ on Casio calculators.

220

## GRAPHS

The number in brackets after each heading indicates the exercise in Book 5 which contains questions on the topic.

### 1 Co-ordinates (8)

In Figure R6:

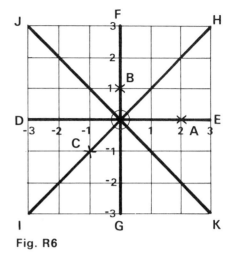

Fig. R6

Point A has co-ordinates (2, 0).
Point B has co-ordinates (0, 1).
Point C has co-ordinates (−1, −1).
Line DE is the x-axis. Its equation is $y = 0$.
Line FG is the y-axis. Its equation is $x = 0$.
The x-axis crosses the y-axis at the origin.
Line HI has the equation $y = x$. Each point on $y = x$ has its x-co-ordinate the same as its y-co-ordinate, e.g. (3, 3); (−2, −2); (1.5, 1.5).
Line JK has the equation $y = -x$. Each point on $y = -x$ has its y-co-ordinate equal to its x-co-ordinate times −1, e.g. (3, −3); (0, 0); (−2, 2).

### 2 Linear (straight-line) graphs (8)

All straight lines can be expressed in equation form as $y = mx + c$, though the three terms may be moved around, e.g. $y = 2x$, $y = 3$, $y = 2x + 3$, $x + y = 2$, $2y + 3x = 4$ and $x = 2 - 7y$ are all equations of straight-line graphs.

Linear graphs are drawn by one of the following methods.

#### (a) Plotting method for y + 2x = 3

Choose three values for x (including zero) and find y for each, e.g.:

If $x = 0$ then $y + 0 = 3 \rightarrow y = 3$. Plot (0, 3).
If $x = 2$ then $y + 4 = 3 \rightarrow y = -1$. Plot (2, −1).
If $x = -1$ then $y - 2 = 3 \rightarrow y = 5$. Plot (−1, 5).

See Figure R7.

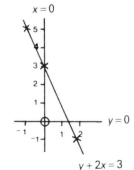

Fig. R7

#### (b) Slope/crossing (y = mx + c) method for y + 2x = 3

When the equation is expressed in the form $y = mx + c$ then c gives the crossing point on the y-axis (0, c) and m gives the slope (see Figures R8(a) and (b)).

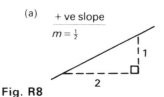
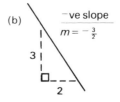

Fig. R8

221

To use this method for $y + 2x = 3$ we first rearrange the terms to change it to $y = -2x + 3$. We now know that $m = -2$ and $c = 3$. Start from 3 on the $y$-axis, then go down and across to give a slope of $-2$. See Figure R9.

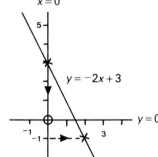

**Fig. R9**

See also Algebra, note 5(a), on the use of linear graphs to solve simultaneous equations.

## 3  Graph regions (8)

Figure R10 shows the line $y = -x + 2$.

For every point on this line the $y$-co-ordinate is equal to $-x + 2$, where $x$ is the $x$-co-ordinate of the point.

Above the line, $y$ is more than $-x + 2$.

Below the line, $y$ is less than $-x + 2$.

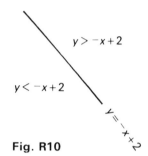

**Fig. R10**

Figure R11 shows the region

$\{(x, y): \quad x < 3 \; ; \; -x + 2 < y \leqslant x\}.$

to the left    above         below or on
of $x = 3$    $y = -x + 2$    $y = x$

Dotted lines are used when the region does not include the line.

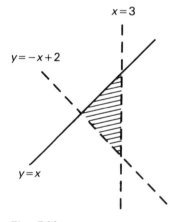

**Fig. R11**

## 4  Parabolas (8)

Equations like $y = x^2$, $y = x^2 + 3$ and $y = 2x^2$ give **parabolas** when drawn as graphs.

Sometimes the equation is given in function notation, e.g. $y = f(x)$ where $f(x): x \to x^2$. This has the same meaning as $y = x^2$.

To draw the graphs, plot values of $y$ for a series of values of $x$. (You are usually told which values of $x$ to use.) It is best to work out the values in a table.

**Example**  To draw the parabola $y = 2x^2 - 3$.

Values for $x$:

Working out: $\left\{\vphantom{\begin{array}{c}a\\b\end{array}}\right.$

Values for $y$

| $x$ | $-2$ | $-1$ | $0$ | $1$ | $2$ |
|---|---|---|---|---|---|
| $2x^2$ | 8 | 2 | 0 | 2 | 8 |
| $-3$ | $-3$ | $-3$ | $-3$ | $-3$ | $-3$ |
| $y$ | 5 | $-1$ | $-3$ | $-1$ | 5 |

$\left.\vphantom{\begin{array}{c}a\\b\end{array}}\right\}$ Add these two rows to find $y$.

The points $(-2, 5)$, $(-1, -1)$, etc. are now plotted and joined with a smooth continuous curve. See Figure R12.

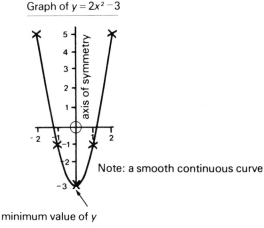

Graph of $y = 2x^2 - 3$

Note: a smooth continuous curve

minimum value of $y$

**Fig. R12**

## 5  Sketching parabolas (8)

(a) All graphs of the family $y = ax^2 + c$ are symmetrical about the $y$-axis.

(b) The value of $c$ gives the crossing point on the $y$-axis.

(c) The value of $a$ affects the width of the curve and which way up it is: the higher the value of $a$ the wider the curve becomes (using the same axes scales); if $a$ is negative then the parabola has its turning point at the top (see Figure R15).

(d) Always draw a parabola with your wrist 'inside the curve', the way that your hand pivots naturally.

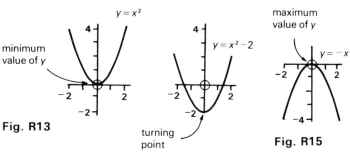

minimum value of $y$

$y = x^2$

**Fig. R13**

$y = x^2 - 2$

turning point

**Fig. R14**

maximum value of $y$

$y = -x^2$

**Fig. R15**

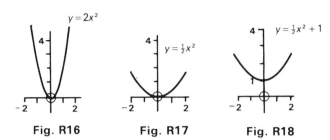

**Fig. R16**     **Fig. R17**     **Fig. R18**

## 6  Using parabolas to solve quadratic equations (8)

A quadratic equation is one involving $x^2$. A very simple quadratic equation is $x^2 = 1$. Unlike the equations you have met before, a quadratic equation may have two solutions. Both $x = 1$ and $x = -1$ make $x^2 = 1$ true. It may also have no solutions, like $x^2 + 1 = 0$.

**Example**   Figure R19 shows the graph of $y = x^2 - 3x + 1$.

To solve the equation $x^2 - 3x + 1 = 0$ (or $x^2 - 3x = -1$).

The parabola's equation, $y = x^2 - 3x + 1$, becomes the equation we have to solve, $x^2 - 3x + 1 = 0$, when $y = 0$. Therefore we find the solutions where the parabola crosses the line $y = 0$ (the $x$-axis). They are $x = 2.6$ and $x = 0.38$ approximately. (You often do not have exact answers to a quadratic equation. Sometimes there are no solutions, e.g. how can $x^2 + 1 = 0$?)

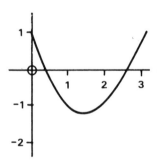

**Fig. R19**

**Example**   To solve $x^2 - 3x + 2 = 0$ using the graph of $y = x^2 - 3x + 1$ (Figure R19).

First we change the left-hand side of the given equation to make it the same as the graph equation; that is, we have to change $x^2 - 3x + 2$ into $x^2 - 3x + 1$. We do this by subtracting 1:

$$x^2 - 3x + 2 = 0 \xrightarrow{-1 \text{ from both sides}} x^2 - 3x + 1 = -1.$$

Now the solutions may be read where $y = -1$.

*Answer*: $x = 1$ and $x = 2$.

Check that $x^2 - 3x + 2 = 0$ when $x = 1$ and when $x = 2$.

## ALGEBRA

The number in brackets after each heading indicates the exercise in Book 5 which contains questions on the topic.

### 1   Basic algebraic notation (10)

When using letters to stand for numbers we do not need to write multiplication signs.

**Example**   $3 \times a \times b$ is usually written as $3ab$.

Note that $3 \times 4 \times 5$ can not be written as 345, and that a computer needs $3 * 4 * 5$ and $3 * a * b$.

When using letters to stand for numbers the division sign is usually replaced by writing the expression as a fraction.

**Example**   $3 \div a$ is usually written as $\dfrac{3}{a}$.

Note that $3 \div 4$ can also be written as $\dfrac{3}{4}$ or 3/4, and that a computer needs 3/4 for both $3 \div 4$ and $\frac{3}{4}$.

### 2   Substitution (10)

**Examples**   If $a = -2$, $b = -3$, and $c = 4$, then:

$$a + b = -2 + -3 \to -2 - 3 = -5$$

> **Note:** $-2 - 3$ can be thought of as 'down 2 then down another 3'. The two minuses do not make a plus here, as they are not multiplied.

$$bc = -3 \times 4 = -12$$

$$ab = -2 \times -3 = 6$$

$$\frac{c}{a} = \frac{4}{-2} = -2$$   **Note:** The same sign rules apply for division as for multiplication.

$$\frac{a}{b} = \frac{-2}{-3} = \frac{2}{3}$$

### 3   Brackets (11)

Any term written directly before a bracket multiplies each term in the bracket.

**Examples**   $2(4 + a) \to 8 + 2a$   Working: $2 \times 4 = 8$; $2 \times a = 2a$

> **Note: Read the $\to$ sign in this course as 'becomes'.**

$-2(4 + a) \to -8 - 2a$   Working: $-2 \times 4 = -8$; $-2 \times a = -2a$

$-2(4 - a) \to -8 + 2a$   Working: $-2 \times 4 = -8$; $-2 \times -a = +2a$

$-(4 + a) \to -4 - a$   Working: $-(4 + a) \Rightarrow -1(4 + a)$; $-1 \times 4 = -4$; $-1 \times a = -a$

> **Note: $\Rightarrow$ is the sign for 'implies' or 'means'.**

$a + 2(b - c) \to a + 2b - 2c$

$a - 2(b - c) \to a - 2b + 2c$

**R**

Note that a computer requires the ∗ (multiply) sign between the term and the bracket, e.g. $-2 * (4 - a)$.

## 4   One letter-term equations (12)

Equations with only one letter-term are nearly always solved (to find the value of the letter) most easily by the 'inspection' approach, not by using 'rules'.

**Examples**   If $b - 2 = 8$ then $b$ must be $\underline{10}$ (as $10 - 2 = 8$).

If $8 + c = 6$ then $c$ must be $\underline{-2}$ (as $8 + -2 = 6$).

If $7 - 2x = 8$ then $2x$ must be $-1$ (as $7 - -1 \rightarrow 7 + 1 = 8$)

so $x$ must be $\underline{-\frac{1}{2}}$ (as $2 \times -\frac{1}{2} = -1$).

If $3e = 2$ then $e$ must be $\frac{2}{3}$ (if 3 $e$'s make 2, then 1 $e$ must be a third of 2).

If $\dfrac{24}{1 - n} = 8$ then $1 - n$ must be 3 (as $24 \div 3 = 8$)

so $n$ must be $\underline{-2}$ (as $1 - -2 \rightarrow 1 + 2 = 3$).

If $4(2a - 7) = 12$ then $2a - 7$ must be 3 (as $4 \times 3 = 12$)

so $2a$ must be 10 (as $10 - 7 = 3$)

so $a$ must be $\underline{5}$ (as $2 \times 5 = 10$).

The above solutions can be written as follows:

$b - 2 = 8 \Rightarrow \underline{b = 10}$

$8 + c = 6 \Rightarrow \underline{c = -2}$

$7 - 2x = 8 \Rightarrow 2x = -1 \Rightarrow \underline{x = -\frac{1}{2}}$

$3e = 2 \Rightarrow \underline{e = \frac{2}{3}}$

$\dfrac{24}{1 - n} = 8 \Rightarrow 1 - n = 3 \Rightarrow \underline{n = -2}$

$4(2a - 7) = 12 \Rightarrow 2a - 7 = 3 \Rightarrow 2a = 10 \Rightarrow \underline{a = 5}$

## 5   Simultaneous equations (12)

When there are two unknown letters to be found you need two equations. For instance, $x + y = 8$ is true for an infinite number of pairs of values for $x$ and $y$. But if we also know that $x = y + 2$ then the only possible solution is $x = 5$ and $y = 3$.

Four methods are possible:

**One**   **Draw intersecting graphs.**

**Two**   **Substitute for one letter its value in the other equation.** This is best used when one of the equations is in the form $x =$ or $y =$. For example, $y = x - 6$ and $3y - 2x = 8$.

**Three**   **Add or subtract the equations to eliminate one of the letter-terms**, having multiplied as necessary to make one letter-term the same absolute value in both. ('Absolute' means 'ignoring the sign'; ABS on a BASIC computer.)

**Four**   **Use matrices.** This is shown in Matrices, Note 4.

**Method One**   **To solve simultaneously $y = 2x - 1$ and $y - x = 1$.**

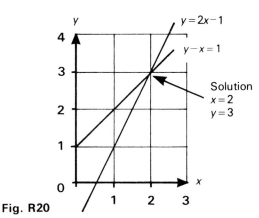

**Fig. R20**

**Method Two**   **To solve $x = 2$ and $2x + 2y = 11$ simultaneously.**

We can think of this as finding where the line $x = 2$ crosses the line $2x + 2y = 11$.
Substitute the value $x = 2$ into $2x + 2y = 11$, giving $4 + 2y = 11$.
Then $4 + 2y = 11 \rightarrow 2y = 7 \rightarrow y = 3\frac{1}{2}$.
Answer: $x = 2$, $y = 3\frac{1}{2}$ (The lines cross at $(2, 3\frac{1}{2})$.)

**To solve $y = x - 6$ and $x + y = 4$ simultaneously.**

Substitute the value $y = x - 6$ into $x + y = 4$, giving $x + (x - 6) = 4$.
Then $x + (x - 6) = 4 \rightarrow x + x - 6 = 4 \rightarrow 2x - 6 = 4 \rightarrow 2x = 10 \rightarrow x = 5$.
We know that $y = x - 6$, so if $x = 5$ then $y$ must be $-1$.
Answer: $x = 5$, $y = -1$.

**To solve $x = 2y - 1$ and $y + 2x = 2$ by substitution.**

Substitute for $x$, giving $y + 2(2y - 1) = 2$.
$y + 2(2y - 1) = 2 \rightarrow y + 4y - 2 = 2 \rightarrow 5y - 2 = 2 \rightarrow 5y = 4 \rightarrow y = \frac{4}{5}$.
Now as we know that $x = 2y - 1$, then $x = \frac{8}{5} - 1 = \frac{3}{5}$.
Answer: $x = \frac{3}{5}$, $y = \frac{4}{5}$.

**Method Three**   **To find the values of $x$ and $y$ that satisfy both $x + 3y = 9$ and $x - 2y = -1$.**

$$x + 3y = \phantom{-}9$$
$$\underline{x - 2y = -1} \quad \text{SUB}$$
$$5y = 10$$
$$\underline{\underline{y = 2}}$$

Substitute $y = 2$
into $x + 3y = 9$,
giving $x + 6 = 9$,
so $\underline{x = 3}$.

Check both equations are true
for $x = 3$, $y = 2$:
$3 + 6 = 9$;   $3 - 4 = -1$.

**Note:** By subtracting, the $x$ terms
have been eliminated. If the
two given equations are
true, then the result of the
subtraction is true.

Compare:   $2 + 3 = 5$
$$\underline{1 + 2 = 3} \quad \text{SUB}$$
$$1 + 1 = 2$$

When subtracting,
$+3y - {-2y} \rightarrow +3y + 2y = 5y$
and $9 - {-1} \rightarrow 9 + 1 = 10$.

227

**R**

**Method Three**

*contd*   **To solve $3x + 5y = 21$ and $7x - 2y = 8$ simultaneously.**

$$3x + 5y = 21 \xrightarrow{\times 2} 6x + 10y = 42$$
$$7x - 2y = 8 \xrightarrow{\times 5} \underline{35x - 10y = 40} \quad \text{ADD}$$
$$41x \qquad\quad = 82$$
$$\underline{x = \ 2}$$

Substitute $x = 2$ into $3x + 5y = 21 \to 6 + 5y = 21 \to 5y = 15 \to \underline{\underline{y = 3}}$.

Check this for yourself.

## 6   Equations with two letter-terms (12)

In solving equations like $3n - 2 = 5 + 2n$ we cannot use the inspection approach (see note 4) until one of the two letter-terms has been removed.

We remove one letter-term by adding to or subtracting from both sides of the equation a term which reduces it to zero, as in the following examples.

**Examples**   (a) $3n - 2 = 5 + 2n \xrightarrow{-2n \text{ on both sides}} 3n - 2 - 2n = 5 + 2n - 2n \to n - 2 = 5$

(b) $5 - 2w = 2 + 3w \xrightarrow{+2w \text{ on both sides}} 5 - 2w + 2w = 2 + 3w + 2w$
$$\to 5 = 2 + 5w$$

(c) $4 - 3x = 5 - 2x \xrightarrow{+3x \text{ on both sides}} 4 - 3x + 3x = 5 - 2x + 3x \to 4 = 5 + x$

(d) $4 - 3z = 5 + 2z \xrightarrow{+3z \text{ on both sides}} 4 - 3z + 3z = 5 + 2z + 3z \to 4 = 5 + 5z$

It does not really matter which letter-term you reduce to zero, but the remainder of the solution is usually easier if you leave a positive letter-term, as we did in the above examples. This can be remembered by the following rule, if you like rules!

**Remove the term with the smaller coefficient.**

The 'coefficient' is the number in front of it. Note that in example (c), $-3$ is smaller than $-2$.

**Note:** Because we perform the same operation on each side of the equation it remains true or 'in balance'. We can see this in number statements:

$$3 + 2 = 5 \xrightarrow{-2 \text{ on both sides}} 3 + 2 - 2 = 5 - 2 \to 3 = 5 - 2$$

$$3 - 2 = 1 \xrightarrow{+2 \text{ on both sides}} 3 - 2 + 2 = 1 + 2 \to 3 = 3$$

**Examples**   Solve $6n + 7 = 4n + 13$.
$$6n + 7 = 4n + 13 \xrightarrow{-4n} 2n + 7 = 13 \Rightarrow 2n = 6 \Rightarrow \underline{n = 3}$$

Solve $7 - 5x = 4x - 2$.
$$7 - 5x = 4x - 2 \xrightarrow{+5x} 7 = 9x - 2 \Rightarrow 9x = 9 \Rightarrow \underline{x = 1}$$

Solve $3(x + 2) = 2(x - 1)$.
$$3(x + 2) = 2(x - 1) \to 3x + 6 = 2x - 2 \xrightarrow{-2x} x + 6 = -2 \Rightarrow \underline{x = -8}$$

If necessary, 'collect terms' on each side of the equation before beginning to solve it.

228

**Example**  Solve $3(a - 2) - 1 = 4(a + 4) + 2a - 2$.

First multiply out the brackets and collect like terms:
$3(a - 2) - 1 = 4(a + 4) + 2a - 2 \rightarrow 3a - 6 - 1 = 4a + 16 + 2a - 2$
$$\rightarrow 3a - 7 = 6a + 14.$$
Now solve the equation:
$3a - 7 = 6a + 14 \xrightarrow{-3a} -7 = 3a + 14 \Rightarrow 3a = -21 \Rightarrow \underline{\underline{a = -7}}$

## 7  How to transpose formulae ('change of subject') (10)

$C = \pi d$ is the formula for the circumference of a circle; $C$ is the **subject**.

When the formula is 'transposed', the subject is changed. The circumference formula can be transposed to make $d$ the subject, giving $d = \dfrac{C}{\pi}$.

If the new subject-letter appears only once in the formula, then the flow-diagram method illustrated below may be used. If the new subject-letter appears more than once, you have to use the 'balance' or 'change sides' algebraic method.

**Examples**  (a) $u = s - t$; new subject $s$

$s \xrightarrow{-t} s - t$
$u + t \xleftarrow{+t} u \quad$ so $s = u + t$

(b) $u = s - t$; new subject $t$

$t \xrightarrow{\text{taken from } s} s - t$
$s - u \xleftarrow{\text{taken from } s} u \quad$ so $t = s - u$

Remember that 'taken from' does not change.

(c) $p = sr$; new subject $s$

$s \xrightarrow{\times r} sr$
$\dfrac{p}{r} \xleftarrow{\div r} p \quad$ so $= \dfrac{p}{r}$

(d) $u = sr - t$; new subject $s$

$s \xrightarrow{\times r} sr \xrightarrow{-t} sr - t$
$\dfrac{u + t}{r} \xleftarrow{\div r} u + t \xleftarrow{+t} u \quad$ so $s = \dfrac{u + t}{r}$

(e) $t = 2\pi \sqrt{\dfrac{l}{g}}$; new subject $g$

$g \xrightarrow{\text{divided into } l} \dfrac{l}{g} \xrightarrow{\surd} \sqrt{\dfrac{l}{g}} \xrightarrow{\times 2\pi} 2\pi \sqrt{\dfrac{l}{g}}$

$\dfrac{l}{\left(\dfrac{t}{2\pi}\right)^2} \xleftarrow{\text{divided into } l} \left(\dfrac{t}{2\pi}\right)^2 \xleftarrow{(\ )^2} \dfrac{t}{2\pi} \xleftarrow{\div 2\pi} t$

so $t = \dfrac{l}{\left(\dfrac{t}{2\pi}\right)^2} = l \div \dfrac{t^2}{4\pi^2} = l \times \dfrac{4\pi^2}{t^2} = \dfrac{4\pi^2 l}{t^2}$

(f) $f = 2uf - v$; new subject $f$

The flow method cannot be used. Bring both $f$ terms to the same side:
$f - 2uf = -v$
Take out the $f$ as a common factor:
$f(1 - 2u) = -v$
Then $f = \dfrac{-v}{1 - 2u}$
If you multiply the top and bottom of the fraction by $-1$ you simplify the answer:
$f = \dfrac{v}{2u - 1}$.

## 8  Indices (11)

$a^2$ is shorthand for $a \times a$.
$b^3$ is shorthand for $b \times b \times b$.
$3a^2$ means $3 \times a^2$, so that if $a = 4$, $3a^2 \to 3 \times 16 = 48$.

$3a^2b^3 \times 2ab^4 \to 6a^3b^7$. You may use the rule 'Add the indices when multiplying powers of the same letter', or think of the terms written out in full:

$3a^2b^3 \times 2ab^4 \to 3 \times a \times a \times b \times b \times b \times 2 \times a \times b \times b \times b \times b$

$3 \times 2$ is 6; the three $a$'s multiply together to give $a^3$; the seven $b$'s multiply together to give $b^7$.

**Example**   To simplify $4a^5b^3c \div 8a^2bc^3$.

$$\frac{4a^5b^3c}{8a^2bc^3} \to \frac{^1\cancel{4} \times \cancel{a} \times \cancel{a} \times a \times a \times a \times \cancel{b} \times b \times b \times \cancel{c}}{_2\cancel{8} \times \cancel{a} \times \cancel{a} \times \cancel{b} \times \cancel{c} \times c \times c}$$

Having cancelled as much as possible, this leaves $\dfrac{a^3b^2}{2c^2}$.

**Or**: Using the 'subtract indices' rule:

$$\frac{4a^5b^3c}{8a^2bc^3} \to \frac{1a^{5-2}b^{3-1}}{2c^{3-1}} \to \frac{a^3b^2}{2c^2}$$

**Note**: The $c$ term is at the bottom in the answer because the bigger power of $c$ ($c^3$) was at the bottom to start with.

**Example**   $c^3(c^4 + 2) \to c^7 + 2c^3$

## 9  Special indices (11)

**(a)  The value of $a^0$**

$a^x \div a^x$ must equal 1, but using the subtraction of indices rule, $a^x \div a^x \to a^{x-x} = a^0$. Hence the fact that $a^0 = 1$.

**(b)  Fractional indices**

$x^{\frac{1}{2}}$ is another way of writing $\sqrt{x}$ because $x^{\frac{1}{2}} \times x^{\frac{1}{2}} = x^{\frac{1}{2}+\frac{1}{2}} = x$.
Similarly $x^{\frac{1}{3}} \times x^{\frac{1}{3}} \times x^{\frac{1}{3}} = x$, so $x^{\frac{1}{3}}$ is the cube root of $x$, $\sqrt[3]{x}$.

**Learn:**   $x^{\frac{1}{n}}$ **is the same as** $\sqrt[n]{x}$.

**Example**   Simplify $8^{\frac{2}{3}}$.

As $8^2$ means '8 squared', and $8^{\frac{1}{3}}$ means 'the cube root of 8', it follows that $8^{\frac{2}{3}}$ means the cube root of 8 squared, that is, $2^2 = 4$.

Always find the root first, then the power; this keeps the numbers smaller.

**(c)  Combining indices**

**Example**   $(2a^2)^3 \to 2a^2 \times 2a^2 \times 2a^2 \to 8a^6$

**Learn:**   $(x^m)^n \to x^{mn}$

## (d) Negative indices

By subtracting indices, $a^2 \div a^4 = a^{-2}$.

By cancelling, $a^2 \div a^4 \rightarrow \dfrac{a^2}{a^4} \rightarrow \dfrac{1}{a^2}$

Therefore $a^{-2} = \dfrac{1}{a^2}$.

Similarly $a^{-1} = \dfrac{1}{a}$ and $49^{-\frac{1}{2}} = \dfrac{1}{\sqrt{49}} = \frac{1}{7}$.

**Learn:** $x^{-n}$ **is the same as** $\dfrac{1}{x^n}$.

## Summary

$a^0 = 1$ for all values of $a$ (except 0??!)

$a^{\frac{1}{n}} = \sqrt[n]{a}$

$a^{-n} = \dfrac{1}{a^n}$

**Example** Simplify $27^{-\frac{2}{3}}$.

The $-$ means one over, giving $\dfrac{1}{27^{\frac{2}{3}}}$.

The third means the cube root, giving $\dfrac{1}{3^2}$.

The two means squared, giving the final answer $\frac{1}{9}$.

## 10 Expansion of quadratic brackets (11)

**Examples** $(x + 2)(x + 3) \rightarrow x^2 + 3x + 2x + 6 \rightarrow x^2 + 5x + 6$

$(m - 3)(m + 2) \rightarrow m^2 + 2m - 3m - 6 \rightarrow m^2 - m - 6$

**Note:** The middle step should be done mentally when you have had some practice.

**Example** $(4 + x)(3 - x) \rightarrow 12 - 4x + 3x - x^2 \rightarrow 12 - x - x^2$

**Note:** Do not attempt to change the order of the given terms.

## 11 Factorisation (11)

### (a) Common factors

If all the terms in an expression have a common factor then the common factor may be 'taken out' and written in front of a bracket.

**Examples** $3 + 6a \rightarrow 3(1 + 2a)$

$2a - ab \rightarrow a(2 - b)$

$3ax^2 + ax \rightarrow ax(3x + 1)$

Make sure that you take out the *highest* common factor.

**Example**  To factorise $3x - 3y + ax - ay$.

$3x - 3y + ax - ay \rightarrow 3(x - y) + a(x - y)$
Note that $(x - y)$ is itself now a common factor and may be 'taken out':
$3(x - y) + a(x - y) \rightarrow (x - y)(3 + a)$

Multiply $(x - y)(3 + a)$ to check the answer.

**Example** $\dfrac{6x + 6}{2xy + 2y} \rightarrow \dfrac{3\cancel{(2x + 2)}}{y\cancel{(2x + 2)}} \rightarrow \dfrac{3}{y}$

### (b) Differences of two squares

If two terms in an expression are both squares and are connected by a minus, then they may be split into 'sum times difference'.

**Examples**  $a^2 - 16 \rightarrow (a + 4)(a - 4)$

$4x^2 - 25 \rightarrow (2x + 5)(2x - 5)$

$2a^2 - 18 \rightarrow 2(a^2 - 9) \rightarrow 2(a + 3)(a - 3)$

This can be useful in arithmetic.

**Examples**  $54^2 - 46^2 \rightarrow (54 + 46)(54 - 46) \rightarrow 100 \times 8 = 800$

Area of an annulus (e.g. a washer) is $\pi R^2 - \pi r^2$.
$\pi R^2 - \pi r^2 \rightarrow \pi(R^2 - r^2) \rightarrow \pi(R + r)(R - r)$

### (c) Quadratics

$(x + 4)(x + 3) \rightarrow x^2 + 3x + 4x + 12 \rightarrow x^2 + 7x + 12$

By reversing this we can factorise a quadratic expression.

By no means will all quadratic expressions factorise into two brackets, but an examiner will not ask you to factorise one that will not.

There is no 'golden rule' which will give you the correct answer first time, but the following will help:

**If the last sign is** + then both brackets have the sign of the middle term. In checking with 'FOIL' (First, Outer, Inner, Last), O + I gives the middle term.

**Examples**  $x^2 + 10x + 21 \rightarrow (x + 3)(x + 7)$
  Check: $+7x + 3x \rightarrow 10x$
  $+3 \times +7 \rightarrow +21$

  $x^2 - 10x + 21 \rightarrow (x - 3)(x - 7)$
  Check: $-7x - 3x \rightarrow -10x$
  $-3 \times -7 \rightarrow +21$

**If the last sign is** − then one bracket is + and the other is −, and you must be very careful to get the correct sign with each number, for example $(2x + 1)(x - 2)$ gives $2x^2 - 3x - 2$, whilst $(2x - 1)(x + 2)$ gives $2x^2 + 3x - 2$.

232

**Examples**   $x^2 + 4x - 12 \rightarrow (x + 6)(x - 2)$
Check: $-2x + 6x \rightarrow +4x$
$+6 \times -2 \rightarrow -12$

$x^2 - 4x - 12 \rightarrow (x - 6)(x + 2)$
Check: $+2x - 6x \rightarrow -4x$
$-6 \times +2 \rightarrow -12$

If there are a lot of factors to choose from, start with the pair closest together and work upwards, e.g. for 12 try $3 \times 4$, then $2 \times 6$, then $1 \times 12$.

## 12   Quadratic equations (12)

If two factors multiply to give zero, one or both of them must be zero.

**Example**   If $x(x - 4) = 0$ then either $x = 0$ or $x - 4 = 0$.
Hence $x(x - 4) = 0$ when $x = 0$ and when $x = 4$.

**Example**   If $(x - 2)(x + 4) = 0$ then either $x - 2 = 0$ or $x + 4 = 0$.
Hence $(x - 2)(x + 4) = 0$ when $x = 2$ and when $x = -4$.

**Example**   If $(2x - 7)(4x + 2) = 0$ then either $2x - 7 = 0$ or $4x + 2 = 0$.
If $2x - 7 = 0$ then $2x = 7$, so $x = 3\frac{1}{2}$ is one solution.
If $4x + 2 = 0$ then $4x = -2$, so $x = -\frac{1}{2}$ is the other solution.

**Example**   Solve $x^2 - 3x + 2 = 0$.

$x^2 - 3x + 2 = 0 \rightarrow (x - 2)(x - 1) = 0$
$\therefore x = 2$ and $x = 1$ are the solutions.

**Example**   Solve $x^2 - 4x = 0$.

Quadratics with no constant term are easy to factorise by taking out the common factor. Make a special point of remembering this.

$x^2 - 4x = 0 \rightarrow x(x - 4) = 0$
$\therefore x = 0$ and $x = 4$ are solutions.

The solutions of the equation $ax^2 + bx + c = 0$ are called its **roots**. These roots are usually referred to as $\alpha$ (alpha) and $\beta$ (beta).

$$\alpha + \beta = -\frac{b}{a} \quad \text{and} \quad \alpha\beta = \frac{c}{a}$$

These two facts can be used to check solutions to a quadratic equation.

**Example**   Find the roots of $2x^2 + 3x - 9 = 0$.

$2x^2 + 3x - 9 = 0 \rightarrow (2x - 3)(x + 3) = 0$

The roots are $x = 1\frac{1}{2}$ and $x = -3$.

Check by letting $\alpha = 1\frac{1}{2}$ and $\beta = -3$, and, knowing that $a = 2$, $b = 3$ and $c = -9$:

$\alpha + \beta = -\dfrac{b}{a} \rightarrow 1\frac{1}{2} - 3 = -\frac{3}{2}$ which is correct, and

$\alpha\beta = \dfrac{c}{a} \rightarrow 1\frac{1}{2} \times -3 = -\frac{9}{2}$ which is also correct.

Many quadratic equations will not factorise; the following two algebraic methods may then be used.

## Method One   Completing the square

**Example**   Solve $x^2 + 5x - 1 = 0$.

$$x^2 + 5x - 1 = 0 \rightarrow \left(x + \frac{5}{2}\right)^2 - \frac{25}{4} - 1 = 0$$

$$\left[\text{Note: } \left(x + \frac{5}{2}\right)\left(x + \frac{5}{2}\right) = x^2 + 5x + \frac{25}{4}\right]$$

$$\rightarrow \left(x + \frac{5}{2}\right)^2 - \frac{29}{4} = 0$$

$$\rightarrow \left(x + \frac{5}{2}\right)^2 = \frac{29}{4} = 7.25$$

$$\rightarrow x + 2.5 = \sqrt{7.25}$$

$$\rightarrow x + 2.5 \simeq \pm 2.69 \text{ [plus or minus 2.69]}$$

So $x \simeq -2.5 + 2.69 = \underline{0.19}$

or $x \simeq -2.5 - 2.69 = \underline{-5.19}$

**Example**   Solve $3x^2 - 2x - 2 = 0$.

$$3x^2 - 2x - 2 = 0 \xrightarrow{\div \text{ all by } 3} x^2 - \tfrac{2}{3}x - \tfrac{2}{3} = 0 \qquad \text{Note: We divide by 3 to reduce the}$$
$$\rightarrow (x - \tfrac{1}{3})^2 - \tfrac{1}{9} - \tfrac{2}{3} = 0 \qquad\qquad\qquad\qquad \text{coefficient of } x^2 \text{ to unity.}$$
$$\rightarrow (x - \tfrac{1}{3})^2 - \tfrac{7}{9} = 0$$
$$\rightarrow (x - \tfrac{1}{3})^2 = \tfrac{7}{9}$$
$$\rightarrow x - 0.\dot{3} = \sqrt{0.\dot{7}}$$
$$\rightarrow x - 0.\dot{3} \simeq \pm 0.882$$

Either $x \simeq 0.\dot{3} + 0.882 \simeq \underline{1.22}$

or $x \simeq 0.\dot{3} - 0.882 \simeq \underline{-0.55}$

## Method Two   The Quadratic Equation Formula

The formula is obtained by applying the completion of the square method to the general quadratic equation $ax^2 + bx + c = 0$. Your teacher will illustrate this.

$$x = \frac{-b \pm \sqrt{b^2 - 4ac}}{2a}$$

**Learn:** 'x equals minus $b$ plus or minus the square root of $b$ squared minus four $ac$, **all** divided by two $a$.'

**Example**   Solve $x^2 + 5x - 1 = 0$.

$$a = 1 \qquad b = 5 \qquad c = -1$$
$$x = \frac{-5 \pm \sqrt{25 + 4}}{2} = \frac{-5 \pm \sqrt{29}}{2}$$
$$x \simeq \frac{-5 \pm 5.385}{2}$$

Solutions are $x \simeq \underline{0.19}$ and $x \simeq \underline{-5.19}$

**Example**  Solve $3x^2 - 2x - 2 = 0$.

$a = 3 \qquad b = -2 \qquad c = -2$

$x = \dfrac{+2 \pm \sqrt{4 + 24}}{6} = \dfrac{2 \pm \sqrt{28}}{6}$

$x \simeq \dfrac{2 \pm 5.29}{6}$

Solutions are $x \simeq 1.22$ and $x \simeq -0.55$

## 13  Problems (12)

Many problem questions are best answered by letting the required answer be a letter ($x$ is traditional), then forming an equation which can be solved to find $x$.

**Example**  The length of a rectangle is 5 cm more than its breadth. If its area is 24 cm² find its dimensions.

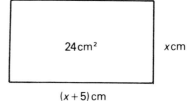

24 cm²    $x$ cm

$(x + 5)$ cm

Let its breadth be $x$ cm.
Then its breadth is $x + 5$ cm.
Area of rectangle = length × breadth
so $x(x + 5) = 24 \rightarrow x^2 + 5x = 24 \rightarrow x^2 + 5x - 24 = 0 \rightarrow (x - 3)(x + 8) = 0$
∴ $x = 3$ or $x = -8$.
$x$ cannot be $-8$, so the only solution is $x = 3$, making the rectangle of breadth 3 cm and length 8 cm.

## 14  Fractional equations (12)

**Example**  Solve $\dfrac{x^2}{2} - x - \dfrac{3}{4} = 0$.

First remove the fractions by multiplying every term by 4, which is the common denominator.
As $4 \times \dfrac{x^2}{2} \rightarrow 2x^2$, and $4 \times \dfrac{3}{4} \rightarrow 3$, then the equation becomes:
$2x^2 - 4x - 3 = 0$.
This can now be solved as in note 12.

## 15  Inequalities (12)

Inequalities can be solved by treating them as equations (but see the note following the example).

**Example**  Find the range of values of $x$ if $2x - 3 < 15 - 3x$.

$2x - 3 < 15 - 3x \xrightarrow{\;+3x \text{ on both sides}\;} 5x - 3 < 15$

If $5x - 3 = 15$, then $5x = 18$, giving $x = \dfrac{18}{5} = 3\frac{3}{5}$.

As $5x - 3 < 15$, then the answer is $x < 3\frac{3}{5}$.

235

**Note:** An inequality statement is reversed if you multiply or divide both sides by a negative amount. Remember that the letter itself may be negative.

For the equation $-3x = 6$:

$$-3x = 6 \xrightarrow{\times \text{ both sides by } -1} 3x = -6$$

Both equations are true when $x = -2$.

BUT for the inequality $-3x \geqslant 6$ the solution is NOT $x \geqslant -2$ (e.g. when $x = 4$, $-3x$ is $-12$, which is not more than 6).

You have to reverse the inequality sign:

so $-3x \geqslant 6 \xrightarrow{\div \text{ both sides by } -3} x \leqslant -2$

or $-3x \geqslant 6 \xrightarrow{\times \text{ both sides by } -1} 3x \leqslant -6 \rightarrow x \leqslant -2$.

Inequalities arise in graphical work on regions, see Graphs, Note 3.

The topic of Linear Programming involves inequalities and graphical regions; your teacher will give you examples if you have to study this topic.

## 16 Functions and mappings (12)

The mapping $f : x \rightarrow (x + 1)^2$ is read 'A function of $x$ is such that $x$ becomes $(x + 1)^2$.'

It may also be written $f(x) = (x + 1)^2$.

For the above mapping, $f(3) = (3 + 1)^2 = 16$ and $f(-1) = (-1 + 1)^2 = 0$.

$\{16, 0\}$ is called the *image* of $\{3, -1\}$ (the *object*) under the function f.

### (a) Combining functions

If $f(x) = (x + 1)^2$ and $g(x) = (x - 2)^2$ then $fg(x)$ means first apply function g to $x$, then apply function f to the answer.

Note the order, g first then f. This is very important.

For the given functions, $g(3) = (3 - 2)^2 = 1$ so $fg(3) = f(1) = (1 + 1)^2 = 4$.

Similarly, $gf(3) = g(16) = 196$. Check this.

### (b) Inverse function

The inverse of a function maps the image back to the object. It is written using the index $-1$.

If $f : x \rightarrow x + 2$ then $f^{-1} : x \rightarrow x - 2$.

If $g : x \rightarrow \dfrac{2}{x}$ then $g^{-1} : x \rightarrow \dfrac{2}{x}$ (this is a 'self-inverse').

You may check the inverse by substituting a number for $x$. In the above, $f(6) = 8$ and $f^{-1}(8) = 6$; $g(4) = \frac{1}{2}$ and $g(\frac{1}{2}) = 2 \div \frac{1}{2} = 4$.

## 17 Variation (13)

### (a) Direct variation

When a quantity $y$ is directly proportional to another quantity $x$ (written $y \propto x$) then $y = kx$, where $k$ is a constant. We also say that $y$ 'varies directly as' $x$.

236

A simple example is the number of 10p's you have ($n$) and their value ($p$ pence). If $n$ doubles then $p$ doubles; if $n$ trebles then $p$ trebles, and so on. Therefore $p$ is directly proportional to $n$. We can write $p \propto n$ and $p = kn$. In this case we know that $k = 10$.

Slightly more difficult to understand is that the area of a circle varies directly as the square of the radius. We can write $A \propto r^2$ and $A = kr^2$. In this case we know that $k = \pi$. (Note that the area varies directly as the *square* of the radius, not directly as the radius. If you double the radius the area increases *four* times.)

Many laws of science involve direct variation,
e.g. Hooke's law for a spring: extension $\propto$ load
Ohm's law for a conductor: voltage $\propto$ current
Snell's law of refraction: $\sin i \propto \sin r$.

## (b) Inverse variation

$$\text{Time} = \frac{\text{distance}}{\text{speed}} \rightarrow t = \frac{d}{s}$$

If the distance travelled is constant, then $t \propto \dfrac{1}{s}$; $t$ is 'inversely proportional' to $s$. If you double the speed, then you halve the time taken.

If the area ($A$) of a rectangle is constant, then the length ($l$) is inversely proportional to the width ($w$):

$$A = lw \rightarrow l = \frac{A}{w} \rightarrow l \propto \frac{1}{w} \text{ when } A \text{ is constant.}$$

Say the area is $36 \text{ cm}^2$. If the length is $9 \text{ cm}$ then the width is $4 \text{ cm}$. If the width doubles, to $8 \text{ cm}$, then the length must halve, to $4.5 \text{ cm}$.

## (c) Joint variation

Often one variable depends on several others.

The volume of a cylinder depends on both its base radius and its height, as $V = \pi r^2 h$. We say that $V$ 'varies jointly as the square of the radius and the height'. (The word 'jointly' is often missed out.)

The volume ($V$) of a given mass of gas varies directly as the temperature ($T$) and inversely as the pressure ($P$). Note that the 'and' does not imply 'add' here.

$$V \propto \frac{T}{P} \rightarrow V = \frac{kT}{P}$$

If the pressure increases then the volume decreases. If the temperature increases then the volume also increases.

Many other laws of science involve joint variation,
e.g. in electrolysis: mass $\propto$ (current $\times$ time)
in thermal and electrical conductivity: conductivity $\propto$ (radius)$^2$/time

**Example** $p$ varies as $t$ squared and inversely as the cube root of $w$.
$p = 1$ when $t = 1$ and $w = 8$.
(a) Find $p$ when $t = 2$ and $w = 1$.
(b) State how $w$ varies with $p$ and $t$.

Variation statement: $p \propto \dfrac{t^2}{\sqrt[3]{w}}$

Equation with constant $k$: $\quad p = \dfrac{kt^2}{\sqrt[3]{w}}$

(a) Substitution to find $k$: $\quad 1 = \dfrac{k \times 1^2}{\sqrt[3]{8}} \rightarrow 1 = \dfrac{k}{2} \rightarrow k = 2$

Equation with $k$ known: $\quad p = \dfrac{2t^2}{\sqrt[3]{w}}$

Substitution for $t$ and $w$: $\quad p = \dfrac{2 \times 2^2}{\sqrt[3]{1}} = 8$

(b) $p = \dfrac{kt^2}{\sqrt[3]{w}}$; change subject to $w$:

$$w \xrightarrow{\;\sqrt[3]{\;}\;} \sqrt[3]{w} \xrightarrow{\text{divided into } kt^2} \dfrac{kt^2}{\sqrt[3]{w}}$$

$$\left(\dfrac{kt^2}{p}\right)^3 \xleftarrow{\;(\;)^3\;} \dfrac{kt^2}{p} \xleftarrow{\text{divided into } kt^2} p$$

$$\text{so } w = \left(\dfrac{kt^2}{p}\right)^3 = \dfrac{k^3 t^6}{p^3}, \text{ so } w \propto \dfrac{t^6}{p^3}$$

## GEOMETRY

The number in brackets after each heading indicates the exercise in Book 5 which contains questions on the topic.

## 1  Straight-line and parallel-line angles (14)

In Figure R22 angle $a$ is **acute**
angle $b$ is **obtuse**
angle $r$ is **reflex**.

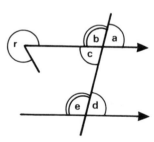

$a + b = 180°$   (**Adjacent ∠s on a straight line**)

$a = c$   (**Vertically opposite ∠s**)

$a = d$   (**Corresponding ∠s**)

$c = d$   (**Alternate ∠s**)

$c + e = 180°$   (**Allied ∠s**) [Also known as Interior ∠s]

**Fig. R22**

Hints: Adjacent ⇒ next-door
Corresponding ⇒ in the same position
Alternate ⇒ on opposite sides (Z angles)
Allied ⇒ joined together

Angles that add up to 180° are said to be **supplementary**.

## 2  Construction methods (18)

Figure R23 shows the compass construction for a 60° angle.

Figure R24 shows the way to bisect an angle.

These two constructions can be combined to draw many other angles, e.g. 30° by bisecting 60°.

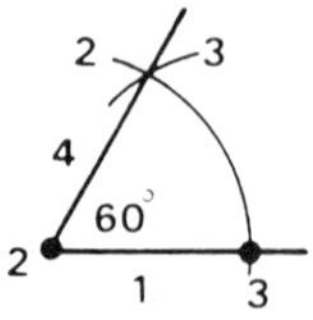

**Fig. R23**

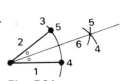

**Fig. R24**

Figures R25(a) and R25(b) show two methods to construct a right angle. The first combines a 60° and a 30° angle; the second bisects a 180° angle.

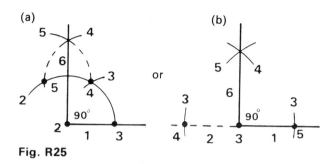

Fig. R25

Figures R26 to R32 show other constructions often required at a 16+ examination.

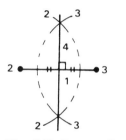

**Fig. R26  Perpendicular bisector**

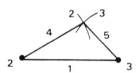

**Fig. R27  Δ given 3 sides**

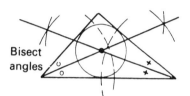

**Fig. R28  Incircle of Δ**

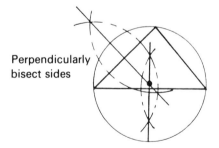

**Fig. R29  Circumcircle of Δ**

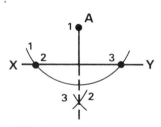

**Fig. R30  Dropping a perpendicular**

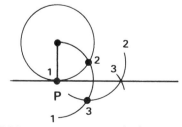

**Fig. R31a  Tangent to a circle**

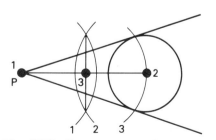

**Fig. R31b  Two tangents from a point**

239

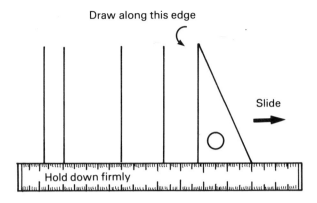

Draw along this edge

Slide

Hold down firmly

**Fig. R32  Using a set-square and a straight edge to draw parallel lines**

## 3  Names and properties of special quadrilaterals (14)

| Name | Sides | Angles | Diagonals |
|------|-------|--------|-----------|
| **Trapezium** | 1 pr // | – | – |
| **Isosceles trapezium** | 1 pr // <br> 1 pr non-// equal | 2 equal prs | equal |
| **Kite** | 2 adjacent equal prs | 1 equal pr | one bisected, cross at 90° |
| **Parallelogram** | 2 prs equal and // | opposites equal | bisect each other |
| **Rhombus** | 4 equal | opposites equal | bisect at 90° |
| **Rectangle** | as parallelogram | all 90° | equal |
| **Square** | as rhombus | all 90° | equal, cross at 90° |

// = parallel

## 4  Similar triangles (15)

**Two shapes are similar when one is an exact enlargement of the other.**

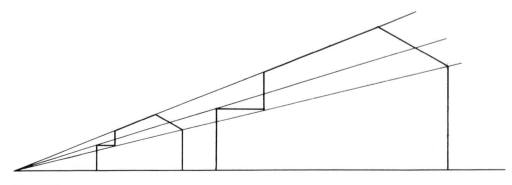

**Fig. R33**

When two shapes are similar, their corresponding (in the same position) sides are in the same ratio, and their angles are the same sizes. For a triangle, and only for a triangle, it is sufficient to know *one* of these two facts to know that the shapes are similar. In Figure R34 the two shapes have angles of the same sizes, but they are not similar. In Figure R35 the two shapes have their sides in the same ratio (2:1) but they are not similar.

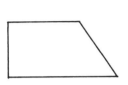 

**Fig. R34**

**Fig. R35**

The triangles in Figure R36 are similar because their angles are the same sizes. By writing the equal angles over each other, $\begin{smallmatrix} A & B & C \\ D & E & F \end{smallmatrix}$, then covering up one column at a time we obtain the ratio of the sides:

$$\frac{BC}{EF} = \frac{AC}{DF} = \frac{AB}{DE}.$$

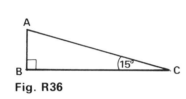

**Fig. R36**

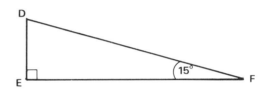

**Example**  Calculate the unknown lengths in Figure R37.

$\Delta s \begin{smallmatrix} G & H & I \\ J & K & L \end{smallmatrix}$ are similar, $\therefore \ \dfrac{HI}{KL} = \dfrac{GI}{JL} = \dfrac{GH}{JK}.$

Substituting the given lengths we have: $\dfrac{6}{8} = \dfrac{GI}{6} = \dfrac{4}{JK}.$

**Fig. R37**

The sides are therefore in the ratio $6:8 = 3:4$.
The sides of the smaller triangle are $\frac{3}{4}$ of the sides of the larger.
The sides of the larger triangle are $\frac{4}{3}$ of the sides of the smaller. Hence

$$GI = JL \times \frac{3}{4} = {}^3\!\!\not{6} \times \frac{3}{\not{4}_2} = 4\tfrac{1}{2}\,cm$$

$$JK = GH \times \frac{4}{3} = 4 \times \frac{4}{3} = 5\tfrac{1}{3}\,cm.$$

## 5  Congruent triangles (15)

**Congruent figures are exactly the same shape and size.**

There are four 'cases of congruency' for triangles. In each case, three equalities must be known.

**3 sides**

**R**

**2 sides, included angle**

(Included means 'between the sides'.)

**Right angle, hypotenuse, side**

(The hypotenuse is the side opposite the right angle.)

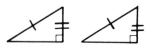

**2 angles, corresponding side**

(Corresponding means in the same position: opposite the same angle.)

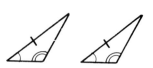

**Example**   In Figure R42, $\Delta$s $\begin{array}{c}\text{ABC}\\\text{CDA}\end{array}$ are congruent (3 sides).

> **Note**: AC is the third side. It is **common** to both triangles, therefore equal in both. We mark a common side with a wavy line.

From $\begin{array}{c}\text{ABC}\\\text{CDA}\end{array}$: covering up $\begin{array}{c}\text{A}\\\text{C}\end{array}$ gives BC = DA

covering up $\begin{array}{c}\text{B}\\\text{D}\end{array}$ gives AC = CA

covering up $\begin{array}{c}\text{C}\\\text{A}\end{array}$ gives AB = CD.

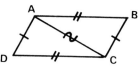

**Fig. R42**

## 6   Pythagoras' Theorem (19)

In all right-angled triangles, the square on the hypotenuse is equal to the sum of the squares on the other two sides.

In Figure R43, $h^2 = a^2 + b^2$

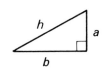

**Fig. R43**

The $\boxed{x^2}$ key is useful for finding the squares.

**Examples**   In Figure R44:
$$h^2 = 5.6^2 + 8.2^2$$
$$h^2 = 98.60$$
$$h = \sqrt{98.60} \simeq 9.9 \text{ cm}$$

Key: 5.6 $\boxed{x^2}$ $\boxed{+}$ 8.2 $\boxed{x^2}$ $\boxed{=}$ $\boxed{\surd}$

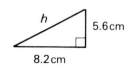

**Fig. R44**

In Figure R45:
$$9.5^2 = 5.7^2 + a^2$$
$$a^2 = 9.5^2 - 5.7^2$$
$$a^2 = 57.76$$
$$a = \sqrt{57.76} \simeq 7.6 \text{ cm}$$

Key: 9.5 $\boxed{x^2}$ $\boxed{-}$ 5.7 $\boxed{x^2}$ $\boxed{=}$ $\boxed{\surd}$

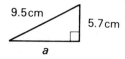

**Fig. R45**

# 7 Polygons (14)

| **polygon: many-sided** | |
| --- | --- |
| pentagon: 5 sides | octagon: 8 sides |
| hexagon: 6 sides | nonagon: 9 sides |
| heptagon: 7 sides | decagon: 10 sides |

The exterior angles of all polygons total 360° (Figure R46).

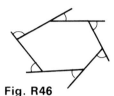

**Fig. R46**

The interior angles of an *n*-sided polygon total $(n - 2) \times 180°$ (Figure R47).

**Fig. R47**

# 8 Circles (16)

## (a) Perpendicular bisector of a chord

The perpendicular bisector of a chord is a diameter. See Figure R48.

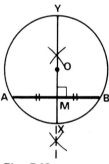

**Fig. R48**

## (b) Angles at centre and circumference

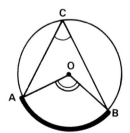

**Fig. R49**

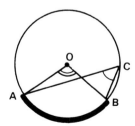

**Fig. R50**

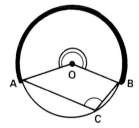

**Fig. R51**

In each of Figures R49, R50 and R51 the arc AB subtends $\angle AOB$ at the centre O and subtends $\angle ACB$ at the circumference.

$$\angle AOB = 2\angle ACB \quad \text{(Angles at centre and circumference)}$$

Note that in Figure R51 it is the major (longer) arc which subtends the angles, and $\angle AOB$ is reflex in this case.

**R**

Hints: (a) The pair of angles must start and finish with the same letters, e.g. $\angle POQ = 2\angle PXR$ could not be correct.

(b) Both angles must 'open out' the same way. This is especially important when the centre angle is reflex, as in Figure R51. This is illustrated in Figure R52.

  and    but NOT

**Fig. R52**

### (c) Angle in a semicircle

The angle in a semicircle is a right angle. See Figure R53.

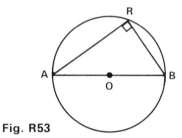

**Fig. R53**

### (d) Angles in the same segment

A chord cuts a circle into two segments. In Figure R54 angles AXB and AYB are **angles in the same segment** (the segment cut off by chord AB). These angles are equal: $\angle AXB = \angle AYB$.

If a chord was drawn from X to Y then angles XAY and XBY would also be 'equal angles in the same segment', though of course it is a different segment to the first one.

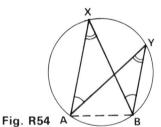

**Fig. R54**

Angles in the same segment must start and finish with the same letter, and the middle letter must be a point on the circumference.

### (e) Cyclic quadrilaterals

A cyclic quadrilateral has its four corners on the circumference of a circle.

The opposite angles of a cyclic quadrilateral add up to 180° (they are 'supplementary').

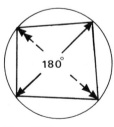

**Fig. R55**

### (f) Tangent

A tangent to a circle makes an angle of 90° with the radius to the point of contact (see Figure R31a page 239).

244

The two tangents from a point to a circle are equal (see Figure R31b, page 239).

The angle between a tangent and a chord is equal to the angle the chord subtends at the circumference of the alternate segment, Figure R56.

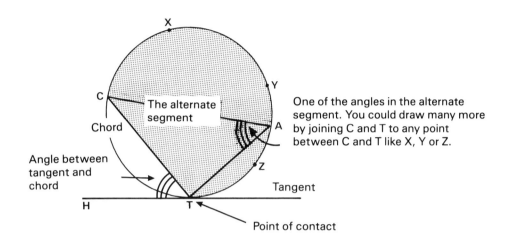

**Fig. R56**

# SYMMETRY

The number in brackets after each heading indicates the exercise in Book 5 which contains questions on the topic.

## 1 Line symmetry (14)

A figure has line symmetry if it can be divided into two parts by a mirror line.

An H has two lines of symmetry.

## 2 Rotational symmetry (14)

The order of rotational symmetry is the number of times a figure fits into a tracing of itself (or 'maps onto itself') in one revolution (one full turn).

All figures have at least order 1 rotational symmetry, but often this is not counted, so an M can be said to have no rotational symmetry. An H has rotational symmetry of order 2.

## 3 Point symmetry (14)

The simplest way to find out if a figure has point symmetry is to see if it looks different when rotated through 180°. An H has point symmetry, but an M has not.

## 4 Planes of symmetry (reflection symmetry) (17)

In the cuboid shown in Figure R57, BDHF is a plane of symmetry (see Figure R58a), and IKSQ is another (see Figure R58b). ABCD is a square.

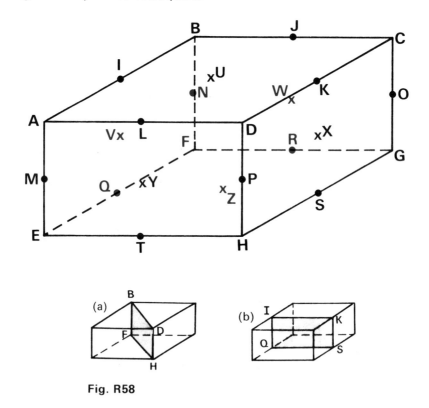

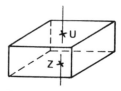

**Fig. R58**

A plane of symmetry acts as a mirror.

Why is ADGF in Figure R57 not a plane of symmetry?

Which are the 2 diagonal planes of symmetry, and the 3 planes of symmetry parallel to the faces, for the cuboid in Figure R57?

## 5 Axes of symmetry (rotational symmetry) (17)

In Figure R57, UZ is an axis of symmetry (see Figure R59). The cuboid in Figure R57 has 5 axes of symmetry. Name each of them.

**Fig. R59**

## 6 Symmetry number (17)

The symmetry number of a solid is the number of ways that it can be put into a mould of itself. The cuboid in Figure R57 has symmetry number 8.

# MENSURATION

The number in brackets after each heading indicates the exercise in Book 5 which contains questions on the topic.

## 1 Areas of plane figures (20)

Rectangle/Parallelogram   Base times height: $A = bh$

Triangle                                    Half base times height: $A = \frac{1}{2}bh$

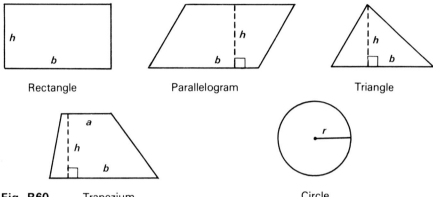

**Fig. R60**     Trapezium                                         Circle

Trapezium                                    Half the sum of the parallel sides times the distance between them: $A = \frac{1}{2}(a + b)h$

Circle                                          *Pi* times the square of the radius: $A = \pi r^2$

## 2 Surface areas of solids (20)

Cylinder   Curved surface area is circumference of base circle times height of cylinder: $\pi dh$

Total surface area is curved surface area plus the areas of the top and bottom circles: $\pi dh + 2\pi r^2$

Cone       Curved surface area is *pi* times the radius of the base times the slant height: $\pi rl$

Total surface area is curved surface area plus the area of the base circle: $\pi rl + \pi r^2$

Sphere    Surface area is 4 times *pi* times the square of the radius: $4\pi r^2$

Cylinder                              Cone                              Sphere

**Fig. R61**

## 3 Volumes (20)

| | | |
|---|---|---|
| Prism | A solid with a constant cross-section; that is, it has the same shape all through it. Examples: breeze block, kitchen roll, Toblerone box, unsharpened pencil, wedge of cheese. | Area of cross-section times length (or height): $V = Al$ or $Ah$ |
| Cuboid | A prism with rectangular cross-sections, like a brick. | Length times width times height: $V = lwh$ |
| Cylinder | A prism whose constant cross-section is a circle. | Area of circular cross-section times height: $V = \pi r^2 h$ |

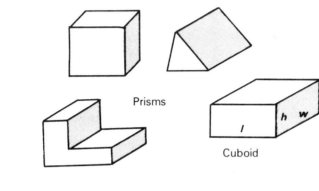 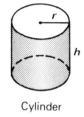

Prisms  Cuboid  Cylinder

   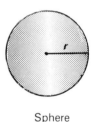

Pyramids  Cone  Sphere

**Fig. R62**

| | | |
|---|---|---|
| Pyramid | May have any shape base, with sloping sides coming to a point. A pyramid on a square base is usually called an Egyptian pyramid. A pyramid with four triangular faces is called a tetrahedron (if the triangles are equilateral it is a regular tetrahedron). | One third of the base area times height: $V = \frac{1}{3}Ah$ |
| Cone | A pyramid with a circular base. | One third of the circular base area times height: $V = \frac{1}{3}\pi r^2 h$ |
| Sphere | A ball. | Four-thirds times *pi* times the cube of the radius: $V = \frac{4}{3}\pi r^3$ |

## 4 Arc and sector of a circle (20)

To find the length of an arc we first find what fraction of the circumference it is by considering the angle it subtends at the centre.

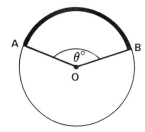

**Fig. R63**

In Figure R63:

$$\text{arc AB} = \frac{\theta°}{360°} \times \text{circumference} = \frac{\theta}{360} \times \pi \times \text{diameter}$$

**Note:** $\theta$ is a Greek letter, pronounced 'theta'.

**Example**   In Figure R64, $\theta = 50$ and the diameter is 36 cm.

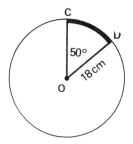

**Fig. R64**

$$\text{Arc CD} = \frac{50}{360} \times \pi \times 36 \rightarrow \frac{5\cancel{0}}{{}_{1}\cancel{360}} \times \frac{22}{7} \times 36^1 = \frac{110}{7} \rightarrow 15\tfrac{5}{7} \text{ cm}$$

In Figure R65, P is the major sector and Q is the minor sector.

Area of sector $Q = \dfrac{\theta°}{360°} \times \text{area of circle} = \dfrac{\theta}{360} \times \pi \times r^2$.

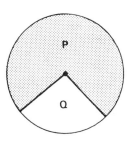

**Fig. R65**

## R

# TRIGONOMETRY

The number in brackets after each heading indicates the exercise in Book 5 which contains questions on the topic.

## 1  Solution of right-angled triangles (21)

$$o = a \times \tan \theta \quad o = h \times \sin \theta \quad a = h \times \cos \theta$$

$$\frac{o}{a} = \tan \theta \qquad \frac{o}{h} = \sin \theta \qquad \frac{a}{h} = \cos \theta$$

one ancient teacher of history swore at his class!

### (a)  Finding sides

$$x = 5 \times \tan 54°$$
$$\simeq 6.88$$

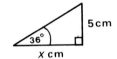

$$x = 5 \times \sin 40°$$
$$\simeq 3.21$$

$$x = 5 \times \cos 25°$$
$$\text{or} \quad x = 5 \times \sin 65°$$
$$\simeq 4.53$$

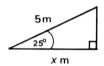

Sample key sequence: 5 $\boxed{\times}$ 54 $\boxed{\text{TAN}}$ $\boxed{=}$

### (b)  Finding angles

$$\frac{7}{6} = \tan \theta$$
$$\theta \simeq 49.4°$$

$$\frac{7}{9} = \sin \theta$$
$$\theta = 51.1°$$

$$\frac{7}{9} = \cos \theta$$
$$\text{or} \quad \frac{7}{9} = \sin \alpha \rightarrow \alpha \simeq 51.1°$$
$$\theta \simeq 38.9°$$

Sample key sequence: 7 $\boxed{\div}$ 6 $\boxed{=}$ $\boxed{\text{ARCTAN}}$        (Note: ARCTAN may be INV TAN or TAN$^{-1}$.)

## 2 Using minutes (21)

Fractions of an angle may be given either as a decimal of a degree, or by using minutes, where 1 minute (1′) is a sixtieth of a degree.

**Example** An angle of $36\frac{1}{4}°$ may be written 36.25° or 36° 15′.

In order to use the trigonometry keys on a calculator you must convert angles given in degrees and minutes into decimals of a degree. Many calculators have a special key to do this; it may be marked $\boxed{\text{o}'''\rightarrow}$. Note: ″ is the symbol for seconds ($\frac{1}{360}°$). We do not usually need to measure angles to this level of accuracy.

If you have a conversion key try it for the above example.

Key:   36.15 $\boxed{\text{o}'''\rightarrow}$ should display 36.25, or try 36 $\boxed{\text{o}'''\rightarrow}$ 15 $\boxed{\text{o}'''\rightarrow}$

Note that the point in 36.15 is not a decimal point, but is used to separate the degrees from the minutes.

If you do not have such a key you can convert by thinking of 36° 15′ as $36\frac{15}{60}°$.

Key:   36 $\boxed{+}$ 15 $\boxed{\div}$ 60 $\boxed{=}$ should give you the required 36.25°.

Note that the calculator must observe the order of signs for this sequence.

## 3 Applications (21)

**Depression** = looking down.

**Elevation** = looking up.

Angle of elevation = angle of depression.

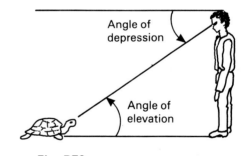

**Fig. R72**

The **altitude of the sun** is its angle of elevation.

At noon the sun is at its highest point; its angle of elevation is at a maximum.

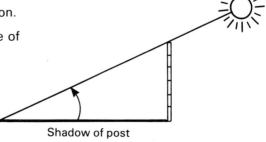

Shadow of post

**Fig. R73**

**R**

Figures R74(a) and (b) show the **vertical angle** of an isosceles triangle and of a cone. Half this angle is called the **semi-vertical angle**.

(a)

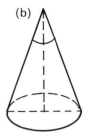
(b)

**Fig. R74**

**Inclination** is usually the angle made with the horizontal, but it can be with a vertical, or any other, plane.

**Slope** is usually the tangent of the angle made with the horizontal.

**Gradient** is mathematically the same as slope, but for surveying (roads, railways, etc.) it is taken as the sine of the angle. For small values of inclination, $\theta$, which will usually be the case for road and railway slopes, $\sin \theta \simeq \tan \theta$, so the difference is unimportant.

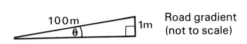
Road gradient (not to scale)

Mathematical gradient (slope)

**Fig. R75** Gradient = $\sin \theta = \frac{1}{100} = 1\%$    **Fig. R76** Gradient = $\tan \theta = \frac{2}{5}$

### Northings and Eastings

Ship B is 1 nautical mile (n.m.) north and 5 n.m. east of ship A.

One nautical mile is $\frac{1}{3600}$ of the length of the equator, so 1 n.m. subtends 1′ at the centre of the Earth.

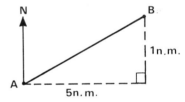

**Fig. R77**

## 4  Sine rule for a non-right-angled triangle (21)

When a triangle is not right-angled, our trig. ratios cease to be true. However it is possible to obtain a rule, called the **sine rule**, that can be used when the triangle is not right-angled. You must, however, know one side and the angle opposite it, together with another side or angle.

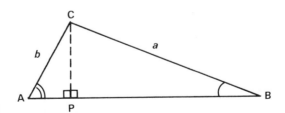

**Fig. R78**

In Figure R78, $\triangle ABC$ is not right-angled, but $\triangle APC$ and $\triangle CPB$ are. From these triangles:

$$CP = a \times \sin B \text{ and also } CP = b \times \sin A.$$

252

Therefore $a \times \sin B = b \times \sin A$. This is the **sine rule**, usually written:

$$\frac{a}{\sin A} = \frac{b}{\sin B}$$ to find a side

or

$$\frac{\sin A}{a} = \frac{\sin B}{b}$$ to find an angle

Always start the rule with the side, or the sine of the angle, that you are trying to find.

You can only use the sine rule if you know a side and the angle opposite to it.

**Example**  In Figure R79:

$$\frac{x}{\sin 27°} = \frac{12\,cm}{\sin 48°}$$

$$x = \frac{12\,cm}{\sin 48°} \times \sin 27°$$

Key: 12 ÷ 48 [sin] [×] 27 [sin] [=]

Answer: $x = 7.33$ cm correct to 3 s.f.

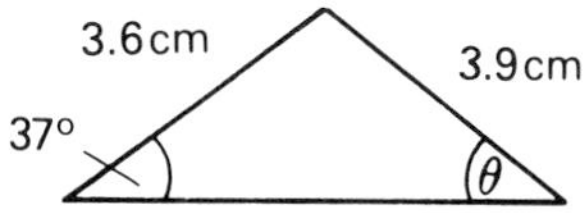

**Fig. R79**

**Example**  In Figure R80:

$$\frac{\sin \theta}{3.6\,cm} = \frac{\sin 37°}{3.9\,cm}$$

$$\sin \theta = \frac{\sin 37° \times 3.6\,cm}{3.9\,cm}$$

Key: 37 [sin] ÷ 3.9 [×] 3.6 [=] [ARCS'N]

Answer: $\theta = 33.8°$ to the nearest 0.1°.

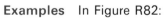

**Fig. R80**

## 5  Cosine rule for a non-right-angled triangle (21)

The cosine rule may be used when there is no opposite side/angle pair (required by the sine rule, see Note 4). It is the general case of Pythagoras' Theorem, and starts in the same way.

In Figure R81:

$a^2 = b^2 + c^2 - 2bc \cos A$

The cosine rule may also be used to find an angle given the three sides.

In Figure R81:

$$\cos A = \frac{b^2 + c^2 - a^2}{2bc}$$

This may be learnt, or worked out from the first version.

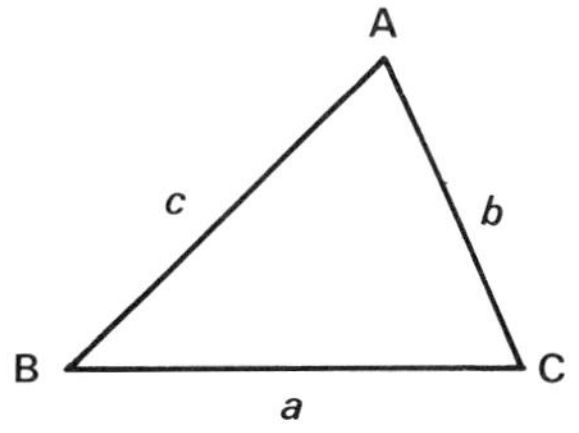

**Fig. R81**

**Examples**  In Figure R82:

$$a^2 = 7^2 + 4.8^2 - 2 \times 7 \times 4.8 \times \cos 28.7°$$

Key: 7 [$x^2$] [+] 4.8 [$x^2$] [−] 2 [×] 7 [×] 4.8 [×] 28.7 [COS] [=] [√]

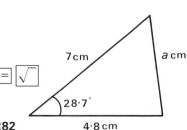

**Fig. R82**

253

In Figure R83:

$$\cos \theta = \frac{6^2 + 5.4^2 - 8.9^2}{2 \times 6 \times 5.4}$$

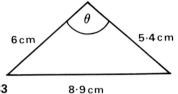

**Fig. R83**    8·9 cm

Key: $6 \boxed{x^2} \boxed{+} 5.4 \boxed{x^2} \boxed{-} 8.9 \boxed{x^2} \boxed{\div} 2 \boxed{\div} 6 \boxed{\div} 5.4 \boxed{=} \boxed{\text{INV}} \boxed{\text{COS}}$

$\boxed{\text{COS}^{-1}}$

$\boxed{\text{ARCCOS}}$

## 6   Which trigonometry rules to use (21)

Right angle?
Use tan/sin/cos.

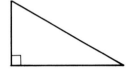

Angle and opposite side?
Use sine rule.

Two sides and included angle?
Use cosine rule.

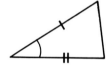

Three sides but no angles?
Use cosine rule.

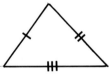

## 7   The area of a triangle (21)

**The area of ΔABC is $\frac{1}{2}ab \sin$ C.**

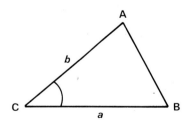

**Fig. R88**

Figure R89 shows the proof of this formula.
Area $\Delta ABC = \frac{1}{2}ah$
$h = b \sin C$
$\therefore$ Area $\Delta ABC = \frac{1}{2}ab \sin C$

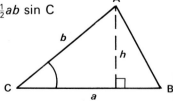

**Fig. R89**

## STATISTICS

The number in brackets after each heading indicates the exercise in Book 5 which contains questions on the topic.

### 1 The three statistical averages (23)

**Mean**
The total score distributed equally to each item. The mean of 2, 7 and 9 is the total (18) divided by 3, giving 6.

**Mode**
The item that occurs most frequently. There may be several modes, or no mode.

**Median**
The middle score of an odd number of items. For an even number of items it is usually taken as the mean of the two middle scores, although it could be anywhere between them.

### 2 Frequency tables (23)

These are used to simplify the arithmetic with a large amount of data. (Processing such large amounts takes a long time, so examples in books usually apply the method to a small amount of data!)

**Example** To find the mean of £16, £16, £17, £17, £17, £18, £18, £18, £18, £19, £19, £19, £20.

| Score ($x$) | Frequency ($f$) | Total ($f \times x$) |
|---|---|---|
| £16 | 2 | £32 |
| £17 | 3 | £51 |
| £18 | 4 | £72 |
| £19 | 3 | £57 |
| £20 | 1 | £20 |
| TOTALS | 13 | £232 |

Mean $= \dfrac{£232}{13} \simeq £18$

Mode = £18 (highest frequency)
Median = £18 (score of the 7th item, which is clearly in the £18 frequency: 2 + 3 = 5; 2 + 3 + 4 = 9)

### 3 Mean from grouped data; modal class (23)

To calculate the mean from grouped data you assume that each frequency scores the mid-value (middle) of the range. This mid-value is the mean of the upper and lower limits of the range, e.g. the middle of 0–9 is $\dfrac{0 + 9}{2} = 4.5$, and the middle of 31–35 is $\dfrac{31 + 35}{2} = 33$.

**Example**

| Class | Frequency ($f$) | Middle ($x$) | Totals ($fx$) |
|---|---|---|---|
| 30–39 | 23 | 34.5 | 793.5 |
| 40–49 | 55 | 44.5 | 2447.5 |
| 50–59 | 32 | 55 | 1760 |
| | 110 | | 5001 |

Mean $\simeq \dfrac{5001}{110} \simeq 45$

The class which has the highest frequency is called the **modal class**. As with the mode, there can be more than one modal class. In the last example the modal class is 40–49.

## 4 Cumulative frequency curve; quartiles; percentiles (23)

| Marks | Frequency |
|---|---|
| 1 to 5 | 1 |
| 6 to 10 | 2 |
| 11 to 15 | 4 |
| 16 to 20 | 7 |
| 21 to 25 | 9 |
| 26 to 30 | 5 |
| 31 to 35 | 2 |
| 36 to 40 | 1 |

| Mark | Cumulative frequency |
|---|---|
| 5 or less | 1 |
| 10 or less | 1 + 2 = 3 |
| 15 or less | 3 + 4 = 7 |
| 20 or less | 7 + 7 = 14 |
| 25 or less | 14 + 9 = 23 |
| 30 or less | 23 + 5 = 28 |
| 35 or less | 28 + 2 = 30 |
| 40 or less | 30 + 1 = 31 |

Marks out of 40 for a class of 31 pupils

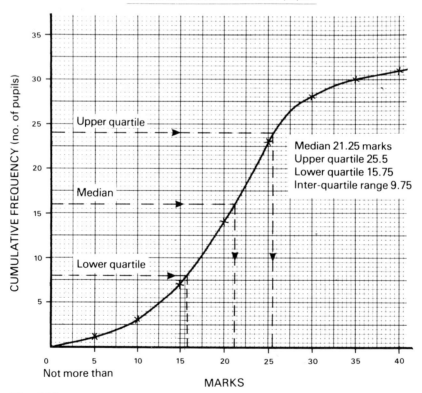

Median 21.25 marks
Upper quartile 25.5
Lower quartile 15.75
Inter-quartile range 9.75

**Fig. R90**

Statisticians usually use 'percentiles', which are more meaningful than quartiles. As the name indicates, percentiles divide the total frequency into 100 equal divisions. However, at the time of writing, examiners are still asking questions about quartiles.

# PROBABILITY

The number in brackets after each heading indicates the exercise in Book 5 which contains questions on the topic.

## 1 The mathematical definition of probability (24)

Mathematicians state the probability of an event happening as a fraction between 0 (impossible) and 1 (certain). This fraction may be written as a common or decimal fraction (e.g. $\frac{1}{4}$ or 0.25), as a ratio (1 : 4 or 1 in 4), or as a percentage (25%).

Betting odds are stated differently. Probability $\frac{1}{4}$ becomes odds of 3 to 1 (3 chances that it will not happen to 1 chance that it will).

The probability of a successful outcome (i.e. that the event you want will happen) is:

$$\frac{\text{number of successful outcomes possible}}{\text{total number of possible outcomes}}.$$

Note: This is only true if all successful outcomes are equally likely. For example, it is not true for a loaded die.

## 2 Combining probabilities: independent events (24)

Outcomes are **independent** when one event happening does not prevent (or exclude) the others from happening. When the successful outcomes are independent the probabilities of each are **multiplied** to obtain the probability of them all happening.

Example   Calculate the probability of drawing first an ace and then a king from a full pack of 52 cards if:
(a) the ace is replaced after being picked
(b) the ace is not replaced.

The two successful outcomes are: (i) drawing an ace first, (ii) drawing a king second. These are independent events because after (i) happens it is still possible to go on to pick a second card to see if (ii) happens.

(a) With replacement:
$P(\text{ace first}) = \frac{1}{13};\quad P(\text{king second}) = \frac{1}{13}$
$P(\text{ace then king}) = \frac{1}{13} \times \frac{1}{13} = \underline{\underline{\frac{1}{169}}}$

(b) Without replacement:
$P(\text{ace first}) = \frac{1}{13};\quad P(\text{king second}) = \frac{4}{51}$
$P(\text{ace then king}) = \frac{1}{13} \times \frac{4}{51} = \underline{\underline{\frac{4}{663}}}$

## 3 Exclusive events (24)

Events are **exclusive** when one of them happening excludes (prevents) the others from happening. For exclusive events, the separate probabilities are **added** to obtain the probability of one *or* the other happening.

Example   Calculate the probability of picking either a king or a queen from a full pack of cards.

The successful outcomes are: (i) picking a king first pick, (ii) picking a queen first pick. Either may happen, but not both, so the two events are exclusive.

$P(\text{king}) = \frac{1}{13};\quad P(\text{queen}) = \frac{1}{13};\quad P(\text{king or queen}) = \frac{1}{13} + \frac{1}{13} = \underline{\underline{\frac{2}{13}}}$

257

## SETS
The number in brackets after each heading indicates the exercise in Book 5 which contains questions on the topic.

### 1 Set notation and terminology (28)

'Describe set A'.     A = {the first four odd integers}

'Describe set B'.     B = {triangular numbers less than 10}

'List set A'.     A = {1, 3, 5, 7}

'List set B'.     B = {1, 3, 6}

| Symbols | Meaning |
|---------|---------|
| $3 \in A$ | 3 is an element (or member) of set A. |
| $2 \notin A$ | 2 is not an element of set A. |
| $n(A) = 4$ | There are 4 elements in set A. |
| $\varnothing$ or { } | A null, or empty, set. It has no elements, e.g. {even numbers in set A}. |
| $\{1, 5\} \subset A$ | {1, 5} is a subset of set A. |
| $A \supset \{5\}$ | Set A contains the subset {5}. |
| $B \not\subset A$ | Set B is not a subset of set A. |
| $A \cap B = \{1, 3\}$ | The intersection of sets A and B. It consists of the elements common to both sets. |
| $A \cup B = \{1, 3, 5, 6, 7\}$ | The union of sets A and B. It is made by joining the two sets together. Note that elements common to both sets are only written once in the union. |
| $\xi$ | The universal set. It defines all the elements that may be used in a particular problem. |
| $A'$ | The complement of set A. It contains those elements that are not in set A. |

### 2 Venn diagrams (28)

Venn diagrams illustrate sets.

In Figure R91, A = {1, 3, 5, 7} and T = {1, 7}.

Set T is a subset of A (T $\subset$ A or A $\supset$ T).

**Fig. R91**

In Figure R92, set A intersects set B.

$A \cap B = \{1, 3\}$     $n(A \cap B) = 2$

$A \cup B = \{1, 3, 5, 6, 7\}$

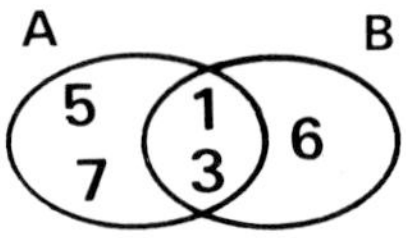

**Fig. R92**

In Figure R93, sets G and T are disjoint. They do not intersect.

$G \cap T = \varnothing$     $n(G \cap T) = 0$

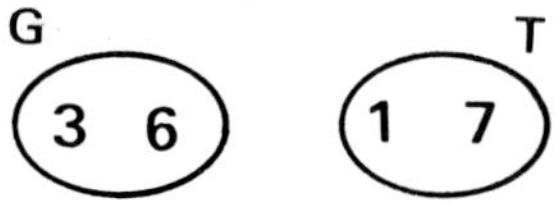

**Fig. R93**

In Figure R94, $\xi$ (the rectangle) is the universal set. The hatched region is D′, the complement of set D.

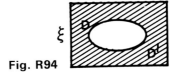

Fig. R94

Figure R95 shows the number of elements in sets $\xi$, A and B. It does not tell you what the elements are.

$n(A) = 2 + 2 = 4 \qquad n(A') = 1 + 3 = 4$

Note: $[n(A) + n(B)] - [n(A \cup B)] = n(A \cap B)$.
$\quad\;\; [\; 4 \;+\; 3 \;] - [\quad 5 \quad] = \quad 2$

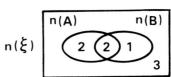

Fig. R95

**Example** Draw a Venn diagram to show: $n(A \cup B) = 16$, $n(A) = 9$, and $n(B) = 10$.

As $n(A) + n(B) = 19$, but $n(A \cup B) = 16$, then $n(A \cap B) = 19 - 16 = 3$. Fill in the 3, then the 6 and the 7, giving the answer shown in Figure R96.

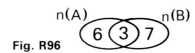

Fig. R96

## 3  Three-set problems (28)

Venn diagrams can clarify complex logic problems. Follow the reasoning used in this example.

Maria has 32 dresses. Of these, 17 have sleeves, 22 have zips, and 15 have belts. 10 have zips and sleeves, 8 have zips and belts, 6 have sleeves and belts. All the dresses have at least one of these features.

Find how many have:
(a) only sleeves      (b) only a zip      (c) only a belt.

**Summary using set notation**

$n(\xi) = 32$;  $n(S) = 17$;  $n(Z) = 22$;  $n(B) = 15$;  $n(Z \cap S) = 10$;  $n(Z \cap B) = 8$; $n(S \cap B) = 6$;  $n(S \cup B \cup Z)' = 0$.

**Solution Method One**

Insert the zero from $n(S \cup B \cup Z)' = 0$.
Let $n(S \cap B \cap Z) = x$. Then as $n(Z \cap S) = 10$ you can insert the $10 - x$; similarly for $6 - x$ and $8 - x$. See Figure R97.

The fourth section of each set can now be completed, e.g. $n(S) = 17$ and so far $n(S) = 10 - x + x + 6 - x = 16 - x$; hence writing $1 + x$ in the last section will give the total 17. See Figure R98.

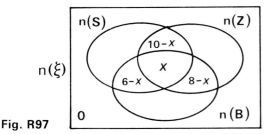

Fig. R97

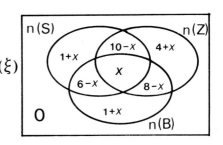

Fig. R98

259

Finally add up all the regions to total 32 and solve the resulting equation to find *x*. The diagram can then be easily completed: see Figure R99.

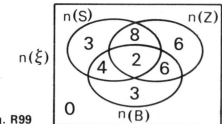

**Fig. R99**

## Solution Method Two

See Figure R100. Compare the union of the sets with their sum: $n(S \cup B \cup Z) = 32$ and $n(S) + n(B) + n(Z) = 54$. The difference is 22, which means that we must 'lose' 22 in the intersections.

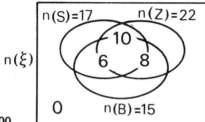

**Fig. R100**

The given intersections total 24, which is 2 too many. This tells you that the intersection of all three contains 2. The diagram may now be easily completed: see Figure R99.

## TRANSFORMATIONS

The number in brackets after each heading indicates the exercise in Book 5 which contains questions on the topic.

### 1 Rotation (26)

To describe a rotation state the centre of rotation and the angle turned (+ve rotations are anticlockwise).

**Example** In Figure R101 triangle ABC has rotated through 270° about O.

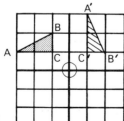

**Fig. R101**

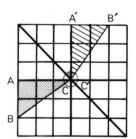

**Fig. R102**

## 2 Reflection (26)

To describe a reflection state the equation, or the name, of the mirror line.

**Example**  In Figure R102 triangle ABC has been reflected in the line $y = -x$.

## 3 Enlargement (26)

To describe an enlargement state the scale factor by which the figure has been enlarged and the centre of the enlargement.

Figures R103 to R106 illustrate four kinds of enlargement. In each diagram $\triangle ABC$ is mapped onto $\triangle A'B'C'$.

Figure R103 is an enlargement of scale factor 2 from centre O.

Figure R104 is an enlargement of scale factor $\frac{1}{2}$ from centre O.
(Note that we refer to the transformation as an enlargement even when the image is smaller than the object.)

Figure R105 is an enlargement of scale factor $-1$ from centre O.
(Note that in a negative enlargement the image is on the opposite side of the centre.)

Figure R106 is an enlargement of scale factor $-2$ from centre O.

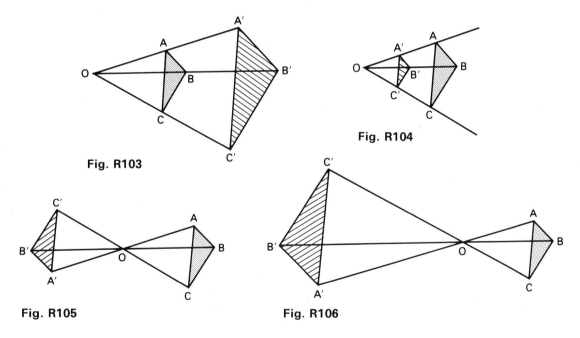

Fig. R103

Fig. R104

Fig. R105

Fig. R106

## 4 Translation (26)

A sliding movement, able to be described by a vector. See Vectors, Note 3.

## 5 Shear (26)

The object is pushed sideways from a fixed line, which may be a side of the shape, or inside it, or outside it.

To describe a shearing state the equation, or the name, of the invariant (fixed) line and the original and transformed positions of one point.

Figures R107 to R109 show three shearings, each with line AB invariant.

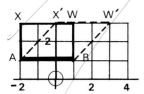

**Fig. R107**

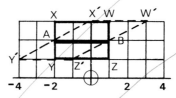

**Fig. R108**

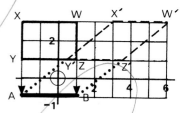

**Fig. R109**

Figure R107 is a shearing from AB, such that (1, 3) → (3, 3).

Figure R108 is a shearing from AB, such that (1, 3) → (3, 3).

Figure R109 is a shearing from AB, such that (1, 3) → (6, 3).

## 6  Stretch (26)

The object is pulled to make it longer, or wider, or both, from a fixed line which may be a side, or inside, or outside the object.

To describe a stretch state the invariant line(s) and the stretch factor(s).

Figures R110 to R112 all show a stretch from AB of stretch factor 2.

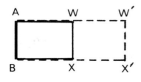

**Fig. R110**

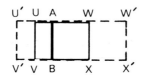

**Fig. R111**

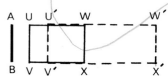

**Fig. R112**

## 7  Topological transformation (26)

The shape is distorted without altering the number of nodes, arcs, or regions.

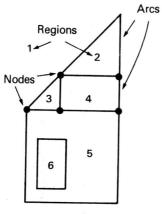

**Fig. R113**

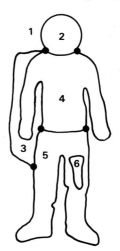

## MATRICES

The number in brackets after each heading indicates the exercise in Book 5 which contains questions on the topic.

## 1 Multiplication of matrices (27)

**Constant times matrix**

Example $\quad 3 \begin{pmatrix} 2 & -1 \\ 0 & 3 \end{pmatrix} = \begin{pmatrix} 6 & -3 \\ 0 & 9 \end{pmatrix}$

**Matrix times matrix**

Example $\quad \begin{pmatrix} 2 & 3 \\ 2 & 5 \end{pmatrix} \begin{pmatrix} 4 & 2 \\ 1 & 5 \end{pmatrix} = \begin{pmatrix} 11 & 19 \\ 13 & 29 \end{pmatrix}$

$\qquad$ Step One $\quad (2 \quad 3) \begin{pmatrix} 4 \\ 1 \end{pmatrix} \rightarrow 8 + 3 = 11$

$\qquad$ Step Two $\quad (2 \quad 3) \begin{pmatrix} 2 \\ 5 \end{pmatrix} \rightarrow 4 + 15 = 19$

$\qquad$ Step Three $\quad (2 \quad 5) \begin{pmatrix} 4 \\ 1 \end{pmatrix} \rightarrow 8 + 5 = 13$

$\qquad$ Step Four $\quad (2 \quad 5) \begin{pmatrix} 2 \\ 5 \end{pmatrix} \rightarrow 4 + 25 = 29$

Be especially careful when negative (minus) numbers are involved. Check the following example carefully:

$$\begin{pmatrix} 2 & -1 \\ -3 & 1 \end{pmatrix} \begin{pmatrix} -1 & -2 \\ 1 & 4 \end{pmatrix} = \begin{pmatrix} -3 & -8 \\ 4 & 10 \end{pmatrix}$$

Remember that most matrices give different answers when multiplied together, depending on which one is at the front (we say multiplication of matrices is 'not commutative').

For example, $\qquad \begin{pmatrix} 1 & 0 \\ 1 & 2 \end{pmatrix} \begin{pmatrix} 2 & 1 \\ 0 & 0 \end{pmatrix} = \begin{pmatrix} 2 & 1 \\ 2 & 1 \end{pmatrix}$

but $\qquad \begin{pmatrix} 2 & 1 \\ 0 & 0 \end{pmatrix} \begin{pmatrix} 1 & 0 \\ 1 & 2 \end{pmatrix} = \begin{pmatrix} 3 & 2 \\ 0 & 0 \end{pmatrix}$

## 2 Matrix transformations (27)

The following three methods can be used to define the position of points A, B and C on the grid in Figure R114.

| Co-ordinates | Position vectors | Matrix |
|---|---|---|

A: (1, 1) $\qquad \overrightarrow{OA} = \begin{pmatrix} 1 \\ 1 \end{pmatrix}$

$\qquad\qquad\qquad\qquad\qquad\quad \begin{array}{cc} & A \ B \ C \\ x & \begin{pmatrix} 1 & 1 & 3 \\ 1 & 2 & 1 \end{pmatrix} \\ y & \end{array}$

B: (1, 2) $\qquad \overrightarrow{OB} = \begin{pmatrix} 1 \\ 2 \end{pmatrix}$

C: (3, 1) $\qquad \overrightarrow{OC} = \begin{pmatrix} 3 \\ 1 \end{pmatrix}$

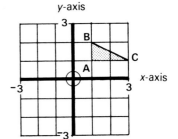

Fig. R114

263

**R**

Using the matrix method to define the triangle, the co-ordinates of the triangle after a rotation of 270° about (0, 0) can be found by multiplying by the matrix $\begin{pmatrix} 0 & 1 \\ -1 & 0 \end{pmatrix}$:

$$\begin{matrix} & A & B & C \\ \end{matrix}$$

$$\begin{pmatrix} 0 & 1 \\ -1 & 0 \end{pmatrix} \begin{pmatrix} 1 & 1 & 3 \\ 1 & 2 & 1 \end{pmatrix} = \begin{pmatrix} 1 & 2 & 1 \\ -1 & -1 & -3 \end{pmatrix}$$
$$\begin{matrix} A' & B' & C' \end{matrix}$$

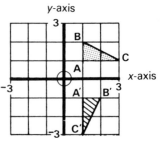

**Fig. R115**

## 3   Identity and inverse (27)

For a given number system, the **identity** is the element that has no apparent effect under a given operation.

For integers: The identity for addition is 0, e.g. 6 + 0 = 6.
   The identity for multiplication is 1, e.g. 6 × 1 = 6.

For 2 by 2 matrices: The identity for addition is $\begin{pmatrix} 0 & 0 \\ 0 & 0 \end{pmatrix}$,

e.g. $\begin{pmatrix} 6 & 5 \\ 4 & 3 \end{pmatrix} + \begin{pmatrix} 0 & 0 \\ 0 & 0 \end{pmatrix} = \begin{pmatrix} 6 & 5 \\ 4 & 3 \end{pmatrix}$.

The identity for multiplication is $\begin{pmatrix} 1 & 0 \\ 0 & 1 \end{pmatrix}$,

e.g. $\begin{pmatrix} 1 & 0 \\ 0 & 1 \end{pmatrix} \begin{pmatrix} 6 & 5 \\ 4 & 3 \end{pmatrix} = \begin{pmatrix} 6 & 5 \\ 4 & 3 \end{pmatrix}$.

For a given number system, the **inverse** of an element combines with the element to give the identity. The inverse can be thought of as 'undoing' the operation.

For integers: The inverse of $n$ for addition is $-n$,
   e.g. **6** + 3 = 9 and 9 + −3 = **6**.

   The inverse of $n$ for multiplication is $\dfrac{1}{n}$,
   e.g. **6** × 3 = 18 and 18 × $\frac{1}{3}$ = **6**.

For 2 by 2 matrices: The inverse of $\begin{pmatrix} a & b \\ c & d \end{pmatrix}$ for addition is $\begin{pmatrix} -a & -b \\ -c & -d \end{pmatrix}$,

e.g. $\begin{pmatrix} 6 & 5 \\ 4 & 3 \end{pmatrix} + \begin{pmatrix} -1 & 0 \\ 7 & 9 \end{pmatrix} = \begin{pmatrix} 5 & 5 \\ 11 & 12 \end{pmatrix}$ and

$\begin{pmatrix} 5 & 5 \\ 11 & 12 \end{pmatrix} + \begin{pmatrix} 1 & 0 \\ -7 & -9 \end{pmatrix} = \begin{pmatrix} 6 & 5 \\ 4 & 3 \end{pmatrix}$.

The inverse of $\begin{pmatrix} a & b \\ c & d \end{pmatrix}$ for multiplication is $\dfrac{1}{ad - bc} \begin{pmatrix} d & -b \\ -c & a \end{pmatrix}$.

$(ad - bc)$ is called the **determinant** of the matrix $\begin{pmatrix} a & b \\ c & d \end{pmatrix}$.

When transforming by a matrix, the determinant is the scale factor of the change in area.

The example below shows step-by-step how to calculate the multiplicative inverse.

The additive inverse matrix is little used, and the multiplicative inverse is always the one implied when you are asked to find 'the' inverse.

**Example**  To find the inverse of $\begin{pmatrix} 5 & 1 \\ 8 & 2 \end{pmatrix}$.

Step One  Write the standard format: $\frac{1}{\phantom{-}}\begin{pmatrix} \phantom{xxx} \end{pmatrix}$

Step Two  Calculate the determinant. This is best done by writing it above the original matrix:

$\overset{10\ -\ 8\ =\ 2}{\begin{pmatrix} 5 & 1 \\ 8 & 2 \end{pmatrix}} \rightarrow \frac{1}{2}\begin{pmatrix} \phantom{xxx} \end{pmatrix}$

Step Three  Swap over the elements on the leading diagonal:

$\begin{pmatrix} 5 & \\ & 2 \end{pmatrix} \rightarrow \frac{1}{2}\begin{pmatrix} 2 & \\ & 5 \end{pmatrix}$

Step Four  Change the signs on the other diagonal, giving the complete inverse:

$\frac{1}{2}\begin{pmatrix} 2 & -1 \\ -8 & 5 \end{pmatrix}$  Note: The $\frac{1}{2}$ may be multiplied through to give $\begin{pmatrix} 1 & -\frac{1}{2} \\ -4 & 2\frac{1}{2} \end{pmatrix}$.

## 4  Matrix solution of simultaneous equations (27)

The Teachers' Manual to Book 3 contains a computer program, SIMUL, which solves simultaneous equations. It uses the following matrix method, which many students find easier than the traditional algebraic approach.

**Example**  To solve $5x + 3y = 11$ and $3x + 2y = 7$ simultaneously.

The equations may be written in a matrix form (rather cunning, this!):

$\begin{pmatrix} 5 & 3 \\ 3 & 2 \end{pmatrix}\begin{pmatrix} x \\ y \end{pmatrix} = \begin{pmatrix} 11 \\ 7 \end{pmatrix}$  (Multiply this out to check it.)

$\therefore \begin{pmatrix} x \\ y \end{pmatrix} = \begin{pmatrix} 11 \\ 7 \end{pmatrix} \div \begin{pmatrix} 5 & 3 \\ 3 & 2 \end{pmatrix}$

To divide by a matrix we pre-multiply by its inverse (compare this with division by a fraction):

$\therefore \begin{pmatrix} x \\ y \end{pmatrix} = \frac{1}{1}\begin{pmatrix} 2 & -3 \\ -3 & 5 \end{pmatrix}\begin{pmatrix} 11 \\ 7 \end{pmatrix} = \begin{pmatrix} 1 \\ 2 \end{pmatrix}$

giving $x = 1$ and $y = 2$.

**Example**  To solve $4x + 5y = 14$ and $2x + 3y = 8$ simultaneously.

$\begin{pmatrix} 4 & 5 \\ 2 & 3 \end{pmatrix}\begin{pmatrix} x \\ y \end{pmatrix} = \begin{pmatrix} 14 \\ 8 \end{pmatrix} \rightarrow \begin{pmatrix} x \\ y \end{pmatrix} = \frac{1}{2}\begin{pmatrix} 3 & -5 \\ -2 & 4 \end{pmatrix}\begin{pmatrix} 14 \\ 8 \end{pmatrix}$

$\rightarrow \begin{pmatrix} x \\ y \end{pmatrix} = \frac{1}{2}\begin{pmatrix} 2 \\ 4 \end{pmatrix}$

$\rightarrow \begin{pmatrix} x \\ y \end{pmatrix} = \begin{pmatrix} 1 \\ 2 \end{pmatrix}$

Answer: $x = 1$ and $y = 2$.

## 5 Route matrix to describe a network (Paper 15)

Figure R116 shows a two-way network. Q is a **node** of order 3 (3 **arcs** leave it). Order-2 nodes, like P, only exist if specially marked. Figure R116 has 4 nodes (*N*), 6 arcs (*A*) and 4 **regions** (*R*). Note that the loop counts as one arc and the regions include the outside of the network.

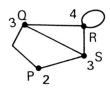

**Fig. R116**

For all networks $N + R = A + 2$ [Euler's (pronounced 'Oiler') Theorem].

A **route matrix** describes a network by stating how many ways there are of passing from one node directly to another. This is the route matrix for Figure R116:

|  |  | to | | | |
|---|---|---|---|---|---|
|  |  | P | Q | R | S |
| from | P | 0 | 1 | 0 | 1 |
|  | Q | 1 | 0 | 1 | 1 |
|  | R | 0 | 1 | 2 | 1 |
|  | S | 1 | 1 | 1 | 0 |

A two-way route matrix is always symmetrical about the leading (\\) diagonal. Note that the loop at R is shown as a 2, clockwise and anticlockwise.

Figure R117 shows a one-way network and its matrix. Note that a one-way matrix is not symmetrical. When drawing a one-way network from a matrix be careful that you do not draw a new arc if you can put a second arrow on an existing one. Figure R118 illustrates this.

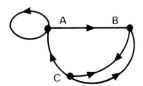

|  |  | to | | |
|---|---|---|---|---|
|  |  | A | B | C |
| from | A | 1 | 1 | 0 |
|  | B | 0 | 0 | 1 |
|  | C | 1 | 2 | 0 |

**Fig. R117**

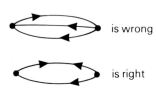

is wrong

is right

**Fig. R118**

A network is **traversable** (can be drawn with one continuous line) if it has two odd nodes or no odd nodes. An odd node must be either a start or a finish. An even node may be both the start and the finish, or an intermediate point.

## VECTORS

The number in brackets after each heading indicates the exercise in Book 5 which contains questions on the topic.

## 1 Definition (25)

A **vector** is a line with both length and direction. It is described by a column matrix, showing how far the end point of the vector is from the start point, measured horizontally and vertically. Positive and negative directions are the same as for graph axes. Figures R119 and R120 show two examples.

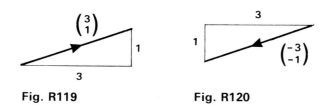

Fig. R119                    Fig. R120

## 2  Position vectors (25)

**Position vectors** always start at the origin, so the position vector $\begin{pmatrix} -4 \\ 2 \end{pmatrix}$ starts at (0, 0) and ends at $(-4, 2)$.

## 3  Shift vectors (25)

**Shift vectors** describe translations (slidings). In Figure R121 the hatched square is translated to the shaded square by the vector $\begin{pmatrix} 3 \\ 1 \end{pmatrix}$. Each corner of the square moves 3 units to the right and 1 unit upwards.

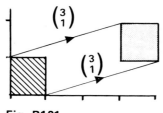

Fig. R121

Shift vectors can start at any point, and the same vector can be at several places on the same grid.

## 4  Vector defined by a matrix; by end letters; by a (25)

Vectors may be described as a matrix, $\begin{pmatrix} 3 \\ 1 \end{pmatrix}$, or by their end letters, $\overrightarrow{AB}$, or by a single letter distinguished with a wavy line underneath (or sometimes, in print, by being thicker, e.g. **a**).

## 5  Parallel vectors (25)

The same letter (or letters) can be used for parallel vectors, but different letters *must* be used for non-parallel vectors.

Figures R122 to R125 show some examples of parallel vectors.

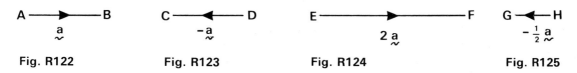

Fig. R122              Fig. R123              Fig. R124              Fig. R125

## 6  Resultant vectors (25)

A **resultant vector** is the single vector that gives the same translation as all the others added together.

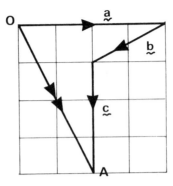

**Fig. R126**

In Figure R126, $\overrightarrow{OA}$ is the resultant of $\underset{\sim}{a}$ and $\underset{\sim}{b}$ and $\underset{\sim}{c}$.

The resultant vector may be calculated by adding the matrices of the given set of vectors.

In Figure R126, $\overrightarrow{OA} = \underset{\sim}{a} + \underset{\sim}{b} + \underset{\sim}{c} = \begin{pmatrix} 4 \\ 0 \end{pmatrix} + \begin{pmatrix} -2 \\ -1 \end{pmatrix} + \begin{pmatrix} 0 \\ -3 \end{pmatrix} = \begin{pmatrix} 2 \\ -4 \end{pmatrix}.$

## 7  Magnitude of a vector (25)

The **magnitude of a vector** is its length. It is often written as $|\overrightarrow{OA}|$, and it is called the **modulus** of $\overrightarrow{OA}$.

In Figure R127:

$(|\overrightarrow{OA}|)^2 = 2^2 + 4^2$ (Pythagoras' Theorem).

Hence $|\overrightarrow{OA}| = \sqrt{20} = 4.47$ to 3 s.f.

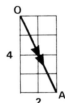

**Fig. R127**

# You Need to Learn

'See Mensuration 1', for example, refers you to Note 1 on Mensuration in the Reference Notes for more information.

## ARITHMETIC

### Areas (see Mensuration 1, page 247)

**Parallelogram:** Base times perpendicular height (two ways).

**Triangle:** Half base times perpendicular height (three ways).

**Trapezium:** Half sum of parallel sides times perpendicular distance between them.

**Circle:** Pi times square of radius.

**Cylinder:** Circumference of base ($\pi D$) times height (plus circles at top and bottom).

### Volumes (see Mensuration 3, page 248)

**Prism:** Cross-section area times height (or length).

**Pyramid:** One-third of base area times perpendicular height.

Note: A cylinder is a prism; a cone is a pyramid.

### Percentages (see Percentages, pages 215 to 217)

**Fraction to %:** Fraction times 100%.

**One amount as a percentage of another amount:** First amount over second amount times 100%.

**Change %:** Change over original times 100%. (Change may be an increase/profit or a decrease/loss.)

**To increase by $r$%:** Multiply by [100 plus $r$] divided by 100.

**Example** To increase by 8% multiply by 1.08.

**To decrease by $r$%:** Multiply by [100 minus $r$] divided by 100.

**Example** To decrease by 8% multiply by 0.92.

**Beware:** Watch out for questions where you know the amount *after* the percentage change.

**Example** Price £50 including 15% VAT. What is pre-VAT price?
It is no good working out 15% of £50, or 85% or £50, because the 15% was on the pre-VAT price which you do not know! See Percentages 7, page 216 for the correct method.

### Arithmetical terms

**Reciprocal:** One over the number.

**HCF:** The highest factor of all the given numbers. It cannot be bigger than the smallest number given.

**LCM:** The lowest multiple of all the given numbers. It must be at least as big as the biggest number given.

# L

## GRAPHS

### Straight line (see Graphs 2, page 221)

$y = f(x)$ or $y = mx + c$

**Example**  $f(x) = 3x + 2$ or $y = 3x + 2$

For $y = mx + c$, $m$ is the slope and $c$ the $y$-intercept (the crossing point on the $y$-axis).

### Curves

$y = ax^2 + bx + c$ gives a parabola ($b$ and/or $c$ may be zero); see Graphs 4 and 5, pages 222 to 223.

$y = ax^3 + bx^2 + cx + d$ gives a cubic curve; see Figure L1 ($b$ and/or $c$ and/or $d$ may be zero).

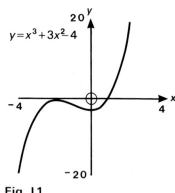

**Fig. L1**

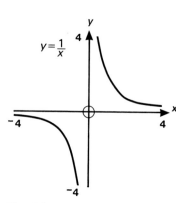

**Fig. L2**

$y = \dfrac{a}{x}$ gives an exponential curve; see Figure L2.

### Equation solution (see Graphs 6, page 224)

Where two graphs cross their $y$-values are equal.

**Example**  Where $y = x + 1$ crosses $y = x^2 + 2x - 1$ the equation solved is
$$x + 1 = x^2 + 2x - 1 \xrightarrow{\text{becomes}} x^2 + x - 2 = 0.$$

To solve an equation from a given parabola, change the given equation to the drawn one, then draw a straight line to cross it.

**Example**  To solve $x^2 + 3x - 4 = 0$ from $y = x^2 + x - 3$.
$$x^2 + 3x - 4 = 0 \xrightarrow{-2x+1} x^2 + x - 3 = -2x + 1$$
Draw $y = -2x + 1$ and read values of $x$ where the graphs cross.

### Tangents to curves

To find **slope of graph** at $(a, b)$, draw tangent at $x = a$.

**Distance/time graph** (time horizontal): slope gives speed. See page 47.

**Speed/time graph** (time horizontal): slope gives acceleration; area under gives distance (use trapeziums). See page 51.

270

## ALGEBRA

### Indices (see Algebra 8, page 230)

**To multiply:** Add indices of same letters.
(Remember that, for example, $b$ is $b^1$ not $b^0$, so $b \times b^2 \to b^3$.)

**To divide:** Subtract indices of same letters.

**Negative indices:** Negative index means 'one over'.

**Fractional indices:** Fractional index is a root.

### Factorisation (see Algebra 11, page 231)

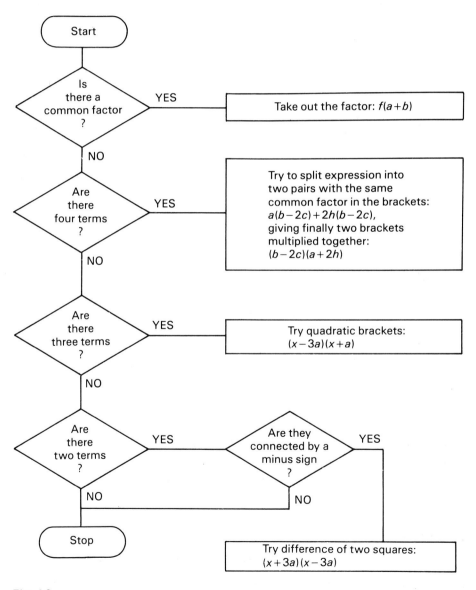

**Fig. L3**

**Functions** (see Algebra 16, page 236)

**fg(x)** means: Use function g first, then use function f on the answer.

## Equations

**One letter-term:** Solve by inspection; see Algebra 4, page 226.

**Two letter-terms:** Reduce to one letter-term by adding or subtracting on both sides so that one of the letter-terms becomes zero; see Algebra 6, page 228.

**Quadratic** (involving a square, like $x^2$): Factorise if possible, otherwise use the formula; see Algebra 12, page 233. For $ax^2 + bx + c = 0$,

$$x = \frac{-b \pm \sqrt{b^2 - 4ac}}{2a}$$

**Variation** (see Algebra 17, page 236)

**Direct proportion:** As one increases so does the other, by the same multiplying factor.

**Inverse proportion:** As one increases the other decreases, by the same fractional multiplying factor.

**Varies as x and y:** Multiply the variables.

**Example**  $p$ varies as $t$ and as the square of $v$.
$$p \propto tv^2 \rightarrow p = ktv^2 \ (k \text{ constant})$$

## GEOMETRY

**Loci** (paths of moving points)

The **locus** of a point moving so that it is a constant distance from:
(a)  a line – is a **parallel line**
(b)  a fixed point – is a **circle**
(c)  two fixed points – is the **perpendicular bisector of the line joining the points**
(d)  the arms of an angle – is the **bisector of the angle**.

### Rhombus/kite/square

Diagonals cross at right angles.

**Polygons** (see Geometry 7, page 243)

**Exterior angles:** Total 360° in all polygons.

**Interior angles:** Total $(n - 2) \times 180°$ in an $n$-sided polygon.

**Circles** (see Geometry 8, page 243)

**Angles in the same segment** are equal. (Start and finish at same points on circumference.)

**Angles at centre and circumference:** Centre angle is twice circumference angle. (Make sure that they open out the 'same way'.)

**Angle in semi-circle** is a right angle.

**Cyclic quadrilaterals:** Opposite angles total 180°. (They are NOT equal unless the quadrilateral is a rectangle.)

**Tangents:** Tangent meets radius at 90°.

The two tangents from a point to a circle are equal.

## Pythagoras

$h^2 = a^2 + b^2$ ($h$, the **hypotenuse**, is the longest side in a right-angled triangle.)

## Bearings

**Three-figure:** Measured clockwise from north.

**Back bearings:** Add 180°; if answer more than 360°, subtract 360°.

**Example**   Town A is on a bearing of 235° from town B. Find the bearing of town B from town A.
$235 + 180 = 415 \xrightarrow{-360} 055°$.

## Circles round the earth

**Great circles:** A great circle is the largest circle that can be drawn on the surface of a sphere. The equator is a great circle, so are all lines of longitude through the north and south poles. On the equator or any line of longitude (meridian), 1 minute of arc is 1 nautical mile long.

**Latitudes:** Circles drawn parallel to the equator. On latitude $\theta°$N or $\theta°$S, 1 minute of arc is $\cos \theta$ nautical miles long.

**Knot:** A speed of one nautical mile per hour.

## TRIGONOMETRY

**Right-angled triangles** (see Trigonometry 1, page 250)

one ancient teacher of history swore at his class

**Sine rule** (see Trigonometry 4, page 252)

$$\frac{a}{\sin A} = \frac{b}{\sin B} \text{ to find side } a; \qquad \frac{\sin A}{a} = \frac{\sin B}{b} \text{ to find angle A}$$

You must know a side/angle pair, e.g. side $b$ and angle B.

**Cosine rule** (see Trigonometry 5, page 253)

$$a^2 = b^2 + c^2 - 2bc \cos A \text{ to find side } a; \qquad A = \arccos \frac{b^2 + c^2 - a^2}{2bc} \text{ to find angle A}$$

Use when you cannot use the sine rule.

**Note:** Do not use the sine rule to find the biggest angle in a triangle; it might be obtuse, but your calculator will only give you an acute angle. Find a smaller angle first, then use angle sum of triangle.

**Area of triangle** (see Trigonometry 7, page 254)

**Area $\triangle$ABC** $= \frac{1}{2}ab \sin C$

## STATISTICS

### Averages (see Statistics 1, page 255)

**Mode:** Most common.

**Median:** Middle.

**Mean:** Total divided by number of items, often called *the* average.

## PROBABILITY

### Independent (see Probability 2, page 257)

All can happen either consecutively or simultaneously. Key word is *and*.

**Rule:** Multiply the probabilities.

### Exclusive (see Probability 3, page 257)

Only one can happen in a given sequence of events. Key word is *or*.

**Rule:** Add the probabilities.

### 'Not'

The probability of something not happening is 1 minus the probability of it happening. This can save a lot of work, e.g. to find the probability of at least one black pencil being picked, find 1 minus the probability of no black pencils beings picked.

## VECTORS

### Identical vectors (see Vectors 5, page 267)

If $a = b$, then $|a| = |b|$ and $a$ is parallel to $b$.

If $ha = kb$, then either $a$ is parallel to $b$, or $h = k = 0$.

## TRANSFORMATIONS

### Descriptions

**Enlargement:** Scale factor, centre.

**Reflection:** Mirror line.

**Rotation:** Angle of turn (+ve anticlockwise), centre.

**Translation:** Vector.

**Shear:** Invariant line, mapping of one point.

**Stretch:** Stretch factor, invariant line.

## MATRICES

### Order

Always pre-multiply by the transforming matrix (i.e. write it in front of the matrix that defines the corners of the shape to be transformed).

PQ(A) means transform shape A first by Q, then apply matrix P to the resulting image.

### Area

The determinant of the transforming matrix gives the change in the area.

### Inverse  (see Matrices 3, page 264)

To find the inverse of $\begin{pmatrix} a & b \\ c & d \end{pmatrix}$:

$$ad - bc = x$$

$$\begin{pmatrix} a & b \\ c & d \end{pmatrix} \rightarrow \frac{1}{x} \begin{pmatrix} d & -c \\ -b & a \end{pmatrix}$$

# Glossary

If you cannot remember what a word means, or cannot find a particular topic in the Reference Notes, this glossary should help you. 'See Geometry 1', for example, refers you to Note 1 on Geometry. Words in *italics* may be looked up in this glossary.

## A

**Adjacent**        Next to: see Geometry 1, page 238.

**Allied**        Joined to: see Geometry 1, page 238.

**Alternate**        On opposite sides: see Geometry 1, page 238.

**Altitude**        Height; a triangle has three altitudes, depending on which side is taken as the base line.

**Amount**        The whole, for example *principal* sum plus interest.

**Apex**        The top point, especially of a triangle.

**Appreciation**        Increase in value.

**Approximate**        About the same: see Basic arithmetic 1, page 208.

**Arc**        Part of the circumference of a circle: see Mensuration 4, page 249.
A line joining two *nodes*.

**Associative**        An *operation* (e.g. +, −, ×, ÷) which is unaffected by brackets when three or more terms are combined, e.g. + is associative as 3 + (4 + 5) = (3 + 4) + 5, but − is not as 3 − (4 − 5) ≠ (3 − 4) − 5.

**Average**        Usually the *mean* of a set of data, but *mode* and *median* are also averages in statistics.

## B

**Bearing**        The direction of one point from another. Cardinal bearings use N, E, S and W. Three-figure bearings are measured in degrees clockwise from north, e.g. east is 090° and west is 270°.

**Binary**        Base two; the number system that uses only the figures 0 and 1.

## C

**Cardinal**        See *Bearing*.

**Change the subject**        See Algebra 7, page 229.

**Chord**        A straight line joining two points on the circumference of a circle. The *perpendicular bisector* of a chord is a *diameter*: see Geometry 2, Figure R29, page 239.

**Circumcircle**        The circle passing through the *vertices* of a *polygon*: see Geometry 2, Figure R29, page 239, and Geometry 8, Figure R55, page 244.

**Class**        In statistics, a group of items between two limits: see Statistics 3, page 255.

| | |
|---|---|
| **Coefficient** | The *constant* multiplying an algebraic term, e.g. the 3 in $3x^2$. |
| **Collinear** | In the same straight line. |
| **Column matrix** | A matrix with only one columns of figures, e.g. the vector $\begin{pmatrix} 2 \\ 3 \end{pmatrix}$. |
| **Commission** | Pay which depends on the value of the goods sold or services supplied. |
| **Commutative** | An *operation* (e.g. +, −, ×, ÷) which is unaffected by the order of the terms: e.g. + is commutative as $2 + 3 = 3 + 2$, but − is not as $2 - 3 \neq 3 - 2$. |
| **Complement** | One of two parts that make up a whole. Complementary angles add up to 90°. Complement of a set: see Sets 1, page 258. |
| **Concave** | 'With a cave'; a concave polygon has at least one angle pointing inwards ('re-entrant'). |
| **Concurrent** | Meeting at the same point. |
| **Congruent** | Exactly the same both in shape and size: see Geometry 5, page 241. |
| **Conjecture** | A guess or forecast without proof. |
| **Consecutive** | Following one after another: 5, 7, 9 are consecutive odd numbers. If $n$ is even then $n$, $n + 2$ and $n + 4$ are consecutive even numbers. |
| **Constant** | Unchanging: a constant term in an algebraic expression will be the same for all values of the letters (the *variables*). |
| **Construct** | Draw accurately, usually using only a ruler and a pair of compasses. |
| **Convex** | 'Pointing outwards'; the opposite of *concave*. |
| **Co-ordinates** | $(x, y)$ defines the position of a point on a graph: see Graphs 1, page 221. |
| **Corresponding** | In the same position: see Geometry 1, page 238. |
| **Cosine** | The ratio '*adjacent* over *hypotenuse*' in a right-angled triangle: see Trigonometry 1, page 250. |
| **Cosine rule** | $a^2 = b^2 + c^2 - 2bc \cos A$ in $\triangle ABC$, which need not be right-angled: see Trigonometry 5, page 253. |
| **Cross-section** | A cut across a solid. |
| **Cubic** | In the shape of, or involving, a cube. $1 \text{ cm}^3$ (one cubic centimetre) is the volume of anything with the same volume as a cube of side 1 cm. A cubic expression involves a letter-term of *power* three, e.g. $4x^3 - 2x + 1$. |
| **Cuboid** | A solid with six rectangular faces, like a brick. If all the rectangles are squares it is called a cube. |
| **Cumulative frequency curve** | See Statistics 4, page 256. |
| **Cyclic quadrilateral** | A quadrilateral with its four corners on the circumference of a circle: see Geometry 8, page 243. |

## D

| | |
|---|---|
| **Decimal places** | The number of figures after the decimal point: see Basic arithmetic 1(a), page 208. |
| **Deduce** | To reach a conclusion by reasoning. |
| **Denary** | Based on ten; our usual number system. |
| **Denominator** | The bottom number in a common fraction; it indicates into how many parts the whole has been divided. |
| **Deposit** | An initial payment to reserve a piece of property; an amount paid into a savings account. |
| **Depreciation** | Loss in value. |
| **Determinant** | For matrix $\begin{pmatrix} a & b \\ c & d \end{pmatrix}$ the determinant is $ad - bc$: see Matrices 3, page 264. |
| **Diagonal** | A line joining two corners of a *polygon* which are not *adjacent*. |
| **Diameter** | The *chord* which passes through the centre of a circle. |
| **Difference** | The result of a subtraction. |
| **Digit** | One of the figures in a number. |
| **Digit-sum** | Used in this course for the result of continually adding the *digits* of a number until a single digit results: see Basic arithmetic 5, page 210. |
| **Directed numbers** | See Basic arithmetic 6, page 210. |
| **Discount** | The amount by which a price is reduced. |
| **Discrete** | Able to be measured exactly, e.g. the number of pages in a book. The opposite is continuous, e.g. the length of a line, which can never be given exactly. |
| **Dividend** | The number being divided, e.g. the 8 in $8 \div 4$. |
| **Divisor** | The number you are dividing by, e.g. the 4 in $8 \div 4$. |
| **Domain** | The set of numbers, or the *region*, on which *operations* are performed. |

## E

| | |
|---|---|
| **Element** | A member of a set; one of the things being combined in an *operation*. |
| **Exclusive** | In probability, events which cannot all happen in the same trial: see Probability 3, page 257. |
| **Expand** | In algebra, to multiply out the brackets, e.g. $(x + 3)(x - 3)$ expands to $x^2 - 9$. |
| **Expression** | A collection of terms with no equality given, e.g. $4x - 2y^2 + 3z$. |
| **Exterior angle** | The angle between a *produced* side of a *polygon* and the *adjacent* side: see Geometry 7, page 243. |

**F**

| | |
|---|---|
| **Face** | The flat side of a *polyhedron*. |
| **Factorise** | Split an *expression* into *factors*; see Algebra 11, page 231. |
| **Factors** | Numbers or *expressions* that multiply by others to make the whole, e.g. 5 and 10 are factors of 100. For algebraic factors see Algebra 11, page 231. |
| **Fibonacci sequence** | A sequence made by adding the previous two terms, usually starting 1, 1, 2, 3, 5, 8. |
| **Formulate** | To express in a clear or definite form. |
| **Frequency** | How often something happens: see Statistics 2, 3 and 4, pages 255 and 256. |
| **Frustum** | The part of a pyramid or cone contained between the base and a plane parallel to the base. |
| **Function** | An algebraic 'event', e.g. a function of $x$ may be such that any value, $x$, becomes $x^2$, often written as $f(x) : x \rightarrow x^2$, or $f(x) = x^2$. Then $f(2) = 4$, as 4 is $2^2$. See Algebra 16, page 236. |

**G**

| | |
|---|---|
| **Generalise** | Express in general terms, usually using an algebraic formula. |
| **Gradient** | The slope of a line; in mathematics the *tangent* of the angle made with the horizontal; in surveying, the *sine* of this angle. See under $y = mx + c$. |
| **Gross** | The whole amount, before any deductions. |

**H**

| | |
|---|---|
| **Hatch** | To define an area by drawing a set of parallel sloping lines on it. |
| **Hexadecimal** | Base sixteen, which uses the letters $a$ to $f$ to represent 10 to 15 in machine-code programming of computers. |
| **Highest common factor (HCF)** | The highest *factor* that divides exactly into each member of a set of numbers or *expressions*: see Basic arithmetic 9, page 211, and Algebra 11, page 231. |
| **Histogram** | A bar-chart in which the area of the bars represents the frequency. There is no vertical scale, but a key showing the area that represents one unit. |
| **Hypotenuse** | The longest side in a right-angled triangle. |

**I**

| | |
|---|---|
| **Image** | The result of a transformation. |
| **Improper fraction** | A top-heavy fraction, like $\frac{13}{2}$. |
| **Incircle** | The circle drawn inside a *polygon* with each side of the polygon a *tangent* to the circle: see Geometry 2, Figure R28, page 239. |

| | |
|---|---|
| **Inclusive** | 'Including everything', e.g. {integers from 1 to 3 inclusive} = {1, 2, 3}. |
| **Independent** | In probability, events which all happen in the same trial; compare with *exclusive* events: see Probability 2, page 257. |
| **Infinite** | Without ending. |
| **Intercept** | Part of a line between two crossing points. |
| **Interior angle** | The angle made inside a polygon by two *adjacent* sides: see Geometry 7, page 243. |
| **Intersection** | The crossing point. |
| **Invoice** | A bill, setting out the payment required. |
| **Irrational** | Unable to be written as a common fraction, e.g. $\pi$, $\sqrt{2}$. |

**K**

| | |
|---|---|
| **Kite** | A special quadrilateral: see Geometry 3, page 240. |

**L**

| | |
|---|---|
| **Linear equation** | An equation with only one *solution*: see Algebra 4, 5 and 6, pages 226 to 228. |
| **Linear graph** | Straight-line graph: see Graphs 2, page 221. |
| **Litre** | The metric unit for capacity; 1 litre = 1000 cm$^3$ (or c.c.); 1 ml = 1 cm$^3$. |
| **Locus** | The path made by a moving point: see page 272. |
| **Loss/Loss%** | The opposite of *profit*. A car bought for £8000 and sold for £2000 is sold at a loss of £6000 or $\frac{6000}{8000} \times 100\% = 75\%$. |
| **Lowest common multiple (LCM)** | The lowest number that is a *multiple* of each member of a set of numbers: see Basic arithmetic 10, page 212. |

**M**

| | |
|---|---|
| **Magnitude** | The size (e.g. length) of something. Magnitude of a vector: see Vectors 7, page 268. |
| **Mapping** | The action of a *function*: see Algebra 16, page 236. |
| **Mean** | A statistical average: see Statistics 1, page 255. |
| **Median** | A statistical average: see Statistics 1, page 255. |
| **Mixed number** | A number consisting of an integer and a fraction, like $3\frac{3}{4}$. |
| **Mode** | A statistical average: see Statistics 1, page 255. |
| **Modulus** | The *magnitude* of a vector: see Vectors 7, page 268. |
| **Multiple** | A number made by multiplying one integer by another. |
| **Multiplying factor** | The fraction used to increase or decrease in a given ratio, e.g. to change in the ratio $x : y$ use the multiplying factor $\frac{x}{y}$. |

**N**

| | |
|---|---|
| **Natural numbers** | Numbers used for counting. |
| **Net** | The plane shape that folds to make a solid. <br> The amount left after deductions. |
| **Node** | Junction in a network: see Matrices 5, page 266. |
| **Notation** | The symbols used in a mathematical problem. |
| **Numerator** | The top number in a fraction. |

**O**

| | |
|---|---|
| **Octal** | Base eight, using the figures 0 to 7 only. |
| **Operation** | A way of combining elements. It may be a standard method, such as $+$, $-$, $\times$ or $\div$, or a combination defined by a special sign, often $*$ or $\circ$. For example $a * b$ could be defined to mean double $a$ then add the square of $b$, so that $2 * 4 = 20$. |
| **Ordered pair** | An alternative name for *co-ordinates*. |

**P**

| | |
|---|---|
| **Parabola** | The curve obtained when a cone is cut by a plane parallel to the *slant height*: see Graphs 4, page 222. |
| **Parallelogram** | A special quadrilateral: see Geometry 3, page 240. |
| **Pentagon** | A five-sided *polygon*. |
| **Percentage error** | An indication of the seriousness of an arithmetical error. Found by the formula: (Error/True) $\times$ 100%. |
| **Percentile** | See Statistics 4, page 256. |
| **Perpendicular** | At right angles. <br> Dropping a perpendicular: see Geometry 2, Figure R30, page 239. |
| **Perpendicular bisector** | A line which crosses the midpoint of another line at right angles: see Geometry 2, Figures R26 and R29, page 239. |
| **Pictogram** | A chart showing information by means of picture symbols that represent a certain amount. |
| **Plural** | More than one. |
| **Point symmetry** | A figure has point symmetry if it looks the same after a rotation of 180°. |
| **Polygon** | A many-sided figure: see Geometry 7, page 243. |
| **Polyhedron** | A solid with flat faces; the five regular ('Platonic') polyhedra are: tetrahedron (4 equilateral triangles); cube (6 squares); octahedron (8 equilateral triangles); dodecahedron (12 regular pentagons); icosahedron (20 equilateral triangles). |
| **Position vector** | A vector giving the *co-ordinates* of a point: see Vectors 2, page 267. |

| | |
|---|---|
| **Power** | The result of multiplying a number by itself a number of times. It can be shown using an index (raised figure), e.g. as $5^3$ (the third power of 5). |
| **Premium** | Payment made for insurance. |
| **Prime** | A number which has only two *factors*, itself and 1: see Basic arithmetic 8, page 211. |
| **Principal** | Money on which interest is paid: see Percentages 8, page 217. |
| **Prism** | A solid with a constant *cross-section*. |
| **Produce** | To make a line longer, e.g. 'Produce AB to C' means lengthen line AB from end B until it reaches point C. |
| **Product** | The result of multiplying numbers. |
| **Profit** | The gain made when something is sold for more than was paid for it. Percentage profit is found from the formula: (Profit/Cost price) × 100%. |
| **Proportion** | Two quantities are in proportion when they are in a constant ratio, e.g. m.p.h. and km/h. They give a straight-line conversion graph. See Ratio 1 to 10, pages 212 to 215. |
| **Pyramid** | A solid with a *polygon* as its base and triangular sides meeting at a common *vertex*. |

## Q

| | |
|---|---|
| **Quadratic equation** | An equation involving a squared term, e.g. $3x^2 - 3 = 4x$. |
| **Quartile** | See Statistics 4, page 256. |
| **Quotient** | The result of a division. |

## R

| | |
|---|---|
| **Rank** | To place in order, e.g. of size. |
| **Range** | The distance between two points. |
| **Rateable value** | The amount allotted to a property on which the rates to be paid to the council depend. For example, if a house has a rateable value of £300 and the rate is 50p in the £, then £150 will have to be paid. |
| **Rational** | Able to be written exactly as a common fraction. |
| **Real number** | A number that exists and can be written as a (possibly endless) decimal fraction; $\pi$ is real but $\sqrt{-1}$ is not. |
| **Reciprocal** | One over a number, e.g. the reciprocal of 2 is $\frac{1}{2}$ or 0.5. |
| **Rectangular numbers** | Numbers that are not prime (except 1). |
| **Recur** | To repeat, as in recurring decimals, the repeating figure(s) being indicated with a dot (or two dots). |
| **Reflex** | An angle more than 180°. If a reflex angle is intended then it will be written as 'Angle ABC reflex'. |

| | |
|---|---|
| **Region** | A special area of a diagram, especially of a graph or network. See Graphs 3, page 222, Matrices 5, page 266. |
| **Resultant** | In vectors, the one vector that gives the same final position as all the others in sequence: see Vectors 6, page 268. |
| **Rhombus** | A special quadrilateral: see Geometry 3, page 240. |
| **Roots** | The *solutions* of an equation. |
| **Rotational symmetry** | The number of times a shape fits into a tracing of itself in one full rotation is the order of rotational symmetry, e.g. a square is of order 4. Rotational symmetry of order 1 is often not counted as true rotational symmetry. See Symmetry 2, page 245. |
| **Round off** | To approximate: see Basic arithmetic 1, page 208. |

S

| | |
|---|---|
| **Scale factor** | The factor by which a figure has been enlarged: see Transformations 3, page 261. |
| **Scientific notation** | See Basic arithmetic 2, page 208. |
| **Sector** | Part of a circle between two radii: see Mensuration 4, page 249. |
| **Segment** | Part of a circle cut off by a *chord*: see Geometry 8, page 243. |
| **Shear** | To push an object sideways from a fixed line: see Transformations 5, page 261. |
| **Shift vector** | A vector which describes a translation (sliding): see Vectors 3, page 267. |
| **Significant figures** | See Basic arithmetic 1 (b), page 208. |
| **Similar** | Exactly the same shape. Two similar objects have *corresponding* sides in the same ratio. For similar solids with sides' ratio $x : y$, their areas are in the ratio $x^2 : y^2$ and their volumes are in the ratio $x^3 : y^3$. |
| **Simplify** | In algebra, to make an *expression* simpler, usually by multiplying out brackets and collecting like terms. |
| **Simultaneous** | At the same time: see Algebra 5, page 226. |
| **Sine** | The ratio 'opposite over *hypotenuse*' in a right-angled triangle: see Trigonometry 1, page 250. |
| **Sine rule** | $a/(\sin A) = b/(\sin B)$ or $(\sin A)/a = (\sin B)/b$ in $\triangle ABC$, which need not be right-angled: see Trigonometry 4, page 252. |
| **Slant height** | The shortest distance from the *apex* of a *pyramid* to the base, measured along a *face*. |
| **Solution** | The value(s) of the letter(s) that make(s) an equation true. |
| **Solve** | To find the numerical value of the letter(s). |
| **Sphere** | The mathematical name for a ball. |
| **Standard form** | See Basic arithmetic 2, page 208. |

| | |
|---|---|
| **Step graph** | See Figure 9:5. |
| **Subtend** | Angle APB is subtended at point P by the lines AP and BP: see Geometry 8, page 243. |
| **Sum** | The result of an addition. |
| **Supplementary** | Adding up to 180°. |
| **Surd** | An *irrational* number. |

**T**

| | |
|---|---|
| **Tangent** | A straight line which touches, but does not cross, a curve. The ratio 'opposite over *adjacent*' in a right-angled triangle: see Trigonometry 1, page 250. |
| **Taxable income** | The amount of your pay on which you have to pay tax: you are allowed to earn a certain amount each year free of income tax. |
| **Tonne** | A metric unit of weight (mass) equal to 1000 kg. |
| **Topological transformation** | Distortion of a shape without altering the number of *nodes*, *arcs* or *regions*: see Transformations 7, page 262. |
| **Translate** | To slide a shape: see Transformations 4, page 261. |
| **Transpose** | To *change the subject* of a formula. |
| **Trapezium** | A special quadrilateral: see Geometry 3, page 240. |
| **Triangular number** | One of a sequence of numbers of dots that make equilateral triangles. The sequence starts 1, 3, 6, 10, 15 . . . The $n$th term is $\frac{1}{2}n(n+1)$. |

**V**

| | |
|---|---|
| **Variable** | A letter which may stand for various numbers. |
| **Vertex** | A corner of a shape. |
| **Vertices** | The plural of *vertex*. |
| **Vulgar fraction** | A common fraction that is not top-heavy. |

**Y**

| | |
|---|---|
| $y = mx + c$ | The general equation of all straight-line graphs. $m$ is the slope or *gradient* and $c$ is the crossing point on the $y$-axis. See Graphs 2, page 221. |
| $y = x^2 + bx + c$ | The general equation of all parabolas. $c$ is the crossing point on the $y$-axis. If $b = 0$ the parabola is symmetrical about the $y$-axis. To find where the parabola crosses the $x$-axis (if it does), solve $ax^2 + bx + c = 0$. See Graphs 4 to 6. |

# Answers

**Note:** The answers to some of the boxed extension questions are omitted; these are left for you to puzzle out.

## Exercise 1

**1**  (a) 17, 19   (b) 16   (c) 20   (d) 18   (e) 15
**2**  1 (or 0)
**3**  4 or 5
**4**  (a) 23.4   (b) 0.12
**5**  (a) $-\frac{1}{2}$ foot   (b) 1 foot   (c) $-1\frac{1}{2}$ feet
**6**  (a) 5   (b) 300
**7**  (a) rational   (b) irrational   (c) rational
**8**  (a) 10   (b) 2   (c) 24   (d) $\frac{2}{3}$, 0.$\dot{6}$; $\frac{3}{2}$, 1.5
**9**  (a) 1894, 119, 24, 1985, 15   (b) 6000, 200
**10**  (a) 340   (b) 0.0638
**11**  (a) $9.85 \times 10$   (b) $4.6 \times 10^{-1}$
**12**  (a) 0.4   (b) 60%   (c) $\frac{7}{100}$   (d) $\frac{3}{20}$
**13**  1, 2, 3, 4, 6, 12
**14**  (a) 1, 3   (b) 2, 3   (c) 1, 4   (d) 1, 2, 4
    (e) 4, 12   (f) 1, 3, 6   (g) 4, 6, 12
**15**  (a) 1000   (b) 1 000 000   (c) 200 056
**16**  (a) $1 \times 10^3$   (b) $1 \times 10^6$
    (c) $2.000\,56 \times 10^5$
**17**  (a) 2.8   $-04$   (b) 3.65   $-02$
    (c) 8.42   $-01$
**18**  (a) 149.9 mm   (b) 14.99 cm
**19**  (a) 20   (b) 126
**20**  (a) $2 \times 3 \times 3$   (b) $3 \times 13$   (c) $2 \times 3 \times 7$
**21**  (a) A, $\frac{3}{4}$;  B, $1\frac{5}{8}$;  C, $2\frac{1}{4}$;  D, $3\frac{1}{3}$;  E, $4\frac{5}{6}$
    (b) A, 0.75;  B, 1.625;  C, 2.25;  D, 3.$\dot{3}$;
        E, 4.8$\dot{3}$
**22**  See Figure A1:1.
**23**  (a) 50%   (b) 25%   (c) 60%   (d) 57%
    (e) 18.75%
**24**  (a) $\frac{3}{4}$, 0.75   (b) $\frac{6}{25}$, 0.24   (c) $\frac{1}{3}$, 0.$\dot{3}$
**25**  (a) 5, 2   (b) 25, 36   (c) 48, 96   (d) 42, 56
    (e) $\frac{1}{32}$, $\frac{1}{64}$   (f) 0.01, 0.001   (g) $-1$, $-4$
    (h) 0, $-0.2$   (i) 125, 216   (j) 1, 2
**26**  12
**27**  6 by 4 by 4; 8 by 3 by 4; 12 by 2 by 4;
    24 by 1 by 4
**28**  £4; £2
**29**  4/5, 2/3, 0.6, 4/7, 1/3, 15%
**30**  33 °C

**31**  (a) 100   (b) $-2$
**32**  11
**33**  (a) even   (b) odd   (c) odd   (d) either
    (e) odd   (f) even   (g) odd   (h) even
**34**  112
**35**  (a) 0.5   (b) 0.143   (c) $\frac{4}{3}$ or 1.$\dot{3}$   (d) $\frac{5}{4}$ or 1.25
**36**  (a) $\frac{1}{2}$   (b) $\frac{1}{9}$   (c) $\pm 2$   (d) $\pm\frac{1}{2}$   (e) 4
    (f) $\frac{1}{2}$   (g) 1000
**37**  7 frames are possible.
**39**  (a) 51 200 km$^2$   (b) about 9 times as many
    (c) Scotland about 66, England about 358

## Exercise 2

**1**  (a) $1\frac{7}{12}$   (b) $\frac{1}{12}$   (c) $\frac{1}{2}$   (d) $1\frac{2}{7}$
**2**  (a) $2\frac{3}{20}$   (b) $2\frac{17}{20}$   (c) $1\frac{1}{3}$   (d) $\frac{3}{5}$
**3**  (a) about 1.2 million   (b) about 930 000
    (c) about 493.6 tonnes   (d) 6 h 55 min
    (e) 524 m.p.h.   (f) 3960 ft   (g) 8.3p
    (h) (i) 7 h 25 min   (ii) 1 h 40 min
        (iii) 9 h 2 min   (iv) 25 h 2 min
    (i) about 438 m.p.h.
**4**  (a) $\frac{17}{20}$   (b) $\frac{1}{21}$   (c) $\frac{1}{3}$   (d) $\frac{3}{8}$
**5**  (a) $1\frac{7}{8}$   (b) $1\frac{1}{6}$   (c) $\frac{4}{5}$   (d) $\frac{2}{5}$
**6**  £36 000
**7**  256
**8**  No; 5 min short
**9**  $\frac{3}{4}$
**10**  54 m.p.h.
**11**  (a) $\frac{1}{2}$   (b) 45
**12**  9
**13**  $8\frac{1}{3}$
**14**  (a) 1   (b) $3\frac{5}{8}$   (c) 5 250 000
**15**  (a) $-17.8$ °C   (b) $-23.3$ °C
**16**  
| | | | | | |
|---|---|---|---|---|---|
| N(1) | 7 | 1 | 1 | 1 | 1 |
| N(2) | 1 | 7 | 4 | 4 | 2 |
| N(3) | 4 | 4 | 7 | 2 | 4 |
| N(4) | 8 | 8 | 8 | 2 | 7 |
| N(5) | 2 | 2 | 2 | 8 | 8 |

## Exercise 3

**1**  £13.50
**2**  French 70%; German 80%. German best.
**3**  £56

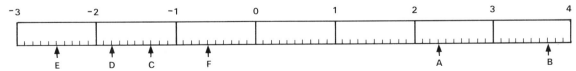

**Fig. A1:1**

**4** 167%
**5** (ii) 0.26   (iii) 2.15   (iv) 2.05
**6** (a) 16   (b) £85   (c) £2.52
**7** £16
**8** £2280
**9** 54p
**10** £13.94
**11** 20%
**12** 67%
**13** (a) £42   (b) 25%
**14** 21p
**15** (a) £2250   (b) £20 250
**16** 25%
**17** (a) £32   (b) £360   (c) £440   (d) £80
**18** (a) £120   (b) £72   (c) £2720; £440
**19** (a) £264   (b) £1.80   (c) £144
**20** (a) Rental, £345.60; Cash, £287.40; HP,
      £365.40
      (b) £101.60
**21** (a) £22.50   (b) £1.28   (c) £39.10   (d) £9
      (e) more than 32   (f) 20%
      (g) £28.80 or £46.80; £10.20
**22** £45 000
**23** (a) 8.4 million   (b) 11.6%
**24** £4913
**25** £741
**26** 2.5%
**27** (a) £10   (b) 26p
      (c) (i) £2.20   (ii) 22%
      (d) (i) the second   (ii) 30p
**28** (a) £4000   (b) 20%   (c) £5376   (d) 16.9%

**Exercise 4**

**1** (a) direct   (b) direct   (c) inverse   (d) direct
**2** graph (d)
**3** (a) 2:1   (b) 1:50   (c) 15:1   (d) 13:10
**4** (a) 3:1   (b) 2.4:1   (c) 0.75:1
**5** 15
**6** 240
**7** 10 m
**8** 5 km
**9** 20 litres
**10** £2.50
**11** (a) 3/8   (b) 37.5%   (c) 3.9 g
**12** Both the same
**13** 96 km/h
**14** 100 cm
**15** 1:3, 1:1, 3:1
**16** 9 h 36 min
**17** $C = zx/y$
**18** 10 ft
**19** 7.2 s
**20** No calculated division widths needed
**21** 500 ml, £1.65; 1 litre, £3.15; 2.5 litre, £7.53

**22** 141:1
**23** About 0.41

**Exercise 5**

**3** (a) 16.92   (b) −1.5   (c) 2.59
      (d) 15.4   (e) 23   (f) 6.4   (g) 0.725
      (h) 0.0452   (i) 6.13   (j) 0.263   (k) 0.273
      (l) 1.21
**4** (a) 4.47   (b) 3.46   (c) 0.143   (d) 7
**5** (a) 265   (b) 500   (c) £2.99   (d) 143 m
**6** (a) 286.84   (b) 493.1   (c) £2.87
      (d) 159.82 m
**7** (a) £13.28   (b) 19.28%   (c) 56%
**8** (a) £9.18   (b) £13.50   (c) £27
**9** (a) 3.45 million   (b) 35.4%
**10** (a) £35.50   (b) £55.10   (c) 26
**11** (a) 153   (b) 60.4   (c) 0.201   (d) 0.939
      (e) 41.1
**12** (a) 966 thousand   (b) 3.85%
**13** (a) 2775
**14** (a) 10.5   (b) 2.71   (c) 0.843   (d) 0.675
**15** (a) 284   (b) 220
**16** (a) 627 thousand   (b) 972 thousand
**17** (a) −3.665   (b) −3.665   (c) 17.48
      (d) −3.75

**Exercise 6**

**1** (a) $4.12 \times 10^7 \, m^2$   (b) $1.51 \times 10^7$
      (c) 9.38 m   (d) $6.114 \times 10^9$ litres
**2** (a) 166 min   (b) 26 min
      (c) A, 24;  B, 81;  C, 60   (d) 39 m.p.h.
      (e) 11.4p   (f) Basingstoke to Winchester
**3** (a) 7 oz   (b) 344 g
**4** 6249 units
**5** (a) 3.2 V   (b) 32 V   (c) 6.5 V   (d) 320 V
      (e) 0.35 MΩ
**6** (a) (i) 120 ft   (ii) 0.7 s   (iii) 2.1 s
      (b) The thinking time is the same, but the
          faster your speed the further you will travel
          while you are thinking.
**7**   30   0.7    5   0.7    6   1.4   10
        60   0.7   10   1.4   25   2.1   35
        90   0.7   20   2.1   50   2.8   70
**8** (a) (i) £3595   (ii) £1800
      (b) (i) £11 176   (ii) £5400
      (c) £259
      (d) There is a higher risk of him not surviving.
      (e) £18; females have a higher life expectancy.
**9** 1270 therms
**10** See Figure A6:1.
**11** Man: about £1810; Woman: about £1750
**12** (a) 46 and 47
      (b) 22

**Fig. A6:1**

(c) Belgrave Gate; Charles Street; Rutland Street; Belvoir Street; Welford Road.
(d) Straight on along Belvoir Street. Take the first left past the Post Office, along Granby Street. Keep straight on until you reach the clock tower, then take the third exit along the Haymarket. The ABC is on your left before you reach the roundabout.

**13** Table should show from 5 rolls to 14 rolls required.
**14** (a) Paddington   (b) 2 h 33 min
   (c) 66.1 m.p.h.
**15** About 49 thousand.

## Exercise 7

**1** (a) 798 marks   (b) 372 francs
**2** £61.16
**3** (a) 18p   (b) £1.89   (c) £2.38
**4** (a) £360   (b) £400   (c) £276   (d) £124
   (e) 182 weeks
**5** £200
**6** (b) (i) £1323   (ii) £1449   (iii) £487
**7** (a) £35 247   (b) £587.45
**8** (a) £5040   (b) £4435.20   (c) £4213.44
**9** £70
**10** £30 000
**11** £2600
**12** £520
**13** Tax relief, £823.60; Net cost, £2016.40
**14** £447.30
**15** £7264
**16** Taxable pay, £7665; After tax, £5442.15
**17** (a) £9450   (b) £10 100   (c) £11 000
**18** (a) £45   (b) £74.94   (c) £31.50
   (d) £391.44
**19** £99
**20** (a) 2126   (b) 96   (c) £21.24   (d) £12.53
   (e) £33.70
**21** (a) £300   (b) £36   (c) £327.20   (d) £36.85
**22** (a) £356.70   (b) 5 years   (c) £607
   (d) £15.56   (e) £57.20
**23** (b) 23.1%
   (c) (i) £19.11   (ii) £9937.20
   (e) £69.72
**24** (a) £45 000   (b) £240
**25** (a) £237.12   (b) £3276.16   (c) £9720.85
   (d) £15 000

**26** (a) £1100   (b) 12   (c) £609.50
**27** £75.50; £93.14
**28** £199
**29** (a) £12
   (b) Bus, by 40p, but he does have the use of the motorcycle at other times too.
   (c) Motorcycle by £215, because he now owns it. However he should allow for depreciation.
**30** Suggested advice:
   (a) Try to find a 100% mortgage, otherwise increase your savings, then find another house at about the same price.
   (b) Go ahead and arrange the mortgage.
   (c) You are being too ambitious on your present income; try to find a cheaper house.
**31** £52.03
**32** £46 452
**34** (a) £9800   (b) £1234.17
**35** (a) £13.65   (b) 30p   (c) 36.5%

## Exercise 8

**1** (a) (i) A, $(-6, -3)$; B, $(6, -3)$ (ii) I, $(0, 1)$;
   J, $(-2, 3)$
   (b) (i) $y = -3$   (ii) $x = -6$   (iii) $y = \frac{1}{2}x$
   (c) IJ
**2** See Figure A8:1.

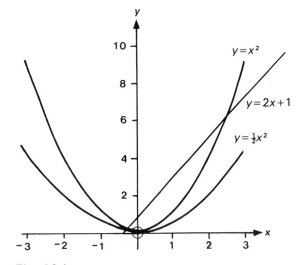

**Fig. A8:1**

<br>

**A**

3   (a) −0.2, −0.22, −0.25, −0.29, −0.33, −0.4,
        −0.5, −0.67, −1, −2, 0.2, 0.22, 0.25,
        0.29, 0.33, 0.4, 0.5, 0.67, 1, 2
    (b) You cannot divide by zero.
4   (a) $\frac{1}{2}$   (b) −1
5   (a) 5   (b) 8   (c) 10   (d) 4   (e) 3   (f) 1
6   See Figure A8:2.

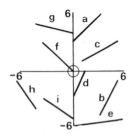

**Fig. A8:2**

7   (a) 1   (b) 2   (c) $\frac{1}{2}$   (d) 3   (e) $\frac{1}{6}$   (f) −1
    (g) $-\frac{1}{4}$   (h) $-\frac{3}{2}$   (i) $-\frac{2}{3}$
8   See Figure A8:3.

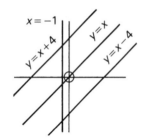

**Fig. A8:3**

9   See Figure A8:4.

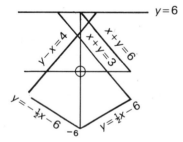

**Fig. A8:4**

10  See Figure A8:5.
11  (a) See Figure A8:6.
    (b) (1, 1); (3, 3); (5, 3); (5, 1)
12  See Figure A8:7.

290

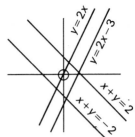

**Fig. A8:5**

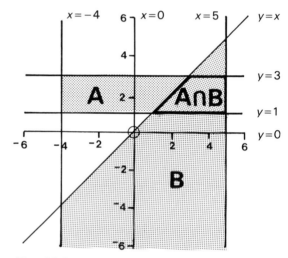

**Fig. A8:6**

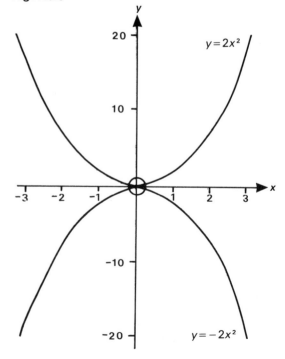

**Fig. A8:7**

**13** (a) See Figure A8:8.
(b) (i) about 32.2 cm² (ii) about 2.5 cm

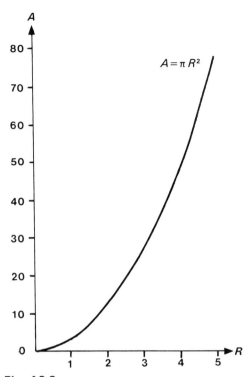

**Fig. A8:8**

**14** See Figure A8:9.

**15** See Figure A8:10.

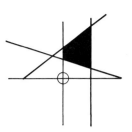

**Fig. A8:10**

**16** (a) −2.6, 1.6 (b) −2.3, 1.3
**17** (a) $x^2 + 2x + 1 = 0$ (b) $x^2 + 2x − 1 = 0$
(c) $x^2 + 2x − 2 = 0$ (d) $x^2 + 2x = 0$
(e) $2x^2 + 2x + 1 = 0$
**18** (a)

| −1 | 0 | 1 | 2 | 3 | 4 |
|---|---|---|---|---|---|
| 1 | 0 | 1 | 4 | 9 | 16 |
| 3 | 0 | −3 | −6 | −9 | −12 |
| 3 | 3 | 3 | 3 | 3 | 3 |
| 7 | 3 | 1 | 1 | 3 | 7 |

(b) $x = 1\frac{1}{2}$
(c) See Figure A8:11 (page 292).
(d) $y = \frac{3}{4}$
(e) 1, 2, $x^2 − 3x + 2 = 0$
(f) (i) 0, 3, $x^2 − 3x = 0$
(ii) −1, 4, $x^2 − 3x − 4 = 0$
(iii) 2.6, 0.4, $x^2 − 3x + 1 = 0$
(iv) 3.6, −0.6, $x^2 − 3x − 2 = 0$
(v) −1.2, 4.2, $x^2 − 3x − 5 = 0$

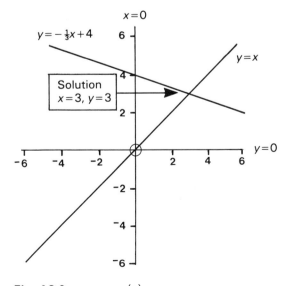

**Fig. A8:9** (a)

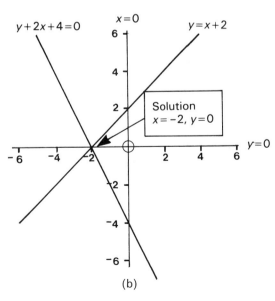

(b)

291

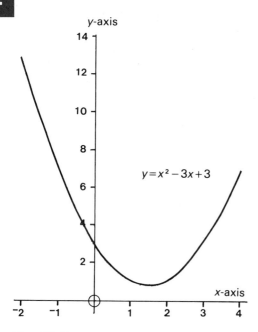

**Fig. A8:11**

19 (a)

| −3 | −2 | −1 | 0 | 1 | 2 |
|---|---|---|---|---|---|
| 18 | 8 | 2 | 0 | 2 | 8 |
| −12 | −8 | −4 | 0 | 4 | 8 |
| −5 | −5 | −5 | −5 | −5 | −5 |
| 1 | −5 | −7 | −5 | 1 | 11 |

(b) See Figure A8:12.

(c) −7, at $x = -1$

(d)   (i) −2, 0, $2x^2 + 4x = 0$

    (ii) −3, 1, $2x^2 + 4x - 6 = 0$

   (iii) −4, 2, $2x^2 + 4x - 16 = 0$

   (iv) 1.4, −3.4, $2x^2 + 4x - 10 = 0$

    (v) 0.7, −2.7, $2x^2 + 4x - 4 = 0$

   (vi) 0.2, −2.2, $2x^2 + 4x - 1 = 0$

  (vii) 1.2, −3.2, $2x^2 + 4x - 8 = 0$

(e) 0.9, −2.9

20 Read the values of $x$ where the parabola crosses the $x$-axis.

21 (a) 8   (b) −12   (c) −4

22 (a) 5   (b) −7   (c) −3   (d) −1   (e) 0

23 (a)

| −4 | −3.5 | −3 | −2.5 | −2 | −1.5 | −1 | −0.5 | 0 | 0.5 | 1 | 1.5 | 2 |
|---|---|---|---|---|---|---|---|---|---|---|---|---|
| 32 | 24.5 | 18 | 12.5 | 8 | 4.5 | 2 | 0.5 | 0 | 0.5 | 2 | 4.5 | 8 |
| −12 | −10.5 | −9 | −7.5 | −6 | −4.5 | −3 | −1.5 | 0 | 1.5 | 3 | 4.5 | 6 |
| −4 | −4 | −4 | −4 | −4 | −4 | −4 | −4 | −4 | −4 | −4 | −4 | −4 |
| 16 | 10 | 5 | 1 | −2 | −4 | −5 | −5 | −4 | −2 | 1 | 5 | 10 |

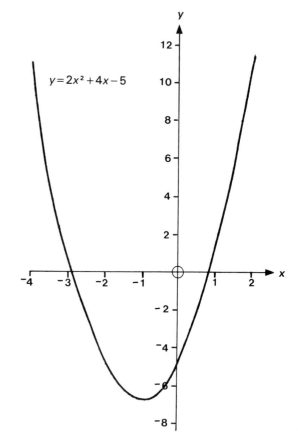

**Fig. A8:12**

(b) See Figure A8:13.
(c) (i) about −9   (ii) about 7

24 (a) 1.3, −2.8, $2x^2 + 3x − 7 = 0$
   (c) 1.5, −2, $2x^2 + x − 6 = 0$
25 (a) $2x^2 − 3x − 4 = 0$   (b) $2x^2 − 3x = 0$
   (c) $2x^2 − 4x − 1 = 0$   (d) $2x^2 − 4x − 3 = 0$
   (e) $2x^2 − 2x − 4 = 0$   (f) $2x^2 − x − 2 = 0$
26 (a) $y = −4x + 4$   (b) $y = −5x + 2$   (c) $y = x$
   (d) $y = −3x − 1$   (e) $y = −x + 5$
27 (a) See Figure A8:14.
   (b) See Figure A8:15.

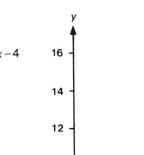

$y = 2x^2 + 3x − 4$

Fig. A8:13

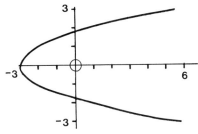

Fig. A8:14

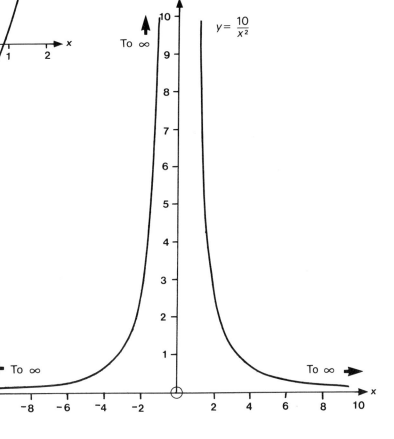

$y = \dfrac{10}{x^2}$

To ∞

To ∞

To ∞

Fig. A8:15

293

**27** (c) See Figure A8:16.

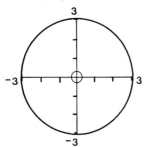

**Fig. A8:16**

(d) See Figure A8:17.

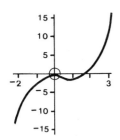

**Fig. A8:17**

**28** (a) See Figure A8:18.

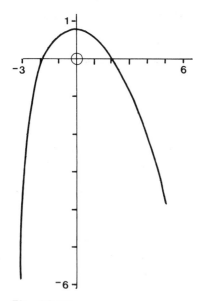

**Fig. A8:18**

(b) −1.28, 0.78
(c) $x^2 - x - 7 = 0$
(d) ∞

## Exercise 9

**2** (a) £14 000   (b) 3.6%   (c) 38.6%
   (d) £2100
**3** (a) 10p   (b) No; zero number ordered and
   zero cost impossible.
**4** (a) 30 min   (b) 0955   (c) 100 km/h
   (d) 50 km/h
**5** (a) (2000, 225); (3000, 325); (4000, 450);
   (5000, 600)
   (c) about £3600
**6** (a) 66 ft/s   (b) 34 m.p.h.   (c) 22 ft/s
   (d) 73 m.p.h.
**7** (b) (i) 45 s   (ii) about 92 s
**8** Figure 9:14   Average speed of 40 km/h for
   $\frac{1}{2}$ h, stationary for $\frac{1}{2}$ h, average
   speed of 20 km/h for 1 h.
   Figure 9:15   Average speed of 40 m.p.h. for
   3 h, stationary for 4 h, return
   journey at average speed of
   40 m.p.h.
   Figure 9:16   Average speed of 80 km/h for
   15 min, stationary for 15 min,
   average speed of 120 km/h for
   15 min, then average speed of
   20 km/h for 30 min.
**9** Figure 9:14   20 km/h
   Figure 9:15   24 m.p.h.
   Figure 9:16   48 km/h
**10** 1115, 50 miles; 1245, 15 miles
**11** 1 km/min
**12** CD
**13** CD, constant speed of 20 m/s; DE, acceleration
   of 20 m/s²; EF, constant speed of 30 m/s
**14** 20; $12\frac{1}{2}$; 45. Total is 112.5 metres.
**15** (a) 5 m s⁻²   (b) 310 m; 25.8 m/s
**16** (b) 64 m   (c) 134 s
**17** (b) (i) 0.9 m/s²   (ii) 0.45 m/s²   (c) 1370 m
**18** 2.7 miles
**20** (a) about 1:24p.m.   (b) about 30 km³/h²
   (c) about 163.5 km³
**21** (a) $\begin{pmatrix} 12 \\ 0 \end{pmatrix}$; $\begin{pmatrix} 11 \\ 3 \end{pmatrix}$; $\begin{pmatrix} 10 \\ 6 \end{pmatrix}$; $\begin{pmatrix} 9 \\ 9 \end{pmatrix}$; $\begin{pmatrix} 8 \\ 12 \end{pmatrix}$; $\begin{pmatrix} 7 \\ 15 \end{pmatrix}$
   (d) 5.4 m

## Exercise 10

**1** (a) 50 °F   (b) 30 °F   (c) 20 °F
**2** 6 m²
**3** (a) 15 ft   (b) 175 ft
**4** (a) 3   (b) 9   (c) −1   (d) −1   (e) 16
   (f) $2\frac{2}{3}$
**5** Figure 10:1, $4a + 4b$;   Figure 10:2, $14a + 4c$;
   Figure 10:3, $12a$;   Figure 10:4, $16a$

**6** Figure 10:5, $4a + 4b + 4c$;
Figure 10:6, $6x + 3y$;   Figure 10:7, $4s + 4b$;
Figure 10:8, $6a$

**7** (a) $T = S + L$   (b) $L = T - S$
(c) $S = T - L$

**8** (a) $z = xy$   (b) $x = z \div y$   (c) $y = z \div x$

**9** (a) $h = \dfrac{V}{wb}$   (b) $r = \sqrt{\dfrac{A}{\pi}}$   (c) $s = \dfrac{v^2 - u^2}{2a}$
(d) $c = 2S - a - b$   (e) $a = \sqrt{16 - b^2}$
(f) $c = \sqrt{\dfrac{E}{M}}$   (g) $h = \dfrac{S - \pi r^2}{2\pi r}$

**10** (a) $3x$ cm   (b) $2x$ cm   (c) $24x$ cm
(d) $22x^2$ cm   (e) $6x^3$ cm$^3$

**11** (a) 483   (b) 987   (c) 2142

**12** Double the number, then write a zero at the
end, then subtract the number.

**13** 10 lb

**14** (a) $3p$   (b) $3p$   (c) $4p$

**15** 36

**16** (a) 5   (b) 30   (c) 150   (d) 6

**17** 60 metres

**18** $(6 + 6p)$ kg

**19** $k/v$ hours

**20** (a) $12s$ cm   (b) $s^2$ cm$^2$   (c) $5s^2$ cm$^2$

**21** $6s^3$ cm$^3$

**22** $600s^3$ cm$^3$

**23** (a) 1   (b) 5   (c) 100   (d) 500

**24** Figure 10:11, $12a$;   Figure 10:12, $12a + 6b$;
Figure 10:13, $4a + 4b$

**25** Wage = $5x + 8y$ pounds

**26** (a) $y = 2nx - p$   (b) $n = \dfrac{p + y}{2x}$

**27** (a) $v = \dfrac{p}{m}$   (b) $s = \sqrt[3]{v}$   (c) $f = \dfrac{m^2 - a}{3}$
(d) $y = 2g - x - z$   (e) $\sqrt{4 - y^2}$

**28** (a) 4   (b) $-3$   (c) 9   (d) 0   (e) 1   (f) 0
(g) 16   (h) 0   (i) $f^{-1}: x \to \dfrac{x}{2}$
(j) $g^{-1}: x \to x + 1$

**29** $x = \dfrac{2ac}{ab - c}$

**30** (a) $c = \dfrac{5a + 3b}{4 - b}$   (b) $b = \dfrac{4c - 5a}{c + 3}$

**31** $a = \dfrac{7 - b^2}{b - 3}$

**32** $b = \dfrac{2a}{a - 1}$

**33** $D$

**34** $D$

**35** $\dfrac{50k}{3t}$ m min$^{-1}$

**36** (a) $f^{-1}: x \to \dfrac{1}{2(x - 3)}$   (b) $f^{-1}: x \to \dfrac{4x + 2}{x - 1}$
(c) $f^{-1}: x \to \sqrt[3]{\dfrac{x}{2}}$

**37** (a) 1000   (b) 1009   (c) 9991

**38** (a) $fg: x \to 2(x + 3)$;   $gf: x \to 2x + 3$;
$f^{-1}: x \to \dfrac{x}{2}$;   $h^{-1}: x \to \dfrac{1}{x}$
(b) $2x + 6$ cannot equal $2x + 3$ because
$6 \neq 3$.
(c) $-3$
(d) $\frac{1}{2}$ and $-2$

**Exercise 11**

**1** (a) $4c$   (b) $c^2$   (c) $2c^2$   (d) 0   (e) $6c^2$

**2** (a) $c + 7$   (b) $3c - 2$   (c) $3c - 2$
(d) $a + 5c$   (e) $2 + 2c$   (f) $2c - 3$

**3** (a) $3a$   (b) $ac$   (c) n.p.   (d) $4a^2$
(e) $4a$   (f) n.p.

**4** (a) $2a + 2b$   (b) $2ac - 6ab$
(c) $-6a + 9b - 6c$   (d) $10a - 2b$   (e) $a - 1$
(f) $2t - 21$   (g) $2a - 6b$

**5** (a) $x(a + b)$   (b) $4p(q - 2)$
(c) $2(a + 2p - 3c)$   (d) $2(ab - 2bc - 3cd)$

**6** (a) $h^3$   (b) $h^3$   (c) $h^4$   (d) $h^5$   (e) $h^5$   (f) $h^6$

**7** (a) $3ab$   (b) $4a^3$   (c) $6a^3$   (d) $4a^2b$
(e) $6ab^2$

**8** (a) $2a^2b^2$   (b) $p^2q^2$   (c) $8p^2c$   (d) $3m^3n^3$

**9** (a) $2a/3b^2$   (b) $b/2a$   (c) $a/b$
(d) $1/ab$   (e) 4

**10** (a) $a^3$   (b) $a^3$   (c) $1/a^2$ or $a^{-2}$
(d) $ab/3$   (e) $2b$

**11** (a) $5a^2b$   (b) n.p.   (c) $3a^2$   (d) $5a^2 - 2a$
(e) n.p.   (f) $4ab^2$

**12** (a) $8x^5$   (b) $x + 6$   (c) $2x + 7$   (d) $4x - 6y$
(e) $24a^2b$   (f) $15x^3y/8$   (g) $2c$   (h) $x^2/2y$
(i) $5a^2b$

**13** (a) $5d$   (b) $3d^2$   (c) $d^3$   (d) $3c$   (e) $8f^2$

**14** (a) $3 + a$   (b) $7a - 1$   (c) 0   (d) $1 + 3c$

**15** (a) $5x - 10y$   (b) $2c^2 + 2c$
(c) $-2 + 8r - 2t^2$   (d) $5a - 4b$
(e) $2q + 4t$   (f) $a^2 - a$

**16** (a) $2(2b - c)$   (b) $r(3t - 4)$
(c) $2m(n - 2m)$   (d) $ab(1 - a)$
(e) $4x(x - y)$

**17** (a) $12c$   (b) $2a^3$   (c) $8c^3$   (d) $5b^2c$
(e) $a^3b^2$

**18** (a) $x^3$   (b) $5r$   (c) $4b^2/5a$   (d) $1/a^3$ or $a^{-3}$

**19** (a) 3   (b) 4

**20** $4x + 3y$

**21** (a) $(a - b)(c + d)$    (b) n.p.
    (c) $(a + c)(3 - c)$    (d) n.p.
    (e) $(a - c)(b - d)$

**22** (a) $(a - b)(c + d)$    (b) $(m + p)(n + t)$
    (c) $(a + 2)(b + c)$    (d) $(a - b)(x - 2y)$
    (e) $(2 - 3c)(3x + 2y)$    (f) $(3 - x)(x - y)$
    (g) $(2p + s)(p - 2t)$

**23** (a) $(a + 5)(a - 5)$    (b) $(a + 5b)(a - 5b)$
    (c) $4(1 + 3x)(1 - 3x)$
    (d) $3(c + 2d)(c - 2d)$    (e) $5(x + y)(x - y)$
    (f) $3(y + 2)(y - 2)$

**24** (a) $x^2 + 3x + 2$    (b) $x^2 + x - 2$
    (c) $x^2 - x - 2$    (d) $x^2 - 3x + 2$
    (e) $6x^2 - 13x + 6$    (f) $4w^2 - 4w + 1$

**25** $(5, 6); (6, 5); (4, 9); (9, 4); (1, 0); (0, 1);$
    $(-3, 2); (2, -3)$

**26** (a) $(t - 3)(t - 1)$    (b) $(x - 3)(x + 2)$
    (c) $(x - 5)(x - 1)$    (d) $(n - 7)(n - 6)$
    (e) $(a - 8)(a + 2)$    (f) $(2a - 5)(a + 2)$
    (g) $(2x - 3)(x + 2)$    (h) $(3a + 2)(a - 8)$
    (i) $(3a - b)(2a - b)$    (j) $(3x - 2)(x + 4)$

**27** 4

**28** 4

**29** (a) $1/a^2$    (b) $1/b^3$    (c) $\frac{1}{36}$    (d) $\frac{1}{8}$

**30** (a) 10    (b) 2    (c) 2    (c) 2    (d) $2d^2$
    (f) $3d^3$    (g) $2c$    (h) $2a^{1\frac{1}{2}}$

**31** (a) 4    (b) 8    (c) 8    (d) 8    (e) 27

**32** (a) $\frac{1}{2}$    (b) $\frac{1}{2}$    (c) $\frac{1}{2}$    (d) $\frac{1}{4}$    (e) 16

**33** (a) 3    (b) 1    (c) $\frac{1}{27}$    (d) 27    (e) 64    (f) 32
    (g) $\frac{1}{4}$    (h) 5    (i) $\frac{1}{8}$    (j) $2\frac{1}{4}$

**34** (a) $a + 1$    (b) $\dfrac{1}{2m - 3n}$    (c) $\dfrac{x + 4}{x}$
    (d) $\dfrac{1}{a - 1}$    (e) $\dfrac{3a + 2}{a - 3}$    (f) $\dfrac{a - 3}{a - 4}$

**35** $10\sqrt{3}$

**36** (a) $\dfrac{9a}{20}$    (b) $\dfrac{9a + 10}{15}$    (c) $\dfrac{a + 1}{6}$
    (d) $\dfrac{a - b}{8}$    (e) $\dfrac{7a + 3}{30}$

**37** (a) $9ac$    (b) $ab/12$    (c) $1\frac{1}{3}$    (d) $m^2/2d^2$
    (e) $8abc$    (f) $8ad/3$

**38** (a) $\dfrac{x^2 + y^2}{xy}$    (b) $\dfrac{x^2 - y^2}{xy}$    (c) $\dfrac{5}{x}$    (d) $\dfrac{9a^2 - b^2}{3ab}$
    (e) $\dfrac{3ab + a}{b^2}$    (f) $\dfrac{4a - 1}{3a}$

**39** (a) $\dfrac{a^2 + b^2}{(a - b)(a + b)}$    (b) $\dfrac{3}{(a + 1)(a + 4)}$
    (c) $\dfrac{3a + 17}{(a - 1)(a + 3)}$
    (d) $\dfrac{a + 18}{(3a - 1)(2a + 3)}$    (e) 1

**40** (a) $b^3 + 3b^2 - 2$    (b) $6a^3 - 2a^2 - 26a + 24$
    (c) $2x^4 - 9x^3 + 5x^2 - 16$

**41** (a) $(x - 1)(x + 1)(x + 2)$
    (b) $(x - 1)(x - 1)(x + 2)$    (c) $(x - 2)^3$
    (d) $(x + 2)^2(2x - 3)$

## Exercise 12

**1** (a) 7    (b) $-1$    (c) $-3$    (d) $4\frac{1}{2}$    (e) $-2$
    (f) 16

**2** (a) 3    (b) $-3$    (c) 1    (d) $-21$    (e) $7\frac{1}{2}$
    (f) 1

**3** (a) $x > 5$    (b) $x \leqslant 6$    (c) $x > 3$    (d) $x > -1$
    (e) $-1 \leqslant x < 3$

**4** $6\frac{2}{3}$

**5** (a) $-3$    (b) $6\frac{1}{2}$    (c) 6    (d) $8\frac{1}{2}$    (e) $\frac{1}{2}$    (f) $\frac{1}{3}$

**6** $1.7 \times 10^{-5}$

**7** (c) (i) 20 cm    (ii) 5 cm$^2$
    (d) (i) $4(x + y)$    (ii) $(x + y)(x - y)$
    (e) (i) 18 cm    (ii) 275 cm$^2$
    (f) (i) $x = \dfrac{P - 4}{4}$    (ii) $x = \sqrt{A + 1}$

**8** (a) 2    (b) 8    (c) 4    (d) 10    (e) $\frac{3}{4}$    (f) $\frac{2}{3}$
    (g) $-\frac{3}{8}$    (h) 3    (i) 5

**9** (a) $x = 3, y = -1$    (b) $x = 3\frac{1}{2}, y = -2$
    (c) $x = 2, y = -1$    (d) $x = 3, y = -\frac{1}{3}$

**10** (a) $0, -3$    (b) $0, 3\frac{1}{2}$    (c) $0, -1\frac{1}{2}$    (d) $0, 4$
    (e) $0, 3$    (f) $0, 4$

**11** (a) $2, 1$    (b) $-3, 1$    (c) $-3$    (d) $12, -5$
    (e) $2, 1\frac{1}{2}$    (f) $2, -\frac{3}{8}$

**12** (a) $-2, 7$    (b) $-6, 1$    (c) $-8, 5$    (d) $-1, 6$
    (e) $-8, 4$    (f) $-3, 5$

**13** (a) $0.59, 3.41$    (b) $-3.45, 1.45$
    (c) $-0.46, 6.46$    (d) $-\frac{1}{2}, 4$    (e) $-1.54, 0.87$

**14** $x \geqslant 4$

**15** $r = 1\,\Omega; E = 1.5\,V$

**16** $z = 4W/3$

**17** (a) $-3, 1$    (b) $\frac{1}{2}$    (c) 1

**18** $x = \frac{3}{5}$

**19** $\sqrt{-1}$ is unreal.

**20** (a) $-6, -11, -2$    (b) $7\frac{1}{2}$
    (c) (i) $6x - 7$    (ii) $5\frac{1}{2}$    (d) $\dfrac{x}{3}, \dfrac{x + 7}{2}, \dfrac{4}{x}$
    (e) $-\frac{1}{2}, 4$    (f) $\dfrac{4 + 7x}{2x}$

**21** (a) (i) $\frac{2}{7}$    (ii) $x = \dfrac{ay}{1 + y}$
    (b) $-6\frac{1}{2}$    (c) $\dfrac{2x + 3}{x + 3}$

**22** (a) (i) 0    (ii) $-3$
    (b) (i) $-1, 1\frac{1}{2}$    (ii) $0, \frac{1}{2}$

**23** (a) $-2 \geqslant x \geqslant \frac{1}{3}$    (b) $-1\frac{1}{2} < x < 5$
    (c) $-2 \leqslant x \leqslant 4$

**24** (a) 2  (b) $\frac{2}{5}$  (c) $-\frac{1}{8}$  (d) $-1$  (e) $3\frac{7}{10}$
**25** (a) $2\frac{1}{2}$  (b) $6\frac{3}{4}$  (c) 9  (d) 8  (e) 10
**26** (a) none  (b) $-1$  (c) none  (d) $1\frac{1}{3}$, 3
**27** (a) $\{-2, -1, 0, 1, 2, 3, 4, 5, 6, 7\}$
 (b) $\{-4, -3, -2, -1, 0, 1\}$
 (c) $x < -1$, $x$ integral [an infinite set]
**28** (a) $x^2 + x - 6 = 0$  (b) $x^2 - 4x = 0$
 (c) $2x^2 - x - 10 = 0$
**29** $-9, 5$
**30** 8 m by 8 m and 8 m by 5 m
**31** 0, 100, 48
**32** £70
**33** (a) $-0.28, 1.78$  (b) $\frac{3}{4}$  (c) $0 < x < 1\frac{1}{2}$
**34** (a) 12.96  (b) 12  (c) 0.34 s, 11.66 s
**35** (a) $P = 6x + 10$
 (b) $A = 2x^2 + 9x + 4$, $x = 3.629$, 31.77 cm
**36** (a) $\dfrac{240}{x}$  (b) $\dfrac{200}{x-1} + 2$ or $\dfrac{240}{x} + 2$  (c) £5
**37** $x = 2\frac{2}{3}$, $y = 1\frac{2}{3}$, $V = 11\frac{23}{27}$ cm$^3$ or $x = 2$, $y = 3$,
 $V = 12$ cm$^3$
**38** (b) 2.2055
**39** (ii) 0.201 64  (iii) 2.1284
**40** Check your solutions by substitution.
**41** 2 feet

## Exercise 13

**1** (a) $c = kn$; $c \propto n$; $c$ varies directly as $n$; $c$ is
 directly proportional to $n$.
 (b) $A = kr^2$; $A \propto r^2$; $A$ varies directly as the
 square of $r$; $A$ is directly proportional to
 $r$ squared.
 (c) $y = \dfrac{k}{x}$ or $y = k\dfrac{1}{x}$; $y \propto \dfrac{1}{x}$; $y$ varies inversely
 as $x$; $y$ is inversely proportional to $x$.
 (d) $y = \dfrac{kx}{z^2}$ or $y = k\dfrac{x}{z^2}$; $y \propto \dfrac{x}{z^2}$; $y$ varies
 directly as $x$ and inversely as the square of
 $z$; $y$ is directly proportional to $x$ and
 inversely proportional to $z$ squared.
 (e) $C = \dfrac{k}{n}$ or $C = k\dfrac{1}{n}$; $C \propto \dfrac{1}{n}$; $C$ varies
 inversely as $n$; $C$ is inversely proportional
 to $n$.
**2** $y = ks$; $y \propto s$
**3** $E = kh$; $E \propto h$
**4** $V \propto AH$
**5** $H \propto V/R^2$
**6** $A \propto F/M$
**7** (a) $\times\frac{1}{4}$  (b) $\times\frac{1}{2}$  (c) $\times\frac{1}{8}$  (d) $\times 2$  (e) $\times\frac{1}{2}$
**8** (a) $y$ varies directly with $x^2$ and inversely with
 $z$.
 (b) $\frac{3}{10}$  (c) 10

**9** (a) (i) $y \propto x^{-1} \rightarrow y \propto \dfrac{1}{x} \rightarrow y = \dfrac{k}{x}$
 (ii) $y \propto x \rightarrow y = kx$
 (iii) $y \propto x^2 \rightarrow y = kx^2$
 (b) (i) 16  (ii) 64  (iii) $\frac{2}{3}$  (iv) $\frac{1}{4}$
**10** See Figure A13:1.

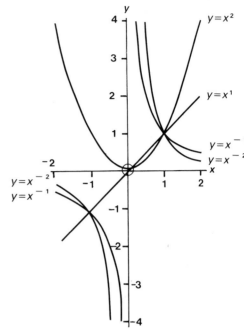

**Fig. A13:1**

**11** (a) $V \propto R^2H$  (b) $\times 16$  (c) $\times 18$  (d) $\times 27$
**12** Decrease of 20%
**13** (a) $H \propto V^2T/R$  (b) $H = kV^2T/R$  (c) $\frac{1}{4}$
 (d) $1\frac{1}{4}$
**14** 11.9 years
**15** (a) 724 K  (b) $1.2 \times 10^5$ N/m$^2$
**16** (a) $n = a + bx$
 (b) $a = 8$, $b = 40$, 900 metres

## Exercise 14

**1** (a) rectangle  (b) triangle  (c) octagon
**2** (a) 360°  (b) 180°  (c) 1080°
**3** (b) 130°  (d) 40°
**4** (a) 60°  (b) 40°  (c) 60°
**6** (a) 3  (b) 2  (c) 5
**7** (b) no  (c) centre of O
**8** (a) 39°  (c) 64°  (d) 206°
**9** (a) duodecagon; hexagon; square  (b) 150°
**10** Rotational symmetry of order 4; point
 symmetry

**11** (c) a kite   (d) 25°
**12** (c) about 063°, 108°, 180°, 243°
   (d) about 5 km
**13** (a) 120°   (b) 60° or 90°
**14** Try drawing it.
**15** (a) 240°   (b) 070°
   (c) Add 180°; if answer is more than 360° subtract 360°.
**16** 162°
**17** 1:2
**18** 60°
**19** 100°
**20** 1440°
**22** (b) about 38 km   (c) about 43 km
   (d) about 235°

## Exercise 15

**1** (a), (b), (d) and (f)
**2** (b) 1:4
**3** (a) 10 cm   (b) 15 cm
**4** (a) 3:2   (b) (i) 9 cm   (ii) 10 cm
**5** (a) (i) A′B′C′   (ii) A″B″C″   (iii) A‴B‴C‴
   (b) (i) 2   (ii) −2   (iii) −6
**6** (a) and (d)
**7** 4 metres; five doors
**8** (a) 150 cm²   (b) 50 cm
   (c) (i) 13.5 cm   (ii) 6 cm
   (d) (i) 3/5   (ii) 9/25   (iii) 9/10
   (e) (i) $1\frac{1}{2}$ m   (ii) £61.50
**9** (a) (i) 8   (ii) 27   (iii) 64
   (b) (i) 600 cm²   (ii) 1350 cm²   (iii) 2400 cm²
   (c) (i) 1000 cm²   (ii) 3375 cm²   (iii) 8000 cm²
   (d) (i) 1:1.6̇   (ii) 1:2.5   (iii) 1:3.3
**10** (b) 2:3   (c) 4:9
**11** (a) RBP   (b) QPC, ABC
   (c) (i) 12 cm   (ii) 3 cm   (iii) 1/16
   (d) 3k cm²
**12** (a) ∠CAD   (b) ∠ADC
   (c) (i) DAC   (ii) CBA   (iii) BAD
   (d) (i) DA, AC, AC   (ii) AB, CA, BD
   (iii) BA, AD, CD
**13** $5\frac{1}{3}$ cm
**14** Figure 15:12   Not necessarily as first angle is not included.
   Figure 15:13   Yes, three sides.
   Figure 15:14   Yes, two angles, corresponding side.
   Figure 15:15   Yes, two angles, corresponding side.
   Figure 15:16   Yes, two sides, included angle.
   (∠ABG = 90° + ∠CBG and ∠CBE = 90° + ∠CBG)
**15** 6 cm
**16** (a) 4:3   (b) 16:9   (c) 64:27

**17** (a) 3 sides, due to triangles being equilateral.
   (c) 1:2
   (d) 4:1
**18** 2:3
**19** 1:7
**20** 0.628

## Exercise 16

**1** A, 16:3   B, 16:2   C, 16:1   D, 16:5
   E, 16:4
**2** Perpendicularly bisect chords to give diameter; perpendicularly bisect diameter to give centre. Or use the perpendicular bisectors of two chords.
**3** 6 cm
**4** (a) 40°   (b) 48°   (c) 48°   (d) 80°   (e) 40°
**5** 115°
**6** (a) OT, OS   (b) ATX, ASY
   (c) (i) 90°   (ii) 90°   (iii) 120°   (iv) 240°
**7** (a) ∠BEC   (b) ∠DCE
   (c) ∠ABE, ∠ACE, ∠ADE   (d) AD
   (e) ABCD, ACDE, ABCE   (f) 20°
**8** (a) radii OA = OB   (b) 50°, 65°, 65°
**9** (a) 120°   (b) 65°, 115°   (c) 160°
   (d) O not on the circumference
**10** (a) ∠Q, ∠R, (∠s in same segment)
   (b) (i) ∠PSQ   (ii) ∠PTR   (iii) ∠QTR
**11** (a) ∠S = 70°, ∠Q = 110°, ∠R = 110°,
   ∠P = 70°
   (b) 90°
**12** ∠s in same segment; vertically opposite ∠s
**13** ∠ sum of right-angled △
**14** ∠s in same segment
**15** 100° (Join AC; ∠s in same segment;
   ∠ sum of isosceles △)
**16** 105°
**17** (a) ∠s in same segment
   (b) opp. ∠s of cyclic quad.   (c) AYXB; AZXC;
   AZPY; CXPY
**18** (a) (i) 90°   (ii) 90°
   (b) (i) 20°   (ii) 70°   (iii) 70°
**19** (a) v = s   (b) r = s   (c) u = q
**26** 4 cm

## Exercise 17

**1** (a) cube   (b) cuboid   (c) cylinder
   (d) sphere
**2** (a) 12   (b) EF   (c) A and E   (d) 10 cm
   (e) 20 cm
**3** A
**4** (a) See Figure A17:1.   (b) 12 cm square.
**5** (a) A rectangle, 4 cm by 3.3 cm.
   (b) A triangular prism.   (c) See Figure A17:2.
   (d) 1.6 cm

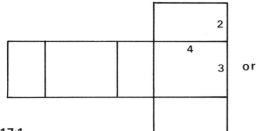
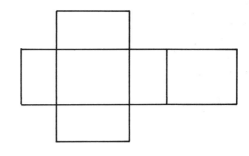

Fig. A17:1

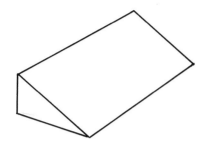

Fig. A17:2

**6** (a) Figure 17:5, Icosahedron
Figure 17:6, Tetrahedron
Figure 17:7, Cube
Figure 17:8, Dodecahedron
Figure 17:9, Octahedron

(b)

| | 17:5 | 17:6 | 17:7 | 17:8 | 17:9 |
|---|---|---|---|---|---|
| $F$ | 20 | 4 | 6 | 12 | 8 |
| $V$ | 12 | 4 | 8 | 20 | 6 |
| $E$ | 30 | 6 | 12 | 30 | 12 |

(c) See Figure A17:3.

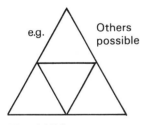

e.g.     Others possible

Fig. A17:3

**7** (a) (i) 60 litres   (ii) 75 litres   (iii) 90 litres
(b) $52\frac{1}{2}$ litres

**8** (a) Figure 17:11, Cube
Figure 17:12, Square-based pyramid
Figure 17:13, Cone
Figure 17:14, Cylinder
Figure 17:15, Triangular prism
Figure 17:16, Tetrahedron
Figure 17:17, Probably a triangular prism

(b) See Figure A17:4.

**9** All right angles except ∠AHC and ∠ACH.

**10**

| | 17:19 | 17:20 | 17:21 | 17:22 | 17:23 |
|---|---|---|---|---|---|
| (a) | 3 | 1 | 7 | 13 | 7 |
| (b) | 3 | ∞ | 7 | 9 | 6 |
| (c) | 4 | ∞ | 12 | 24 | 12 |

**11 to 13**   Ask your teacher to check these.

### Exercise 18

**6** (b) 471 mm
**8** 7.5 km
**9** 7.4 cm
**10** (b) 1.44 km   (c) 10.8 km
**11** (c) (ii) 28 hours
**12** (c) 129°   (d) 321°   (e) (i) A   (ii) 10 min
**13** (a) (i) 10.6 cm   (ii) 41°
(b) (i) 6.9 cm   (ii) 41.4 cm$^2$
**16** (b) 174 cm
**18** 72°
**19** 240 m; 150°
**20** 6.9 m; 4 m; 0.4 m
**21** (c) 46 m

11    12    13    14    15    16    17

Fig. A17:4

## Exercise 19

**1** (a) 6.55 cm  (b) 3.66 cm  (c) 3.54 cm
**2** (a) acute  (b) obtuse  (c) acute
(d) impossible  (e) right-angled
(f) impossible  (g) acute  (h) acute
**3** 8 m
**5** 11.1 cm
**6** 7 cm, 17 cm
**7** (a) 6.32 cm  (b) 7 cm
**8** 20.8 cm
**9** 5065 km
**11** 13.42 cm
**12** (a) 8.6 cm
**13** 6 cm
**14** $x = 7.5$ or 5

## Exercise 20

**1** (a) 257 m  (b) 6.12 m/s  (c) 1363.5 m$^2$
(d) 25.1
**2** 57.3 cm
**3** (a) 3.40 m  (b) (i) 4  (ii) 3  (iii) 2
(c) (i) 21 m$^2$  (ii) 1.1 m$^2$  (iii) 3.9 m$^2$
(iv) 7 litres for £14
(d) 283.5 kg  (e) 62.5 cm$^2$; 37 500 cm$^3$
(f) 196 litres  (g) 20.4 m$^2$  (h) about 9.6 mm
**4** 97
**5** (a) 12.5 kg  (b) 4091 cm$^2$
**6** 593.4 g
**7** £129.60; yes
**8** £1125
**9** 50
**10** (a) £26  (b) 5 m$^2$  (c) 0.5 m$^3$  (d) £13
(e) £16.25
**11** (a) 25 cm  (b) 4710 cm$^3$  (c) 94.2 cm
(d) 25 cm  (e) 94.2 cm  (f) 216°
(g) 1204.76 cm$^2$
**12** (a) 457 cm$^3$  (b) 7.18 cm
**13** (i) 18  (ii) 2  (iii) $43\frac{1}{3}$; 42%
**14** (a) 5.66 cm  (b) 9 cm  (c) $74\frac{2}{3}$ cm$^2$
(d) 50.9 cm$^2$  (e) 4.40 cm
**15** (a) 6.2 cm  (b) 14.1 cm$^2$  (c) 96.7%
**16** (a) 12 m
(b) (i) 1018 m$^3$  (ii) 2413 m$^3$; 1395 m$^3$
(c) $1.39 \times 10^6$ litres
(d) (i) 20 m  (ii) 5 m
(e) (i) 330 m$^2$  (ii) 254 m$^2$  (iii) 98 litres
**17** 1470 m$^2$
**18** 3183 cm/min

## Exercise 21

**1** (a) 4.66  (b) 4.23  (c) 26.6°  (d) 30°
(e) 8.39  (f) 6.43

**2** (a) 9.42 cm; 10.2 cm  (b) 1.7 cm; 4.35 cm
(c) 3.68 cm; 1.56 cm
**3** (a) 59°; 31°  (b) 36.9°; 53.1°
**4** About $11\frac{1}{2}$ metres
**5** About 27 metres
**6** 63.4°
**7** 11.5°
**8** 44°
**9** 2.9°
**10** $6\frac{1}{4}$ km
**11** 15 n.m. south; 10 n.m. east
**12** (a) 2.66  (b) 2.6  (c) 1.32  (d) 5.49
(e) 56.3°  (f) 41.8°  (g) 31°  (h) 48.6°
(i) 6.06  (j) 1.46  (k) 38.7°  (l) 60.3°
(m) 44.4°  (n) 53.1°  (o) 34.8°  (p) 33.7°
(q) 8.66  (r) 32°  (s) 10.3
**13** 45°
**14** (a) 7.99 cm  (b) 7.54 cm  (c) 0.754
**15** (a) 65 cm  (b) 52 cm  (c) 0.385  (d) 0.923
**16** 45°
**17** (a) 4.87 cm  (b) 10.2 cm  (c) 17.5 cm
**18** (a) 4.46 cm; 16.5°; 138.5°
(b) 4.60 cm; 41.8°; 88.2°
(c) 75.5°; 46.6°; 57.9°
(d) 78.5°; 57.1°; 44.4°
(e) 3.40 cm; 48.9°; 59.8°
(f) 85.7°; 57.7°; 36.6°
(g) 4.6 cm; 9.2 cm; 11.5 cm; 49.5°; 22.3°;
108.2°
**19** 3.66 km; 4.48 km; 3.17 km
**20** 21.8 m
**22** 6.14 cm$^2$
**23** 17.3 m$^2$
**24** (a) 35.4 n.m.  (b) 21.7 n.m.  (c) 11.8 n.m.
(d) 16.3 n.m.
**25** (b) (i) 312 m  (ii) 26°
(c) 206°
**26** 150°;  21.3 m  (a) 7°  (b) 721 m
**27** (a) 5.50 m  (b) $\angle$PAV = 30°
(c) $\angle$QCN = 51.3°  (d) $\angle$CQD = 77.3°
**28** (a) 2.24 m; 4.66 m  (b) 4.47 m
(c) 43.8°  (d) 47.2°

## Exercise 22

**2** (a) 36.9 °C  (b) beats/min; breaths/min
(c) 71 beats/min  (d) 18 breaths/min
(e) Yes. High temperature; high pulse rate;
low respiration rate.  (f) 28 Feb.
**3** (a) 7% r.m.p.; 48% manufacturing;
45% services
(b) See Figure A22:1.
**4** (a) 135°  (b) $1.5 \times 10^5$
**5** (a) £9  (b) £27  (c) £36  (d) 150°

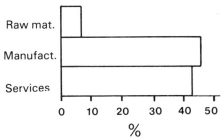

Fig. A22:1

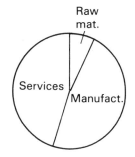

**6** See Figure A22:2.

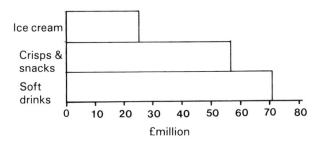

Fig. A22:2

**7** (a) B  (b) £400  (c) £300  (d) £24  (e) A

**8** See Figure A22:3.

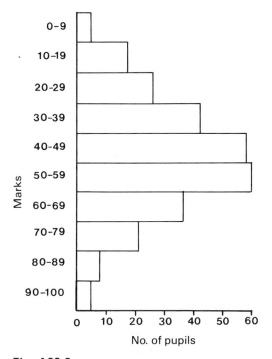

Fig. A22:3

**9** (a) See Figure A22:4.
   (b) (i) £1980  (ii) 27°  (iii) $6\frac{2}{3}$°

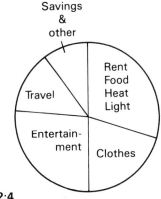

Fig. A22:4

**10** See Figure A22:5 (page 302).
**11** See Figure A22:6 (page 302).

## Exercise 23

**1** (a) 8, 8, 8  (b) 8 & 15, 11, 11
   (c) 8 & 9, 8, 6.7  (d) 10, 8, 7.625
**2** (a) 30  (b) 2  (c) 2.7
**3** (a) 20–29  (b) 20–29  (c) 26.57
**4** 28
**5** (a) 7 & 9, 7, 5.64  (b) 12, 11.5, 11.3
**6** (a) 4, 8, 5, 4, 0, 0, 2, 1
   (b) (i) 24  (ii) 49  (iii) 1  (iv) 2.04  (v) 1.5
**7** (a) no effect  (b) increases to 2.12
   (c) increases to 2
**8** (a) 191  (b) 5–7  (c) 5–7  (d) 10
**9** About 47 m.p.h.
**10** 47.34
**11** (a) 40  (b) 1
   (c) See Figure A23:1 (page 302).
   (d) $2\frac{1}{6}$  (e) (i) 200  (ii) £500
**12** −0.19 °C
**13** £1620
**14** £3.04

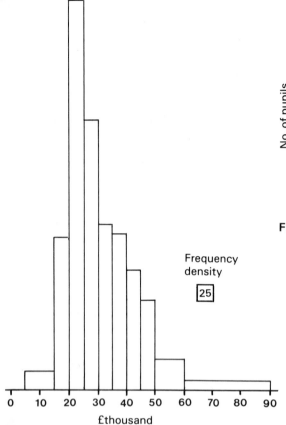

Frequency density

25

£thousand

**Fig. A22:5**

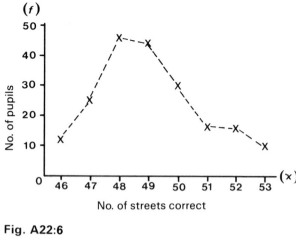

(f)

No. of pupils

No. of streets correct

**Fig. A22:6**

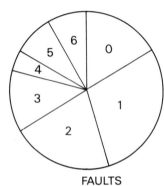

FAULTS

**Fig. A23:1**

**15** (a) £45   (b) £50   (c) £56.77
**16** $23\frac{1}{3}$
**17** (a) 3   (b) 4   (c) 3.7   (d) 3.6
**18** 1, 2, 6
**19** 2, 10, 10, 22
**20** (a) 60   (b) 40   (c) 36   (d) 43   (e) 31–54
**21** (a) 80%   (b) £5000   (c) about £13 000
**22** (b) 108 g   (c) 112
**24** (a) 79   (b) 58   (c) 40   (d) 12
   (f) (i) about 22 years   (ii) about 28
**25** (b) 33   (c) 83   (e) 34.83
**26** All averages are 3.
**27** Test 1, 1.581;   Test 2, 1.0;   Test 3, 1.871;
   Test 4, 2.151
**28** 11

**Exercise 24**

**1** (a) $\frac{1}{2}$   (b) $\frac{1}{4}$   (c) $\frac{1}{13}$   (d) $\frac{1}{52}$
**2** 3 in 4

**3** $\frac{3}{8}$
**4** $\frac{5}{24}$
**5** (b) (i) $\frac{1}{64}$   (ii) $\frac{20}{64}$   (iii) $\frac{1}{64}$   (iv) $\frac{22}{64}$
**6** (b) (i) $\frac{1}{6}$   (ii) $\frac{2}{3}$
**7** (a) $\frac{3}{14}$   (b) $\frac{3}{7}$   (c) $\frac{9}{14}$
**8** (a) $\frac{1}{120}$   (b) $\frac{1}{80}$   (c) $\frac{1}{960}$   (d) $\frac{11}{12}$
**9** (a) $\frac{1}{125}$   (b) $\frac{64}{125}$
**10** (a) $\frac{1}{4}$   (b) $\frac{1}{51}$   (c) $\frac{13}{25}$   (d) $\frac{13}{5100}$
**11** (a) $\frac{8}{27}$   (b) $\frac{2}{27}$
**12** (a) $\frac{3}{118}$   (b) $\frac{29}{118}$   (c) $\frac{10}{177}$   (d) $\frac{10}{177}$
**13** (a) $\frac{1}{4}$   (b) $\frac{5}{78}$   (c) $\frac{3}{52}$   (d) $\frac{25}{1482}$   (e) $\frac{9}{35}$
   (f) $\frac{21}{190}$
**14** (a) $\frac{2}{5}$   (b) $\frac{6}{50}$   (c) $\frac{1}{10}$
   (d) (i) $\frac{9}{100}$   (ii) $\frac{1}{15}$   (e) $\frac{7}{10}$
**15** (a) $\frac{1}{18}$   (b) $\frac{1}{6}$   (c) 0   (d) $\frac{5}{18}$   (e) $\frac{5}{6}$
**16** (a) $\frac{1}{4}$   (b) $\frac{1}{3}$   (c) $\frac{3}{4}$   (d) $\frac{1}{64}$   (e) $\frac{5}{36}$
**17** (a) $\frac{1}{13}$   (b) $\frac{4}{663}$   (c) $\frac{13}{204}$   (d) $\frac{1}{11050}$   (e) $\frac{2}{17}$
   (f) $\frac{28}{1105}$

**18** $\frac{1}{1000}, \frac{3}{500}, \frac{3}{1000}, \frac{3}{500}, \frac{9}{250}, \frac{9}{500}, \frac{3}{1500}, \frac{9}{500}, \frac{9}{1000}, \frac{3}{500};$
$\frac{9}{250}, \frac{9}{500}, \frac{9}{250}, \frac{27}{125}, \frac{27}{500}, \frac{9}{250}, \frac{27}{500}, \frac{27}{250}, \frac{3}{500}, \frac{9}{1000}, \frac{9}{500}, \frac{9}{1000};$
$\frac{9}{500}, \frac{27}{250}, \frac{9}{500}, \frac{9}{1000}, \frac{27}{500}, \frac{27}{1000}$
  (a) (i) $\frac{27}{125}$ (ii) $\frac{3}{1000}$ (iii) $\frac{27}{250}$ (iv) $\frac{27}{500}$
  (b) $\frac{27}{1000}$ (c) $\frac{81}{625}$

**19** (a) $\frac{1}{150}$ (b) $\frac{3}{125}$ (c) $\frac{17}{100}$ (d) $\frac{71}{1500}$

**20** (a) $\frac{1}{16}$ (b) $\frac{3}{8}$ (c) $\frac{15}{16}$

**21** (a) $\frac{1}{45}$ (b) $\frac{2}{9}$ (c) $\frac{1}{6}$ (d) $\frac{1}{120}$ (e) $\frac{4}{15}$ (f) $\frac{11}{20}$

**22** (a) $\frac{1}{17}$ (b) $\frac{1}{26}$ (c) $\frac{1}{26}$ (d) $\frac{13}{34}$

**23** $\frac{9}{1\,000\,000}$

**24** (a) $\frac{1}{15}$ (b) $\frac{2}{5}$ (c) $\frac{8}{15}$
  (d) (i) 91 (ii) 130

**25** (a) $\frac{1}{6}$ (b) $\frac{11}{15}$ (c) $\frac{2}{87}$ (d) $\frac{1}{10}$ (e) $\frac{3}{290}$

**26** (a) $\frac{1}{6}$
  (b) (i) $\frac{1}{7}$ (ii) $\frac{6}{35}$
  (c) $\frac{1}{42}$ (d) $\frac{2}{7}$; $n = 9$

**27** (a) $\frac{1}{140}$ (b) $\frac{11}{28}$ (c) $\frac{33}{70}, \frac{2}{5}$

**28** (a) $\frac{3}{4}$
  (b) (i) $\frac{9}{16}$ (ii) $\frac{1}{16}$ (iii) $\frac{3}{8}$ (iv) $\frac{15}{16}$
  (c) (i) $\frac{1}{5}$ (ii) $\frac{1}{10}$ (iii) $\frac{9}{160}$

## Exercise 25

**1** (a) $\begin{pmatrix} 0 \\ 2 \end{pmatrix}$ (b) $\begin{pmatrix} 1 \\ 0 \end{pmatrix}$ (c) $\begin{pmatrix} 1 \\ -1 \end{pmatrix}$ (d) $\begin{pmatrix} 2 \\ 2 \end{pmatrix}$
  (e) $\begin{pmatrix} 0 \\ -4 \end{pmatrix}$

**2** (a) $2\underset{\sim}{a}$ (b) $-2\underset{\sim}{b}$ (c) $\underset{\sim}{c}$ (d) $\frac{1}{2}\underset{\sim}{b}$
  (e) $3\underset{\sim}{a}$ (f) $\underset{\sim}{d}$ (g) $-1\frac{1}{2}\underset{\sim}{b}$ (h) $-2\underset{\sim}{d}$

**3** (a) 2 (b) $\sqrt{8}$ (c) $\sqrt{18}$

**4** (a) 5 (b) $\sqrt{29}$

**5** (a) $\begin{pmatrix} 5 \\ 0 \end{pmatrix}$ (b) $\begin{pmatrix} 1 \\ 1 \end{pmatrix}$ (c) $\begin{pmatrix} 1 \\ -1 \end{pmatrix}$ (d) $\begin{pmatrix} -3 \\ -3 \end{pmatrix}$

**6** (c) $\underset{\sim}{a}$; $2\underset{\sim}{b}$; $-\underset{\sim}{d}$; $-2\underset{\sim}{d}$; $\underset{\sim}{a}$; $2\underset{\sim}{d}$; $\underset{\sim}{a}$; $1\frac{1}{2}\underset{\sim}{c}$; $1\frac{1}{2}\underset{\sim}{a}$

**7** See Figure A25:1.

**8** (a) $\begin{pmatrix} -1 \\ 7 \end{pmatrix}$ (b) $\begin{pmatrix} 13 \\ 11 \end{pmatrix}$

**9** $\begin{pmatrix} 4 \\ 3 \end{pmatrix}$

**10** (a) (i) $\underset{\sim}{b}$ (ii) $-\underset{\sim}{b}$ (iii) $\frac{1}{2}\underset{\sim}{b}$ (iv) $-\frac{1}{2}\underset{\sim}{b}$
    (v) $\frac{1}{2}\underset{\sim}{b}$ (vi) $-\frac{1}{2}\underset{\sim}{b}$
  (b) (i) $-\underset{\sim}{b} - \underset{\sim}{a}$ (ii) $-\underset{\sim}{b} + \underset{\sim}{a}$ (iii) $\underset{\sim}{a} + \frac{1}{2}\underset{\sim}{b}$
    (iv) $-\frac{1}{2}\underset{\sim}{b} - \underset{\sim}{a}$ (v) $\frac{1}{2}\underset{\sim}{b} - \underset{\sim}{a}$ (vi) $\underset{\sim}{a} - \frac{1}{2}\underset{\sim}{b}$

**11** (a) $-2\underset{\sim}{a}$ (b) $2\underset{\sim}{a} + 2\underset{\sim}{d}$ (iii) $\underset{\sim}{a}$ (iv) $\underset{\sim}{d} - \underset{\sim}{a}$

**12** (a) (i) $-\underset{\sim}{a}$ (ii) $\underset{\sim}{b} - \underset{\sim}{a}$ (iii) $\underset{\sim}{b} - 2\underset{\sim}{a}$
    (iv) $3\underset{\sim}{b} - 3\underset{\sim}{a}$
  (b) (i) $\overrightarrow{EF}$ (ii) $\overrightarrow{FG}$ (iii) $\overrightarrow{GB}$ or $\overrightarrow{FC}$ (iv) $\overrightarrow{DH}$

**13** (a) $-\underset{\sim}{x}$ (b) $\underset{\sim}{y} + \underset{\sim}{x}$ (c) $-\frac{1}{2}\underset{\sim}{x} - \underset{\sim}{y}$
  (d) $-\underset{\sim}{x} + \underset{\sim}{y}$

**14** (a) (i) $\begin{pmatrix} 2 \\ 0 \end{pmatrix}$ (ii) $\begin{pmatrix} 2 \\ 1 \end{pmatrix}$ (iii) $\begin{pmatrix} 3 \\ -2 \end{pmatrix}$
  (b) (i) AB//DC; AB = 2DC (ii) 110°
    (iii) $2\underset{\sim}{a} - 2\underset{\sim}{b}$ (iv) $-\underset{\sim}{a} + \underset{\sim}{b}$
    (v) DE//CA; DE = $\frac{1}{2}$CA

**15** (a) $\begin{pmatrix} 3 \\ -1 \end{pmatrix}$
  (b) (i) $-\underset{\sim}{a} + \underset{\sim}{c}$ (ii) $-\frac{1}{2}\underset{\sim}{a} + \frac{1}{2}\underset{\sim}{c}$ (iii) $\frac{1}{2}\underset{\sim}{a} + \frac{1}{2}\underset{\sim}{c}$
    (iv) $\frac{1}{3}\underset{\sim}{a} + \frac{1}{3}\underset{\sim}{c}$ (v) $-\frac{1}{6}\underset{\sim}{a} - \frac{1}{6}\underset{\sim}{c}$
    (vi) $-\frac{2}{3}\underset{\sim}{a} + \frac{1}{3}\underset{\sim}{c}$ (vii) $-\underset{\sim}{a} + \frac{1}{2}\underset{\sim}{c}$
  (c) $\overrightarrow{BG} = \frac{1}{3}(-2\underset{\sim}{a} + \underset{\sim}{c})$; $\overrightarrow{BE} = \frac{1}{2}(-2\underset{\sim}{a} + \underset{\sim}{c})$
    ∴ BG//BE and BGE is a straight line; also
    as $\frac{2}{3} \times \frac{1}{2} = \frac{1}{3}$ then BG = $\frac{2}{3}$BE.

**16** (a) (i) $\underset{\sim}{a} + \underset{\sim}{b}$ (ii) $\frac{1}{2}\underset{\sim}{a} + \frac{1}{2}\underset{\sim}{b}$ (iii) $1\frac{1}{2}\underset{\sim}{b} - \frac{1}{2}\underset{\sim}{a}$
    (iv) $\frac{3}{4}\underset{\sim}{b} - \frac{1}{4}\underset{\sim}{a}$ (v) $\frac{3}{4}\underset{\sim}{b} + \frac{3}{4}\underset{\sim}{a}$ (vi) $\frac{1}{4}\underset{\sim}{b} + \frac{1}{4}\underset{\sim}{a}$
  (b) QV//PS and QV = $\frac{3}{4}$PS (c) 3:1

**17** (a) (i) $\frac{1}{2}\underset{\sim}{p}$ (ii) $\underset{\sim}{q} + \frac{1}{2}\underset{\sim}{p}$ (iii) $\frac{1}{3}\underset{\sim}{q}$ (iv) $\underset{\sim}{p} + \frac{1}{3}\underset{\sim}{q}$
    (v) $\underset{\sim}{p} - \frac{2}{3}\underset{\sim}{q}$ (vi) $\frac{2}{3}\underset{\sim}{q} - \frac{1}{2}\underset{\sim}{p}$
  (b) $\frac{3}{4}\underset{\sim}{q} + \frac{3}{8}\underset{\sim}{p}$ (c) $\frac{3}{4}$

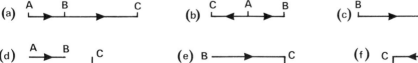
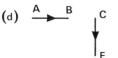

**Fig. A25:1**

**18** (a) (i) $-\underset{\sim}{a} + \underset{\sim}{b}$  (ii) $-\frac{1}{4}\underset{\sim}{a} + \frac{1}{4}\underset{\sim}{b}$  (iii) $\frac{3}{4}\underset{\sim}{a} + \frac{1}{4}\underset{\sim}{b}$

(b) (i) $\begin{pmatrix} 3 \\ 4 \end{pmatrix}$  (ii) 5  (iii) (2, −1)

(c) $l = 3$, $m = -7$

**19** (a) (i) $2\underset{\sim}{q} + \underset{\sim}{p}$  (ii) $2\underset{\sim}{p} + \underset{\sim}{q}$  (iii) $-\underset{\sim}{q} + \underset{\sim}{p}$

(b) $\underset{\sim}{p} - \underset{\sim}{q}$

(c) Parallel and same length

(d) $2\underset{\sim}{p} - 2\underset{\sim}{q}$

(e) Parallel with RT = 2DB

(f) $\begin{pmatrix} \sqrt{3} \\ 1 \end{pmatrix}, \begin{pmatrix} -\sqrt{3} \\ 1 \end{pmatrix}$

(g) $(2\sqrt{3}, 2)$; $(\sqrt{3}, 3)$; $(-\sqrt{3}, 3)$; $(-2\sqrt{3}, 2)$

(h) $4\sqrt{3}$

**20** (a) $-\underset{\sim}{a} + \underset{\sim}{b}$; $2\underset{\sim}{a}$; $-2\underset{\sim}{a} + 2\underset{\sim}{b}$

(b) $-4\underset{\sim}{a} + 4\underset{\sim}{b}$; $-2\underset{\sim}{a} + 4\underset{\sim}{b}$; $2\underset{\sim}{a} - 3\underset{\sim}{b}$

(c) $k\underset{\sim}{a}$

**21** (a) $2\underset{\sim}{a}$  (b) $\frac{1}{2}(\underset{\sim}{a} + \underset{\sim}{b})$  (c) $\frac{2}{3}\underset{\sim}{b}$  (d) $\frac{1}{2}\underset{\sim}{a} - \frac{1}{6}\underset{\sim}{b}$

(e) $1\frac{1}{2}\underset{\sim}{a} - \frac{1}{2}\underset{\sim}{b}$

MN = 3NM; NML are in a straight line.

$OQ = \frac{2}{5}(\underset{\sim}{a} + \underset{\sim}{b})$; $OR = \frac{2}{5}(\underset{\sim}{a} + \underset{\sim}{b})$

Q is at the same point as R.

## Exercise 26

**1** (a) (i) D2, E3  (ii) C5, D4  (iii) C1

(b) (i) E3, D4  (ii) B4, C5, D4, E3, D2, C1

**2** D1

**3** (b)  (i) (6, 6), (6, 12), (12, 6)

(ii) (−2, −2), (−2, −4), (−4, −2)

(iii) (1, 1), (1, 2), (2, 1)

(iv) (−4, −4), (−4, −8), (−8, −4)

**4** (a) (2, 2), (2, 6), (6, 2)

(b) (4, 0), (2, 0), (4, −2)

(c) (5, 5), (4, 5), (5, 4)

**5** 1001, 1111, 1691, 1881, 1961, 6009, 6119, 6699, 6889, 6969, 8008

**6** (a) 2  (b) 1  (c) 0  (d) 1  (e) infinite

**7** (b) (i) $13\frac{1}{2}$ cm$^2$, $2\frac{1}{4}$ times

(ii) $1\frac{1}{2}$ cm$^2$, $\frac{1}{4}$ times

**8** See Figure A26:1.

**9** (a) $\begin{pmatrix} 5 \\ 4 \end{pmatrix}$

(b) (i) $+90°$  (ii) (−3, 4)

(c) (i) $y = -x$  (ii) (−7, −2)

(d) (2, 4)

**10** (a) rectangle, rhombus

(b) kite, isosceles trapezium

(c) parallelogram  (d) square

**11** (b) (−3, 4), (−4, −3), (0, −5), (5, 0); isosceles trapezium

**12** (a) (i) (4, 3)  (ii) (−3, −1)

(b) (i) 40°  (ii) 100°

(iii) AB = A′C, AD = BC, A′B = BC − A′C, BD = AD − AB, ∴ A′B = BD

**13** See Figure A26:2; P is invariant under DTM(Q), ∴ rotation $+90°$ about (1, 3).

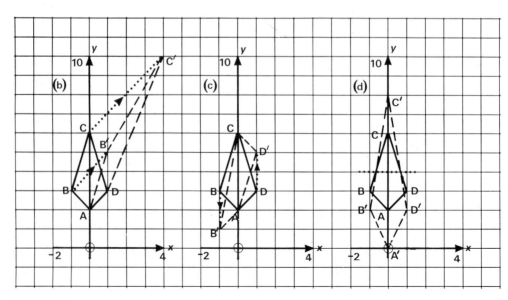

**Fig. A26:1**

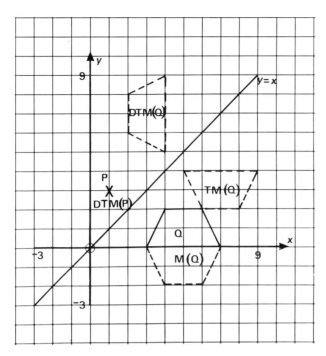

**Fig. A26:2**

## Exercise 27

**1**  (a) $\begin{pmatrix} 2 \\ -1 \end{pmatrix}$  (b) $(2 \quad 2)$  (c) not possible

(d) $\begin{pmatrix} 9 \\ 6 \end{pmatrix}$  (e) $(-1 \quad \frac{1}{2})$  (f) $\begin{pmatrix} -2 & 6 \\ 0 & -4 \end{pmatrix}$

(g) $(-7)$  (h) not possible  (i) $(0 \quad -2)$

(j) $(2 \quad -8)$  (k) $\begin{pmatrix} -3 \\ -2 \end{pmatrix}$  (l) $\begin{pmatrix} 6 & 1 \\ 8 & 2 \end{pmatrix}$

(m) $\begin{pmatrix} 2 & 4 \\ 2 & 6 \end{pmatrix}$  (n) $\begin{pmatrix} 0 & -2 \\ -2 & 6 \end{pmatrix}$

(o) $\begin{pmatrix} 6 & -1 \\ -4 & 0 \end{pmatrix}$

**2**  (a) $\begin{pmatrix} -6 \\ -2 \end{pmatrix}$  (b) $\begin{pmatrix} 1 \\ \frac{1}{2} \end{pmatrix}$  (c) $\begin{pmatrix} -1 \\ 0 \end{pmatrix}$

(d) not possible  (e) $(3)$  (f) not possible

(g) $(-1 \quad 0)$  (h) $(2 \quad -1)$  (i) $\begin{pmatrix} -2 & 1 \\ 2 & -1 \end{pmatrix}$

(j) $\begin{pmatrix} -3 & 0 \\ 7 & 0 \end{pmatrix}$  (k) $\begin{pmatrix} 2 & -11 \\ -3 & 19 \end{pmatrix}$

(l) $\begin{pmatrix} 17 & -21 \\ -3 & 4 \end{pmatrix}$  (m) $\begin{pmatrix} -1 & 5 \\ 1 & -5 \end{pmatrix}$

(n) $\begin{pmatrix} -6 & 0 \\ 1 & 0 \end{pmatrix}$

**3**  (d) $\begin{pmatrix} 1 & 0 \\ 0 & 1 \end{pmatrix}$  identity

$\begin{pmatrix} 0 & -1 \\ 1 & 0 \end{pmatrix}$  rotation $+90°$

$\begin{pmatrix} -1 & 0 \\ 0 & -1 \end{pmatrix}$  rotation $180°$

$\begin{pmatrix} 0 & 1 \\ -1 & 0 \end{pmatrix}$  rotation $+270°$

$\begin{pmatrix} -1 & 0 \\ 0 & 1 \end{pmatrix}$  reflection in $y$-axis

$\begin{pmatrix} 0 & 1 \\ 1 & 0 \end{pmatrix}$  reflection in $y = x$

$\begin{pmatrix} 0 & -1 \\ -1 & 0 \end{pmatrix}$  reflection in $y = -x$

$\begin{pmatrix} 1 & 0 \\ 0 & -1 \end{pmatrix}$  reflection in $x$-axis

**4**  (a) shear, $x$-axis invariant, $(1, 1) \rightarrow (3, 1)$
(b) shear, $y$-axis invariant, $(1, 1) \rightarrow (1, -1)$
(c) enlargement, scale factor 2, centre $(0, 0)$

305

**4** (d) enlargement, scale factor $-2$, centre $(0, 0)$
(e) stretch from $y$-axis, stretch factor 2
(f) stretch from $x$-axis, stretch factor 2

**5** (a) $\begin{pmatrix} 2 & 3 \\ 3 & 5 \end{pmatrix}$ (b) $-\frac{1}{6}\begin{pmatrix} -1 & -1 \\ 0 & 6 \end{pmatrix}$

(c) $-\frac{1}{2}\begin{pmatrix} 4 & -2 \\ -3 & 1 \end{pmatrix}$ (d) $-\frac{1}{2}\begin{pmatrix} 1 & -2 \\ 1 & -4 \end{pmatrix}$

**6** (a) $x = 2, y = 3$ (b) $x = 2\frac{1}{2}, y = 1$

**7** (a) $\begin{pmatrix} 1 & 1 \\ -1 & 1 \end{pmatrix}$ (b) $\begin{pmatrix} 4\frac{1}{2} & -1 \\ \frac{1}{2} & 1 \end{pmatrix}$

**8** (a) $x = -3, y = 1$ (b) $x = \frac{1}{2}, y = -\frac{1}{3}$
(c) $x = -4, y = \frac{1}{2}$

**10** (a) no change
(b) 5 times bigger
(c) twice as big
(d) no change

**11** (a) shear, $y = 0$ invariant, $(2, 1) \rightarrow (4, 1)$
(b) enlargement, centre $(0, 0)$, scale factor 2

(c) $\begin{pmatrix} 1 & 2 \\ 0 & 1 \end{pmatrix}$ (d) $\begin{pmatrix} 2 & 0 \\ 0 & 2 \end{pmatrix}$

(e) 4 square units; $\begin{pmatrix} 2 & 4 \\ 0 & 2 \end{pmatrix}$

**12** (a) $y = \frac{1}{2}x$

(b) Inverse of $\frac{1}{5}\begin{pmatrix} 3 & 4 \\ -1 & 7 \end{pmatrix} = \frac{1}{5}\begin{pmatrix} 7 & -4 \\ 1 & 3 \end{pmatrix}$,

hence final matrix is $\frac{1}{5} \times \frac{1}{5}\begin{pmatrix} 7 & -4 \\ 1 & 3 \end{pmatrix}$

$= \frac{1}{25}\begin{pmatrix} 7 & -4 \\ 1 & 3 \end{pmatrix}$.

**13** (a) $(0, 0), (2, 2), (1, 3)$ and $(0, 0), (0, 4),$
$(-2, 4)$
(c) rotation of $+45°$; enlargement, centre
$(0, 0)$, scale factor $\sqrt{2}$

(d) $n = 8, (0, 0), (32, 0), (32, 16), \begin{pmatrix} 16 & 0 \\ 0 & 16 \end{pmatrix}$

**14** (b) $(2, -1), (2, 2), (5, 2), (5, -1)$
(c) Determinant of matrix gives enlargement
factor, hence $\frac{1}{4}$ of 9 square units $= 2\frac{1}{4}$
square units.
(d) $(2a, -a); (4b, 4b)$
(i) no change
(ii) moved four times as far from the origin.

**15** (a) $(0, 0), (0, -1), (4, 1)$
(b) $(0, 0), (0, -1), (4, -1)$
(c) shear, $x$-axis invariant, $(3, 1) \rightarrow (4, 1)$
shear, $y$-axis invariant, $(3, 1) \rightarrow (4, -1)$

(d) $ad - bc = 1$ (determinant $= 1$) (see
answer to question 14(c))
area $= 2$ square units

(e) $\begin{pmatrix} 1 & 1 \\ -\frac{1}{2} & \frac{1}{2} \end{pmatrix}$

**16** (a) 2 square units
(b) See Figure A27:1.

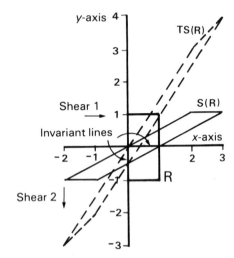

**Fig. A27:1**

(c) 2 square units (shearing does not affect
area)

(d) $\begin{pmatrix} 1 & 2 \\ 1 & 3 \end{pmatrix}$

(e) inverse of (d) $= \begin{pmatrix} 3 & -2 \\ -1 & 1 \end{pmatrix}$

(f) They are both shearings, but one shears
towards $y = 0$ and the other shears away
from $y = 0$.

## Exercise 28

**1** (a) F; $n(A) = 2$ (b) F; $n(B) = 2$ (c) T
(d) F; $D \supset F$ (e) T (f) T
(g) F; $A \cup B = \{a, b, c\}$ (h) T (i) T (j) T
(k) T (l) T (m) F; $n(G) = 4$

**2** (a) $\{a, b\}$ (b) $\{d, e, f, g\}$ (c) $\{e, f, i, j, k\}$
(d) $\{d, e, f, g, i, j, k\}$ (e) $\{l, q, r, s\}$
(f) $\{e, f, i, j\}$ (g) $\{l, s\}$ (h) $\{l\}$
(i) $\{n, o, p, s, r\}$ (j) $\{o\}$

**3** (a) (i) B (ii) A (iii) C
(b) See Figure A28:1.
(c) See Figure A28:2.

**4** See Figure A28:3.

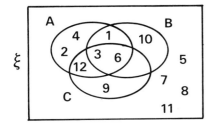

**Fig. A28:1**

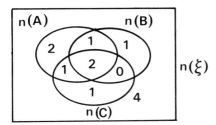

**Fig. A28:2**

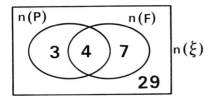

**Fig. A28:3**

**5** (a) F; $n(K) = 5$ (b) T
(c) F; M = {0, 7, 9, 12} (d) T
(e) F; $n(M \cup N \cup K) = 11$ (f) T
(g) F; P = {1, 3, 6, 7}
(h) F; $n(P \cup Q \cup R)' = 1$ (i) T
(j) F; $n(R') = 4$
**6** (a) N = {1, 4, 6, 7, 12, 15} (b) {3, 7}
(c) {1, 2, 3, 5, 6, 7} (d) {2, 4, 5, 9}
**7** See Figure A28:4.

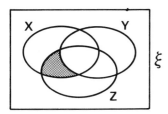

**Fig. A28:4**

**8** (a) Y (b) W and X, X and Y, X and Z
(c) 12, 14, 16, 18, 20 (d) 31, 37, 41, 43, 47
**9** See Figure A28:5. Five boys.
**10** See Figure A28:6.

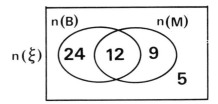

**Fig. A28:5**

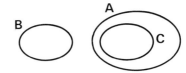

**Fig. A28:6**

**11** See Figure A28:7.
(a) 2 (b) 12

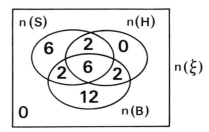

**Fig. A28:7**

**12** (a) {d, f, g} (b) {a, b, d, f}
**13** (a) Smallest is 0, see Figure A28:8. Largest is
35, see Figure A28:9.
(b) 15

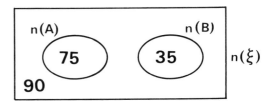

**Fig. A28:8**

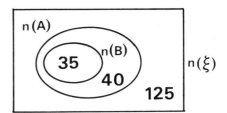

**Fig. A28:9**

307

14 (a) See Figure A28:10.
(b) A′ ∩ (B ∩ C)
(c) (i) P ⊂ Q   (ii) S ⊂ R
(d) P ⊂ Q, Q ⊂ S, S ⊂ R

15 3, 4, 5, 6

16 (a) (i) 11   (ii) 10   (iii) 26   (b) 38

17 See Figure A28:11.
(a) −0.73   (b) −0.5

18 (a) $x = 5, y = 9$   (b) 16
(c) (i) $\frac{1}{8}$   (ii) $\frac{3}{52}$

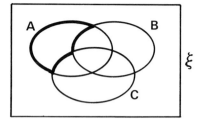

**Fig. A28:10**

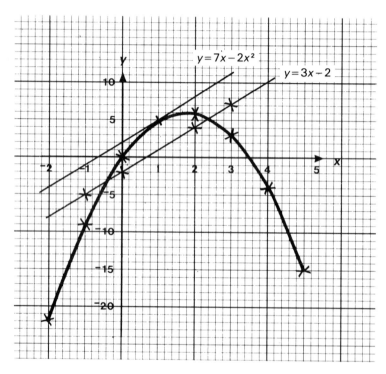

**Fig. A28:11**